THE NATION'S CHILDREN

GOLDEN ANNIVERSARY
WHITE HOUSE CONFERENCE ON
CHILDREN AND YOUTH

HONORARY CHAIRMAN
The President of the United States Dwight D. Eisenhower

HONORARY VICE CHAIRMAN
The Secretary of Health, Education, and Welfare Arthur S. Flemming

CHAIRMAN: Mrs. Rollin Brown

VICE CHAIRMEN

Hurst R. Anderson
Philip S. Barba, M.D.
Mrs. James E. Blue
Robert E. Bondy
Erwin D. Canham
Donald K. David
Luther Foster
Msgr. Raymond J. Gallagher

Mrs. Frank Gannett
Edward D. Greenwood, M.D.
Daryl P. Harvey, M.D.
Donald S. Howard
Ruth A. Stout
Rabbi Marc H. Tanenbaum
Rev. Dr. William J. Villaume

SECRETARY: Mrs. Katherine B. Oettinger
ASSOCIATE DIRECTOR: Isabella J. Jones
EXECUTIVE DIRECTOR: Ephraim R. Gomberg

COMMITTEE ON STUDIES
Chairman: Eli Ginzberg *

Leona Baumgartner, M.D.
Mrs. Fitzhugh W. Boggs
Mrs. Wright W. Brooks
Sister Mary de Lourdes *
Jack R. Ewalt, M.D.
Mrs. Otto L. Falk
Mrs. David Graham
Margaret Hickey
Reuben L. Hill, Jr.*
A. John Holden
Rt. Rev. Arthur Carl
    Lichtenberger

Harry M. Lindquist
Mrs. Alvin A. Morrison
Captain Frank J. Popello
William L. Pressly
Milton J. E. Senn, M.D.*
Joseph Stokes, M.D.*
Ruth A. Stout *
Rabbi Marc H. Tanenbaum *
John Tannehill
Ralph W. Tyler *
Whitney M. Young, Jr.*

* Members of the Steering Committee.

THE NATION'S CHILDREN
(Three Volumes in One)

EDITED BY ELI GINZBERG

*With a New Introduction
by the Editor*

Transaction Books
New Brunswick (U.S.A.) and Oxford (U.K.)

Library of Congress Catalog Number: 86-19334

ISBN: 0-88738-676-8

Printed in the United States of America

Library of Congress Cataloging in Publication Data

The Nation's children.

   Originally published: New York: Published for the Golden Anniversary White House Conference on Children and Youth by Columbia University Press, 1960.
   Includes bibliographies.
   1. Children—United States. 2. Family—United States. I. Ginzberg, Eli, 1911-   . II. White House Conference on Children and Youth (1960: Washington, D.C.)
HQ792.U5N38 1986   305.2′3′0973   86-19334
ISBN 0-88738-676-8 (pbk.)

PREFACE

THE PLAN for these three volumes was developed by the Steering Committee of the Committee on Studies for the Golden Anniversary White House Conference for Children and Youth at its meetings early in 1959. The Steering Committee quickly decided that it should not seek to stimulate new research for the Conference since the results could not possibly be available before the convening of the delegates in March, 1960. It recognized, however, the desirability of providing the delegates with materials that would help to outline the major developments in the field of children and youth since the 1950 Conference and would provide a basis for charting directions for the next decade.

These volumes were designed to meet this twofold purpose. The speedy approval by the Taconic Foundation of a grant to cover the expenses involved in preparing the materials, and assistance from other foundations to facilitate their distribution, proved a major boon, and grateful acknowledgment is hereby made of these generous and constructive contributions.

The Steering Committee set high goals for these volumes: contributors were to be recognized experts in their respective fields; they were to write for the educated layman; not for the specialist; the contributors were to strive for balance and eschew extremes; they were to limit themselves to about 5,000 words; and their essays were to be in hand by September, so that the published volumes could be sent to the delegates at least two months before the Conference.

These ambitious objectives could not have been met had it not been for the splendid cooperation of the contributors. Only one person who accepted an assignment failed to complete it and then only for reasons of health.

Most contributors recommended a limited number of books and articles that are more or less readily available so that an interested reader can pursue any subject further. These recommendations have been consolidated into a reading list appended to each volume.

The observant reader may be perplexed by differences in the figures cited. For instance, one author uses $4,800 and another $5,000 as average family income for 1957. Still another refers to average family income as being "well over $6,000 in 1958." The difference between $4,800 and $5,000 reflects a rounding off of median total income. The "well over $6,000" figure reflects primarily the use of the mean as an average and a more complete coverage of income, including an estimate of the value of income in kind. In general, differences reflect choices as to dates, sources, and averages. It should be emphasized that each author is responsible for the selection of his material and its interpretation.

The willingness of the Columbia University Press to accept a very difficult schedule and its success in meeting it warrants special note.

PREFACE

Ruth Szold Ginzberg helped to style the three volumes for press under great pressure of time, and contributed significantly to their readability.

Robert W. Smuts, Research Associate of the Conservation of Human Resources Project, Columbia University, read the galleys carefully and made helpful suggestions which led to many clarifications.

Eli Ginzberg, CHAIRMAN
COMMITTEE ON STUDIES
THE GOLDEN ANNIVERSARY WHITE HOUSE
CONFERENCE ON CHILDREN AND YOUTH

CONTENTS

CONTENTS

INTRODUCTION TO THE TRANSACTION EDITION: A RETROSPECTIVE

Eli Ginzberg

Twenty-five years ago planning was started for the White House Golden Anniversary Conference on Children and Youth. There was a short meeting of the National Committee in 1959 and when it ended my friend John W. Gardner, at that time president of the Carnegie Corporation, told me that he was going to propose that I be named Chairman of the Committee on Studies to help assure that essential background papers be developed to guide the conference's discussions.

We started out with the assistance of this larger Committee on Studies (see back of half-title page of *The Nation's Children*, Columbia, 1960, Three Volumes in One), a small steering committee, and a generous grant from the Taconic Foundation to pay honoraria to the prospective authors. But not before two awkward problems were constructively resolved. The first related to religion, the second to the participation of Black scholars—hardly minor matters even in the Eisenhower era of peace and goodwill.

It was established practice, it was reported, that at each decennial conference, leaders of the dominant faiths prepared papers. No one was opposed to following this practice although I, and several others whom I persuaded, considered it unnecessary, even undesirable, to have separate presentations submitted by each of the principal denominations. We needed, we decided, one paper on the role of religion in the nurturing and development of children and youth. A recent visit to the Vatican had led me to believe that if requested, permission for a joint paper would be forthcoming. And it was.

At the first meeting of the steering committee it was clear from the remarks made by Whitney M. Young, at the time dean of the school of social work at Atlanta University, that the role to be played by Black scholars in this conference had surfaced among the leadership but had not been resolved. I asked Whitney Young, whom I had not previously known, to hold his comments and I promised to have a satisfactory solution within sixty days. When my slate of invited scholars was ready it included Hylan Lewis, then Program Director, Child Rearing Study, National Capitol Area; Horace Mann Bond, Dean, School of Education, Atlanta University; and Louis W. Jones, Director, Social Science Research, Tuskegee Institute.

The Conference resulted in 31 chapters in three volumes; 32 authors participated with Gardner and Lois Murphy collaborating. From this distance, it appears that I took initiative in inviting about one-third of the contributors after formal clearance with the steering committee and that I was guided in extending invitations to the others by suggestions of either steering committee members or others whom I consulted.

In addition to these "background papers" which were initially published in three separate volumes, *The Family and Social Change, Development and Education,* and *Problems and Prospects,* the Committee on Studies had responsibility for inviting persons to address the plenary sessions. Their contributions were later published in an accompanying volume entitled *Values and Ideals of American Youth,* Columbia, 1961.

More than 6,000 delegates attended the conference; the sessions were dull; President Eisenhower's address was pedestrian, and my summary judgment at the time was that because of its scale the decennial conference could no longer serve a useful purpose as either an assessment device or in setting new goals. Both the Nixon Administration and the Carter Administration pursued alternative approaches but informed opinion concluded that these later conferences were even less successful than the Golden Anniversary effort. We do not know of course whether the administration in office in 1990 will sponsor a new conference or whether it will be able to find a purpose and a structure that will yield valuable results.

A Rereading

When Irving Louis Horowitz first broached the idea of this retrospective, I was intrigued not only because I agreed

with him that the problems of children and youth are still on
the nation's agenda or should be, since so many of the older
issues had not been satisfactorily resolved and since many
new ones had surfaced since 1960 for which no satisfactory
solutions were at hand. Dr. Horowitz's proposed retrospective is not unbounded; it is focused on the core problems
singled out by the distinguished authors and their suggestions about how best the nation might respond. Horowitz
wants to consider these issues with the benefit of a quarter
century's perspective.

Here in brief are my reactions to what I reread grouped
around the three principal themes—family, individual development and policies. I will note first the findings of the
contributors and then call attention to the different ways in
which history tripped them up.

- Several of the writers noted that the twentieth century
  had led to the reconstruction of American society from
  one characterized by farms and small communities to one
  composed primarily of cities and suburbs; further technology had led to major gains in income per family and
  per individual.
- Rising individual and family incomes provided the average person with more discretionary income and their
  gains were associated with improved health and personal
  freedom.
- In the view of one writer, affluence made it easier for
  young professionals to move up the socioeconomic ladder
  because they no longer had to accumulate the capital
  required to establish a professional practice, such as law

or medicine. Many, by joining the ranks of management, were on their way right after college or graduate school.

- One contributor recorded his parochial reactions to the fact that although the nuclear family is dominant in most high-income countries, it is not universal. Most Americans then as now have parochial views of the world beyond their borders. Nevertheless, various types of extended families have survived the test of time.

- Today, even our nuclear family is undergoing changes; fathers are playing larger roles in housekeeping and child-raising. Other changes which were noted twenty-five years ago, sometimes emphasized, included the tendency to earlier marriage, early childbearing, larger families.

- The one contributor from overseas, highly knowledgeable about United States developments, set forth his strong belief that continued industrialization was the wave of the future and that on balance it would add more than it would detract from human well-being. Several others were concerned about the new stresses and strains that industrialization cum urbanization were bringing in their wake but they did not raise the alarm.

The chapter on religion noted that formal membership in churches and synagogues was at an all-time high, that progress could be speeded if men (and women) collaborated more, that labor itself has a dignity, and that parents must close ranks against the disorganizing forces in modern society.

As these chapters were being prepared the country was entering a new demographic era which could not yet be discerned. The changes were major, not minor: a radical decline in the birth rate; a significant increase in the average age of marriage; frequently a delay in childbearing until the parents were in their thirties; further increases in divorces; more and more children being reared in single-parent homes; a significant change in sexual mores which resulted in large numbers of couples living together outside of marriage.

The projection of trends which did not persist was only one type of error; the other related to new developments that had not been detected. We will delay considering the latter until we review briefly the contents of the other two volumes, on individual development and policy.

The first three chapters of the volume on *Development and Education* emphasized the importance of genetic factors in human development, what we know and what we still do not know about growth and development and particularly the role of the psyche. Readers were reminded that in the past many children suffered from malnutrition but in modern affluent countries, such as the United States, the danger was from the side of over-nutrition, fat children, and the deleterious consequences of excessive weight.

Two other themes dominated the volume: the first raised perennial questions about the appropriate educational objectives for American democracy. The answers included the importance of the country's not asking the school to do everything and that, instead, we realize that a complete education must involve family, the military, church, voluntary organizations as well as the school. With regard to the school, the important point was to insist that it perform, and perform well, what could legitimately be viewed as its responsibilities.

Reinforcement for this view was in special chapters which provided new and interesting information about the role of the Armed Forces as a training institution and which looked once again at the interface between religion and youth, this time from the vantage of the institutional structure and the participation of young people in church and synagogal activities and the meaning of such participation on their value formation. After reviewing a great number of facts and figures, the author concluded on a cautionary note that there does not appear to be a "revival" of commitment to historic religion.

The two themes which dominate the second volume involve the interface between education and the economy and society and questions of equity, specifically, greater equality of opportunity. With respect to the former, a leading member of the scientific establishment made a strong plea for large-scale improvement in "scientific literacy" to be achieved by a strong improvement in the quality of science instruction in the secondary school, including improved text books.

A senior official of the United States Department of Labor who wrote on "Education and Employment" made two critical contributions. First he called attention to the vast increases in the number of young people reaching working age which would occur in the decade of the 1960s, a reflection of the "baby-boom" generation which would then come of age. Second, he stressed the continuing shift of the industrial-occupational structure away from goods production in the direction of services with their expanded demands for literacy and intellectual competence. There would be less and less room, he warned, and fewer and fewer career prospects for the high school dropout.

The equity theme elicited three complementary approaches. A distinguished southern Black educator presented an empirical analysis of the role of community and school support in the higher education of southern Blacks. Those who had the advantages of a benign environment did much better than the vast majority who were denied such support. The child psychologist stressed the wide range of differences in the potential of children and made a strong plea for letting the child choose among his options. Closely aligned to the foregoing was the chapter that emphasized the longstanding commitment of American society to equality of opportunity but which went on to emphasize that excellence is a multifaceted phenomenon and worthwhile contributions can be made by individuals with wide-ranging talents and skills.

On rereading these chapters, I was struck by the neglect of several critical facets of the development-education theme. Let me call attention to some of the more important omissions.

The economic barriers (income) to equality of opportunity were muted to almost total silence. From these chapters one would have to conclude that a child with low-income parents growing up in the Delta had approximately the same chances of "making it" as did the offspring of a

Scarsdale executive. Discrimination visited on women, Blacks and other minority groups had scarcely a nod of recognition. The malfunctioning of inner-city schools and the consequences of these on the young people who had to use them also escaped notice. Considering the popularity at that time of dynamic psychology, it is surprising that the emotional scarring that results from failures in the nurturing process were not identified and surely not explored. One possible explanation for these shortcomings is that the contributors to this volume considered the formulation of remedies to be the task of their colleagues who contributed to the third and final volume on "Problems and Prospects." But, as we shall soon see, this explanation may not be far off the mark.

The opening chapter in Volume 3 noted in passing that the new generation of adolescents might differ from earlier generations. It observed that the concept of a generation as measured from birth of father to birth of first child had collapsed from 30 to 20 years, and also that the new generation had an opportunity to work out new domestic and international strategies which might result in peaceful coexistence with the USSR. The author of this chapter, together with other contributors, speculated about the societal shift in focus from the role of work to play which had taken place. The opening salvo of this chapter suggested that the new problems and new prospects were both strong and imaginative but a closer reading suggests that the author did not believe that his speculative formulations would come to pass. He concluded that the new generation would probably be much like the old.

The next three chapters are directed to handicapped young people—rural youth who would have to relocate to urban centers, Black youth in the south who had heard the song of freedom but who would have to make their way in a world still characterized by racial discrimination, and Spanish-speaking children among whom the author differentiated Mexican-Americans, the largest subgroup, Puerto Ricans, and the Spanish-American child.

The problems of the rural young people included the need for more stimulation to realize their potentials; the need for access to better schools in order to cope more effectively with the increased needs and demands of employers, and the need for a new balance between themselves and the communities into which they were born, bred and where some considerable number might remain.

It was clear to the analyst of Black youth that most of them would not remain in the rural south but would relocate to cities in the south and north. The author realized that poorly educated migrants from the rural south were responsible for large increases in urban delinquency, crime, dependency, but he asked that these young people be assisted so that the costs of migration would be reduced. He emphasized the issue of self-image and warned that the accepted belief in their inferior status was no longer part of ther mental and emotional inheritance and that Black youth would insist that society accept them as fully endowed citizens.

The analysis of Spanish-speaking children stressed their handicaps of language and education but warned that the current enthusiasm for bi-lingualism was not likely to help. The Puerto Rican child was most disadvantaged; in additon to other handicaps many Puerto Ricans also faced the color bar.

The next three chapters contained forecasts and policy prescriptions. The first, dealing with juvenile delinquency, made the important point that confinement in prison for an average of 18 months to two years of many youngsters who may have breached the law in only minor regards was a poorer solution than a probationary system with effective staff for counseling and other support services.

The following two chapters looked more closely at the potentials and limits of social welfare institutions, the first under voluntary, the second under government auspices. The conclusions were cautious. It was admitted that the United States had a long history of volunteerism and continued to raise sizable sums to assist the poor and the handicapped, including many children and youth. But the authors pointed out that the scale of need far exceeded the resources available to voluntary agencies even when account was taken of the rise in their gift income and the flow of government dollars to assist them in the performance of their several missions.

While acknowledging that government had been willing and able to make more tax funds available to a wide variety of needy citizens, from children in broken homes to the elderly, the writer concluded that the gap between need and revenues was indeed large and the only conclusion that could be reached is that many children and young people would grow up under such disadvantaged conditions that the promise of equal opportunity for all would remain a promise delayed.

The three concluding chapters were set in a broader historical perspective. The first addressed the issue of women, work and children, and highlighted the revolution that was occurring in the role of married women in the world of work. The author suggested that a revolution of this magnitude must have a significant if still unknown impact on the children of working mothers.

The penultimate and final chapters looked at the different ways in which Americans have dealt with "childhood." Each generation of adults projects its fears, anxieties and aspirations onto their children in a search for the "right" way to bring them up. The author suggests that the young people be able to participate in the decisions which affect them.

The final contribution to the three volumes entitled "The Human Commonwealth," presents a major plan whereby the United States must work out its own problems with awareness of and responsiveness to the rest of the human commonwealth. The discovery and use of atomic energy have placed the world on a new path—one that must provide the leit-motif for educating the young so that they will be prepared for tomorrow. Parochialism and chauvinism, never attractive traits, represent suicidal threats in a world in which there is no longer a separation of West and East, North and South.

Let us now consider briefly what the contributors did not include in their identification of problems and prospects. The greatest oversight was to minimize the impact of the explosively large increase in the numbers of young people on established institutions—colleges and universities, the job market, the capacity of urban centers to absorb the inflows of migrants and the additional interfaces where the new large numbers pushed against existing structures and caused the development of fissures.

The writers also saw the racial issue from too narrow a focus. North as well as south were soon to erupt. And there was much more to the women's revolution than the impact on children of working mothers. The new feminism turned out to be a broad-based effort to lower the longstanding barriers against women in all sectors of our national life, from the nursery to the executive suite, the Cabinet, and the Supreme Court.

It is always easy to take advantage of hindsight and to fault the analysts for their failures to assess and project current trends correctly. On balance, they did as well as any other group of carefully picked academicians, government officials and publicists.

Hindsight and Foresight

Let us consider briefly the major events which erupted during the 1960s and which affected children and young people which the writers did not include in their analyses and projections. The point of this exercise is not to fault them but to see how history has a way of putting social scientists in their place. We will call attention to a few major unexpected events.

The first was the Great Society programs launched by President Johnson during the wave of public remorse which followed the assassination of President Kennedy. Only the assassination and a new president determined to reshape the country could have brought about so much new legislation aimed at expanding the number of opportunities for all citizens especially those mired in poverty and suffering from discrimination. Children and young people were assisted by major federal initiatives in manpower training and employment policy; in federal assistance for schools with large enrollments of children from low income families; in the complex of antipoverty programs including Head Start, the Job Corps, and Medicaid.

The Vietnam War was another unforeseen event. Never before had the United States engaged in such a war without prior or concurrent congressional approval—a war of such questionable aims that many draft-eligibles chose jail or exile over a uniform. And it was the war which was the direct precursor of the explosions on university campuses, although the first at Berkeley was ignited by other factors.

The Black revolution which resulted in torched sections of Detroit, Chicago, Newark, New York and other large cities, was also unexpected. After all, the *Brown* decision has been handed down in 1954 and while it was being implemented slowly, there was considerable movement on several civil rights fronts including the first federal legislation (1957) since the early years after the Civil War.

Although the chairman of the rules committee of the House of Representatives believed that he could derail the Civil Rights bill in 1963 by adding the word "sex" to "race," he merely helped to assure its passage the following year and thereby helped to accelerate the women's revolution that was soon to overtake and outdistance the racial revolution.

There was one more revolution which was not foreseen by experts in 1960—the revolution of sexual mores and the associated changes in values and life styles. While the last two are not easy to sort out and assess, the revolution in sexual mores among all groups and particularly among the young has been amply documented.

We have identified six happenings of major import that occurred during the 1960s which we did not foresee at the onset of the decade. Most of them burst on the national scene with little or no forewarning. If we were indeed to follow the conventional wisdom, three of these happenings—the Great Society, the Vietnam War, and the campus uprisings—are now no more than footnotes to the history of a turbulent decade. But the conventional wisdom has been wrong in the past and I believe that once again it will be found wrong. The Vietnam

War has seared our national soul permanently. Those who were directly affected and all others who were indirectly affected by it will carry the scars as long as they live. Despite Ronald Reagan's election and reelection, neoconservatism is not the dominant ideology of this country and time will provide a successor to the Great Society programs which we hope will be better conceived and better executed. Although the epigones insist that contemporary undergraduates are interested only in marks and careers, I believe them to be wrong. Let's hope that the campus riots of the late 1960s are a thing of the past but there is no basis for believing that the campus cannot erupt again.

We need no long list of arguments to buttress our position that the unprecedented revolutions involving women, minorities and sexual mores are still with us and will be with us for years to come. One thing is certain: the 1960s left their mark.

Concluding Observations

What can the social scientist interested in learning about the processes of societal change extract from this retrospective? Here are my brief conclusions:

- The social scientist relies heavily on trends. But since trends do not persist, here is one important source of error.
- The contemporary world is exposed to a great amount of inflammable materials in every arena—international relations, group relations, family relations, relations between employers and employees, teachers and students, men and women, adults and children—in fact in every

arena. There is no way to forecast where the next fire will erupt and whether it will get out of control. Only time will tell.

- Despite these instabilities in the environment, elements of continuity can be discerned. The American people are uneasy about gross differentials in income and wealth, especially about the considerable numbers at the bottom of the income distribution. And they are restive about the continuing maltreatment of minorities. They have not turned their backs on societal interventions, on taxing themselves to help their less fortunate neighbors. But they have become more skeptical of grandiose solutions with bureaucrats in the cat-seat.

This observer concludes that these lessons ingrained by our experiences in the 1960s have not led to the establishment of a new ideology which holds that each person/family is solely responsible for its own members. The United States will continue to be concerned with children and youth, perhaps not as much as some of us would like but more than the neoconservatives would have us believe.

ELI GINZBERG

1: THE FAMILY AND SOCIAL CHANGE

FROM FRONTIER TO SUBURBIA

by FOSTER RHEA DULLES

IN THE YEARS that have stretched from the close of the nineteenth century to the present—the years that one historian has characterized as those of "The Big Change"—there have been far-reaching transformations in every phase of American life. Of course transformations characterize every period of history. What has so dramatically distinguished the first half of the twentieth century, however, is the extreme rapidity of change. The amazing acceleration of scientific and technological advance has made over the face of America and had momentous consequences in industry, in agriculture, in transportation, and in the waging of modern war.

These developments have also revolutionized American home life. Never within so short a span of time have the conditions affecting family relations, and both the problems and the opportunities in bringing up children, changed so drastically. Young people today face an entirely different world from that which their parents, let alone their grand-

Foster Rhea Dulles is Professor of American History at The Ohio State University.

parents, knew in their youth. They take for granted scientific marvels that only a relatively few years ago were hardly envisaged. Their ways of life and their sense of values are founded upon circumstances and premises which are greatly different from those that governed the generation preceding theirs—to the continued confusion and at times consternation of their parents.

It is only since the beginning of the present century that electric power has invaded the home and made possible the myriad machines and gadgets that characterize modern housekeeping. The automobile which has given such incredible physical mobility to the American people was an erratic and very expensive plaything of the rich less than sixty years ago. Travel by air, which has now become so commonplace that even the introduction of jets causes hardly a ripple of excitement, did not begin until the Wright brothers made their first flight at Kitty Hawk as recently as 1903. The movies were no more than the faintly flickering images of the vitascope at the opening of the century, and the immensely significant experiments in the field of communications which introduced radio and television were brought to fruition in the last forty years.

These so recent developments of technology, together with many others, have contributed not only to a higher standard of living, greater leisure, and broader opportunities for a full and satisfying life than any people have ever before known, but also to many of the stresses and strains of present-day living. They have created problems that not only seriously affect our domestic economy and foreign relations, but every phase of day-by-day family life and the always difficult adjustments of youth to the society in which they live.

What are the responsibilities of children when household tasks are in some instances immensely simplified by modern gadgets, and in more wealthy families seemingly complicated by the substitution of machines for servants? How can playtime be most advantageously used against the background of a recreational pattern revolutionized by the movies, television, and the automobile? How can discipline be upheld under conditions which make for so much individual freedom for young people and often seem to encourage license? In what ways can children be most effectively trained and educated to play their future role in a society wherein manners, customs, and values are subject to the constant assault of technological advances so rapid that adjustment can hardly hope to keep up with them?

Herein lies the challenge of how the present adult population can most effectively promote the opportunities that will enable today's children and youth "to realize their full potentialities for a creative life in freedom and dignity."

An Industrial Society

The basic underlying change reflecting this growth of technology that America has experienced in the modern era has been the transformation from an agricultural to an industrial community. This is clearly apparent not only in the constant expansion in manufactures but in the rise of industrial towns and cities. Even farming itself has tended to become a business rather than a way of life under the impact of these industrial forces. The twentieth century has produced a vastly different economic structure for the nation from that which characterized the nineteenth century.

Until relatively recent times a major factor in our national growth was still the frontier—the frontier as both symbol and actuality. It represented free land, an expanding agricultural community, and an ever beckoning opportunity for new settlers on the western prairies. It was only in 1890 that the Census reports officially announced that the frontier, described as an unbroken line of western settlement, had finally disappeared. Even then there remained vast areas of free land still to be taken, and agricultural expansion would continue into the new century. But a great epoch in our national history came to a close when the traditional frontier disappeared; the future clearly belonged to industry rather than agriculture, to the city rather than to the farm.

This shift in emphasis soon began to have far-reaching effects. It had its political as well as its economic and social implications. A dramatic instance was the election of 1896 when William Jennings Bryan, who more than any other political leader of the day represented the agrarian interests of the country, went down to defeat before William McKinley, the spokesman of big business and industry. Sang Vachel Lindsay:

> Defeat of the wheat.
> Victory of the letterfiles
> And plutocrats in miles
> With dollar signs upon their coats.[1]

[1] From *Bryan, Bryan, Bryan, Bryan.* Copyright 1914. Quoted with permission of The Macmillan Company.

The victory for industry and the city can also be illustrated by the movement of population that took place in the ensuing years and by the occupational shifts within the labor force. Between 1890 and 1930, the number of people living in communities with more than 2,500 persons rose from about one-third to something more than one-half the total population. Another twenty years and the urban population was nearly two-thirds of the total. This trend has continued through the 1950s.

This change from a rural to an urban America is also shown by the employment statistics. Out of the total number of employed civilians in 1958, approximately 58 million were engaged in nonagricultural activities and only 6 million in farming.

These are broad generalizations about significant trends but their potential effect on the nation's youth is readily apparent. Whereas a half century or more ago, the traditions and mores of the farm, the village, or the small town greatly influenced family relationships and the position of children in the home, urban and suburban standards have come to supersede them almost completely. Something of the old simplicity and informality of life has been lost in the mounting complexity of a society that centers about the city. Even for children still brought up in rural communities, the quiet—sometimes deadening monotony—of isolated farm life has given way to the more rapid pace of modern living, while in the urban communities—and suburbs—there is no escaping the consequences of today's crowded, congested conditions.

More Equitable Income

As this new industrial urban America has developed, a further significant change affecting family life has been an increasing and more equitably distributed national income. This trend has been most pronounced in very recent years, particularly since the depression of the '30s. For the first time in our history the great majority of wage earners, as well as white-collar workers and other better-paid members of the labor force, are able to purchase the wide range of products that they themselves are producing. This was not generally the case in the 1890s. America was then engaged in the rapid expansion of basic industry, financed in part through the export of agricultural products and raw materials. By 1914, when Henry Ford raised the base wage of his employees to $5 a day, the consumer durable goods industries were becoming an important part of the economy and a few far-sighted businessmen had begun to recognize that high wages were the foundation for a growing domestic market. The constant pressure of militant labor unions, especially since the mid-1930s, has also helped to bring about a great change in this regard. Wage earners now make up the great bulk of the consumer market, not only for food and clothing, but for the automobiles, the refrigerators, the television sets that have become the staples of American life.

The statistical evidence of the increase in wages, and the consequent phenomenal rise in the standard of living for the American people as a whole, is often confusing. It has to be related to changes in the price level and to changes in the quality of goods. In very general terms, however, real wages —that is wages adjusted to the price level—rose only moderately in the period from 1897 to 1914, about one-half of 1 percent annually. In the latter year it was estimated that anywhere from one-third to one-half the labor force were still earning less than enough to support their families in decent conditions. The war and postwar years saw more substantial gains; the depression of 1929–33 then reversed the trend with not only wage cuts but spiralling unemployment. Since then however, the upward pace in real earnings has not only been renewed but greatly accelerated. Between 1939 and 1950, real earnings for production workers in the field of manufacturing, for example, rose more than 40 percent, and they were further supplemented in many instances by old-age pensions and other fringe benefits largely unknown in earlier periods.

Current figures show that average earnings for such workers had risen to about $90 weekly in 1959, while a comprehensive study showed that the median family income from wages and salaries in the United States was $4,800 in 1957. In these circumstances the American people as a whole have been able to spend an increasingly greater proportion of their income on nonessentials, and often luxuries, beyond anything to which previous generations could aspire.

Children no less than their parents have benefited from this phenomenal rise in living standards. It has in many cases freed them from traditional household tasks and chores, provided them new means of recreation or amusement (as will be subsequently considered in discussing the increased

leisure in modern life), and in broad terms made their life
easier and more free through greatly reducing child labor.
In addition very significantly increased family incomes have
made possible a longer term in school or college for the
great majority of the nation's young people. While there
would seem to be little change in the accepted tradition of
young people seeking to earn money for themselves as soon
as possible, the improved economic status of their parents
has enabled them to use such earned money for their own
purposes rather than contribute it entirely for household
expenses.

Other Changes

There have been many other changes in the pattern of
American life importantly affecting the family and children.
The twentieth century has witnessed immense gains in people's health. Education has expanded greatly in response to
new needs and new demands. There have been developments within the broad field of religion affecting people's
attitude toward manners and morals and altering the place
of the church in family life. From a quite different angle, the
participation of the United States in two world wars has had
important repercussions on the attitudes and mores of young
people especially. It is necessary only to recall the revolt of
the younger generation in the 1920s, the strange manifestations of the Jazz Age, the effects of worldwide overseas service during World War II, and the confusing consequences
of today's continued compulsory service in the armed forces.

HEALTH. The nation's improved physical well-being, resulting from both medical advance and more effective measures in the area of public health, may perhaps be especially singled out. This is often forgotten in the somewhat complacent attitude that prevails in an age when so many of the diseases of the past have been almost entirely eradicated. And this is true for children to an extent that would have seemed miraculous to earlier generations. This is not to suggest that disease and ill-health do not remain important problems for modern society. Of course they do. But medicine and public health research have won victories even more significant than those of engineering and industrial technology.

The tremendous gains in reducing infant mortality, the successful attacks that have been made upon the diseases of childhood, the improvement in child health due to inoculations and sanitary precautions, the emphasis upon more healthy dietary procedures—these are among the most significant developments of the modern age for children. Whatever may be said of other consequences of scientific advance, those that may be attributed to medicine would appear to be wholly beneficial for young people as well as for society as a whole.

It may be that the tensions of the modern world have an adverse effect upon the emotional stability of children as well as adults, and are responsible for problems that earlier generations did not encounter. But physical health is better and life expectancy greatly increased. It remains an amazing fact that the American child born today has a life expectancy of some seventy years—nearly twenty-five years more than that of the child born in the rural America of the 1890s.

BIRTH RATE. At the same time, changes in the birth rate have had important consequences for family life. Over the past half century there has been a pronounced trend with one sharp fluctuation. The steady decline which continued until the mid-1930s led to anguished cries of possible race suicide. Since World War II, however, the birth rate increase has been a surprising and notable phenomenon—the number of births per 1,000 of population has risen from approximately 18 to 25. Earlier marriages, a conspicuous fact of life on university campuses throughout the country, and the apparent desire of young couples to have more offspring, are primarily responsible for this reversal of the long-time trend. Today's children have more siblings than their parents generally had and thus at least the opportunity for a more emotionally satisfying life within the family circle.

EDUCATION. Relatively more children now attend school than ever before, starting at an earlier age and leaving at a later age. The total enrollment in public schools, indeed, has more than doubled since the beginning of the century, with the greatest growth at the two ends of the public education system—the high schools and the kindergartens. The estimated totals for 1958 show over 33 million pupils in public schools out of a population of 42 million between the ages of five and seventeen years.

The problems of education are today more important than ever before because of this great increase in pupil enrollment

ing up new vistas upon the world, television is playing a tremendously significant role in setting up the values of a child's universe and in molding his attitudes.

A danger that is often pointed out, for both adults and children, is the part both radio and television have had in impressing uniformity upon American life. It is charged that the omnipresent commercials tend to force upon society patterns of behavior that are destroying the individuality of an earlier age, and that herein lies one of the greatest changes in American society since the days still symbolized by the frontier. In the case of children, who are particularly susceptible to all influences making for conformity, television does often appear to spell out attitudes from which the child departs at his peril. The first of these is the compulsion to watch television. And then there are all the behavior patterns which television suggests as the accepted norm for well-adjusted boys and girls. Somewhat ironically, in the light of complaints that the freedom and individualism of frontier days have been lost, it might be noted that the popularity of Westerns remains one of the most intriguing features of television programming. Witness how the child world can be swept by such a craze as the Davy Crockett fad!

The more traditional forms of recreation for children have also undergone marked changes as a consequence of the new circumstances of modern life. The trend is away from simple, spontaneous activities to more formal organized sports and games. The casual vacant lot baseball game has given way to the little leagues; the old swimming hole has been replaced by the community pool. In fulfillment of their obligations to their children, modern parents tend more and more to rely upon arranging for their participation in various forms of highly organized activity. This reflects perhaps a comparable trend in the adult world toward the professionalization of sports and even "spectatoritis" as a substitute for active play. In any event, play today is regulated and controlled to an extent that earlier generations—on the farm, in the country—could hardly have imagined.

A NATION ON WHEELS. A further change in family life has been brought about by the automobile. Its role obviously extends far beyond the field of recreation, for both parents and children. While motoring for pleasure constitutes a large part of the use of the automobile, no single product of the technological revolution has had more far-ranging consequences on every aspect of American living. The cars parked about factories, places of business, and shopping centers, our crowded highways and congested city streets, offer constant and incontrovertible evidence of a complete dependence upon the automobile in present-day society.

The visual evidence of the number of cars on the roads is amply supported by the statistics: there were some 78 million motor vehicles in the United States in 1958—more than twice the number for as recent a year as 1940. Including bus and truck drivers, nearly 80 million persons (almost half the country's population) were licensed to drive. In the perspective of history, there may be something astounding about such figures, but they can be readily accepted by anyone who has had occasion to motor on a summer weekend in almost any part of the country.

The automobile provides a basic means of transportation in business and industry, entirely apart from the role of trucks and buses; it has served to link the country and the city by breaking down the one-time isolation of the farm, and it has greatly widened the horizons of the American people through holiday trips and vacation travel throughout the country. But the automobile has affected the world of children quite as much as the adult world. It has caused the general disappearance of the Little Red School House and substituted the new consolidated schools. It has made possible the convenient transportation of children for a host of social activities that were impracticable in the pre-automobile era. It has given teen-agers an independence and freedom of movement (when they are able to obtain use of the family car or somehow buy their own second-hand jalopies) which their counterparts in earlier generations never knew.

But the automobile has consequently created a host of problems as well as providing so many obvious benefits. Questions revolving about the use of the family car by the young, the age at which driving licenses should be granted, practical precautions to minimize the hazards of reckless driving, possible safeguards for manners and morals in the broad area of adolescent dating, point up only some of the issues which the motorizing of America has created.

Suburbia

A final development in our evolving twentieth-century civilization which importantly influences family life and children is one that is at once a consequence of the technological revolution of our times and also brings together and exemplifies many of its most distinctive features. This is the growth of suburbia. There are still millions of persons living on farms or in small villages; there are many more living in thriving industrial towns or big cities. But the growth of the suburbs clustering about our great urban centers is once again altering the face of America. The number of metropolitan areas has itself increased in the past two decades, but the suburbs embraced within their geographic limits have grown much more rapidly than the central cities themselves. In some cases, for example New York, there has actually been a decline in the city population while that of the surrounding area has increased enormously. The new garden apartments in the city's outskirts, the workers' housing developments, the more expensive suburbs away from city limits—these are increasingly distinctive features of the national landscape.

Suburbs themselves are not new. But those of an earlier day were restricted by the existing means of transportation: railroads and suburban trolley lines. The automobile has made possible their extension farther and farther into the countryside by providing the means to take the head of the family from home to railway station, if not the entire way to factory or office. It is in the world of suburbia, indeed, that the automobile is really indispensable. It transports the children to school and conveys the housewife to her supermarket and shopping center. It provides not only a popular form of recreation in itself, but enables the family to go to those places where they may either play themselves or watch others play. It is the very basis of the suburb's strange and wonderful life.

These growing communities still attract primarily members of the business and professional classes, salesmen and distributors, white-collar workers. Nevertheless the improving economic status of wage earners has made it possible for an ever larger number of families in this category to seek out the relatively greater open spaces and broader benefits for children that suburban developments offer in comparison with towns and cities. They are a compromise answer to the conflicting pulls of city and country which is designed to meet the housing problems posed by an industrialized society. Carefully graded according to economic and social status, with homes ranging from two-room apartments to split-level ranch houses, embodying all the features of the technological revolution, suburbs are more and more setting the standards and establishing the mores of our civilization. They are the pacemakers in the new culture and new value system of modern American society.

Nothing can suggest more graphically the contrast between the world in which today's children and young people are growing up and the world which the children and young people at the close of the past century confronted than a comparison of suburbia with that earlier period's small town. Neither are entirely typical of the society of their day. That is obvious. They are nevertheless contrasting symbols of how American culture has changed under the impact of technological advance in the past seventy years.

The small town of the 1890s, enveloped by its outlying farms, had a certain stability as well as leisurely atmosphere that even its counterpart today has largely lost. The spacious, comfortable houses with their deep yards and flowering gardens, set well back from quiet elm-shaded streets; the relatively little traffic, and that little composed of slow-moving wagons, carriages, buggies; the country stores that have been replaced by today's supermarkets and shopping centers—all this marked a quite different world than ours. Nor were the families who lived in these towns rushed and harried by the strident demands of a booming amusement industry which sought to mechanize—or at least professionalize—every possible form of entertainment. The traveling theatre company, staging its performances at the local opera house, the Chatauqua meeting, the annual county fair, the occasional visit of the circus—"trailing clouds of glorified dust and filling our minds with the color of romance," as Hamlin Garland has written—these were the only forms of recreation available to supplement village sports and games, church sociables, the meetings of the fraternal orders, and informal family visiting.

There was rarely any electricity, let alone refrigerators or deep freezes, in the comfortable homes along Main Street in the 1890s, and none whatsoever in rural areas; there were no automobiles (although the bicycle was becoming popular); there were no motion pictures, and no radio and no television; there were no multi-lane highways skirting the town or crisscrossing the countryside; there were no zooming jet planes to outrage the quiet air. Nor was there as yet any atomic bomb or any imaginings of the dangers of nuclear warfare!

And what of suburbia? The new real estate developments, whether vast housing projects for factory workers or more expensive, restricted middle-class subdivisions, have by their very nature a quality of sameness, are more uniform, than the towns and villages that grew up gradually in the past. They are congested and crowded as a consequence of a rapidly increasing population. An almost constant flow of traffic is a raucous interruption to everyday life, and the ubiquitous automobile, for all its benefits, emphasizes the hectic pace of suburban living. The shopping centers and supermarkets have a certain impersonality about them which contrasts sharply with the friendliness of the erstwhile local grocery store or meat market. If families have more actual leisure, there is still little of the leisurely atmosphere of earlier days. The suburbs are highly organized, for both adults and children, and present a pattern of living to which almost everyone is under heavy pressure to conform. There is often a competitive spirit in the air, giving a new urgency to the need "to keep up with the Joneses."

The children in these new communities may have greater educational opportunities than those in the small town of the 1890s, enjoy better health than those of earlier generations, have in some ways broader contacts, but they are also subject to pressures which have greatly changed the child's world. There is often no escape for them from the conventions and customs that circumscribe suburbia; it is more difficult for them than in the past to develop independence and individuality. The children living in this world of structured activities, more formalized recreation and amusement, and neighborhood prescribed conventions, may well be confused about their own individual responsibilities.

Family Life in a Complex Age

Looking back over the years, indeed, it is all too apparent that the scientific and technological revolution that has so rapidly carried the nation from an agrarian to an industrial society, from the frontier to suburbia, has brought with it highly divergent consequences for American family life. It has created a more "affluent society" than any other people have ever enjoyed, increased leisure beyond anything former generations envisaged, and opened up new possibilities for a richer and fuller life for all members of society. Yet to offset these actual or potential gains, this technological revolution has also greatly accelerated the pace of modern life, causing new stresses and strains in everyday living, and brought about a measure of crowding in city and even suburb that has immensely complicated all social organization.

This means ever new problems in family adjustment, in the relationship between parents and children, and in the direction of youth along the difficult path to maturity. Perhaps the basic issue is how young people can be brought up with a proper sense of responsibility in a situation that has freed them from so many of the obligations and duties that were theirs in a society that did not enjoy such a high standard of living and so many luxuries. Children today have a new freedom whose advantages and benefits are very real, but which obtain only if this freedom is held within reasonable bounds. Each generation must work out its own set of values in the light of changing circumstance. Something essential may well be lost, however, if such values do not remain fundamentally based upon principles that have grown out of established truths and past experience.

The continued rapidity of the changes taking place in modern society, even more than change in itself, remains the most complicating factor in the endless process of seeking to help children to adjust themselves, intellectually and emotionally, to the world in which they live. And with the potentialities for still further economic and social advance implicit in the discoveries relating to nuclear power (if the adult world somehow gains the wisdom to utilize such power for constructive rather than destructive purposes), there is little to suggest that the pace of technological progress is going to slow down.

We stand today on the threshold of a new age—the Age of Space. In some ways it is easier for children to accept this strange, new world than it is for their parents. Yet only so far as the older generation is able to realize how much—and how rapidly—the world has changed since its own youthful days, will it be in a position to help effectively today's children. Such understanding of both the past and the present is essential if society is to provide its young people with the guidance that will secure for them in an uncertain future a life of free and independent creative activity.

DEMOGRAPHIC TRENDS
AND IMPLICATIONS

by ELEANOR H. BERNERT

KNOWLEDGE of the numbers of children and youth in the United States and their social and economic characteristics, as well as changes in numbers and characteristics, has been accumulating rapidly in the past several decades.[1] With the growth of knowledge has come considerable understanding of the problems of young people, resulting in a variety of programs and policies to meet their needs. A grasp of the demographic materials provides a basis and a perspective for the planning and implementation of many of these activities.

Though the responsibility for care of children in a democracy centers largely in the family, conscious effort and planning by both private and public agencies is predicated on the assumption that specific measures are required to as-

Eleanor H. Bernert is Associate Research Sociologist at the University of California at Los Angeles. This paper was prepared with the assistance of Sherri E. Cavan.

[1] Unless otherwise specified the data provided in this essay are derived from: U.S. Bureau of the Census, *Current Population Reports*, P-20, Nos. 32, 67, 84, 88, 93; P-25, Nos. 187, 193; P-50, Nos. 83, 87; P-60, No. 30.

sure that family needs are met and to provide opportunities for children essential for personal and social development. The rapid growth in the numbers of children, their increasing concentration in urban (and particularly suburban) centers, the new importance of the day care of children of working mothers are merely illustrative of changes emerging from the changing demographic structure of the nation.

The most recent comprehensive discussion of the demographic characteristics of young people, the interrelations of these characteristics and their probable future trends, summarized the available data from the turn of the century to 1950.[2] This essay will present only a brief review of the earlier analyses; the discussion will be focused upon the most recently available materials and the probable future trends with respect to the size and distribution of the nation's child and youth population, the changing ratio of children to adults of working age, the living and family arrangements of children, their educational and labor force participation, and the children of working mothers.

Ten years ago, on the occasion of the last White House conference on children and youth, the following demographic trends were noted:[3] 1) an upsurge in the child population; 2) an increase in the number of younger children and a decrease in the number of older children, with the most

[2] Eleanor H. Bernert, *America's Children* (New York: Wiley, 1958). See also Paul C. Glick, *American Families* (New York: Wiley, 1957); and Conrad Taeuber and Irene B. Taeuber, *The Changing Population of the United States* (New York: Wiley, 1958).

[3] Paul C. Glick, "Population Changes: Their Effect on Children and Youth." Paper presented at the Mid-century White House Conference on Children and Youth (mimeographed), Washington, 1950.

marked increase among children under five; 3) an accelerating trend toward urbanization and suburbanization; 4) though the largest number of children resided in the Southern states, considerable gains among children under five years of age in the Northeastern and Western states; 5) increasing migration of young children; 6) increasing elementary school and college enrollments and declining high-school enrollment; 7) an increase in part-time work among those attending school; 8) a shift among the older teen-agers to more responsible and remunerative jobs with concomitant increases in income; 9) an increasing propensity of older youths to leave parental homes; 10) most children living with relatives, usually both parents, though one-tenth living with only one parent; 11) improving economic levels of families with children.

Now, some ten years later we may summarize the intervening years as follows: 1) a continuing rise in the number of children, though leveling off among those under five, the earlier marked upsurge among the youngest shifting to an older group; 2) a continuation in the urbanization of children, though at a lower rate than formerly; 3) the largest number of children continuing to reside in the South, though considerable gains in the West and North Central states; 4) an upsurge in enrollment rates among five-year-olds (kindergarten), and for those in advanced high-school and college ages; 5) a considerable increase in part-time work among those attending school, reflecting both the expansion in the size of the school population and the continuing increasing propensity to work among students; 6) a continuation in the upgrading of the occupations among youth in the labor force, both those in the compulsory school ages and the older youth; 7) as in earlier years, most children living with relatives, primarily with both parents, though the number living with only one parent is increasing; 8) the economic levels of families with children continuing to improve, in some part due to the persistent increase in the number of working wives and mothers.

Growth in Numbers of Children

The number of children under eighteen years of age is estimated to have reached over 61 million in 1958 (the most recent estimate available at the time of writing, August 1959), an increase of almost 2 million children from the preceding year and an increase of almost 15 million from the date of the last census (1950). The rate of growth in the number of children from 1950 to 1958, over 30 percent, is twice as large as the comparable rate for the total population of all ages. Recent projections of the total number of children under eighteen for 1960 range from about 64 million to 65 million, representing a gain of about 35 to 40 percent from 1950. Comparable gains in the total population, which is estimated for 1960 at from 179 million to 181 million, amount to about 18 to 20 percent.

In contrast to the changes in the preceding decade when children under five showed the most marked increases, during the 1950s children of elementary school age (five to thirteen years) showed the most rapid gains. Within this age group there has been a shift in the growth rate from the younger to the older sectors of the group, due primarily to past fluctuations in the annual number of births. In recent years most of the increase occurred among the ten- to thirteen-year-olds, whereas in earlier years the five- to nine-year group represented most of the increase.

In 1958 there were over 31 million children in the elementary school ages as compared with 22 million in 1950, an increase of 40 percent. Children of preschool age (under five years old) numbered about 19.5 million in 1958 as compared with 16.1 million in 1950. Some of these preschool children of 1958 are already entering school; in the next few years close to 4 million children a year will become old enough to enter school for the first time. It is estimated that by 1960 the population of kindergarten age will reach almost 4 million, as compared with 2.7 million in 1950. Children of grade-school age, who numbered 19.5 million in 1950, will increase to about 29 million in 1960. An estimate of 21 million preschool children in 1960 appears reasonable.

Youths of high-school ages (fourteen to seventeen years) are approaching an all time peak; children born during the war are entering this age group, replacing the smaller number born during the prewar years. In 1958 the group numbered 10.6 million as contrasted with 8.4 million in 1950. It is estimated that the age group in 1960 will comprise about 11.5 million youths and that it will continue to grow for the next several years due to the sizable number of births during the late war and early postwar years, and will reach about 14 million by 1965.

The downward trend which was characteristic of the

college-age population (eighteen to twenty-one years) in earlier years (from the middle 1940s) came to an end in 1954, when small annual gains began to occur. In 1958 the group numbered about 9 million persons. It is estimated that this year (1960) the group numbers about 9.9 million. During the next several years it is anticipated that the age group will increase more rapidly as the larger number of young people who were born during the war and early postwar years enter the group, replacing the smaller number born during the closing years of the depression decade and the early years of the 1940 decade. By 1965 the number of youths aged eighteen to twenty-one years will reach about 12 million.

School Enrollment

School enrollment is to a large extent dependent upon customs which regulate who goes to school and for how long, and which relate to legal regulations about school attendance and labor force participation, the necessity and opportunity to find work, the availability of educational facilities, and progress made in advancing from one grade to the next in the usual age-grade cohorts. Increasingly in the United States factors enabling and encouraging children and youths to attend school have yielded mounting enrollment rates for almost all age groups. Thus have the combined effects of an expanding population and a steady rise in enrollment rates produced a phenomenal growth in the numbers of children and youth enrolled in the nation's schools: from about 30 million in 1950 to 34 million in 1953, 39 million in 1956, and 41 million in 1957. The total number of persons enrolled in the schools and colleges in the fall of 1958 was about 43 million. Approximately 2 million were in kindergarten, 28 million were in elementary school, 9.5 million were in high schools, and 3.2 million were enrolled in colleges and professional schools.

Enrollment rates among children of compulsory school age have already reached a maximum, while the peak in high school is yet to be realized. Between 1950 and 1958 the rise in enrollment rates was most marked for children five years of age, and only somewhat less pronounced for persons beyond compulsory school age. Among the five-year-olds, mostly because of a rise in kindergarten attendance, the percentage enrolled increased from 52 to 64 percent. For youths sixteen and seventeen years old the rates increased from 71 to 81 percent; and for those eighteen and nineteen years old the rates went up from 29 percent in 1950 to 38 percent in 1958. The rates also increased from 9 to 13 percent for persons twenty to twenty-four years old, and from 2 to 4 percent among those aged twenty-five to thirty-four years.

Rises in the enrollment rates have been common to both the white and nonwhite population, though in each age group nonwhite enrollment rates are below those for the white population.

Assuming the age enrollment rates of 1958 to prevail in 1960, it is estimated that there are over 31 million children of kindergarten and elementary school ages enrolled in school today. Among youths in the high-school ages there are over 10 million attending school. Two million youths eighteen and nineteen years old are enrolled in the nation's schools;

1.5 million are aged twenty to twenty-four years, and about another million are twenty-five to thirty-four years old.[4]

Projecting these rates ahead five years, population growth in the various age groups would yield enrollments of 34 to 35 million in the elementary school ages; 13 million in the high-school ages; about 2.5 to 3 million among the eighteen- and nineteen-year-olds; and 2.7 million aged twenty to thirty-four years.

Projecting these enrollment rates to 1970 (and assuming no decline in fertility, which would primarily affect the range shown for elementary school ages) would produce the following range of enrollment figures: 37 to 40 million in the elementary school ages; 14 million in the high-school ages; 3 million among the eighteen- and nineteen-year-olds; and 3 million twenty years of age or over.

Thus, assuming stability in the 1958 enrollment rates during the 1960s, we can expect that our schools must be prepared to absorb additional enrollments of about 8.5 million by 1965 and possibly 14 to 15 million by the end of the decade.

A recent analysis of the effect of demographic factors on school enrollment trends indicates the increasing importance of population change in determining school enrollment levels.[5] Enrollment rates are already maximized among chil-

[4] The United States Office of Education has estimated the 1959–60 enrollment at 46.5 million. These estimates are somewhat higher than those presented here due to differences in definitions, time references, enumeration methods, and our assumptions concerning enrollment rates.

[5] Charles B. Nam, "Demographic Factors in School Enrollment Trends, 1951–1958." Paper read at the Fifty-fourth Annual Meeting of the American Sociological Society, Chicago, September, 1959.

dren of elementary school ages; therefore, future gains in the size of this age group will determine the size of the population attending elementary school. At the high-school level enrollment rates have been increasing, especially for persons sixteen and seventeen years old. Mainly because of the increase in the size of the age group of high-school level, but also because of the continuing rise in enrollment rates, the number of youths enrolled in high school will continue to rise markedly. The largest relative gain in enrollment in future years will occur among the college ages. Enrollment rates have been rising most sharply in this age group, although they are still far below their demographic maximum. The age group itself will increase due to the larger number of persons born during the post-depression years and to the exit from the group of the relatively smaller number of depression-born persons. In summary, the future school and college enrollment levels will depend to a considerable extent upon the number of births in preceding years. Persons born during the persistent "baby boom" are already in all the various school levels and will continue to enter them; the future promises more rapidly rising school and college enrollment.

Dependency Ratios and Educational Expenditures

The rise in the birth rate in the past decade as well as the continuous expansion in life expectancy has resulted in mounting increases in the percentage of dependent population groups, while the percentage in the productive ages has declined. This trend toward an increasingly unfavorable balance between dependent and productive age groups became particularly marked during the 1940s. The past decade saw a continuation of this trend. In 1940 there were 1.67 persons of productive ages (eighteen to sixty-four years) for each dependent person aged under eighteen years or sixty-five years and over. By 1950 there were 1.56 persons of productive ages to each young or aged dependent person. The total dependency ratio in 1958 amounted to 1.31 producers per child or aged dependent. The ratios of productive persons to each dependent child, exclusive of the aged population, for 1940, 1950, and 1958 were 2.04, 1.96, and 1.50, respectively.

As in the past, urban populations enjoy a more favorable balance between dependent and productive age groups than do rural nonfarm and rural farm populations. In recent years there have been about 1.79 urban persons of productive age for each urban child under eighteen years of age, as contrasted with 1.32 and 1.28 for the rural nonfarm and rural farm populations, respectively. If the aged (sixty-five years and over) are added to the dependent children group, there is a ratio of 1.40 producers per dependent in urban areas, 1.11 in rural nonfarm areas, and 1.04 in rural farm areas.

As in earlier years, those states which are characterized by a high ratio of dependent to productive age persons are also characterized generally by relatively low family income, low expenditures for schooling, a low degree of urbanization, low educational attainment among adults, and poor educational performance.[6] Migration from areas of comparative disadvantage to areas of relatively greater opportunity makes the difference in the training and welfare services offered to young people in the various states a matter of nationwide concern. To the extent that public support for educational and welfare programs is derived chiefly from state resources, inequalities in state dependency loads and economic resources are particularly pertinent.

In the past decade, due to the rise in the number of births throughout the entire nation, each state has experienced an increase in the ratio of children to productive age persons. Generally those states which had the most favorable population age balance in 1950 again had the most favorable ratio in 1960. Similarly those states which experienced the least favorable child dependent-producer ratio in 1950 maintained the same comparative position in 1960. At both dates the most favorable demographic dependency burdens were found in the urban Northeast, urban North Central, and Pacific states. The Southeast and West North Central states maintained relatively high dependency ratios throughout the 1950s. Mississippi, New Mexico, and Utah had the highest ratios in both 1950 and 1960.

As child dependency throughout the nation increased, so did expenditures for schooling. Expenditure per pupil in average daily full-time attendance in 1949–50 was $209 for the United States and reached $294 in 1955–56,[7] represent-

[6] See Bernert, *America's Children*, Chapter 3. Educational performance is measured in terms of deviations from an expected age-grade school progress. See also Chapter 6.
[7] U.S. Department of Health, Education, and Welfare. Office of

ing a 40 percent increase over the earlier date. Though proportionate increases were greater in the Southern states, the South still spends considerably less for schooling than states in the other regions. With a third of the nation's children and youth in the Southern states, school expenditures per pupil in average daily attendance in 1955–56 came to only $222 as compared with expenditures in the Northeast, where less than a fourth of the children in the United States reside, of $323 per pupil. About 30 percent of the children live in the North Central States, which expend on the average $304 per pupil attending school. The states of the West, containing less than 15 percent of the children, expend an average of $318 per pupil in average daily attendance.

Mississippi, despite almost doubling its school expenditure between 1949–50 and 1955–56 ($88 per pupil 1949–50 and $157 per pupil 1955–56) still spends considerably less for schooling than any other state. New York, on the other hand, spends more than any other state, reaching $426 per pupil in average daily attendance in 1955–56.

Living and Family Arrangements

Nearly all children in the United States live with one or both parents or other relatives. Of over 60 million children in 1958 about 97 percent were living with one or both parents or other relatives, and about a quarter of a million were living away from relatives, as residents of institutions, as foster children, or as wards.

Education, *Biennial Survey of Education in the United States, 1954–56,* "Statistics of State School Systems," Chapter 2, Table 41.

Most children were living with one or both parents in their own households, though about 2.5 million were with one or both parents who were sharing the living quarters of someone else. Over 90 percent of these children whose parents were sharing living quarters were living in the homes of grandparents or some other relative.

Although the average size of families has not changed significantly since 1950 (3.5 in 1950 and 3.6 in 1958), in the past several years the number of families with two or more children living at home increased more than the number of families with no children or with just one child. In 1958 there were 16.4 million families with two or more of their own children at home—an increase of 5.2 million families or 46 percent over a ten-year period. During this same period the number of families with no children or with only one child showed much less change, 27.3 million in 1958, as compared with 26.1 million in 1948.

The increase in the number of children per family during the past decade or more has been far greater among nonfarm families than among farm families. In 1958, 40 percent of the nonfarm husband-wife families had two or more children living with them. Ten years earlier only 31 percent of these families had two or more children living at home. Comparable figures for farm husband-wife families are 42 percent in 1958 and 40 percent in 1948. These recent gains in the number of children in nonfarm families have almost removed the differences between the two groups of families in this respect.

CHILDREN IN BROKEN FAMILIES. The family as an institution

has changed in many respects in the past several decades, with many of its earlier functions and activities now met by outside agencies. Clothing is usually bought ready-made; there is considerably less food processing in the household; there is considerable commercial recreation outside the home; and into the hands of the school has fallen a variety of educational, disciplinary, health, and socialization functions. However, the family is still regarded as the central mechanism for the transmission of culture, and as the most practical means of caring for children until they can assume their adult responsibilities. Generally, to fulfill this purpose there is a differentiation of roles, or a division of labor, among family members. Typically the father is provider and the mother is homemaker. Circumstances which alter or interfere with the performance of these roles often create problems which threaten the survival of the family itself and give rise to problems of adjustment for the children.

In 1950 there were 4.1 million and in 1958 about 5.6 million children under eighteen years of age, who were not living with both their mother and father; most of these children were living with one parent. These one-parent families, numbering about 3 million in 1958, represent "broken" families and are the result of marital discord and widowhood, as well as service in the armed forces, civilian employment elsewhere, and extended hospitalization. The largest number of children not living with both parents, about 4.7 million, were in families headed by a woman, generally the mother. Separated, widowed, and divorced parents comprise the vast majority of family heads in "broken" homes and a much smaller proportion are parents who are living apart for reasons other than marital discord or military service.[8] A larger proportion of nonfarm families than of farm families are among those which have been disrupted for various reasons.

Women carry the major burden of broken homes, not only because of their longer life span, but also because children usually remain with the mother when a marriage is disrupted by divorce or separation. Furthermore, the evidence suggests that the role of children as deterrents upon family disruption has been steadily weakening. Both the number of broken families and the number of dependent children involved in these families have been rising gradually during the past few decades.[9]

Any break in the home is likely to be a critical experience in the life of the child. In some instances it may draw the remaining members of the family closer together, making for greater integration. However, it is more likely, especially in cases of divorce and separation, to create problems of adjustment for the child and parents, often leading to further disintegration of the family unit, and possibly of the personality of the child. Also, a large proportion of the broken family units are not self-supporting, giving rise to many other derivative problems.

[8] Glick, *American Families*, p. 41, analyzes comparable data for 1953. Of 5.8 million children living with one parent, 1.5 million were living with a separated parent, 1.5 million with a widowed parent, 1.1 million with a divorced parent, .5 million with a mother while father was absent in military service, and 1.1 million were living with one parent while the other was absent from home for reasons other than marital discord or military service. In 1955 there were about 5.8 million children living in "broken families."

[9] Bernert, *America's Children*, pp. 36–39.

Income of Families with Children

Recent estimates of family income levels indicate that median income for all families in 1958 continued its upward trend, although the increase was smaller than previously. The median family income amounted to about $3,100 in 1949, $3,700 in 1951, $4,400 in 1955, $4,800 in 1956, and $5,000 in 1957. Half of the children in the nation (30 million) in 1957 were living in families whose total income was less than $5,000, and 15 to 20 percent of the children (about 11 million) were living in families whose annual income in 1957 was less than $2,500. Over 40 percent of the children in 1957 were living in families whose annual income was $5,000 to $10,000, and about 7 percent were in families earning $10,000 or more.

The weight of cumulative evidence in the past has demonstrated that families with larger numbers of children tend to be in lower income brackets than do those with fewer children. This pattern of differentials is again demonstrated in the data for the past decade. In both 1952 and 1957 the median income of families with one or two children exceeded the median income for all families. The median income among families with four or more children was lower than the median income for all families at both time periods. It is interesting to note, however, that at the latter date the highest median income was achieved in families of three children, while at the earlier date the income of families with three children was about the same as that for all families.

Among families with children in 1958, there was an

average of 2.6 children in families which earned a median income of less than $2,500 as contrasted with 2.1 average number of children in families with $10,000 or more income. Similar figures for 1950 were 2.4 children where the family income was less than $1,000 and 1.9 where the family income was $6,000 or more during the preceding year.

WORKING MOTHERS. The mother often enters the labor market for the purpose of raising the level of family living. In 1958, there were about 6 million families with children under eighteen where both parents were in the labor force. In addition there were almost 1.5 million mothers of dependent children in the labor force who were widowed, divorced, or living apart from their husbands for various reasons. In March, 1958, about 20 percent of the mothers of pre-school age children were in the labor force—following a gradual increase in this proportion from the time of World War II. (The comparable figure in 1950 was less than 15 percent.) Included in this group of 2.85 million working mothers of children under six were 450,000 who were widowed, divorced, or living apart from their husbands for other reasons.

About 40 percent of the mothers of school-age children were in the labor force in 1958, as compared with about 25 percent in 1950. Included in this group of over 4.5 million mothers were about 1 million who were not living with their husbands.

Labor force participation rates were highest for wives without children in the household, intermediate for wives with children six to seventeen years old, and lowest for those with children under six years of age. Also, as the husband's income increased there was a decline in the labor force participation of wives who had children in the household.

Undoubtedly the employment of mothers of young children involves some readjustment in family life patterns, particularly with respect to the care of children. In the spring of 1958 there were about 2 million children under six years of age whose mothers were working full time. The largest proportion of these children—about 40 percent—were being cared for by relatives, other than their parents, including older children, usually siblings. About 20 percent were in the care of their own mothers or fathers who either worked different shifts or who were able to have the children with them at their work. Approximately 25 percent were cared for by neighbors or other nonrelatives. Only 5 percent were placed in care centers such as nursery schools, settlement houses, etc.[10]

There are many aspects of the absence of the mother from the home and such items as time and duration of her employment are of obvious importance. To the extent that the hours and place of employment are adjusted to permit the mother to fulfil her domestic and maternal duties, the effect upon young children may be different from what is usually the case when working hours and place are not adjusted.

[10] Henry C. Lajewski, "Working Mothers and Their Arrangements for Care of Their Children," *Social Security Bulletin* (August, 1959), Vol. 22, No. 8.

Youth at Work

Available data on the labor force participation of youths have shown a rapid decline in rate of participation from the turn of the century to World War II. In contrast to 1900 when almost 45 percent of the youths aged fourteen to nineteen years were in the labor force, in 1940 about one-quarter of the youths were labor force members. By 1950 over a third of those fourteen to nineteen years of age were numbered among the civilian labor force. In 1959 there were still almost 5 million youths aged fourteen to nineteen years in the civilian labor force, representing about a third of the population of these ages. An additional 6 million young persons, twenty to twenty-four years of age, were in the labor force, which at that time totaled about 69 million.

Since the time of World War II the predominant pattern of work for young people of high-school age has been the part-time employment of students. A 1957 survey shows that of 2.7 million youths fourteen to seventeen years of age in the labor force, about 2 million were enrolled in school and most of them were working part time. Among those doing nonagricultural work only a small percentage were employed full time and about two-thirds worked less than fifteen hours per week.

Young workers in recent years, as in previous years, were employed predominantly in industries and occupations which require relatively little skill or previous work experience. Wholesale and retail trades (where young boys are primarily engaged as newsboys and delivery boys) and agriculture (which employs youngsters as farm laborers) account for over two-thirds of the employment of males of high-school ages. Young female workers were employed primarily in the service industries, largely as private household workers; a smaller, though considerable, proportion were employed by retail trade establishments as salesgirls.

In general, changes in the industrial affiliations of young workers were similar to changes in the affiliations of all employed persons. To this extent these changes may be said to reflect shifts in the economic structure of the nation, but the difference in changes which occurred between young workers and total workers may be said to reflect more the variations in the employment opportunities offered to youthful and to mature workers. For example, the teen-age exodus from employment in agriculture has been more pronounced during the past few decades, though agriculture still provides employment for a larger proportion of young people than of total workers. Similarly in retail trade, growth has been more marked in teen-age employment than in total employment. Increases in manufacturing industries, on the other hand, were much greater for the total employed than for the teen-agers.

There are pronounced shifts in the type of work young people do as they advance in age. Among the eighteen- and nineteen-year-old boys, for example, less than 20 percent were employed in agriculture in contrast to those of high-school ages where agriculture accounted for over a third of their total employment (generally as unpaid family workers). Greater employment in manufacturing industries and the trade industries as operators, craftsmen, and clerical workers indicate the increasing responsibility and remuneration achieved by the older boys.

Similarly among the young women clerical jobs in manufacturing and trade and service work other than in private households predominate among the eighteen- and nineteen-year-olds, whereas domestic and retail sales work provide the largest share of employment among the younger girls.

In July, 1957, a special inquiry was made on the summer work activity among children ten to thirteen years of age—who normally are not covered in labor force figures. Of the 12 million children of these ages at that time about 1.8 million or 15 percent were doing some kind of work. This compares with 1.1 million children (12 percent) of the same ages similarly employed in the summer of 1950. At both periods young boys comprised the bulk of this child-worker group—about 70 percent of the total. In 1950 17 percent of these young boys were working. In 1957 the proportion of working boys increased to 21 percent. The percentage of working girls increased from 7 to 9 percent between the two dates.

Though there are considerably more white children engaged in some kind of work activity (over 85 percent of the total) the proportion of nonwhite girls who were working was almost double that of white girls. Among boys the proportion was about the same.

About a million children, or 55 percent of the ten- to thirteen-year-olds who work, work as farm laborers—more than half of whom were family workers. Most of the others were employed as newsboys, laborers, and private household workers (probably on odd-jobs, or as babysitters).

The hours of work reported by these youngsters were considerably shorter than those for workers of high-school age. It also appears that the work weeks were shorter for the ten- to thirteen-year-olds in 1957 than in 1950. Almost 80 percent of the youngsters working in nonagricultural endeavors reported a work week of less than fifteen hours and all but about 5 percent of them worked less than thirty-five hours a week.

When children of these ages are working on farms, however, especially as unpaid family workers, they put in considerably longer hours on the job. Over a third of the youngsters on farms worked thirty-five or more hours a week.

Summary and Conclusions

The rise in the numbers of children and youth in the United States which began during World War II continued during the decade of the '50s, although it leveled off among those under five years of age. Coupling this growth in the actual numbers of children and youth with continuous improvement in school enrollment rates (already maximized in the compulsory school ages and rising among the pre- and post-compulsory school ages) gives rise to one of the most pressing concerns today—the provision of adequate educational facilities. Within the next five years our elementary schools will be faced with enrollments of 34 to 35 million children; by 1970, this figure may reach 37 to 40 million children. High schools will greet some 13 million youths in 1965 and about 14 million in 1970. An additional 2.5 to 3 million youths eighteen and nineteen years old may be enrolling in schools in 1965 and later. Potential students among those aged twenty to thirty-four years will add more than another 2.5 to 3 million students during the years ahead.

To further complicate the issue of providing adequate educational and other facilities for the swelling numbers of children and youth is the concomitant decline in the proportion of population in the productive ages, the group whose efforts usually provide the support for these services and facilities. Ten years ago there were about two persons of productive ages for each child under eighteen years of age. Today there are only 1.5 persons of productive age for each child. With a decline in the ratio of producers per dependent, the population may find it increasingly difficult to provide the required services for both the child and aged dependents.

The balance between the dependent and productive age groups continues to favor urban areas over rural and farm areas. And the balance remains most favorable in those states where economic resources are greater. In those states where economic resources basic to the provision of facilities for dependent groups are relatively low, the dependency ratios are high. The South, which produces over a third of the nation's children and youth, has the least favorable child dependent-producer ratio, relatively low average family income, low expenditures for schooling, low educational attainment among adults, and relatively poor educational performance among school children. Large numbers of migrants leave the South for the North and West. The segregated social environment of white and Negro children in the South also has significant effects on the adequacy of the training for adulthood which is provided in these states.

Most children in the United States live with one or both parents or other relatives. There has been an increase, however, in the number of children living in broken families caused primarily by marital discord or widowhood. Women continue to bear the major burden of broken homes.

The income of families having children has risen gradually over the past several decades, as has the total income of all families in the United States. However, there are over 10 million children in the country today who live in families whose income is grossly inadequate for the provision of even minimum opportunities for growth and development. It is these children particularly, whose families earn less than $2,500 a year, who need special services.

The number of children with working mothers has also been increasing in the past decade. Although a recent survey shows that most of these children who are of preschool age are being cared for by relatives or neighbors, the quality and nature of this mother-surrogate care might well be assessed along with the possible use and services provided by professional care centers.

From the early days of social enlightenment there has been much talk and concern about youngsters being put to work. The activities of several generations of interested persons and agencies coupled with the maturation of our modern industrial life have resulted in effective child labor laws, compulsory school regulations, and attitudes generally favorable to a minimization of child labor. The employment of youngsters ten to thirteen years old is now largely confined to family farms, paper routes, and babysitting or household chores.

Among the youths of high-school age the predominant pattern of work has been the part-time employment of students—combining the advantages of continued schooling with an early and gradual introduction into the adult world. Among the older youths, between eighteen and twenty-four years of age, full-time employment is, of course, more common than is the combination of school and work. However, school enrollment rates among these age groups have increased considerably, suggesting marked improvement in the holding power of our schools beyond the compulsory attendance ages.

Much attention has been paid of late to the numbers of young people, still largely economically dependent, who are being married. Though the number and percentage of married teen-agers increased markedly during the late 1940s and early '50s, a review of the data indicates that there has been little change since the early 1950s. In 1950 1.1 million teenagers or 9 percent were married as compared with 1.5 million or 8 percent in 1958. To the extent that marriage disrupts the continued schooling of these youths, sending them into the labor market prematurely, a penalty is paid in the form of lost opportunities for economic, cultural, and personal advancement. To the extent that parental attitudes and resources as well as increased employment opportunities for student-workers encourage these youths to complete their education, it is conceivable that early marriage and family formation may reap the advantages of providing alternative pathways to adult life. Here is an area about which little is known and one which is ripe for future investigation.

THE AMERICAN FAMILY IN THE PERSPECTIVE OF OTHER CULTURES

by CONRAD M. ARENSBERG

THAT the family is part of the universal experience of mankind we know to be true. It is also true, however, that the family experience of the modern United States has very special features. In considering American families and their effect upon children at home and in society, it is necessary to be clear as to universal characteristics of the American family and as to its special or unique features.

In part, of course, the special features of the American family, in comparison with the family of other parts of the world, are twentieth-century products. In far greater part, however, they are enduring particularities of American culture, built upon American inheritances from Europe. This specificity of the cultural tradition which has shaped the American culture and its characteristic family life is quite striking when we match American family experience against that of most of the extra-European world of both today and yesterday. The family traditions of Europe, like other aspects

Conrad M. Arensberg is Professor of Anthropology at Columbia University.

of European civilization, have been reworked and reshaped here, rather than those of Asian, African, or other civilizations, in the succeeding stages of our national development and amalgamation. Much American custom, modern and self-evident as it may seem to us, is both unique in the world and old and special in kind because it happened to have the particular special European beginnings on which it was built.

In world perspective, then, we must first note that the American family, seen generally, shares many aspects of family life and organization, first of all and very deeply, with Great Britain and the other European countries, particularly the northern and western ones. Some of these European roots are very ancient. The United States has been and is still a great mixture of peoples and conditions. Seen comparatively, its culture is new, recently unified from an assemblage of diverse regions, classes, and ethnic groups. Majority and minority ethnic strains, yielding American subcultures, have evolved an American family life, perhaps not yet completely unified but making a fairly well-understood common ideal pattern which continues to show variations dependent upon different social traditions and different past and present circumstances of economic, religious, and social life.

The common or generally perceived ideal pattern of family life in the United States today shapes our formal institutions and our legal system, lends its values to popular culture and public education, and influences strongly many of the national characteristics of our people. Nevertheless, in dealing realistically with problems of intercultural and intergroup contact and understanding, with difficulties over juvenile delinquency, with the responsibilities of social work, public and private, one must also recognize and cope with many deviations from this general majority culture pattern, anchored in the variant ethnic, regional, and class traditions and circumstances. In discussing the American family as it compares with those of other lands and civilizations both the general pattern and the exceptions to it must be presented.

To put the American family and its variants in proper perspective, then, there are two possible courses. One is to discuss the historical factors that have been at work to produce American civilization in general and lay before the reader their influence upon the family within that civilization. But such a task is better left to the historian. Another course is to outline the kinds and varieties of family organization and experience which anthropological science has revealed in its study of comparative social structure among all human cultures both primitive and civilized, in all epochs and on all the continents, and then to place the American ways with family life in their right place among these.

Our present paper will take the second course. The highly particular, in some ways unique, features of American family life come to the fore better in such a presentation, where contrasts between the familiar and the unfamiliar customs of mankind help the reader see his own American way in sharper outline. In such contrasts well-known facts of American historical development take on added meaning when they are seen operating against the different traditions still continuing in the world outside of Europe but nevertheless in essential continuation of the original and specially European cultural and familial traditions which gave them their beginnings. In taking the world-wide, fully anthropological perspective, we can trace the American family's evolution to its own maturity from its European origins and see more fully the cultural continuities involved. We can avoid thus the temptation to think of our own American family experience as much like others in kind but somehow different chiefly because it is luckier, more progressive, and more modern than that of the rest of mankind. Modern anthropological science, indeed, has come to reveal how very rich, complex, and diverse have been the differing forms of family life and organization of human beings round the world, in cultures both primitive and civilized. This complexity and diversity, indeed, continues to exist even in the "one world" of modern communication. The perspective of this revelation is necessary if we are to see American family life as others must see it from Asia, from Africa, from Oceania, even from Europe itself.

In comparing the families of the cultures of the world, it is possible to distinguish between the immediate family and household, surrounding children from their births through their maturation and until they establish families of their own, on the one hand, and the larger "kinship system," uniting immediate families in larger, extended relationships and groupings, on the other. This "kinship system," as the anthropologists call the circle of relatives about each person, obviously unites families across the generations and through marriages, weaving a network of associations and obligations, perhaps even forming a community of succor, cooperation, or defense among the relatives of his own and of his spouse which nearly every man possesses.

The Immediate Household

It is, of course, the universal experience of mankind, in every culture, that a person has a family in which he is born and grows up, providing him for good or ill with a father, a mother, perhaps with brothers and sisters. If this group of parents and siblings fails to exist, we of course take special note that the man is an orphan or product of a "broken" family, an unusual, fateful case. It is equally universal that many if not most of the adults, but not all, in a society, whether primitive tribe or modern civilization, come to head similar families in which they in their turn are parents of children of their own and thus create the next generation. The two families most persons experience have been aptly called the family of orientation (the one in which a person grows up and is oriented toward his world), and the family of procreation (the one in which he is a parent in his turn). The names, naturally, reflect subjective experience; seen more objectively the two families are merely two in a repetitive succession of like social organisms, families, endlessly transmitting cultural and social experience.

Cultural anthropology has gathered up good evidence of the universal occurrence of these elementary human groupings in all the cultures of mankind, past and present. Yet they are not always alike. It is difficult to believe the evidence that has now been amassed as to how various, underneath this universality, the particularities of organization and experience are from country to country and culture to culture and how special is modern American experience. Roles of the sexes, duties of parents, definitions of father, mother, brother, sister, sizes of the household, durations of the obligations and the affections, longevity of the family grouping, any and all of the behaviors, attitudes, and relationships so universal to human experience leave us little more certainty than that some kind of family life is to be counted on in every human community. The details telling us what kind are much more variable than we expect them to be.

The Kinship System

Equally universal is the existence of some sort of kinship system, as we have called the circle of relatives beyond the immediate family. In normal social life—apart from the accidents of orphanhood, the breaking up of families by emigration or discord or the decimations of population brought by war, famine, or pestilence; and also apart from the special individualizing changes of modern life such as rapid and impersonal urbanizations and industrializations—most of mankind have been and still are born into a web of relationships uniting other families to their own. Through their parents they are brought into a circle of secondary relatives large or small, alive or dead but remembered, giving them their grandparents, uncles, aunts, cousins, and so on, like the ones "reckoned up by dozens" in the song of Gilbert and Sullivan. Later on most persons who marry spouses not orphans or isolates acquire upon marrying another such circle or "family" of inlaws, technically called affinal relatives, as opposed to the first set, their "blood" kin or consanguinal relatives, now relatives who are in turn relatives of their children.

The existence of both types of relatives, consanguinal and affinal, still "family" in the larger sense of relationships of familial and kinship sort, is another universal of human culture. Groupings of such sort mark the social organization and the customary moralities of every culture and society and always have. Their weakening, their disappearance, or their supplantation or disestablishment by the state or by individualism is a matter of interest and comment to social scientists, and it is only recently in political evolution that law and civil right have come to strip them of legal and political force over individuals as in our modern civil codes. Here again, if modern conditions seem to have diminished the importance of such kindreds for Americans, to the point where American discussion of the family tends to omit them altogether, and if modern life seems sometimes to weaken the customs of kinship obligation and responsibility almost to nothing, and even to increase markedly the number of persons in society who are without such relatives or think themselves free of them, then these facts of change away from the usual expectancies of human social life are unusual and deserve special comment.

Today social scientists, moralists, reformers, social workers, and persons concerned with the welfare of dependent persons, old people, women, as well as children, all note alike the decay of kinship in modern life. They all alike note the growing isolation of the immediate family and the small household, not only from ties of neighborhood and residential community but also from those of kinship with other families, from parents and relatives of any sort. The decay of kinship ties is not always regretted. It seems to have been specially marked under American historical conditions calling for great mobility, for free movement from place to place, occupation to occupation, the prerequisites of an "open" society such as ours. American moral and ethical imperatives of personal and small-family self-reliance seem also to have supported the man who could "go it alone," "make a fresh start," "make his own way," free of entangling kindred. But here again the special American accent on kinship does not exempt American family experience from participation in the universality of kinship organization in human cultures; it merely shows us the radical character of the American treatment of kindreds.

Here again, however, the universality of some type of kinship extending beyond the immediate family is merely the first comparative fact we must note. The types of kinship system and the groupings, obligations, the moral imperatives upon persons, the reliances and entanglements to which they put most people in the many and varied societies of the world, past and present, are unbelievably varied and differing. Modern anthropological science has revealed, here too, how strong and ruling kinship customs still are in the world of today, and how various they continue to be in their not yet relaxed hold upon the nationals of country after country in the world nowadays, not only in the underdeveloped areas where premodern conditions still persist but into the upper ranks of civilized persons everywhere, despite the attacks of every kind of modern doctrine, from Communism to democratic idealism, upon such remnants of a pre-individualist order. Anthropology can place modern American custom quite precisely in its likeness and unlikeness to kinship systems in other countries and continents, and is beginning to understand better the effects upon psychology and upon welfare of the especial decay of the institution in our land. Here, too, once more, both the remarkable diversity of custom extant in the world and the special character of the European beginnings upon which American kinship has been built will probably surprise us.

The Institution of Marriage

Another universal of human organization we must mention in order to place the American family in proper comparative perspective is the existence of some sort of marriage in every recorded human society. Every culture anthropology has studied carries some sort of customary legal or moral sanction upon the recognized near-exclusive association of particular male and female human beings. Usually but not necessarily always these are mates, partners in the procreating of and the caring for the children of an immediate household or small family. Thus, we can speak of a "biological" family man shares in some ways even with the higher animals. This serves to unite sex partners at least for the years when children require care and extends sexual association into parental association and cooperation.

But here again we must be careful not to mistake American custom and morality for universalities of human experience and social organization. In many cultures and civilizations the conjugal relation and the cooperation of married partners may well not be the central family relationship at all. Filial and fraternal relationships may be stronger; grandmothers and aunts may have more to do with bringing up children than mothers; mothers' brothers, not fathers, may discipline children, transmit inheritances, represent the family before the community, etc. The immediate equation we make between a married couple and a family, when we think instinctively of the family as a small group dominated by immediate parents of minor children, betrays us into error. Especially, our notion that each married couple lives by itself and by itself constitutes a family, so that we can even speak of a childless married pair as a "family without children" or call a wife or a husband "my family," fails us in many parts even of the modern world.

The anthropological facts are simply that marriages and families always exist, but they differ from ours quite often and interconnect in different ways from ours. While all cultures show some sort of marriage, in the sense of a sanctioned preferential right of association, sexual, economic, proprietary, between one or more men and one or more women, in many parts of the world still today and in many civilizations in history marital unions have not necessarily been nor are they now monogamous, nor even theoretically permanent, nor need husband and wife always live together, nor do necessarily they "cleave together and forsake all others," nor need they be the main source of either their own livelihood or the care, protection, discipline, and legal identification of their children. Other family systems than ours can and do assign all these functions to other relatives and groupings of relatives than the father and mother as husband and wife in a small family. Our American assumptions, equating marrying, setting up an independent household, and supporting a spouse and children as coincident responsibilities of a family life, take our custom for granted and mistake it for an inevitable and universal fact of human life. But once again we must see American family experience, particularly where it makes a successful marital partnership a principal, if not the sole source of love and security for children and of happiness and self-esteem for adults, as in some ways a special product of a highly particular and limited European and American social and legal evolution.

Indeed, in some ways our equation of family stability and successful marital partnership, which American ideals urge upon us, is almost a world extreme both in the reduction of the family in size as a social unit and in central emphasis upon the conjugal tie, with its interspouse adjustment and cooperation, as a basis for family living. Our democratic and individualist traditions and our feminine revolution have brought us costs as well as victories. The imperatives of our family system, basing the small household on the conjugal pair, isolating that pair to free them to command their own destinies and satisfactions and to confer on them nearly complete and untrammeled authority over minor children (ex-

cept where the state and community limit them), are not
easy ones. Nor is the task our educational ideal assumes a
simple one: to prepare each and every man and woman to
be in adulthood spouse, parent, householder, and family
head all at once. These imperatives of our present small, conjugal type of family, with its minimum of kinship entangle-
ment and support, ideally require each person to find a mate
for himself, to love that spouse, to share the upbringing of
children with him or her, to maintain a household with him,
to find chief emotional identification in the little family
growing up around this spouse and partner freely chosen and
freely retained. To carry all these roles is not easy and to put
so many eggs in one basket is certainly risky; few other family customs or national cultures seem to require such concentration of emotional effort in individual responsibility
for self-directed personal adjustment and for unaided child-
training. Here again, American family custom has special
features, imperatives, and problems, arising out of a special
past and responding, perhaps, to special present conditions.

These, then, are the universalities. Families, marital unions, kinship systems are present in every human society and
culture. But they are shaped differently; they interconnect
in many various ways; they assume different relative impor-
tances in the functions of support of every kind, from livelihood to affection, they perform for human beings, both the
grown-up ones and the children. Let us see more closely
where American family, marriage, and kinship, with their
special American interconnections, fit in.

The Middle-Class Ideal

First, the American family is distinguished by the great importance, emphasis upon, and independence of the small, immediate or "biological" family of father and mother and minor children. American custom attempts to generalize this small unit, free it, trains most persons for roles heading it in adult life, delegates societal and legal authority over and responsibility for children almost exclusively to immediate parents in it. In spite of some recent increases in the birth rate this unit is small; on an average households are four and five persons at most; they begin with a marriage of two potential parents, the spouses, who are urged to take up residence, ideally, by themselves and away from others, "undoubling" the larger households of larger, three-generation families still common in many of our recent European immigrant and even our Southern populations; they swell for some years while minor children appear and grow to young adulthood; they contract thereafter as children leave for an existence and a family life of their own.

The unit is not only small, so that households are small and mobile, the family following the husband as he moves from job to job, position to position, or town to town, increasing its isolation not only from kindred but from neighbors and fellows of the community, in the great fluidity of American occupational and residential life, but it is often very short-lived. Not only are divorces common, contributing the major cause of family dissolution (rather than war deaths or famine or emigration of husbands, as in less fortunate countries) but the termination of family life in a period of "the empty nest," with the spouses returned to a life together without children, is a standard, approved, and even planned-for regularity of American social life. Just as the children are trained for the day when they will "leave home" and "have a family of their own," so old people are (ideally) expected to live apart and alone, visited perhaps by adult children but not sharing a household with them, an eventuality perfectly natural in most parts of the world, where gaffers and dowagers may even rule the roost and certainly more often continue in it than leave it as here. But here even the small family endures, in an American's life time, only twenty years or so, especially when the parents ideally have all their children in their younger married years.

All this custom, most of it ideal middle-class American family life whose real prevalence in our mixed and varied population we can only guess at, reflects, obviously, the individual and equalitarian ideals of our country's social and political life, the spread of a wage-earning and money-and-credit consuming way of economic life among most of our people as well as the already mentioned traditional cultural emphasis upon the small family, with its connections to the free choice of mate and residence and occupation and to the open mobility between places and statuses of our society. All those things, together with the reduction of extended family relationships of kinship, inherent in the freeing of individuals from fixed and hereditary placements and categorizations, have marked our civilization since the overthrow of the "ancien régime." We have already cited the historical influences. But the special traditional cultural descent of this kind of family custom which present American conditions continue to deepen and generalize should be noted as well.

The Joint-Family

The best anthropological classification of the families of mankind treats them first as they vary in progressive size of the family unit, particularly as that unit forms the usual households of a society. Largest are the joint-families of India, the patriarchal families of the Chinese gentry of yesterday, the large households of the Middle Eastern countries, of much of Africa where they may be also polygynous, the *zadrugas* and other patriarchal households of the peasant lands which in the the remote Balkans still today practice a household economy like that of ancient Rome. Here a founder, his sons, his sons' sons and all their wives, children, grandchildren, dependents and servants or slaves live their lives out in a house or compound of many rooms with common fields, gardens, and larder under central authority and in common defense for a lifetime. Eventually such a family usually splits to make more like it; the common lands or joint economy make greater size of household equivalent to strength and security; and the continually splitting households often retain ties of common defense, including even blood vengeance, to form far-flung clans of common unilineal descent.

We tend to forget how widespread even today, especially in the underdeveloped countries, are such great families and how common such clans, with the security and the trammels they bring, still are in the world. Because we have forgotten them, or belong to traditions which never knew them, does not mean they are any the less viable alternate ways of organizing individual and community life, imposing imperatives, and requiring virtues of their own kind, in many parts of the world where the national state is still new and where kinsmen and patrons rather than the national police protect individuals. In such lands they are still to be found, still opposing or braking the individualizing forces of modern pecuniary economics and of modern civil law. Some of our American ethnic groups, both immigrant and native, have strong and recent memories of joint households and clan ties, so different from the individuation of the small family of our majority tradition. When their households, for example, give over child care to grandmothers or take in nephews and cousins on the same basis as immediate children, sometimes in direct clash with our family law and our welfare procedures based on our small-family custom in which such relatives have no claim or right of care and protection, the difference in custom and family organization goes unacknowledged and the clash between public procedures and private interests and capabilities unresolved.

The Stem-Family

Our small-family tradition is based, of course, on quite other cultural antecedents than the joint-family and the clan uniting forever all the sons and grandsons of so-and-so. The next classification of families and households common in many parts of the world bases them on a size intermediate between the great households of the joint families and our own small ones. American experience, indeed American social science, does not recognize this classification and fails to note that it is very widespread in the world, particularly in Europe, but also in Asian peasant lands, especially where small proprietorship has fostered the growth and transmission of inherited family farms. In the European countries, especially in those of small peasant holdings, France, Germany, Ireland, northern Italy and northern Spain, etc., but also in Japan, the Philippines (Ifugao, for instance) and in parts of peasant India and China both, an intermediate size of family and household, living for generation after generation on a family holding, has often become standard and customary. This counted in the homestead in each generation the peasant holder, his wife, his minor children, his unmarried brothers or sisters, living as unpaid farm laborers and helping him until they should move away or marry off, his father and mother, perhaps retired from active work but still influential and assisting. If one of the standard disasters of peasant subsistence agriculture was to be avoided, namely the endless equal subdivision of the plot among children until no one child inherited land enough for subsistence, then in each generation the family homestead and plot should be kept intact and undivided. One child, or at most two, should be heirs of the whole, becoming the new holder in turn, and his noninheriting brothers and sisters should have to find for themselves some other provision in life than a bit of the family lands or else remain at home forever in a minor, farm-helper status.

Through matchmaking and other mechanisms such restriction of inheritance to a single heir in each generation often became standard, acceptable, even ideal. The household and lands remained a stem or source of new heirs and new emigrants in each successive generation; a long line of holders kept the homestead in the line or stem; it even, usually, carried the name of the farm as a family name. Each generation knew a three-generation household of retired parents, heir and his spouse (either a son or a daughter might get the land as heir of the intact holding and Norman-French primogeniture and estate entail was merely one version of such custom). Each generation knew new waves of brothers and sisters, noninheriting children who must go out into the world to "make their fortunes" elsewhere, on new farms, in marriages outside, in the apprenticeships leading to artisan or other work in the cities.

This kind of family organization became and is still standard in most of the European countries, whence its name coined by the great French family sociologist LePlay comes: the *famille-souche* or the stem-family (*Stammfamilie*, in German). It seems historically in Europe to have grown up with the medieval transition between tribal landholding and peasant tenancy and proprietorship.

So deeply is it ingrained in European tradition, whether peasant or of higher class, that many discussions between Anglo-Saxons and Europeans founder on the unrecognized adherence of Anglo-Saxon tradition to the small-family and the usual European to the stem-family. Where an American, and an Englishman, in the small-family tradition, may be enjoined by his own desires, his wife, and his columnist of manners and personal problems, such as a Mary Hayworth, to set his old mother up to live alone and think it a hardship to have her under the same roof with his wife and children, a Frenchman may define the *foyer* (intimate family) to include her and regard it as unthinkable that grand'mère live anywhere else. Much of the "Americanization" of modern Americans involves undoubling of such stem-family households today, the dissolution of family kitties which pool the incomes and the salaries of even adult children, a usual and expectable European practice in many countries—indeed even necessary where "family allowances" and state pensions do not even presume individual wage equalities or reckon a living wage to include a family livelihood as with us. Countless thousands of Americans of second-generation or third-generation immigrant origin or even of American Southern and Southern Hill background are new and transitional to the small-family, individualizing family tradition, moving toward it from the other moralities of the stem-family tradition, in a way analogous to that in which we can today find Yugoslavia moving from joint-family (*zadruga*) to stem-family (European peasant) organization with attendant difficulties of social change and adjustment. Our social sciences are still too young to let us know and recognize the many modern cultural and social transitions of this kind and to let us deal adequately with their personal and psychological costs. Only in recent years have the social work and welfare professions begun to recognize such transitions and to learn that caseworkers must be prepared to face them. Public and legal recognition of private customary differences of family interests and definitions is, indeed, not yet in sight.

Family Transformations

The general European movement of family organization during the Middle Ages seems to have been much that of Yugoslavia in recent decades, a movement from joint-family and clan protection for individuals and great-household economy, even for peasants, to smaller peasant subsistence holdings, of stem-family kind, with proprietorship passed down the line of family heirs. There is reason to believe that some parts of Europe, like some parts of the non-European world, never took part in this transition, chiefly because, as we shall see, small families and weak kinship units were aboriginal, part of another way of life than peasant subsistence. Deferring that suggestion for a moment, let us see what kind of kinship evolution took place as stem-families, if not conjugal small ones like ours, succeeded, at least in Europe, joint-families and great-households.

One change was certainly the spread of bilateral as opposed to unilateral kinship units, a shift from exclusive clans of the kind we have mentioned, to diffuse and general kindreds of the sort we know today, in which all the blood descendants of the same grandparents and great-grandparents as our own, are our cousins, regardless of whether they come through the male or through the female lines. We still reckon as relatives upon whom we have some claim, if only a bed in emergencies, the whole diffuse circle of such natural kin; no longer can the world be divided into the sons of my fathers, whom I must defend to the death, and the sons of my mother's clan, who may have to shoot me on sight. Only the family name still, with us as with other Europeans, descends down the paternal line, as a vague identifier. We can trace through European history, as we can trace it still in the spread of the national state today, the shift over to such stem-names, giving each man a family name. The custom reached Turkey only with Kemal Atatürk's reforms, and has yet to reach either Indonesia or (oddly enough) Iceland. We can likewise trace the dissolution of clans and phratries, still alive in Arabia or Pakistan, with the shift to the kind of bilateral, diffuse, cousin-counting kinship we ourselves know. In this shift to diffuse, relative reckoning of significant kinship, from a former counting instead of exclusive and corporate groups of special legal and moral force, we can still see a background to the individuation and the liberation from status and adherence prescribed at birth that has gone so far, as we have pointed out, in our own American treatment of kinship.

Let us at last return to that part of the European tradition in which, as with our own Anglo-Saxon heritage, neither the stem-family of the peasantries nor the fixities of joint-family and clan figured. Other parts of the world, as we said, have been found by social anthropologists to possess small-family organization. Notably these are some of the hunting peoples organized for a subsistence requiring great movement and fluidity among small bands of persons and, oddly enough, many of the civilized peoples of South East Asia; Malays,

Thai, Burmese, etc. There is some evidence, too, that in periods of rapid urbanization, as in ancient Roman days, great movement and migration of persons and extreme fluidity of occupational life and easy social mobility have tended more than once to dissolve kinship rigidities, to isolate and free individuals and generalize small families, just as in recent British and American history.

A great argument of social science can be waged today whether pecuniary civilization, industrialization, the factory system in themselves do not force a generalization of small families, and indeed the European practice is to treat the small family, which we call the "democratic" type of family organization, as the "proletarian" or the "disorganized" one. But the argument is better left to one side, the more so as Japan, India, the Middle East, and even such countries as Belgium and Germany seem to be able to undergo industrialization without a wholesale or even a widespread adoption of American and British small-family social patterns. The only causative argument or association we can advance for the distribution in the world of small families as the standard family system of a culture is that any pattern of economic subsistence requiring fluid movement of persons and alternate sources of hands for impermanent productive units, whether bands of gatherers or hunters, or crews of fishing boats, or short-lived reindeer herds, or new factories recruiting temporary labor forces, seems to favor small-family generalization.

The historical dominance of small-family organization in Great Britain and the nearer parts of North Europe is another problem, not at all to be solved by reference to the Industrial Revolution. The villages of North Europe and of Britain, under the manorial system, seem to have known both stem-families and small-families, and the precarious conditions of medieval farming, with their requirements that a fluid, quickly formed plowteam be formed from any and all neighbors, whether kinsmen or no, at the end of the winters in which only a few oxen or plow-cattle survive to plow the next spring, may well be thought of as favoring the small-family, unobligated peasant, ready to turn to a chance neighbor in the village as quickly as to a cousin or clansman. Certainly by the time the Enclosure Acts had cleared the English villages, destroyed the yeomen who might have duplicated the Grossbauer (big, homesteading peasant) of the continent, and sent out the Puritans and other Dissenters into town life and overseas colonization, the English tradition of small-family life, the generalization of independent starts for children, and the whole apparatus of our modern family system seem already to have been well established.

Our own frontier seems to have spread the Scots-Irish, Southern-Appalachian stem-family tradition. But it also served to spread the Anglo-Saxon, post-medieval, and Puritan small-family way as it spread the English tongue. The Middle West combined and generalized the regional-sectional traditions of our earlier colonial times. Sociologists could note, as late as 1925, that homesteading in Iowa in the sense that farms went to heirs and stayed on with the family line—a definition of the term that stresses holding on to a farm rather than originally "nesting" it—was confined to German and Polish and Czech Americans. The Old Americans, "Anglo-Saxons," in that state as elsewhere preferred to start all the children alike and "independently," setting a boy upon the "agricultural ladder," helping him "start on his own," eventually selling out and dividing the money equally among all the children, moving on to the West or to an old age in which the family was dissolved and the retired farmer and his wife lived apart. The average period of a farm's stay in one owner's hands became twenty-five years, the exact duration indeed of a small-family's life, from the time the young tenant managed (or was helped) to buy his own farm (if only from father) to the time that he in his turn retired, sold, and divided the money equally among his heirs.

The Iowan procedure we are describing here is an excellent example of the American small-family way, with its independent, self-reliant children, all equally on their own, in contrast to the European *famille-souche*: the peasant household forever in the family line, in which a grown man is still a boy, still under the family council headed by his mother and his father, pooling the family's resources, arranging match and dowry for him and sister to the end of the old people's lives. The attendant dissolution of kinship, in which a neighbor or fellow-community member is oftener to be relied on than a cousin, let alone a now nonexistent clansman, is just another step in the reduction of household and family size, in the concentration of roles on small-family

personnel, and in the sweeping away of intermediate supports or obligations between the small-family on the one
hand and the community and state on the other.

The particular North European and British, even village
and Puritan English, descent of the American small-family
system is thus quite fateful in the especial evolution of our
family system and its values. The special features of American family experience we noted earlier have legitimate origins in the cultural history of the country as well as in the
special economic, legal, and political historical conditions of
the country's growth. These special features pose special
problems, psychological or other, for Americans. They pose
such problems for Americans both in their own persons as
sharers and movers of the American customs of family life
and in their special difficulties of child welfare and child care.
Many of these latter problems we have already cited: the
isolation of the small family; the brittle dependence for
physical and emotional security, as well as home training and
discipline, upon the competence, cooperation, and adjustment of the spouses; the great and growing age separation
segregating old people and their experience out of family
and even occupational life; the unacknowledged transitions
and exceptions from the ideal small-family morality of the
majority, middle-class, and institutionally-official traditions,
with their conflicts for individuals torn between values taught
at home and values taught in school and community. Most
recent indeed is the continuing weakening of what parental
authority still remains in the parent-spouses, in the spread of
permissive and "democratic" doctrines of family consultation

and enlistment of child interests and prejudices. The father who is not so much a man, a model of adult manhood for his son, as a "pal" and another boy, absent and out of sight in the important, nonfamilial roles of his work existence, has already worried psychiatrists, especially in our newer, dormitory metropolitan suburbs, with their enforced segregation of women and children of limited like age and interests.

Most of these problems, social, legal, and psychological, seem to flow from the continuing evolution of our particular traditions, with the attendant individuation and dissolution of stabilizing and assisting personal contacts in our lives and their replacement by professional and community services. The trend is one that our long evolution of small-family independence and diffusion of kinship and other fixed-status ties long ago began. It is certainly irreversible, even if we wished to reverse it, which our people do not seem to wish to do. But if some information about its special historical character, its special place in the alternate ways of family and community organization in the history of mankind, and its special demands upon ourselves can help us manage better the trends and currents of social change in which we are caught, then perhaps this brief summary of the place of American family life in the perspective of other cultures will have served a purpose.

THE AMERICAN FAMILY TODAY

by REUBEN HILL

AT THE TURN of the century, most people had the greatest respect for the institution called the family, yet they were loath to learn much about it. The family was taken for granted, ignored, shunted aside, and expected to do the nation's patching and mending without reward or attention. According to the cherished beliefs of the period, all husbands and wives lived together in perfect amity and all children loved their parents, to whom they were indebted for the gift of life. Moreover, even if one knew that these things were not true, he ought not to mention it!

Today much of that has been changed. Gone is the concealment of the way in which life begins, gone the irrational sanctity of the home. The aura of sentiment which once protected the family from discussion clings to it no more. It is no longer considered a virtue to be naive or ignorant about the family. We want to learn as much about it as we can and to understand it as thoroughly as possible, for there is a rising recognition in America that vast numbers of its fam-

Reuben Hill is Director of the Minnesota Family Study Center and Professor of Sociology at the University of Minnesota.

ilies are in trouble—sick from internal frustrations and from external pressures in a society which expects the individual family to act as buffer between a poorly integrated sòcial order and the country's children. If fiscal policies are bungled and inflation results, the family purse strings are tightened; if real estate and building interests fail to provide housing, families must adapt themselves to obsolete dwellings or be shoehorned into quarters shared with other families.

The now famous Bill of Rights for Children of the 1930 White House Conference would be no more than a list of platitudes if individual families did not secure these rights for their children. Alas, this is too much to expect of economically and educationally marginal families. This is one reason subsequent White House Conferences have included analysis of the optimum relationship between the family and government and between the family and community planning. We are engaged in the process of reconstructing our family institutions in these conferences through criticism and discussion.

As the ban on discussion of the family has been lifted many have assumed expertness in diagnosing the American family's ills—and their approach usually begins "What's Wrong with the Family?" A wide variety of writers have addressed themselves to this theme recently, and the range of national magazines carrying their articles suggests the high readership provoked by problems of courtship, marriage, and the family. *Life, Look, McCall's, Ladies Home Journal, Better Homes and Gardens, Harper's,* and *The Atlantic* have featured the family and its problems in recent months. College presidents, psychiatrists, ministers, social workers, and judges appear frequently, but included among the authors can be found a labor leader, a motion picture arbiter, an anthropologist, a political commentator, and the American Mother of the Year. Each touches the ailing body of the American family in a different place, but all agree she is ailing. They point to the high divorce rate, to the changes in our sex morality, to juvenile delinquency, and to the rise in forced marriages of teenagers as proof of the breakdown of the family. The causes they list are most varied:

It's the breakdown of character.

It's modern women—they ought to stay home and take care of their children.

It's the search for happiness—we need to return to the old-fashioned virtues of responsibility and adherence to duty.

Alcohol is the key to it all.

There aren't enough parks and playgrounds.

It's poor sex adjustment—what people need are the facts of life.

The trouble is easy divorce—people know they can get out of marriage if it doesn't work.

It's dissimilarity of family backgrounds and temperament.

I regard much of this hue and cry in the public press as useful and healthy, but I do not have too much confidence in the diagnoses advanced by America's self-styled family experts. My approach is that of a family sociologist who has been greatly impressed by the universality of the family as an institution in all countries and in all times, and by its great capacity for adaptation and survival. The social scientist studying the family takes the comparative approach and asks what troubles experienced by the American family are also reported for families in industrializing and urbanizing societies in other parts of the world. From this vantage point it is possible to conclude that many of the disorders of the American family appear to be "growing pains," discomforts incident to adaptive change, normal symptoms of reorganization following adjustment to a new and baffling industrial urban society. Let us examine these changes in some detail, remembering that there is still much to be learned about the 40-odd million American families in this country and that research is just beginning to answer some of our questions.

A major shortcoming of the diagnoses formulated by writers in the mass media is the fact that they have been based on a limited number of observations. The psychiatrists drew primarily from the biased sample of cases they observed in clinical practice. Judges are prone to write from the distorted view of marriages sick enough for couples to seek adjudication of their troubles through divorce. Other writers relied heavily on the accumulated personal contacts of a lifetime of shrewd observations, often involving no more than a hundred families all told. I hope to improve on this by turning to the several research studies and surveys by social scientists in recent years covering several thousand families, and the findings of the censuses and sample surveys of the Bureau of the Census which cover the country as a whole.

In quick review I hope to answer three major questions: 1) What long-term and what short-term changes are occur-

ring in marriage and family patterns in America? 2) Is the
family any less important to its members and to American
society today than formerly? and 3) What are some implications for conference discussion and for social action of these
changes in family patterns?

Changes in Marriage and Family Patterns

A number of changes in the family tend to be tied to the
highly interrelated phenomena of industrialization, urbanization, secularization, and democratization. These we term
long-run trends since they have been more or less continuous
and cumulative in their impact on family patterns since well
before the Civil War. Another set of changes should be designated as short term because they tend to be relatively temporary fluctuations around a long-term trend line. They may
occur as a consequence of changes in the age and sex composition of the population, or may flow from the vacillations
of the country's economy and polity best seen in the cycles
of depression and prosperity, of inflation and deflation, and
hot wars and cold wars.

As a backdrop for discussing long-term trends let us identify the typical family pattern of a century ago when we were
largely a rural frontier society. There were, to be sure, several
coexisting minority family patterns which differed in some
respects, the colorful but numerically insignificant plantation
family of the Southern upper class to mention only one. John
Sirjamaki is our source:

The majority family of the nineteenth century tended to be
typically of large size because, although the matter was never

put so crassly, many persons were needed for the ceaseless, back-breaking labor of the farms. In 1790 the median family had 5.4 children, and the birth rate which sustained it, 55 per 1,000 population. This high fertility resulted in such a volume of children that the median age of the population in 1790, the first year in which a federal census was taken, was sixteen years. Relatives of course multiplied in consequence, and the social obligations of kinship were well observed. Kinship was traced bilaterally, that is, on both the male and the female sides of the family, although the former may have been of slightly greater social significance in that it was better supported by the patriarchal practices of the society.

Authority in the majority family was lodged in its male head. European practice and law alike fostered such patriarchy, and American experience appeared to justify it. At any rate, the concentration of power in one person who could organize family members in common enterprise and safeguard their welfare was genuinely necessary in farm life, and this command seemed to rest naturally with the husband and father. His rule was, however, considerably tempered by the fact that women did not always bend easily in obedience to their mates. The rugged frontier existence developed competence and self-reliance in them, and from an early time they had high prestige in frontier society.

The custom of separate domicile by newly wedded couples was adapted to the rural economy of family-sized farmsteads. Such farms were frequently too small to support the related families of two generations, and children upon marriage therefore established themselves apart from parents, often on land or with funds or tools partly provided by them.

Another majority family pattern was the comparative freedom young people exercised in their choice of marriage partners. For a while this was hindered by the requirement that a bride bring a dowry in money, goods, or estate to her husband in marriage. But this custom did not long persist because women, often in short supply, were gladly taken in wedlock without the added lure of a dowry, and many families had little enough property to bestow anyway. Moreover, because the bringing of a dowry was based upon arranged marriages and necessitated haggling over property settlements, it came to seem excessively gauche and unsentimental.

Of the quality of family living in the nineteenth century it is difficult to generalize, since Americans were of many conditions and domestic felicity is never constant or universal. More was then required than now of the family as an institution in the struggle for existence; hence, successful marriages were judged by their permanence, or fertility, or affluence, and less by the private happiness of the mates. Parent-child relationships were amiable, but often, because mothers were kept busy with household chores, older children were required to take charge of the younger ones. . . . But the hardships of frontier existence often reached into family living, constraining it and removing its joy. The struggle to survive was so relentless that family members had to labor ceaselessly. Houses were often meanly built and small, and the standard of living within them low. Loneliness was frequently the fate of many families, especially those on farm and frontier. Many mothers, worn out by excessive childbearing, died in early middle age, average life expectancy was below forty years in the first half of the nineteenth century. Amelioration of many of these hardships eventually arrived with the industrial development of the country, but for some families it was slow in coming and for others it did not come at all.[1]

LONG-TERM TRENDS. One can recognize in this majority family pattern of the nineteenth century many characteristics which have survived into the twentieth century: freedom of mate selection, separate domicile for newlyweds (although one couple in five begin marriage even today in the home of one of the parental families), parental subsidy of marriage (although the support today may need to be more subtle

[1] John Sirjamaki, *The American Family in the 20th Century* (Cambridge: Harvard University Press, 1953).

and less openly admitted). In other respects there have been tremendous changes as America has industrialized and urbanized, changes which we identify as long-term trends: changed ways of making a living, decreased self-sufficiency of families, smaller households, increased mobility of families, changed authority patterns, and changed age and sex roles within the family, to mention only a few. Activities once centered in the home, such as production of food and clothing, family recreation, vocational apprenticing, and religious instruction, have been shifted to canneries, factories, recreation centers, vocational schools, and Sunday Schools.

From 1890 to 1960 the proportion of American families subsisting from farming changed from almost half to less than one-tenth. With this changed mode of making a living, the authoritarian, economically integrated, self-sufficient form of family which for centuries had been functionally adapted to rural living has become obsolete. As the family ceased to be a producer of goods and services, the need for an authoritarian foreman in the family disappeared. But as the family ceased to make its own living, and the father left the home to earn money to buy the goods the family once produced, the self-sufficiency of the family also disappeared. The rugged familism which extended the frontier and gave the tenor of individualism to America has disappeared except as it is found in isolated rural and mountain areas.

The family became dependent upon the availability of jobs, on continued prosperity, and on the productivity of the wage earner. Where the father's productivity was not great enough, mothers left the home to supplement the father's pay check. Children, once viewed as potential added hands who soon could earn their keep, have become in the industrial age mouths to feed, bodies to clothe, and minds to educate. Today children are financial liabilities from birth through their schooling. Conservative estimates place the cost of rearing a child to age eighteen at $20,000, and there is still his college education ahead of him.

In order to get ahead in the world young families have become mobile, migrating for added education, better jobs, and in response to the demands of military service. Compared with other countries of the world we are a people on wheels—1 family in 5 moves annually and 1 in 3 of these crosses county lines every year.

In the course of these long-term shifts in the economy and the larger society the family has given up many services it once provided its members: schooling, religious instruction, recreation, medical care, and job placement. Many see in these changes evidences of family decay and disorganization, but I find abundant proof that there is no repudiation of the basic business of families; namely, reproduction, housing, feeding, socializing, and guiding children from infancy to adulthood. Indeed, the family is now more of a specialized agency concentrating on personality development of its members, providing warmth, love, and sanctuary from the anonymity of urban existence, services no other agency in society is prepared to offer.

SHORT-RUN CHANGES. Let us turn now for a moment to the examination of some short-run changes which have occurred in recent years. Family behavior has become increasingly subject to short-run fluctuations integrally related to the economic and political shifts in our highly interdependent type of society. Individuals are increasingly making their marital and reproductive decisions deliberately, taking into account their personal outlook of the moment. The result is often that millions make the same kind of decision at the same time. If conditions are bad as they were during the depression of the '30s, for example, people postpone marriage or if married put off childbearing. At that time hundreds of thousands of young women, after waiting for several years to marry, had to face the specter of spinsterhood because the men, when they did marry, turned to a younger age group for their brides. Later when conditions improved, young people who might have waited decided to marry, or if married decided to have children, and the marriage rates and birth rates responded violently.

The propensity to marry has been so affected by the prosperity of the past decade and a half that a greater increase in the proportion of the population married has occurred than in the previous half century. Among men twenty to twenty-four years of age the proportion married nearly doubled from 1940 to 1955, from 27 percent to 51 percent. Among women of the same ages the percentage married also increased sharply, from 51 percent to 70 percent. The number of marriages in America during the war and postwar years has been increasing very rapidly, only divorce among the vital statistics being more volatile.

Divorce has been subject both to long-term and short-term changes. The long-term trend has been on the increase since the first census covering divorce in 1870, reflecting among other things the emancipation of women through education and industrialization. As a short-term phenomenon the divorce rate follows the marriage rate, which in turn reflects so closely the fluctuations of the business cycle. A cynic once said the basic cause of divorce is marriage! It is true that when marriage rates are low as in a depression so is divorce, and when marriage rates go up so does divorce, for most divorces occur in the early years of marriage. Henry Bowman has used the analogy of a great throng of people on an open drawbridge. As more crowd to get on, others fall off the open end into the water below.

Divorce reached a high of one divorce for every two and one-half marriages in 1946 and has since declined to one in five marriages (the lowest figure since 1941), in line with the more recent decline in the marriage rate. Most vulnerable to divorce during this period have been the childless, the teen-age couples, veterans, the grammar-school educated, and low income groups. Not only are grammar-school educated persons more likely to become divorced (the rate is twice that of persons with a college education), but they end their marriages on the average nine years earlier than college people who do divorce.

A corollary trend which is noteworthy is the high rate of remarriage of the divorced, three-fourths of whom marry again within five years, and 87 percent of whom eventually remarry. Most likely to remarry are divorcees whose first marriage occurred before the age of eighteen. We are in effect operating a type of trial marriage system in this country in which the first marriage breaks in and domesticates the parties, and the second marriage reaps the benefits.[2] The remarriage rate is good evidence that the high rate of divorce in our society constitutes no repudiation of marriage itself. Marriage has never been more popular; about 70 percent of the population between the ages of fourteen to ninety were married in 1958. Eighteen percent were single and most of them will eventually marry. Eight percent were widowed, 3 percent separated, and only 2 percent were in divorced status.

A British social scientist commented on these statistics: "You Americans talk a lot about divorce, but in Europe we worry about the fact that people don't bother to marry. Over 90 percent eventually marry in America, but only 70 percent do in Sweden and Switzerland, and fewer yet in Ireland. The age at first marriage of men in rural Ireland is almost forty, more than ten years later than in America." Americans have indeed been very legal in their channeling of the sex drive in wedlock. They have had low rates of illegal cohabitation, concubinage is unheard of, and common law unions are rare. Yet we have one of the highest rates of change of married partners of any Western civilization. Paul Landis has called our form of marriage serial polygyny! You may wish to reverse it and call it brittle monogamy.

Let us turn to another trend which like divorce looks different when viewed as a long-term than when viewed as a short-run phenomenon—namely, the size of completed families.

[2] A highly readable serious study of second and third marriages of the divorced and widowed is Jessie Bernard's *Remarriage* (New York: Dryden Press, 1956).

Since frontier days the size of households has been shrinking steadily. In 1700, 7.4 children had been born to the average mother forty-five years of age and over. By 1910 the number had dropped to 4.7, by 1940 to 2.9, and by 1950 to 2.5 children.

A reversal of this long-term trend is in the making as a consequence of the prolongation of the baby boom of the 1940s and '50s. When a boom continues beyond ten years it begins to look like a trend. The increase in the birth rate was a direct result of the rapid increases in marriages of the war and postwar years beginning first with many more first babies, later with more second and third babies, and now fourth babies. Since 1950 the number of first babies has declined sharply just as the marriage rate has, both examples of short-run changes, but the number of second babies has held up, and third and fourth babies continue to increase. Comparing 1940–41 with 1954–55 the birth rate of third and fourth babies is up 70 percent.

The shift in family size, however, is not to large families of seven or more children, which have continued to decline from 15 percent of completed families in 1910 to less than 4 percent of completed families in 1957. Childlessness, at the other extreme, is also in decline, having dropped from 20 percent in 1940 to less than 10 percent in 1957. A recent nation-wide study [3] could uncover no interest in childless or one-child families and found the most favored family size to be between three and four children. In successive polls the

[3] Ronald Freedman, Pascal K. Whelpton, and Arthur A. Campbell, *Family Planning, Sterility, and Population Growth* (New York: McGraw-Hill, 1959).

proportion favoring the four-child family has increased from 20 percent in 1941 to 41 percent in 1955, while the proportion favoring two children has declined from 40 to 19 percent over the same period. This same study provides evidence that the higher birth rates of the last fifteen years and the prevailing favorable climate for medium-size families will soon affect completed family size in the United States. Asking women not yet forty-five years of age how many more children they expect to have, the researchers found women born 1916–20 (who reach the end of childbearing in 1960–64) have had or expect to have 2.9 children, women born 1921–25 expect 3.0 children, and women born 1931–37 expect 3.2 children, which is substantially more than the 2.4 children produced by mothers who had completed their childbearing by 1950. It is rather exciting to see a long-term trend change directions.

Closely related to the trend of number of children is the pattern of spacing children, which has undergone some changes with the widespread use of birth control. There is now a tendency to bunch all the children in the early years of marriage, so that women complete childbearing in their late twenties and early thirties. The average mother in the United States in 1950 had her last child at age twenty-six. Coupled with an earlier age at marriage for husbands, which has dropped in sixty years from 26.1 to 22.6 and for women from 22.0 to 20.4, husband and wife have a much longer period of companionship together than their parents enjoyed. With her children in school by the time she is in her early thirties, the wife is freer to re-enter the labor force—40 per-

cent of wives aged thirty to forty with children in school are
gainfully employed. Indeed, there has been a 77 percent increase in married women ages thirty-five to forty-four in the
labor force in the last decade.

Needless to say, this shortening of the period in which the
husband must be the sole breadwinner makes marriage less
of a financial commitment for men and brings to the relation
a more companionate quality. The traditional sentiment that
a new husband must support his wife as her father did has
now been attenuated in nearly all strata of our society by
the growing desire of wives to share in their husbands' financial struggles.

CHANGES IN SEX ROLES. As a consequence of these many
changes—younger age at marriage, changes in child spacing,
as well as changed ways of making a living and the changed
emphasis on services performed in the family—the relationships between husband and wife and between children and
parents have changed sharply with respect to the locus of
power and in the division of duties and responsibilities in the
family. Wives and children are becoming economic partners
with the husband-father in spending as well as in earning the
family income. The family is becoming democratized in the
process.

Participation by wives in family decision making extends
beyond financial matters and is concurrently being strengthened by their higher education, wider contact outside the
home, exercise of responsibility in civic associations, activities
in professional organizations, and by explicit encouragement

by experts. Male pretensions to superior authority are widely ridiculed in contemporary comedy, cartoons, children's literature, and other forms of popular art. Moreover, when family decision making is viewed as a symbol of power the superiority of shared power in creating and maintaining warmth and affection becomes evident. It is easier to love a reasonable, companionable man, and harder to love an authoritarian husband and father today.

Equally striking in the blurring of sex lines are the changes in the division of tasks and responsibilities in the home. Here the middle classes lead the way, according to a recent study covering hundreds of Omaha families at various educational and occupational status levels. The investigator asked who was primarily responsible for the performance of each of a hundred homely tasks that must be performed to keep a family going. His findings may be stated briefly:

1. The middle classes have gone farthest in bringing the husband into taking responsibility for family tasks, and also designate more tasks as the *joint responsibility* of husband and wife.

2. The lower classes placed more of the burdens on the mother and the children, while the upper classes were the only group to turn to outside help for any substantial proportion of family jobs.

3. For all classes, to be sure, the majority pattern is for the wife to assume responsibility for the greatest number of tasks (40–50 percent). Second most popular pattern is that of *joint responsibility* (25–28 percent); third in line is the hus-

band assuming chief responsibility for 20–23 percent of tasks, followed by children with 6–10 percent, and outside help 1–14 percent of tasks.

4. Joint responsibility was the majority pattern for certain types of tasks involving especially control and decision making, such as disciplining children, training in manners, supervising school work, deciding when to buy a new car, planning the budget, and so on.

There remain today only two or three tasks securely monopolized by one sex: childbearing and sewing by the wife, and the most arduous physical maintenance chores by the husband. Painting, repairing, fueling, and car washing are increasingly taken on by the wife, sometimes alone, often with the husband. Her dress on these occasions will be male work clothes and her language will also often be appropriate to the task!

The same crossing of ancient boundaries by the husband is also fast becoming commonplace—diaper changing, dishwashing, cooking, house cleaning, laundering, and shopping are duties shared with the wife, especially if she is gainfully employed—and he has learned to wear an apron, a butcher's apron, to be sure, but an apron! Such sharing of tasks fluctuates, rotates, and changes unevenly, frequently provoking conflict, but the net effect is greater companionship between husband and wife and more freedom for later leisure time pursuits together. Some women and men resent this as a usurpation of their prerogatives, indeed some feel bereaved of function, but most welcome it.

Still another source of marital integration is the trend in

America to undertake leisure time pursuits together. Except in family enterprises like farming, or small family retail enterprises, very few couples have been able to coordinate their work lives at the same vocation, but the decline of segregated amusements "for men only" and "for women only" in favor of recreation for couples more than offsets this handicap. It has become impolite to invite husbands only or wives only to most social functions; today as a consequence agreement upon friends and outside interests now appears as important in predicting marital adjustment as approval by the parental families once did. It appears probable that the urban husband spends more hours per week in the company of his wife than in any decade since factories removed manufacturing of goods from the home. Recreation and social activities now integrate the sexes.

But companionship in marriage is more than sharing common tasks in the home and participating in common leisure time activities. Nelson Foote has advanced the concept of "matching careers" to describe the phenomenon of mutual stimulation to development which occurs in a highly companionable marriage.

To expect a marriage to last indefinitely under modern conditions is to expect a lot. The conception of marriage as continually requiring the incitement of new episodes of shared activity will have more consequences than can be foreseen, but a few implications can perhaps be inferred. Happiness as a criterion of success, for instance, is inherently unstable over time. And even at a given time, the prospect of future achievement of aims may have more effect on the judgment of a marriage by its partners than their current state of gratification. Certainly marriage counselors report many cases of mates who

disclose no specific cause of dissatisfaction yet complain that
they have lost interest in their marriages. Successful marriage
may thus come to be defined, both by married people and by
students of marriage, in terms of its potential for continued
development, rather than in terms of momentary assessments of
adjustment. . . .

In particular the notion of matching careers need not imply
that husband and wife pursue identical professional careers outside the home. . . . Though their careers be differentiated both
in and out of the home, the point that seems decisive in understanding the quality of their marriages appears to remain in the
degree of matching in their phases of distinct but comparable
development. A simple test may be this, how much do they have
to communicate when they are together? [4]

How is this self-conscious appetite for a marriage that will
lead to further development of the partners distributed
within the occupational classes? Our information on this
question is inadequate, but it would appear that it is primarily
in the professional classes that companionship and mutual
development is sought. In rural and working classes the relative prominence of functional economic interdependence as
the basis for family stability seems much greater than in the
more leisured white-collar, business, and professional levels.
Moreover, the trend is for more and more of the working
force to move from agriculture and manufacturing into the
services. If in turn they shift in their interests in marriage to
the focus of the professional classes the implications for
family stability are provocative, for repeated studies show

[4] Nelson N. Foote, "Matching of Husband and Wife in Phases of
Development," in *Transactions of the Third World Congress of Sociology* (London: International Sociological Association, 1956), IV, 29.

that the professional classes are the least vulnerable to divorce of all occupational strata.[5]

The standard view that industrialization and urbanization are inexorably destructive of family stability and solidarity is thus contradicted by the fact that the professional group, which has a low divorce rate, is also the fullest beneficiary of such aspects of industrialism and urbanism as the reliance on science, spatial and social mobility, and emphasis on the welfare and freedom of the individual. The professional group is most liberal in its views about divorce, and is most egalitarian in its views on the propriety of employment of married women and in espousing the notion of equal authority for husband and wife within the family. It appears to be the most cosmopolitan in the range of its choice of marriage mates; most heterogamous in crossing ethnic, class, and religious lines; least affected by propinquity and closest in ages at marriage. It would seem that voluntary commitments emphasized by the professional groups may be stronger bonds for marriage than the economic and legal sanctions which held together traditional families. To adapt an old saying, what is poison to the rural, traditional family may be meat to the urban, professional family.[6]

PROFESSIONALIZATION OF FAMILY ROLES. What do these trends I have cited add up to? Increasing specialization by the family in services performed for its members, increased

[5] W. J. Goode, *After Divorce* (Glencoe, Ill.: The Free Press, 1956), see especially Chapters IV and V, which summarize these studies, pp. 43–67.
[6] Foote, in *Transactions of Third World Congress of Sociology*, IV, 30.

emphasis on quality of performance, shift in focus from production of goods to interest in personality development of children, and high affirmation of companionship in marriage and parent-child relations. Possibly Nelson Foote's term, "The Professionalization of Marital and Family Roles," describes best what is taking place in America today.

Marriage is increasingly viewed as a kind of joint career for which preparation can provide the skills and insights to achieve success. Miller and Swanson have been tempted to call the emerging family the "colleague" family. "As specialists at work may find in each other skills they lack, but skills they equally need, and as they may defer to one another's judgment on the grounds of different competence without feeling that they have personally lost in prestige, so husband and wife may now relate in this way." [7] They see this trend toward specialization leading to the professionalization of the wife's functions. She can no longer learn them satisfactorily from her mother's tutelage and example; they must be rationalized. Intuitive processes give way to formal rules and special technical knowledge. Moreover, the skills employed are subject to improvement as they are submitted to critical appraisal and functional selection. In career terms, the women's magazines provide a kind of in-service training, supplemented with the postgraduate work of the mother study clubs, the meetings with the specialists at the nursery school, the cooking classes, and the growing number of handbooks for preparing unfamiliar or exotic foods.[8] The rise of

[7] Daniel R. Miller and Guy E. Swanson, *The Changing American Parent* (New York: Wiley, 1958), pp. 200–1.

[8] Miller and Swanson, *Changing American Parent*, p. 201.

college and high-school courses in preparation for marriage and parenthood attended by men as well as women and the development of counseling services further affirm this desire on the part of young people to get professional training for their marital and parental roles.

Planning for parenthood today actually goes beyond planning for the control of conception, although a recent nation-wide study reveals that children born today are more likely than ever to be wanted, planned children. They are more likely to be seen as a fulfillment rather than a frustration of marriage goals today than in the depression and post-depression period. Planning for parenthood today includes programs of education for parenthood to facilitate the understanding of children in general and one's own children in particular and thereby to help parents contribute to the maximum development of their personalities. This is a trend of vast significance for personality development and mental health.

Not only are parents professionalizing their marital and parental roles, they are undertaking once again training of the child for the job world, not by providing technical skills but by helping him in human relations. The child must learn the nuances of interpersonal relations to function in the large and complex organizations of industry, business, and government. The child must study his own relations to others and gain better control over himself and his associates. Parents in the professions today do have relevant, hard-bought skills to make the critical judgments of social situations that their children will need. Miller and Swanson expect, moreover, a reappearance of the parent as the counselor and aid of his children after they have become adults and parents in their own right, thus enabling children to serve as a means of self-continuity and companionship as well as fulfillment.[9] In sum, parents have learned that in the contemporary world, a parent is far better advised to endow his child with competence in interpersonal relations than to leave him with "a competence" in the old sense of the word.

How Important Is the Family Today?

With this background in the vast changes that have occurred in the American family, how should we answer my second question, Is the family any less important to its members and to American society than formerly?

It must be granted that the present-day family is not the giant in numbers and functions that it was a century ago. We no longer count as members of our families our kin out to third cousins on either side, and often forget both sets of grandparents and any great-grandparents when we reckon our family size. The modern family, shorn of kinship attachments and bearing two to four children, is smaller and less of an all-purpose organization—but is it therefore less important?

It would be a mistake to assume that because many families are free floating and geographically rootless, most urban families are separated from significant supportive relationships. Recent studies in London, Detroit, Cleveland, and Minneapolis attest to the perseverance of reciprocal relation-

[9] Miller and Swanson, *Changing American Parent*, p. 204.

ships of gift giving, visiting, mutual aid, and advice seeking between grandparents and their married children, and between nuclear families and their kinfolk. In charting the social network of families they still tend to list relatives above friends and neighbors as the first place to turn when crisis strikes.

Yet there have also been social losses in the streamlining and specializing of the modern family. The modern nuclear family focuses primarily on the maintenance of the marriage and the provision of services to the immediate offspring of the marriage. In specializing, the family has not only given up *services* once provided by the traditional family but it has given up *people* who once could find a meaningful place there: maiden aunts, bachelor uncles, widowed and orphaned kin, and grandparents. As a consequence, many more individuals today live outside organized family groups in semi-isolation from the love and support families might give them.

American families are on the whole probably happier than they were in earlier times, yet so much is asked of marriage and the family today that many otherwise sound families experience relative deprivation. The standards of success today go beyond providing and getting ahead economically, beyond the maintenance of minimum goals of health and education for children, to include happiness and self-realization. Few families appear to measure up, yet every man regards a happy marriage as his right. The defects of the modern family develop primarily from the disabilities of the specific persons who marry and rear children. If greater stability of the family is ever to be assured, increasing the competence of young people in interpersonal relations and selecting people for marriage who are ready for parental responsibilities must be undertaken much more systematically.

Granting that marriages today are intrinsically less enduring, evidence can be brought to show that they are greatly improved in quality of performance and are more stimulating climates in which to rear children. In addition, the modern family has the virtue of fitting well the demands of our democratic and urban industrial society, something that would have been impossible to the larger, rooted, and authoritarian family of the past century.

Since the modern family is smaller, it is more mobile, moving where opportunities are to be found. The medium-sized family fits the occupational structure better, relying as it does on achievement on the job over kinship preference for getting ahead in the job world. Small nuclear families of husband, wife, and children, as contrasted with great extended families of the past, appear to be ideally adapted to the different degrees of social movement required by our open competitive type of class society—permitting movement both horizontally in geographic space and vertically in climbing the occupational ladder.

Extended families of the past, in sharp contrast, tended to standardize a single class status among all family members and impose barriers of vested family interests to thwart the principle of equal opportunities of all persons to strive for social mobility. To be sure, parents in nuclear families also confer their own class position initially upon their children, but this transfer of status is never sure or permanent, and eventually must be earned in occupational achievement. Great extended families have in the past constituted a threat to the integrity of public service, undermining democratic processes and the principles of career civil service by nepotistic manipulation of government in behalf of family members. They would seem to be much less well adapted to the economic and political structure of our contemporary society than present-day nuclear type families which are too small to participate in coalitions or to build pyramids of power within business or government.

Is the family any less important to American society than formerly? By virtue of its specialization and its close adaptation to the economic and political structure, the family fits contemporary American society remarkably well. Moreover, the modern family is fully as needed today as formerly since it has no serious competitors among the other agencies in our society for the performance of the personality-building functions in which it is currently specializing. We depend almost exclusively on the family today for the performance of the vital functions of reproduction, infant care, and socialization without which our society would disintegrate.

Implications for Social Action

What are some implications for discussion and social action of the changes in family patterns we have identified? Two specific changes in family patterns require our attention.

HIGH MOBILITY AND NEIGHBORHOOD DEVELOPMENT. Although nonmobile families continue to maintain a nest of kin and neighbors within which they can function in reciprocal assistance and support, what of the mobile families who have separated themselves by geographic movement from kin and home town neighbors? To whom do they turn for counsel and help when they want to spill their troubles? How do they become integrated into a new neighborhood or community? The high mobility of young families results in feelings of "aloneness" and "lockedupness" as they move into new communities or join the stream moving out of the central city into the suburbs.

The challenge is to develop institutions less commercial than the "welcome wagon" and more neighborhood oriented. We need community organization and neighborhood development activities in this direction such as Milwaukee supported for a time. We need to institutionalize the status of "newcomers" and utilize it to provide orientation and welcoming activities into neighborhood and community.

DIVORCE ADJUSTMENT AND SOCIAL AMBIGUITIES. The high rate of divorce and remarriage suggests the need for attention to inventing ways of easing postdivorce adjustment and facilitating successful remarriages. We are better prepared to deal with bereavement of widows and widowers than we are with the adjustments of the divorced. For example, there are no ethical imperatives for relatives or friends that would make them feel constrained to furnish material or emotional support during or after the divorce to the divorced. There is no clear definition of responsibility for readmitting divorce participants back into their former statuses as members of the parental family. Pathways to forming new male or female friendships and remarriage are poorly charted, and there is a distinct ambiguity concerning the proper behavior of the spouses after the divorce. Do they remain forever distant and alienated, or do they re-establish friendships for the children's sake? These ambiguities beg clarification.

NEED FOR NATIONAL AND LOCAL POLICIES FOR FAMILY WELL-BEING. There is still another dimension in which we can move in conference discussion, the dimension of recommending national and local policies for family well-being. The United States is one of the few civilized countries of the world which has not yet formulated an explicit family policy on which a coherent program for families could be built. The federal government, having ceded the issues of family life to the states, has taken little initiative in promoting programs of family betterment. Indeed, the constitution writers avoided the problem by failing to acknowledge the family as a legal entity. Since the issues of family life have few interstate ramifications they have appeared beyond the power of the federal arm of government. Consequent to the denial to the federal government of powers related to the family, we have fifty states with conflicting laws controlling marriage, divorce, responsibility of parents to children, and so on.

It took years of depression to bring the recognition to legislators that family self-sufficiency was no longer feasible in an industrial economy, and that no family can be held entirely responsible for its own destiny. The various extensions of the Social Security Act are important steps toward expanding the role of government in shoring up family resources, but this is only the beginning of a national policy for family life. It seems not incorrect to suggest that the principles of laissez faire have been applied to the relation of government and families with considerably more success than is true in the case of government and business. No pressure group has yet made of government a positive instrument for the benefit of family life. A family policy for America would include not only general goals but specific means appropriate for their realization.

FIVE RECOMMENDATIONS FOR ACTION. In conclusion, may I share with you selected recommendations for action which Dr. Emily H. Mudd, director of the Marriage Council of Philadelphia, and I obtained in an idea-getting survey of sixteen selected practitioners from the major disciplines influencing family life in the United States three years ago. They are embodied in a memorandum prepared for the Commissioner of the Social Security Administration, at his initiative and with his active collaboration.

1. The recommendations begin with a proposal for education for family life at every stage of human development, timed at critical points of maximum readiness when members are most teachable.

   a) It is felt that education has the virtue of intervening before trouble strikes, that it is preventive and helps families help themselves. Moreover, education can be carried out in a variety of settings by social workers, marriage counselors, and writers, as well as teachers.

2. A second recommendation on which there was high consensus among members of our interview panel involved

ways of intervening to improve family life through the courts and legal agencies of government.

    a) Uniform marriage and divorce laws were urged which would prevent hasty marriages and impulsive divorces.

    b) Enabling legislation empowering domestic relations courts to provide counseling services was also recommended.

3. Guidance and remedial measures were recommended, although there was a noticeable reluctance to make them the primary emphasis in future program planning.

    a) Marriage counseling and mental health clinics were recommended for every community, possibly in the neighborhood high school where everyone would feel free to come.

4. A fourth cluster of recommendations appears novel indeed and refers to the need to build the morale of family members engaged in the significant task of rearing the nation's children.

    a) Family morale might be strengthened with a government department which protects family interests as the interests of labor, commerce, and agriculture are already protected—particularly against the stresses which emanate from government policies affecting inflation, unemployment, selective service, and war.

    b) A White House Conference on Family Life to lay the groundwork for a national policy for families would surely have the effect of improving family morale in the United States.

5. A final suggestion involves programs of training and re-
fresher work for the personnel of the family-serving
agencies of the country. Such programs would consider
ways of relating the agencies to families so as to facilitate family development rather than to defeat them.
If families are to be strengthened rather than weakened
as a consequence of contact with helping agencies, what
principles might guide workers?

a) Workers will do best who permit high participation by
families in setting the goals and determining the outcome of service by involvement of all family members
on a group basis.

b) Workers and family members are optimally engaged
if they are dedicated to bringing about *full family
development* rather than the restoration of any pre-
conceived status quo.

c) To reach this high goal, workers should actively seek
to make available their professional insights and secrets
to family members in the interest of leaving parents
and children better able to cope with the task of becoming an adequate and effective family.

These proposals may seem ambitious to some but are
merely suggestive of the kind of help which agencies can offer
for improving the performance of American families. I see
the family, with these aids, surviving even the amazing technological developments now being forecast for the atomic age,
and surviving the impact of urbanization, of social mobility,
of wars and economic depressions, with a minimum of scars
and a maximum of vitality. I see great possibilities in the

family of tomorrow as an improved medium-sized family organization, geared to assure maximum self-expression of family members while maintaining integrity and inner loyalty to the whole. My optimism is predicated on the universality of the family phenomenon, on its survival powers in the past, on its present adaptability, and on the anticipated shape of things to come.

THE CHANGING NEGRO FAMILY

by H Y L A N   L E W I S

IN *An American Dilemma* (1944), Gunnar Myrdal began the section, "The Negro Family," in this way: "The recent book by E. Franklin Frazier, *The Negro Family in the United States* (1939), is such an excellent description and analysis . . . that it is practically necessary only to relate its conclusions to our context and to refer the reader to it for details." Twenty-one years after Frazier's classic treatment, Myrdal's acknowledgement and recommendation are still highly appropriate, especially if one wishes to understand the forces that have shaped the Negro family, and its various expressions, in American life and its responsiveness to economic and social changes.

There have been significant changes in the pace and scope of change since this study was made. These make it the more regrettable that the expected revision of Frazier's basic work is not yet available.

This chapter is not an effort to bring earlier studies of the Negro family up to date, but rather, an effort to examine

Hylan Lewis is Program Director, Child Rearing Study, Health and Welfare Council of the National Capital Area.

and interpret family structure, functions, roles, and values among Negroes, mainly in the context of changes that have occurred, matured, or become salient in American society during the last ten years. There is a concern for what these mean or might mean for the larger community, as well as for the Negro family.

A significant part of the recent expansion of the economy, and of related changes in economic organization and control, and in the social and political climate were stimulated and made more urgent by commitments and pressures inherent in the United States' new international role as leader and partner of non-Communist nations. Negro individuals, families, and organizations—and segments of the total population interested in or committed to improvement—now have increased leverage for their efforts, additional alternatives, and increased flexibility. And they are likely to function now, and to plan for the future, with sharply revised estimates of what is possible and what is probable.

Desegregation

The net effects of recently stepped-up rates of change in processes which for a long while have been changing the United States, and the Negro family in particular—specifically the trend towards desegregation—have been beneficial for the country as well as for the Negro segment of its population. However, the effects of these changes are unevenly spread, and involve considerable lag, disorganization, waste, and anxiety. These reflect "the disorganization of transition" as well as the heavy heritage of inequality.

In estimating any improvement in well-being or participation in the American economy, the base from which Negro gains must be measured is smaller than for the white population. The Negro group as a whole is handicapped by a smaller base of social capital and experience, a higher incidence of problems and unused potential, and "sticky" but unevenly spread discrimination. In a sobering estimate, Ginzberg points out: "Within the short span of fifteen years, the economic opportunities of the Negro have vastly increased. Yet, complacency is unwarranted, for even in the cities of the North and West the Negro is far from having equality of opportunity. . . . No matter how rapid the migration from Southern farms continues to be, the birth rate there is so high that large numbers of Negroes will undoubtedly continue to till the soil for several generations." The task in the urban South is to increase the kinds and quality of the jobs open to Negroes: "Their position in Southern industry today is not too different from what it was in many sectors of the North twenty and thirty years ago. . . . At present most jobs available to them in Southern industry lead nowhere." Outside of the South, "large numbers of employers still refuse to hire Negroes. This is particularly true in the major fields of female employment, many of which have only recently been opened to Negro girls and women. Furthermore, even in the North, the majority of Negroes are still concentrated in jobs which are not likely to lead to advancement. These are serious problems, but progress toward solving them is already substantial."[1]

[1] Eli Ginzberg, *The Negro Potential* (New York: Columbia University Press, 1956), pp. 40–41.

Confronted with a current picture and an outlook that combine shadows and light, it is neither surprising nor inconsistent that individual Negro families should exhibit both identification with and detachment from the lumped characteristics and the perceived chances of the Negro as a category—the modal picture. Recent changes, particularly those accompanying urbanization and desegregation, have made it more practicable, and possibly more urgent, for individual Negro families to try to detach themselves in aspirations and conduct from the conventional image of the modal Negro. This probably reflects not so much a denial of the Negro or "Negroness" as such, as it does a denial or repudiation of a single-mode picture or some of its implications for them.

The problem of identity and, therefore, the function of family in relation to it comes now to be less that of training children and adults to live as Negroes in a restricted, but slowly changing, world with a traditional set of rules; and more that of preparation for a world in which the public rules and practices are changing rapidly, and inevitably—albeit unevenly and reluctantly. It is, and promises to be even more, a world in which being a Negro does not as frequently mean automatic discrimination and arbitrary exclusion.

It is also a world in which the chances are better of correcting images of oneself, one's group, and of other groups and other individuals. Shortly after Central High School in Little Rock was integrated in 1958, Kenneth Clark asked one of the nine Negro students involved what was the most important lesson she had learned as a result of her experience.

Clark reports her answering in a rather deliberate manner: "When I used to go to Horace Mann School I thought that white people were different. When I saw the colored kids at Horace Mann acting silly or doing something that I didn't think they should do, I guessed they used to do this because they were colored. Now that I am at Central High School I see the white children do silly things, too. Just like there are some dumb colored children there are some dumb whites. There are some average colored and there are some average whites, and there are some smart whites and some smart colored. I guess what I have learned is that they are not so different and we aren't so different."

Something of one type and level of parental involvement is suggested in this added observation: "When her father suggested that maybe she was working a little harder on her school work than she worked at Horace Mann, she refused to accept this and insisted that she worked as hard as she could at Horace Mann and she is working as hard as she can at Central High School. She stated this with firm matter-of-fact conviction and her father had to accept her interpretation in spite of the fact that it did not agree with his."

It is probably easier for the Negro family and person to live with the fact of being Negro, but there is more anxiety about being or becoming the "right" Negro—and citizen.

The problems of socialization and adjustment in this more fluid society may temporarily be more difficult and productive of anxieties in Negro families on all levels. This is because of the very fact that the social scene will continue to exhibit, and sometimes chaotically, elements of the old and new. There is acute need for some families—and potential need for all—to reconcile the conflict between the values of protection and security; and dignity, advance, and innovation. Greater freedom of choice and movement and the recognition of the potentiality of a better life improve morale. They also make persons more acutely sensitive about the persistent modal image and its factual basis. And they increase dissatisfactions over the fact that changes are not occurring in some areas. It seems reasonable to believe that new developments and trends related to desegregation and enlarged opportunities (and challenges) force the Negro family to take a more direct and positive role in helping the child and young adult define and interpret that world and their chances in it.

There is reason to believe that heretofore the Negro family itself, characteristically, has not directly or systematically provided the child with its education in race. The need to do this directly now is greater—the occasions are more numerous and public; and importantly, it can be done with less ambivalence and shame. How the Negro family meets this challenge and opportunity is the crucial question.

One of the significant aspects of recent developments has been the key role of government in reaffirming the rights of Negroes and in moving to improve opportunities both as a matter of law and morals and national and community self-interest. Connected with these are the underscoring of the Negro's need and disposition to look toward, and use, the national government, and local and state governments where his vote is a factor, for assistance in erasing disabilities in

education, housing, employment, public facilities, and courts
of law.

The Negro family necessarily reflects and is affected more
frequently by a pragmatic linkage of key wants and expectations to government. Affected in varying degree are its sharing of public education in the South and North; its chances
and hopes for better housing; and its access to some jobs
and industries. And of course it is touched disproportionately
by the law and social agencies because of higher dependancy,
crime, delinquency, and illegitimacy rates—and just the
physical fact of being slum dwellers.

Since this involvement is tactical, rather than ideological,
it would be interesting to investigate the social-psychological
implications of this for the future of Negro family functions
and values.

New Urban Frontiers

The main frontier on which the Negro family will shape, and
have shaped, its forms and functions and make its contributions to American life is the city. And it is in the city that we
can see written now the effects of the rapid influx of new
migrants, increased occupational mobility, educational improvement, and desegregation of public services and facilities
on all Negro families.

Urbanization means, particularly for the new migrants from
rural areas, the beginnings of a kind of delayed acculturation,
introduction of more Negro wage earners into the nonagricultural labor force, better educational opportunities, increased political participation and power, and more direct

sharing in public welfare and protective services. It also means immediate acute problems for both old and new Negro families, and for the white population. However, the economic, political, and social imperatives of urban life are such that the Negro family in the city gets an automatic increment in the struggle for realization and recognition merely by the fact of being there.

The recent rapid urbanization has affected Negro families unevenly and in a variety of ways. One reason is that all of the movement is not that of poorly educated, unsophisticated rural persons and families. It is likely, despite their generally poor background, that recent migrants are on the whole better equipped than their predecessors of a generation or more ago. Yet, they are relatively at a greater disadvantage because of changes in the quality of the demand for workers in industry, service, and commerce. On the other hand, particularly in the urban communities of the North and West, their public rights and interests are better protected—if for no other reason than the political strength of Negroes already settled in those communities.

Today, 2 out of every 3 Negroes live in urban areas; and more than one-third of all Negroes now live in urban areas outside of the South. If present trends continue, it is estimated that by the end of the next fifteen years one-fourth to one-third of the population of a number of the larger cities, and as much as one-fifth of the population of some of the larger metropolitan areas will be Negro. An extreme example, and special case in many ways, is Washington, D.C., where Negroes now represent about 45 percent of the population.

About 9 out of every 10 Negroes in the nation's capital live
in the central city. Washington is likely to be a predominantly Negro community in 1970. It is important to note that
among Southern cities there is a tendency for the proportion
of Negroes to decline.

The gross statistics reveal that Negro families in urban
areas significantly exceed the total population with respect to
rates of residence in older parts of the central city, female
heads of families, working wives, sub-families, doubling-up
in households, separations, widowhood, illegitimacy, and
participation in the Aid to Dependent Children program.

In standard metropolitan areas, approximately 4 out of 5
Negroes live in the central cities in contrast to about 3 out
of 5 of the white population. Concentrated in the central
parts of metropolitan areas, the Negro family has less housing available. And much of the new housing available is that
vacated by whites moving to suburban areas and new developments, from which Negroes are excluded by policy or
high costs.

The Negro population increased slightly more than one-
sixth between 1940 and 1950, but there was an increase of
only one-seventh in the number of their dwelling units. On
the other hand, the white population increased about one-
seventh and there was an increase of nearly one-fourth in the
number of dwelling units.

Between 1940 and 1954, the doubling rate among nonwhite couples was close to twice that for white couples.[2] The

[2] Many of the family statistics cited here and following are taken
or adapted from Paul C. Glick, *American Families* (New York: Wiley,
1957).

significantly higher doubling rate in Negro households is not only a function of lower income, although it is an important factor. It reflects also the smaller supply of housing for all Negroes and the significant role of kinship, particularly among low-income families. As Frazier points out, this does not mean that the urban Negro family has retained the character of an extended family. This is a pragmatic urban cultural form. The rate of doubling for Negroes in 1954 was about the same as the rate for whites in 1940.

Despite the fact that fertility rates are higher for Negro couples than white couples, proportionately fewer Negro sons and daughters under eighteen years old still live with their parents. Larger proportions of Negro youths in their teens live apart from relatives or live in families of relatives other than their parents. This is also true of younger Negro children but to a lesser extent. In urban areas both in and out of the South, the proportion of middle-age Negro families with young sons and daughters in their homes is significantly lower than that for white families. For farm areas, the reverse is true.

The likelihood that a Negro family is a "project dweller" in a public housing unit is much greater than the likelihood that a white family is—and the Negro ratio appears to be increasing. In 1954, Negro families occupied more than a third (37.7 percent) of all such units available; in 1957, the proportion exceeded two-fifths (43.7 percent.) This represents an upgrading of housing for some Negro families. An increasing proportion of low-income urban Negro families are either aspirants to or graduates of public housing projects.

There are many relative gains for Negro families that live in public housing projects, but complaints and invidiousness with respect to these units and their residents are increasing within the Negro community, as well as the larger community.

Public housing continues to be both the first and last best hope of low-income, marginal families, and those involved with social and welfare agencies. The fact that such housing is under attack for a variety of reasons threatens, and increases the invidiousness with respect to, an important setting for a large slice of Negro family life. The gap between the housing project dweller and the rest of the Negro community is likely to widen as general upgrading of living and status standards occurs.

More than 25,000 Negro families are "living under conditions of open-occupancy," according to Public Housing officials. Housing experts point out, however, that experience has shown that where racial barriers in public housing have been broken by public policy or law, there is a tendency for the units to become all-minority.

Negro families are disproportionately involved in the displacement and relocation problems related to slum clearance, urban redevelopment, and urban renewal programs. Overall approximately 2 out of every 3 persons displaced are Negroes. In seventeen communities in the Southeastern Region, for example, 95 percent of the families displaced were Negro; and less than 2 out of 3 of these families were relocated in "decent, safe, and sanitary" houses. One of every 5 families went into substandard housing.

Improved job opportunities and increased incomes since

the 1940s have contributed to the marked increase in home ownership among Negroes and significant upgrading in housing among the middle and upper-income families in urban areas, as a result of both individual efforts and new, privately sponsored but government-insured housing projects for Negroes. Despite this improvement, with the increased population and concentration in the central city, the housing market for the Negro family continues severely restricted. The chances are overwhelming that the Negro family will live in a segregated area or a new transition area that will soon become segregated—a slum or a housing project for low-income groups; and an upgraded all-Negro development, or fringe area for middle- and upper-income groups. And the chances are overwhelming that the Negro family will be paying premium prices for the housing it has.

The Negro family has become increasingly self-conscious and anxious about housing. This development is related not only to scarcity, lack of free choice, and neighborhood and community tensions, but also to changes in comfort, success, and status models. Added to the heightened family and personal value of decent housing and good neighborhoods as proper settings for child-rearing and family living, is the increased importance of housing as a status symbol and measure of mobility. This is, of course, a value that the Negro family shares with all American families. For the Negro family there is additional emphasis—and therefore added possibilities of frustration—because of what housing means now as an overt demonstration of achievement and worth to both the Negro and white communities.

The problem of public school education is directly related

to, and aggravated by, the housing situation for Negroes, particularly in urban communities; and it is marked by similar values, needs, and anxieties among the Negro families. Because of the residential concentration of Negro families in the central and older parts of the city, a high proportion of Negro public school pupils are in older, overcrowded school buildings that tend to be segregated in fact, if not in law. The effects on the family are direct not only in terms of the quality of the education of the child but also in terms of the anxieties and resentments this situation arouses in Negro parents of the stable working class and middle class. The effects are the more acute because of the high values placed on education as a means of advancement in all levels of the Negro community; of the effect of the Supreme Court decision and desegregation in the South, which spotlight and make more onerous segregated schooling in the North; and because of the great current public concern over the quality of public education.

Negro families, and organizations representing them, are showing increased sensitivity over what are perceived as any competitive disadvantages their children have, for whatever reasons. Negro family heads are likely to be concerned not just about the availability of schooling as such, but about the quality of education available to their children and the characteristics of particular schools. For the second successive year a group of Negro parents in New York City are refusing to send their children to what they describe as an inferior, overcrowded school.

The added value placed on education of children as a

means of escaping low and achieving higher status is a myth-like cultural theme. It induces anxiety on all levels. The "compensatory projection of parental ambition" onto children in middle-class, white-collar Negro families is expected and understood; however, Merton points out that "in a recent research on the social organization of public housing developments, we have found among both Negroes and whites in lower occupational levels, a substantial proportion having aspirations for a professional career for their children." Reiss and Rhodes, in a Nashville study, found that "Negroes require a somewhat higher level of educational attainment than the general population and place a substantially greater value on schooling than do whites."

If, as Merton suggests, the "syndrome of lofty aspirations and limited realistic opportunities . . . is precisely the pattern which invites deviant behavior," [3] the conclusions of Reiss and Rhodes provide an important clue to reasons why, and ways in which, Negro mothers might prime both achievement and deviant behavior in children:

White mothers in the lower stratum of American society are less likely than Negro mothers to project high aspirations on to their children if they are low rather than high I.Q. children. . . . [We] suggest that the importance of schooling to the Negro family makes their members more likely than those of the white family to project unrealistic educational goals in the low I.Q. child. There is only a small race difference in subjects' educational aspirations such that Negroes are somewhat more likely to aspire toward a college education.[4]

[3] Robert K. Merton, *Social Theory and Social Structure*, Revised and Enlarged Edition (Glencoe: Free Press, 1957), p. 159.
[4] Albert J. Reiss, Jr. and Albert L. Rhodes, "Are Educational Norms

The absolute chances of Negro youths for higher education are increasing: In 1950 more Negroes graduated from college than had graduated from high school in 1920. The rate of increase of Negro college enrollment during that period was six times that of whites. The fact that slightly better than 1 in 10 Negro families include an adult with some college education in contrast to slightly more than 1 in 4 white families, shows a sizeable gap still. Further, as suggested earlier, general anxiety about education is likely to make Negro families more concerned and anxious about the educational future and prospects of children. And all the more so when the increased costs of education are juxtaposed to the generally low income of the Negro family.

One of the most persistent and popular stereotypes is that lower-class parents have little or no interest in the education of their children. Refutation and an indication of the need to examine other factors are furnished in a study made in a New York school with a pupil population predominately Puerto Rican and Negro. A field worker was assigned to work with the parents. The results:

A year and a half later there were forty-five Negro and Puerto Rican mothers working on the Executive and seven other committees that formed the leadership core of the PTA; the Executive Committee of fifteen Negro and Puerto Rican mothers had felt confident enough to visit the superintendent of all the elementary schools and make a request in non-hostile terms; a parent chorus was giving concerts in schools; the PTA had compiled and mimeographed a directory of available health services

and Goals of Conforming, Truant, and Delinquent Adolescents Influenced by Group Position in American Society?" *Journal of Negro Education*, Vol. XXVIII (Summer, 1959), pp. 258, 261.

and had set up a polio clinic for the neighborhood; and one of the mothers, a Negro, had become president of the Community Health Committee. These parents, who had seemed to take no interest in their children's education, proved that, although oppressed with problems of living conditions, health, and economic security, they were deeply concerned with their school and had the capacity for positive action and leadership.[5]

The foregoing suggests the heavy impact now of housing and schooling values and anxieties as factors affecting one aspect of child rearing and the roles of adults. However, the ways in which, and the relative success with which, Negro families carry out these functions, are primarily related to family size and structure and class position.

During the past generation, the decline in the average size of Negro households has been much less than that of white households, due to differences in the birth rate and in the practice and necessity of doubling. Negro households are significantly larger, containing on the average more children and more adults. Since 1950, the number of Negro households has been increasing at a rate more than twice that for white households. And Negroes have a relatively larger proportion of both small and large households. This is related to the large proportion of childless women, the high proportion of women with large numbers of children, and the high proportion of lodgers.

The chances continue disproportionately high that much of the socialization of the Negro child will take place in a household headed by a woman, not headed by both or either

[5] John H. Niemeyer, "Splitting the Social Atom," *Saturday Review,* September 12, 1959, p. 18.

of his own parents, with relatives other than his own parents and brothers and sisters, or with nonrelatives, and with direct support or subsidy from public funds.

Since the conventional and stable type of family or household is not the instrument of socialization for many children, or of community-orientation and status-giving for many adults, it is probable that persons, institutions, and experiences outside of the family or household are relatively more important, and make their influence felt earlier, in the Negro family. And the relatively larger role played by nonfamily factors in socialization in the Negro community probably applies on all levels and for all family types. Evidence supporting this is found in one of the few recent examples of a follow-up study of Negro family functions. In 1953–56 John H. Rohrer and his associates in New Orleans did a follow-up investigation of the adolescent subjects used in Allison Davis' and John Dollard's 1937–38 study published as *Children of Bondage*. They studied "group patterning of primary social identification" in child training in a class-stratified sample of Negro women householders as well as among the original subjects of the Davis-Dollard study. Their study "failed to reveal that there was any universal systematic training given in caste etiquette, at least before school age." [6]

All that this finding suggests, however, is that the Negro child probably gets most of his racial training by absorbing

[6] John H. Rohrer, "Sociocultural Factors in Personality Development," National Conference on Social Welfare, *The Social Welfare Forum, Official Proceedings, Philadelphia,* 1957 (New York: Columbia University Press, 1957), p. 195.

informally and unsystematically clues and cues from members of the household and from outside the family. Merton points out: "Nor is the socialization confined to direct training and disciplining. The process is, at least in part, inadvertent . . . Not infrequently, *children detect and incorporate cultural uniformities even when these remain implicit and have not been reduced to rules*." [7]

Edward K. Weaver asked children at an elementary school in the South to write answers to the question "When did you first discover that you were a Negro?" In only three of the thirty replies cited as "typical" did a child report the first explicit revelation as having come from direct family instruction or from inside the home. And in these instances it was the grandparent who gave the instruction or warning. [8]

Statistics continue to confirm the classic pictures of disorganization, dependency, and inadequacy, and larger proportions of broken families and female heads. However, we have little or no recent data to tell us what these facts and forms mean and represent in the present context. It may be that the classic explanations are still valid, but we cannot be sure, and there is a risk in assuming or guessing, without the facts that go beyond the statistics and older studies.

The proportion of Negroes married but living apart from spouses is three to four times higher than that of whites. Approximately 1 in 9 Negro married women and 1 in 12 Negro married men are living apart from their spouses. Ne-

[7] Merton, *Social Theory*, p. 158.
[8] Edward K. Weaver, "Racial Sensitivity Among Negro Children," *Phylon*, Vol. XVII (First Quarter, 1956), pp. 52–60.

groes constitute about 1 in 11 of all families in the United States, 1 in 14 of all husband-wife families, and 1 in 5 of all families with female heads.

Much of the incidence of these and the related characteristics is, of course, explained, as Frazier has done so effectively, by the persistence of rural-folk traditions and ways in interaction with urban, secular imperatives. However, not enough is known about the dynamics of present family forms and functions and about the behavior patterns which are distinctly urban products with a dynamic and history of their own. The forms, as in the case of the family headed by the female, may be the same but the context in which they fit and function has probably changed in important details. Knowledge of background and of a tradition, which itself is changing, are necessary but probably not sufficient to explain and understand the Negro family, particularly in the changing cities of today.

In this connection, it is probable that even the time-honored reference to desertion as "the poor man's divorce" needs closer examination and discrimination, although it is abundantly clear that the racial difference in desertion remains very significant. In a study made in Philadelphia, Kephart found that "when the bottom three occupational classes are combined . . . for the whites these classes are slightly overrepresented in desertions, while among Negroes, surprisingly, these classes are slightly underrepresented. . . . [Among] the Negroes the greatest overrepresention is found in the semiskilled category." He suggests as explanatory factors possible underreporting because of ignorance of the law

and the "lingering tradition" among Negro lower classes—
the wives may not want husbands back. Balancing these,
however, he adds, is the fact that lower-class wives must have
family support and cannot get public assistance unless the
husband is reported.[9]

The census data indicate that "color is a differential in
marriage impermanence only in separation and widowhood."
Divorce rates for Negro women tend to rise as education rises
up to, but not including, college graduation.

Increases in illegitimacy rates among Negroes and in the
proportion participating in the Aid to Dependent Children
program are associated with recent increases in urbanization.
For the general population, the number of births to unmarried mothers has been rising at a faster rate than births to
married mothers. The illegitimacy rate in 1956 was 46.5 per
1,000 live births as compared with 37.9 per 1,000 live births
in 1940. Teen-agers contributed nearly half the number of
illegitimacies in 1940, and 40 percent in 1956. The predominant part of the increase between 1940 and 1955 is to
be accounted for by nonwhite illegitimate births, which increased at a rate more than twice that for whites. There has
been a tendency for the nonwhite rate to be higher in
Northern urban centers than the estimated nonwhite percentage for the entire country including the Southern states.
It is undoubtedly true now as Frazier points out that "illegitimacy, like other forms of family disorganization, tends
to become segregated in the poorer sections of the Negro

[9] William M. Kephart, "Occupational Level and Marital Disruption,"
American Sociological Review, Vol. 20 (August, 1955).

community located in the slum areas of our cities." The fact
that illegitimacy rates are increasing in urban areas at the
same time that the general economic and educational level
of the Negro population is improving may reflect a short-run
rise attributable in the main to the disorganization related to
the rapid influx and piling up of low-income groups. There
are certainly other factors operating currently about which we
know little, which are independent of race.

Another measure of family inadequacy or disorganization
closely associated with increasing urbanization of the Negro
is the rate of participation in the Aid to Dependent Children
program. This is not surprising inasmuch as the family crises
leading to need for ADC (absence or incapacity of father)
occur relatively more frequently among low-income groups.
Urbanization of ADC recipients is increasing, particularly
among Negroes who make up an increasing portion of the
ADC load—31 percent in 1948; 40 percent in 1956. More
than one-half of the nonwhite family recipients live in cities
of over 50,000 population; nearly two-thirds of the Negro
recipients are in metropolitan counties. The overrepresenta-
tion of Negro families on ADC rolls is a political and administrative issue in both many Southern states and Northern
communities with large concentrations of Negroes. This is
another example of the acutely "political" character of the
needs and rights of disadvantaged Negroes.

The increase, and the differential, in the labor force participation of Negro wives reflect different values and pressure
among them: the greater need to work to maintain or supplement a basically low family income, particularly among lower

occupational and educational levels; increased incentive or wish to work, in order to improve or maintain a desired level of living, particularly among mobile, better-educated, middle-class families; and possibly, more favorable conditions for leaving children with relatives or others. The significance of this last is questionable, particularly among low-income newcomers to the large cities. Social workers report an increase in "door-key children" and an acute current shortage of low-cost nursery care in impoverished urban areas.

Negro wives in just over two-fifths of all Negro husband-wife families work; about half of those with no children under six work; and nearly 1 in 4 of those with children under six is in the labor force. The mothers of children under six are less than half as likely to be working as other mothers, regardless of race and other variables. And the differences in labor force participation of mothers, Negro and white, who share family responsibilities with a husband and those who are themselves the head of the family, as in the case of a disproportionate number of Negroes, are growing less. That this does not imply the same values and pressures is indicated by the fact that the income level of nearly one-half the broken families with female heads is below $2,000. There is some convergence in the employment rates of Negro and white wives, but the differences remain large.

Class Changes

The heavy wave of professional concern and popular preoccupation with social class values, tastes, and behavior has had telling and, on the whole, favorable effects on the Negro community and the Negro family. One result has been the casting up for popular recognition of features of the Negro community which had been blurred, ignored, not too well understood, and attributed to color. First came the necessary assumption and then the recognition and acceptance that there are class differences within the Negro community. As a result, the Negro's self-esteem and aspirations have received a decisive boost. The impact of the idea, and the demonstration of class in the Negro community have now done what the old, poignant protest, "All Negroes are not alike!" could not do. Applying the class approach to the Negro has helped the public to enlarge and correct its image of the Negro, and it has provided a new, nonthreatening basis for discrimination. It improves the chances of identification, communication, and contact; and it tends to cut across or transcend racial lines. Now, one pauses and asks, "Is this a class or a race trait?"

Very American, and "hopeful" for all concerned, is the assumption that better education and better jobs help more Negroes to acquire middle-class characteristics. For the American middle-class mind, the fewer lower-class Negroes, or Negroes with lower-class characteristics, the less the threat and the cost of disorganization and dependency associated with Negroes. For middle-class Negroes and their families, the fewer Negroes with lower-class characteristics, the less the threat to their own status is the old custom of lumping all Negroes, and the better the chance to work out with minimum anxiety just who they are and with whom they identify.

In addition to what has been said above about the class concept as a catalyst of favorable change it should be pointed out that some of the assumptions and clichés with respect to class values and behavior, particularly lower-class, are among the factors that deter better understanding and policy-making. Using any of the usual socio-economic indices, proportionately more Negro families are in the lower-class. Although it is probably true, this fact alone does not mean necessarily that proportionately fewer Negroes adhere to middle-class values or aspire to middle-class goals. The Negro family's generally low socio-economic status, and discrimination, affect the chances to afford, cultivate, and enjoy some of the American middle-class success values—education, respectability, thrift, etc.; however, the appreciation and grasp of these is another matter. The force of education as a value on all levels of the Negro community has already been discussed.

Among the lower-income or working class Negro families, there have been some postwar changes in income and education, and increased exposure to and absorption of mass culture through the press, radio, and television. These have altered images, aspirations, and practices—and conspicuously along lines of consumption and leisure time. Probably not at the same rate, but certainly along with the rest of America, the Negro family is undergoing an upgrading of tastes and of its ability to satisfy them. This "deproletarianization" of the working class, and the rise and spread of the Negro middle-class tend to make class and ethnic differences less significant and less invidious. Of course, there will be lags and resistant ethnic and class strongholds—but all of the pressures, both outside the Negro community and within it, are enhancing the ability and the opportunity to conform in essentials to middle-class American ways. The desire and design for conformity, even "over-conformity," the American Negro has always had, and the results at times seem to border on caricature as Frazier points out in his portrait of the middle class in *Black Bourgeoisie* (1957).

The force of class changes and the diffusion of middle-class standards and ways shows up not only in the consumption behavior of the Negro family, as in automobiles, housing, dress, etc., but more importantly in child-rearing and family roles.

Davis and Havighurst concluded, in their influential study made in 1943, that "there are *cultural differences* in the personality formation of middle-class compared with lower-class people, *regardless of color*, due to their early training. And for the same reason there should be further but less marked cultural differences between Negroes and whites of the same social class." [10] The logic of events and some evidence since 1943 would indicate that some convergence has occurred with respect to the influence of both class and color factors in child-rearing, if regional differences are held constant. In a recent review of research in this area Bronfenbrenner compared "the traditional view of the differences between the middle- and lower-class styles of life, as docu-

---

[10] Allison Davis and Robert J. Havighurst, "Social Class and Color Differences in Child-Rearing" in Guy E. Swanson, T. M. Newcomb, E. L. Hartley, and others, *Readings in Social Psychology*, Revised Edition (New York: Holt, 1952), p. 550.

mented in the classic descriptions of Warner, Davis, Dollard, and . . . Spinley, Clausen, and Miller and Swanson." He concluded: "To the extent that our data even approach this picture, it is for the period before World War II rather than for the present-day. . . . As for the lower-class the fit is far better for the actual behavior of the parents than for the values they seek to instill in their children." [11]

Since, beyond the social class factor, "child-rearing practices are likely to change most quickly in those segments of society which have closest access and are most receptive to the agencies or agents of change," it is probably true that the Negro family as a category, like the rural family as a category, lags in the rate and extent of change in child-rearing practices.

Clues to some of the dynamics of lag as well as those of change are to be found in the differences in adoption practices between the Negro community and the white community, and in the efforts to encourage change in the Negro family's practices. Among the reasons suggested as affecting adoption behavior are these: many Negro couples come from or live in areas where adoptive facilities are not developed or not available; fear of rejection; limited income and inadequate housing. Special agency and community programs in Chicago, New York, Los Angeles, and San Francisco represent the first organized efforts on a significant scale to solve this program.

Such efforts are similar to those established or proposed to change other practices or circumstances affecting Negro

[11] Uri Bronfenbrenner, "Socialization and Social Class Through Time and Space," in E. E. Macoby, T. M. Newcomb, and E. L. Hartley, *Readings in Social Psychology* (New York: Holt, 1958), pp. 400–25.

family life. They reflect public and professional awareness of the threat and social costs involved as well as increasing recognition that such nonmiddle-class behavior is a result of neither inherent racial nor immutable class characteristics. They show the desire, if not the "need," to grant middle-class potentialities to Negro families; and, frequently, to implement their attainment—both under segregated and unsegregated conditions—with public and private funds.

Notable changes in the roles of Negro family members are due to class mobility and the resulting closer adherence to prevailing American sex role patterns, as well as to the gains and dilemmas of desegregation. For well-known reasons, the influence of the Negro woman in the Negro family has been very strong. It is likely to continue strong in different segments of the Negro community but for different reasons. The reasons with respect to the low-income working class family that is broken are clear, and they will continue to operate. In the mobile or middle-class family the influence of the woman becomes stronger because parents in this type of Negro family tend to be sensitive to the same images, if not precisely the identical pressures, related to the organization and values of present-day business life and the rituals of status, notably place and style of living, that affect their white prototype. And as Frazier points out, the pressures may actually be stronger. Although influence of the Negro woman is increasing, there are gains or changes for the male parent, also. Job, salary, and educational improvement tend to increase confidence and permit him to play and to see himself in the part of the more conventional wage-earner, husband, parent, and participant in community affairs.

In his *Black Bourgeoisie*, Frazier suggests that "In the South the middle-class Negro male is not only prevented from playing a masculine role, but generally he must let Negro women assume leadership in any show of militancy." [12] This is probably less true now—though how much less, we do not know—than it was ten years ago, and than it will be ten years from now, yet dramatic changes are not to be expected. Although it is still "safer" for women—both Negro and white—to act in a strong manner in matters affecting race relations in the South, there are differences between what it is "safe" for the male to do in the cities of the South today and what it is "safe" to do in rural areas. Even here it should be pointed out that with few exceptions in both urban and rural areas, the leadership for recent moves challenging segregation has come mainly from business and professional groups—ministers, lawyers, insurance men, and in many instances medical practitioners—who have been protected by their relative independence from direct economic pressure. And they have been able to use most effectively the support and technical assistance of national organizations as well as their own local strategic political power. These situations have provided new opportunities for the male to play a more positive role; and they have provided models and images for other Negro males. One of the reasons why more males are

[12] E. Franklin Frazier, *Black Bourgeoisie* (Glencoe: Free Press, 1957), p. 221.

not militant or under severe pressure to be so is that much
of the struggle for rights does not involve person-to-person
conflict or the need for direct confrontation. Important
aspects of the struggle are waged by organizations which in
this sense are surrogates that relieve the direct pressure on
the individual. The demand and real need is for Negro families to supply and support the local innovator who will make
the initial challenge. In Montgomery, this part was played by
Mrs. Rosa Parks; at the University of Alabama by Miss Lucy;
in Little Rock by Mrs. Bates (effectively backed by Mr. Bates,
and other men), and notably by the female students (Minnie
Jean Brown, Elizabeth Eckford, et al.); and in New York
City by the mothers of Harlem school children.

The family role and the community position of the average
Negro male, in contrast to the average white male, are affected in direct and subtle ways by the continuing differences
in the following: the industry in which the Negro husband
and father works, the job level or area, the earnings associated with it, the degree of certainty he has with respect to
maintaining it and the chances of advancement he sees in it,
and dependence on wages—in contrast to salary, commissions, profits, investments.

Since the job is a crucial determinant of where and how
the family fits in the society, and of the effectiveness of its
claim on many of the society's rewards, probably the most
important single clue to the quality of change in the Negro
family and in the Negro community is found in the job picture, particularly for the male. In this sense, then, any recent
improvements in that picture as a result of increasing de-

segregation and urbanization represent the most solid and significant of recent gains for the Negro family. And continued changes in the employment picture are necessary to underwrite in practical terms the salutary changes in self-conceptions, movement, participation, and tastes that have recently come rapidly to the Negro family.

A HEALTHIER WORLD

by GEORGE ROSEN, M.D.

IT IS almost impossible to overemphasize the effect the development of microbiology and immunology have had on the health of the community. Action in the interest of community health today comprises an intricate maze of activities involving the services and energies of a wide variety of professional and lay people. Much of this work stems from the application of bacteriological and immunological knowledge to the actual problems of disease control.

Public health departments, as set up in the nineteenth century, were concerned essentially with the control of contagious diseases through environmental sanitation. However, as the microorganisms responsible for specific diseases were identified and their mode of action uncovered, the way was opened for the control of infectious diseases on a more rational, accurate, and specific basis. Such activity by public health authorities became possible on an unprecedented scale. The first decade of the twentieth century saw a solid basis for the control of a number of infectious diseases, and

George Rosen, M.D. is Professor of Public Health Education at the School of Public Health and Administrative Medicine of Columbia University.

throughout succeeding decades advances along this line have continued with increasing tempo.

The meaning of this trend is clearly evident in the case of diphtheria. By 1900, diphtheria could be diagnosed by precise bacteriological methods; the sick person could be treated with diphtheria antitoxin, and well carriers could be detected, thus making possible effective control. The next important step was the direct prevention of the disease by active immunization, a method developed logically from earlier knowledge on the use of diphtheria antitoxin as a passive immunizing agent as well as a therapeutic agent. By 1920 knowledge and tools were available for a full-scale mass attack on diphtheria. In that year active immunization of school children began, and by 1940 the disease had been virtually eliminated as a cause of death: the mortality rate of diphtheria was 1.1 per 100,000 in 1940, in striking contrast to the rate of 785 per 100,000 which obtained in 1894.

The drop in diphtheria morbidity and mortality was not due to preventive immunization alone. This rapid decline actually began in the nineteenth century before diphtheria antitoxin was generally used, and continued progressively even before preventive immunization became widespread. Nor was the decline of diphtheria an isolated instance of the control of disease. Many other major infectious diseases had begun to wane before the full effects of the bacteriological discoveries made themselves felt. Beginning about 1870, there was a continuing downward trend in deaths from such diseases as yellow fever, smallpox, typhoid and typhus fevers, malaria, and tuberculosis. These developments undoubtedly reflect in part the impact of the sanitary reform movement of the nineteenth century. Acting on the theory that a clean city is a healthy city, city governmental and private agencies sought to clean up the physical environment, and made efforts to provide unadulterated food and clean water; in short, action was taken to provide decent living conditions.

Yet, whatever factors were involved in the decline of specific infectious diseases, we must note that children were the chief beneficiaries. The degree of benefit obtained from measures taken for the improvement of milk and water is clearly shown by the trend of the infant mortality rate in New York City. In 1885 the infant death rate was 273 per 1,000 live births; by 1915 it had dropped sharply to 94 per 1,000. Equally beneficial results were obtained through the widespread adoption of smallpox vaccination after 1870. Children also benefited from a decline in the virulence of scarlet fever.

This brief account of the decline in specific infectious diseases and its significance for child health need not be pursued in detail. What it meant in simple quantitative terms can be seen from the following estimates. According to W. S. Thompson, the probable number of survivors to age sixty-five from 1,000 births in the United States increased from 325 in 1875 to 695 in 1940.

While communicable diseases were increasingly being brought under control, and action was being taken for more effective sanitation, new developments occurred during the first decade of the twentieth century which vastly broadened the horizons of public health workers and turned their attention to new tasks. Surveying the community with a critical eye, some of those engaged in health and social work were not entirely satisfied with what they saw. Investigations of the poorer classes of the community showed that their health and environment were highly unsatisfactory. Malnutrition was rife, maternal mortality was high, and while infant mortality had declined, the health of children attending school as well as that of preschool children was found to be extremely poor.

On the basis of these findings, socially minded citizens, physicians, clergymen, social workers, and government officials concerned themselves with all phases of child life. This movement to improve the health and welfare of children was directed at first toward reducing the high child mortality rate. Experts recognized that a large part of infant mortality was preventable—that it was caused by malnourishment, parental ignorance, contaminated food, and other factors attributable entirely or in part to poverty. Some of these factors were remediable, while the effects of others might be greatly lessened. Since the problem had many ramifications, it was attacked along a number of different lines: by instructing mothers in the proper feeding and care of children; through the provision of clean milk; through legislation regulating the work of expectant mothers; and by providing facilities for the care of babies of working mothers.

These endeavors to improve child health were a characteristic and prominent feature of the larger movement for social reform and the amelioration of poor health conditions which marked the United States during the two decades preceding its entry into World War I. The orientation of this movement was empirical and pragmatic; its proponents had confidence in what might be accomplished by conscious social action. In varying degrees the same phenomenon could be found in other countries at this time, and it is evident that this was a response to the problems thrown up by an advancing industrialization accompanied by urban expansion. Protest and affirmation, vigorous discontent and abounding confidence in constructive social endeavor led to action in various directions.

The beginnings of child welfare efforts at the turn of the century followed the same general lines in both European and American urban communities. At first, stations were set up to provide clean milk; later these became well-child stations where the health of infants and young children was supervised, and mothers were instructed in the care of the child at home. It was known that the diarrhea from which so many babies younger than two years of age died, especially in the summer, was due largely to unsafe, highly contaminated milk. It was also known that the mortality among breast-fed babies was considerably lower than among those artificially fed. Consequently, the prime objective of all those concerned with infant health was to encourage breast feeding or, when this was not possible, to provide a safe and effective substitute.

There was yet, however, little or no emphasis on community responsibility for the promotion of child health. During the nineteenth century there were sporadic efforts in

Europe and the United States towards this end, but it was not until the turn of the century that facilities and programs for infant and child care began to appear in rapid succession. In 1889, an American physician, Henry Koplik (1858–1927), established a "milk station," which was actually a very simple consultation center for mothers and children, at the Good Samaritan Dispensary in New York. However, demonstrations initiated in France along these lines exerted a wide effect in other countries. Most important was the work of Pierre Budin, who established a pioneer system of infant consultation centers, which served as a model for other countries.

In these efforts it was recognized that mothers who could not breast-feed their babies should be able to obtain clean cow's milk at a reasonable price. This concept first took hold in France, and milk stations, known as *gouettes de lait*, were set up in Paris. This example was soon followed in New York City by the philanthropist Nathan Strauss, who was interested in health problems. In 1893, he began to set up a system of milk stations which was widely copied and which he supported for twenty-six years until 1919. The milk was modified according to formula, pasteurized, and dispensed in nursing bottles, and mothers were instructed in feeding their babies. In 1902, these stations distributed 250,000 bottles monthly.

The Strauss milk stations provided the impetus for governmental action along these lines in the United States. Set up under health department auspices, experiments in child feeding were carried on, pasteurized milk was distributed at cost, and mothers were instructed in the proper care and feeding of infants.

Provision of clean milk, teaching mothers to care for their babies, and creation of clinics where this could be done properly were the three basic elements that entered into the development of well-child services. Toward the end of the first decade of the twentieth century, a number of private and governmental agencies in various countries had already demonstrated what might be accomplished along each of these avenues in promoting child health. Recognition that the execution of these activities as a total program was a community responsibility to be borne by the agency officially concerned with the health of the community was first achieved in New York City.

The establishment in 1908 of a Division of Child Hygiene in the New York City Health Department is a landmark in the history of child health work. This unit was the first of its kind in the world and was to set a pattern for other health departments in the United States and abroad. S. Josephine Baker, a physician who had been a child health inspector in the Department, was put in charge. Early in the summer of 1908, she had shown how infant deaths could be greatly reduced through prevention of disease. In a congested section of New York's lower East Side the name and address of every newborn baby in the district was obtained from the registrar of records the day after its birth. On that day, a public health nurse visited the mother and taught her how to keep the baby well. When the results were tabulated after about two months, it was found that there were 1,200 fewer deaths in the district than there had been in the preceding summer during the same period. This demonstration of how to give babies a healthy start in life provided the basis for the work of the division.

One of its first achievements was to employ milk distribution as a way of coming into contact with mothers to teach them proper child care. Attention was also directed to the health of babies in foundling hospitals and to children of school age. Long before the idea of maternal deprivation was conceived, Josephine Baker pointed out that good hygienic conditions during pregnancy were fundamental to the health of babies. Similarly, before the term "health education" was invented, the educational process was being employed as a fundamental tool in the campaign to save infant life. An instance in point is the development of the Little Mothers' League. Recognizing that the "little mother," that is, the little girl in a poor family who has to take care of younger children because her mother works, was an important factor in infant deaths, Dr. Baker organized a flock of Little Mothers' Leagues among school girls. These children were given practical instruction in child care and served as missionaries of the new gospel in tenements and slums.

The Division of Child Hygiene represented one avenue of attack on the preventable deaths of children. However, this was a battle waged simultaneously on many fronts. As we have seen, of outstanding importance was the provision of clean milk. In 1901, W. H. Park of the New York City Bacteriological Laboratory showed that milk delivered to customers in the summer was generally highly contaminated with bacteria and might contain more than 5,000,000 organisms per cubic centimeter. The following year, together with L. Emmett Holt, he addressed himself to the problem of infantile diarrhea and its relation to the bacteriology of the milk consumed. The results clearly showed that the quality of milk fed to infants during hot weather influenced the amount of illness to which they were subject and their mortality.

In 1910, the New York City Board of Health began to require that all milk used for drinking purposes be properly pasteurized, and two years later the Board adopted a grading system and standards for all milk brought into the city for sale. Clean milk became available for New York's babies, rich and poor. The degree to which infants benefited by the measures is indicated by the virtual elimination of deaths from summer diarrhea. By 1923, scarcely a vestige remained of the great rise in infant mortality that generally came with the hot weather.

The beginnings of official action on behalf of child health in New York City have been described in some detail because they illustrate the elements and interrelationships that entered into the development of this field of health action in the United States. What New York City had done on a local level was carried forward by the states and the federal government. Federal recognition was accorded to the field of child health when President Taft, on April 9, 1912, signed a bill creating a Children's Bureau which was charged with investigating and reporting "upon all matters pertaining to the welfare of children and child life among all classes of our people."

The idea for such a Bureau came from Florence Kelley and Lillian Wald, both members of that dedicated, militant group of men and women who at the end of the nineteenth century and during the first quarter of the present century undertook to curb some of the worst abuses created by industrialization and who prepared the way for the social legislation we take for granted today. Its initial appropriation was only $26,640, and the Bureau wisely devoted much of its activity to a reconnaissance of the field assigned to it by Congress. Much of the data collected before the 1930s provided a solid basis of fact for later federal action in the interest of mothers and children.

That infancy could not be protected without the protection of maternity was one of the principles on which the Children's Bureau developed its program. In the United States, the first organized program of health care during the prenatal period was provided in 1908 by the Pediatric Department of the New York Outdoor Medical Clinic. Visiting nurse service for pregnant women in their homes followed a year later in Boston, under the sponsorship of the Women's Municipal League. In 1912 such services were initiated in St. Louis. Initially, the Children's Bureau participated in the field of maternal health by studying maternal mortality, and by providing instruction for mothers. For the latter purpose, the Bureau, in 1913, published a pamphlet entitled *Prenatal Care*, which has been a best-seller ever since.

Since then, great strides have been taken in maternity care

in the United States. These have gone hand in hand with and are in part the result of important social and scientific developments. For example, in 1935, 63 percent of all babies were born in places other than hospitals, and 13 percent of all live births were not attended by physicians. By 1956, almost 95 percent of all babies born in this country were delivered in hospitals, and 97 percent of all registered births were attended by physicians. Increased public awareness of the value of maternity care coupled with advances in medical knowledge have been responsible for the sharp declines in the mortality of mothers and infants over the past thirty years, and the general improvement in their health. While there still are areas and groups in the United States—chiefly rural, low income, and of lower-than-average educational level—that do not fully enjoy these benefits, even these have shown improvement in recent years.

To a very considerable degree, this is a result of action by the federal government. During and after World War I developments in the care of mothers and children came rapidly, especially with the passage of the Maternity and Infancy (Sheppard-Towner) Act in 1921. Through the extension of grants-in-aid to private and public agencies, a strong stimulus was given to prenatal care and child welfare work. For seven years, a successful program based on federal-state cooperation was carried on, but in 1929 it failed to secure further appropriations from Congress. Six years later, however, it was reenacted on a much more ambitious scale as Title V of the Social Security Act. This section authorized grants to be made each year to the various states through the

Children's Bureau to help them extend and improve their maternal and child health services, as well as services for handicapped children.

During World War II, the Children's Bureau also administered through state agencies a vast emergency program of infant and maternity care for the wives of service men. By holding unswervingly to a broad conception of child welfare as concerned with all the social aspects of child life, by insisting on the use of qualified personnel in all programs, and by encouraging communities to develop programs on the local and state levels to improve the health and welfare of mothers and children, the Children's Bureau has played a leading role in developing these aspects of community health in the United States.

Action in the interest of mothers and infants during the past half-century was paralleled by the development of health services for school children. Medical examination of school children was initiated to control contagion. Much of the early work in this field was sketchy. It was simply a crude attempt to screen out the worst cases of infectious diseases, though many minor ones could be brought to light by physicians who were conscientious and experienced. After a while, however, it was recognized that this was not enough. In addition to such diseases as diphtheria, measles, and scarlet fever, school children in large urban centers, especially in slum areas, suffered from skin diseases (pediculosis, scabies, ringworm, impetigo), eye conditions (trachoma), malnutrition, and physical defects. It was recognized that education of parent and child was necessary to combat these conditions.

An effective method of dealing with the situation was first developed in New York City. In 1902, at the request of the Health Commissioner, Lillian Wald of the Henry Street Settlement loaned one of her best qualified nurses to carry out a pilot demonstration in a particularly bad school. After a few months, this nurse had evolved an educational approach that was effective in checking the minor infections. In consequence, she was appointed as the first full-time school nurse in the United States, and soon additional nurses were employed to work along the lines she had developed. This approach was eminently successful and contributed in large measure to the eventual disappearance of many of the conditions listed above.

With the passage of time, many changes have taken place in the provision of health services for school children. There has been a shift of emphasis from the initial limited objectives to a broader concept of the field of school health. From a concern with the control of contagion had come the introduction of public health nursing in schools. The program was then expanded by the introduction of periodic medical examinations and follow-up procedures for the correction of discovered physical defects. Once interest in the health problems of children was aroused in the United States developments occurred in a number of other directions.

The school lunch movement had its inception in New York in 1908 as an effort to supplement the diet of undernourished children. Philadelphia, Chicago, and other large cities followed the lead of New York in the supplementary feeding of poor children. Originally, the program provided a warm lunch for children whose parents found it inconvenient to have them come home. The need for further work in this field was underscored by Dr. Josephine Baker who in 1917 estimated that 21 percent of the children in the New York schools were undernourished. In 1918, Dr. Thomas Wood estimated that this was true of 15 to 25 percent of the school children in the United States.

The most important single factor in developing the school lunch program was the depression of the 1930s. Following its reorganization in 1935, the Federal Surplus Commodities Corporation undertook an active program of reducing agricultural surpluses. One phase of this work was the school lunch program. At the end of 1938, forty-five states and the District of Columbia were participating in the program, and over a period of five years of operation about 130,000,000 meals were served. There is no doubt that this program was of direct benefit in improving children's health. At the same time, emphasis was also put on nutrition education, a subject that had been introduced into the school curriculum in 1918, and has since become a regular part of both elementary and secondary education. The lunch program was formalized in the National School Lunch Act of 1946, which provided grants-in-aid to states for school lunch programs. This Act was important in stimulating the further development of such programs throughout the United States.

Free clinics for school children were established in 1912 in New York City, as a service of the municipal health department. These included a general medical clinic, a skin clinic, an eye clinic, and a tonsil and adenoid clinic. Similar facilities have been established by many other communities. Today, they may include dental clinics, mental hygiene clinics, as well as clinics for cardiacs and other handicapped children.

Dental health service got off to a slow start in the United States. Only since the 1930s has there been a broad development of active programs. The growth in public health programs since then is indicated by the organization in 1938 of the American Association of Public Health Dentists. Since 1948, the fluoridation of community water supplies promises to reduce considerably the burden of dental care in the school-age population.

It is manifestly impossible to develop in detail all the trends in school health work. One tendency, however, should be noted. Beginning in the 1920s and continuing into the 1930s, health workers and educators began to question the methods of school health work. It was felt that a hurried routine examination of a child without parent present and with little attention to follow-up procedures was a sterile activity. To break out of this web of routine and to develop better means of providing health care, a number of studies were undertaken, beginning with that launched in 1923 by the American Child Health Association. Eventually, in July, 1936, the Astoria Health District Study was initiated in New York City and carried on for four years.

Much of what has happened since then in the administration and practice of school health work is based on the Astoria demonstration and its results. Today, greater emphasis is placed on more adequate, though possibly less frequent, medical examinations by the family physician or the school physician. Teacher-nurse conferences on suspected health problems and special examinations by the school doctor are being used to see that children most urgently in need of care receive it.

Nevertheless a more fully effective school health service in the United States is still a goal to be attained. One obstacle is the division of responsibility that exists in many communities between educational and health authorities in the administration of health services for school children. A second is the frequently unclear and truncated role of the school physician, who screens and diagnoses but does not treat, and his relation to the family doctor when a family has one. Thirdly, the family must work with teacher, doctor, and nurse to give the child the care he needs, and this as we are only too well aware is dependent in considerable degree on economic, social, and cultural factors. In short, as long as the care of the "total" child is divided among several agencies and a variety of personnel, often inadequate in some respect, one cannot expect the full benefits of school health work.

Yet, despite inadequacies and defects still to be found in the health of the American people, the past fifty years have witnessed an unprecedented overall trend toward the improvement of community health. This advance, however, has not been uniform either within communities or among various parts of the world. A large group of countries generally underdeveloped in an economic and technological sense, and often new as independent nations, still have problems of preventable disease like those with which the countries of western Europe and the United States had to cope three-quarters of a century ago. Their problems are still the control of infectious diseases, the provision of uncontaminated water supplies and proper sewage, and the elevation of the general standard of living to a minimum acceptable level. In economically more fortunate countries, however, such as the United States, Great Britain, and a number of others in western Europe, the actual problems of community health are very different. To be sure, much unfinished business remains; at the same time, a whole set of new problems has appeared. The diseases of infancy, youth, and early adulthood have been reduced to such an extent that people are no longer dying of them in large numbers. As the problems of communicable disease have declined in urgency, the community health program has broadened to include, wherever feasible, other elements and situations that may adversely affect the physical and mental well-being of people in the community. The widening horizons of public health have in recent years come to include such problems as mental health and illness, prevention of accidents, as well as renewed emphasis on the control of the physical environment. With our expanding and changing industrial technology have come environmental alterations of increasing complexity. Recent years have also brought an increasing amount of discussion of the social and psychological changes accompanying our expanding urbanism.

All these trends have their reflection in the area of child health. Some of the problems are more recent than others. The effects of radiation on child health whether through diagnostic radiology or fall-out are still largely unknown and remain to be elucidated. Similarly, the long range genetic effects of radiation are still in dispute.

On the other hand, while specific aspects of the mental health of children have indirectly received attention for well over a century, it is only recently that direct attention has been given to these matters from a more scientific viewpoint. For the most part, the earliest knowledge on the mental health of children came from persons with the responsibility of providing care for neglected, dependent, and delinquent children. During the last two decades of the nineteenth century social workers were particularly active in trying to find ways of dealing with the problem of "child saving." Behavior problems of children received attention, the importance of the home and good mothering were stressed, and on an empirical basis welfare workers developed points of view which in more recent years have either been rediscovered or reinforced in terms of dynamic theories of behavior and personality development.

Initially, the emphasis was on rehabilitation and therapy. As the value of preventing abnormal child development became increasingly apparent, efforts were directed at assisting parents in helping their children during the formative years of infancy and childhood. Nursery schools, kindergartens, parent education all played a part in helping children toward healthy physical and mental development.

To be sure, much remains to be done in the field of child health. The world in which our children live is in many ways better than it was in 1890 or 1900. Our retrospective glance showed clearly how far we have come, but it is just as clear that we cannot be satisfied with the present. The Mid-Century White House Conference on Children and Youth of 1950 took as its theme the total well-being of children or "how we can develop in children the mental, emotional, and spiritual qualities essential to individual happiness and responsible citizenship and what physical, economic, and social conditions are deemed necessary to this development." This is still the problem for the years ahead.

To achieve this purpose more effort must be focused on unsolved health problems. Most prominent among these are perinatal mortality and certain handicapping conditions, chiefly convulsive disorders, cerebral palsy, and mental retardation which appear to be associated with conditions and circumstances affecting fetal development and birth. In this connection the significance of nutrition requires further intensive investigation. The accumulation and application of new knowledge about premature births would probably make it possible not only to reduce neonatal mortality considerably, but also to prevent a large amount of later physical and mental disability.

More needs to be accomplished also in the prevention of human malformations. Except for the cases of rubella infection and of radiation, little has yet been done to translate existing knowledge of the factors involved in the experimental production of congenital malformations in animals into tools that may be useful for human populations. Similarly, there are large areas in the field of mental health that remain to be tilled. For example, the hypothesis of maternal deprivation and its effects requires more critical investigation.

Various social services to families also require expansion if we expect children to develop and grow up in a wholesome environment. The broadening concept of how home-makers can be used is an instance in point. Still another is the development of methods for prepaying and providing medical care so that continuity and quality of needed medical services may be maintained.

These are only a few indications pointing to fruitful areas of action in the next decade. Research will undoubtedly be carried on, and new knowledge relating to health and disease in children will undoubtedly accumulate. Equally important, however, is to see that such knowledge is applied for the benefit of those who need it. Social inventiveness and innovation must go hand in hand with scientific investigation if the world of the 1960s is to be a healthier one for children.

GROWING UP
IN AN AFFLUENT SOCIETY

by MOSES ABRAMOVITZ

RELIGION apart, no aspect of human affairs has such pervasive and penetrating consequences as does the way a society makes its living—and how large a living it makes. And few societies have experienced such radical alteration in the level of their income and in the manner in which it is earned as has this country during the last seventy-five years. In this period, in common with most of the countries which share in the civilization of the Western world, America has been passing through the complex series of changes we associate, however vaguely, with industrialization. Wherever this process has held sway, the application of science to industry and the accumulation of capital have transformed the economic life of peoples. But in America, these forces have operated in a peculiarly favorable environment and the transformation in the modes of living and working have been especially profound.

Industrialization has reshaped our lives, not only during

Moses Abramovitz is Research Associate of the National Bureau of Economic Research and Professor of Economics at Stanford University.

the years people work, but during those in which they are
not yet old enough to work and during those in which they
are too old. In this essay, however, I will try to write about
the impact of industrialization, not on the whole of our
mortal span, but rather on those peculiarly malleable, im-
pressionable, and seminal years of youth—not "from the
cradle to the grave," but from the cradle to the job. I will try
to say something about the economic developments which
have been transforming the position and prospects of American youth. And I will try also to say what I can about the
significance of these changes, although this is far from clear.
Indeed to descry this significance is a major challenge to
study and insight so that we may, so far as we can, put ourselves in a position to understand our fate and, in some
degree, to shape it.

The Rise in Income and the Change in its Distribution

The most obvious effect of industrialization upon the young
has come through the change it has wrought in the incomes
of the families in which they grow up. In terms of the dollar's purchasing power in 1957, the average income of American families in 1870 was roughly $1,750. This date does not
represent the beginning of industrialization in this country,
but it is the earliest date for which fairly reliable figures are
available and it carries us back ninety years to a time when
nearly three-quarters of our population was still classified
as rural and when some 53 percent of those gainfully employed were still engaged in agricultural pursuits. By 1958,

however, the level of living had risen beyond recognition. Average family income had increased about three and one-half times and stood at well over $6,000 per family. And since the size of families has declined—from slightly over 5 persons per family in 1870 to about 3.5 in recent years—family income today is devoted to the support of fewer children. Income per capita, in other words, has increased still faster than family income. During 1958 disposable income per head of the population stood at about $1,800, a figure five times as large as per capita disposable income in 1869 when measured in dollars with today's purchasing power.

The effects of this great rise in income upon the growth of the country ramify in many directions. Our children, like their parents, are far better fed, clothed, and housed than they used to be. This more generous provision for the physical necessities of life is reflected in their health and in that of their parents. It is well-known that the great increase in life expectancy at birth, which has risen some 50 percent since 1870, manifests itself most strikingly in the proportion of all children born who survive the dangers of infancy and childhood and live to enter adult careers. It is less well-known that the lesser, but still significant, improvement in the life expectancy of adults has significantly reduced the proportion of our children who must grow up in broken families. As late as 1900, approximately 1 out of 4 widows was under forty-five years of age. In 1956, the corresponding figure was 1 in 12.

No doubt the advance of medical science and of the scientific basis of public health has been a necessary condition for the improvement recorded in the health of children and of the population at large. But just as clearly, the rise of income has been required to provide the resources needed to support scientific work, to exploit its findings, and to spread its benefits to the mass of the population. Some portion of responsibility for the improvement of health is to be ascribed to the mere fact that a much larger portion of the population now enjoys the varied diet and the more sanitary living conditions which only the rich could afford a century ago. Some portion too must be assigned to the resources which richer communities can provide for safeguards against the contamination of water and food, against the spread of epidemics, for the sanitary disposal of waste, and for the extension of hospital and other medical facilities to every section of the population. Nor should we forget that, in contrast to conditions one hundred or even fifty years ago, very few children now grow up in families in which medical care, more especially hospital care, is denied them because of mere geographical isolation. Industrialization has implied urbanization and has bound even the most remote places to centers of population and of medical facilities with an efficient system of transport and communication.

The rise of income then has enlarged the potential of youth in the fundamental physical sense that it has contributed to a great increase in the proportion of infants born who survive throughout the entire span of childhood and adolescence and live to become adults. In short, one of the most important things about living in an affluent society is that children stand a better chance of growing up, at least in the minimal sense of reaching adulthood. The rise in income, however, has helped to enlarge the scope of youth in another, equally important, respect. Childhood and youth are vivid, active years of life, important in themselves; but they are also years of preparation for adult careers. Indeed, one of the more significant ways in which the period of youth may be defined is by the age at which a young person makes the transition from preparation for work to work itself and, by obtaining gainful employment, secures the prerequisite for a life no longer in dependence upon his parents.

In this sense too, industrialization has extended the period of youth for the mass of young people. It has done so in two ways: by placing a greater premium upon formal education as a qualification for successful participation in a career of work, and by providing the means by which a longer period of education could be extended to a larger portion of our youth.

The level of a country's income supports, or restricts, its educational system in two ways. It provides the resources from which the staffs of its schools and their physical facilities are supported, and it affords that necessary surplus of income which makes it possible to dispense with the contribution of children to the family budget. In this country, partly because the level of income was relatively high, provision for public education developed earlier than in many countries of Western Europe. Yet in 1900, while 96 percent of American children between six and fourteen were attending school, the percentage of those between fourteen and seventeen was only 15, while those attending colleges and universities were 4 percent of the population aged nineteen to twenty-two.

Thus in 1900, we were well on the way to universal elementary education, but this was as yet hardly true of secondary education, while a college education was still restricted to a very few. Today, as we know, these figures are very different. The percentage of children between six and fourteen attending school in 1957 was 99; that for the youngsters of high school age was 89; and in addition, no fewer than 20 percent of those between eighteen and twenty-four were in school, the bulk attending some institution of higher learning. We have, therefore, reached a period when secondary education, while by no means universal, is the norm, and when college or university training has been put within reach of a very large and growing minority of young people.

In so far, then, as we look on youth as a period of dependency and of preparation, the rise in income has brought us the means and, also the need, to extend the period of youth for the mass of the population. Both these aspects of the enlarged scope of youth call for our closest consideration. We have extended the years of dependency and postponed the age when young people, by earning their own living, assume a role of responsibility as well as of independence of their parents' guidance and control. But this portentous change is qualified by another which we have already noted. If the average period of dependency has been extended, so has the life expectancy of young people at the age at which they pass into the work force. The latter may not completely offset the former in the sense of keeping the proportion between years of preparation and years of activity constant, but there has been a substantial offset.

The other aspect of the enlargement of youth through education is perhaps more nearly obvious but not less fundamental. The extension of schooling means, on the whole, better formal training and, therefore, a larger range of ultimate opportunities for the much larger portion of our youth who share in them. As we shall see, however, the larger provision of education has been accompanied by a larger need, and, therefore, has aggravated the disabilities imposed on the substantial fractions of our youth who may be deprived of a chance to gain all the formal training from which they are able to benefit.

The great rise in average income during the last century has been accompanied during much of the period by a trend towards greater equality in the distribution of income. In the last thirty years, the money incomes of the relatively poor families have increased considerably more rapidly than those of the relatively rich. This was not clearly true of money incomes in earlier decades, but there is good reason to think that it was, nevertheless, true of real income. For the goods and services whose supply is especially cheapened by the introduction and improvement of power machinery and mass production are typically the kinds of goods consumed by the lower income groups. And to this we must add the considerable contribution of state services, chiefly in aid of the lower income groups, which has grown apace with the burgeoning role of government.

The more equal distribution of income is working together with the extension of education and with the change in conditions of work to make the conditions of adolescence and the prospects of youth of all classes more similar to one another than they have ever been before. The extension of education fits a larger proportion of youth for work of a type requiring formal training and makes this central experience of youth more nearly the same for large sectors of the population. At the same time, the reduction in the inequalities among their families' incomes makes their lives at home less different and brings them together in neighborhoods less divided in external appearance and in the character of the activities they harbor. The net result is presumably that youths share a more nearly similar outlook and a more nearly similar set of aspirations. It goes without saying that, in this country, the outlook and aspirations which are coming to be more widely shared are those of the middle class—but what this ever-growing, long-dominant sector of American society is becoming, thinking and aspiring to are matters I must leave to other writers.

The Changing Character of Work

The rise in income about which we have spoken is the most obtrusive aspect of industrialization and certainly the one in which we can take the most unalloyed satisfaction. But industrialization involves many great changes in the mode of economic activity and in nothing so much as in the nature of the daily jobs we do.

The most general way to characterize this change is to say that it involves a shift from the relatively direct manipulation and fabrication of things to jobs concerned with the organization and regulation of production and distribution, from hard-handed to soft-handed work, from blue-shirt to white-collar occupations. We may see this first in the great decline of farming which in 1870 still engaged some 53 percent of those gainfully employed but in 1957 employed under 10 percent of our labor force. We see it next in the lesser relative decline of the other great "commodity-producing" industries—manufacturing, mining, and construction, and in the relative growth of those departments of the economy concerned with the organization and regulation of production and the distribution of its products—that is, the services, trade, finance, the professions, and government itself. Finally, we may see it in the great increase of clerical, administrative, and overhead activity within *all* branches of economic activity. For it is in the nature of the process of industrialization and the basis of its efficiency that productive activity becomes more specialized and that machines take on more of the physical work, while men become increasingly concerned with the supervision of machines, with the coordination of specialized productive activity and the routing of its product.

Two aspects of this change are especially noteworthy in their impact on the position and prospects of youth, and both fit in with and support the forces set in motion by the income changes already described. In the first place, the change in the nature of work from unskilled to skilled occupations, from blue-shirt to white-collar, from manual manipulation to distribution, administration and regulation involves a vast increase in our need for educated people and, therefore, in the opportunities our economy affords to the educated. With regard to the kind of education that is needed, it is clear that a highly industrialized and rich society needs people with education at every level, starting with mere literacy and going on to specialized and profound training of every kind and degree. It cannot prosper without it. The process, therefore, which has given us the resources to support a longer period of preparation for an ever larger portion of our youth, has also greatly increased our need for that kind of preparation, and one of the central social questions of our time is whether we have so used our resources as to make provision for education to match our need. Nor should we forget that if one side of the coin of industrialization is the greater opportunity which is afforded to skill and education, the reverse is the barrier it sets up against the employment and advancement of young people who are deprived of formal training. Individual development, no less than social, demands that adequate provision be made for the education of every young person who can use it and that each such person be put in a position to avail himself of the facilities provided.

The change in the character of work is also acting to soften the class divisions of our society. For in this country, the chief social boundary has been the line dividing the manual, or, if one likes, proletarian occupations, from the nonmanual. Those engaged in the latter, however important the differences due to income, are broadly associated with the business, or middle, class in our society and, in a general way, share a common set of attitudes and aspirations and identify themselves with one another. Since the most prominent change in the character of work has been to effect a vast enlargement in the proportion of our population engaged in nonmanual occupations, we may assume that a larger proportion of families now identify themselves with the middle class. And, therefore, on this account, as well as on account of the extension of education and the more equal distribution of income, their children are growing up under more nearly similar circumstances and coming to share the outlook and ambitions of the middle class to which their parents see themselves as belonging.

We may well believe that such a change in the class divisions of our society has effects of the most far-reaching character upon the position of the young, their prospects, and their aims. It is far less easy to guess what these effects are and to evaluate them. We may well speculate upon the increase in social mobility when many more young people feel themselves to be members of the same dominant class, and upon the ease with which they will see themselves as moving to occupations, regions, and social strata still strange to their parents. And we may think too about what this widespread identification portends for the stability of our economic and political system. But if these vague directions of speculation give rise to any feelings of satisfaction or complacency, we should think also about what the change signifies for the variety of life in our country. And we should, in particular, consider what it means for the division between those growing up with an outlook proper to what Thorstein Veblen called "industry," as distinct from "business."

Few aspects of living shape our values and our interests more powerfully than does the concrete nature of our work-a-day lives. *Industry* is the fabrication of goods. It provides an education in the relations between physical causes and effects. Those who are concerned with it learn the properties and possibilities of materials and tools. They take from it a matter-of-fact concern with the direct and unadorned adaptation of goods to their functions, and they are led to conceive the functions of goods in their relations to the more solid needs and wants of human beings. *Business* is the making of money. As a social institution, it is the basis of the complex mechanism by which our labor and capital are guided towards the production of the goods people demand—as these demands register in markets. To those engaged in business, however, it is only in part an education in the adaptation of goods to people's needs and in the design and operation of efficient productive organizations. It is also an education in the manipulation of our needs and in the restriction of output, in the arts of bargain and maneuver, of speculation and promotion. It is an experience in the strategies by which advancement is gained in large corporations and in the tactics by which income and wealth are preserved in the face of the vagaries of markets and the exactions of governments. As the characters of children are formed in their homes rather more than in their schools, we must be deeply concerned with the impact of the changing nature of work on the everyday concerns of their parents.

The New Security in Business and Professional Careers

In view of the growth of the middle class, as distinct from the manual worker, or proletarian, class, it is worth considering some of the important ways in which the differing eco-

nomic and career outlooks of these classes are reflected in
the patterns of life of the youths who belong to them. For,
it turns out, the career outlooks of these classes have changed
along with the change in their relative size.

One of the chief differences between proletarian and middle-class life used to be that a proletarian youth left school
and got a job relatively early, and fairly soon thereafter
achieved a secure status relative to the standards of his
class. By contrast, a youth entering a middle-class occupation,
unless he was very rich, took much longer to obtain a secure
foothold. If he were going into business, he needed years in
which to accumulate the capital with which to start the
independent venture which was the normal form of business
activity, and even if he were fortunate enough to have access
to a small capital, a considerable period was needed to obtain the experience with which to use capital effectively.
Similarly, if he were entering a profession, he not only faced
many years of preparation but also an indefinite period of
insecurity thereafter while he built up at least a modest
private practice. As a result of this difference in the time-
patterns of their careers, working-class youths courted and
married relatively early, and they had more children and
had them earlier than did youths going into business and
the professions. In this respect, the working-class youth re-
sembled the young people of very rich families—though for
very different reasons.

This important point of differentiation between the life
patterns of the different classes, however, has now changed
both in its incidence and its character in the further course

of economic development. On the one hand, a larger proportion of young men, as already noted, are destined for occupations associated with the middle class and, therefore, adopt middle-class standards with regard to the time and character of courtship and marriage and with regard to the number and spacing of their children. On the other hand, it is now possible to obtain a foothold in the more characteristic middle-class occupations earlier and more easily than used to be true. Business is now generally organized in the form of large corporations rather than in small independent ventures. Young businessmen, therefore, enter their careers at the lower levels of large firms and advance through their managerial bureaucracies. Capital is not required for entrance, and experience is gained on the job.

The prospects for young professional and semi-professional aspirants have similarly improved. For one thing, the demand for people with such training has, in recent years, far outrun the growth of supply. Independent practice is, therefore, more easily established. For another, the growth in the size of business firms, in the scope and variety of governmental activities, in the importance and size of labor unions, and of medical, scientific and educational institutions, has created a host of professional and semi-professional posts within the staffs of these organizations. At the same time, what amounts to the corporate practice of professions has grown in importance. Thus, the problem of establishing an independent practice may now be by-passed by a large fraction of those entering the learned middle-class pursuits. On all these counts, the aspiring young businessman or professional may now look forward with unprecedented confidence to a secure career upon the completion of his training. Finally, although the period of training is now somewhat longer in several of the major professions than was the case a generation or two ago, it is now probably easier for a young man to obtain the means to support himself during his training. For this there are a number of reasons. The rise of incomes has made it easier for parents to provide liberal support for their children. At the same time, philanthropic and governmental support of education has provided more scholarship aid than used to be the case. Finally, students themselves, profiting by the rise of earning power, find it easier to supplement their funds by work. And when, as is not uncommon, they marry in the course of schooling, their wives can contribute to their support by exploiting new opportunities for women in industry.

The net outcome of this complex of supporting changes has been to place the future of men entering middle-class occupations upon a secure basis at a much earlier age than was true even a generation ago. As a consequence early courtship, marriage, and family foundation are now more feasible for this group. In this respect, as in others already noted, the attitudes and life patterns of middle-class youth have come to resemble those of the working class and of the very rich. It would, of course, be imprudent to assert that the relatively new patterns of high-school courtships, much earlier marriage, of larger numbers of children more closely spaced, which has become characteristic of middle-class youth, as well as of the young of other classes, can be accounted for entirely, or even chiefly, by the economic developments traced above. Whatever the contributing circumstances, however, we can be confident that so large a change in the life patterns of middle-class youth could not have taken place except upon a firm economic basis.

The New Position of Women

Because men have been, and still are, more closely concerned with economic activity than women, much of the discussion so far has been concerned more with the position and prospects of boys and young men, rather than with those of girls and young women. In the more recent development of our economy, however, the working life of women, with some inevitable differences, has come to resemble that of men more closely than ever before. This, in turn, has affected the prospects of women, it has had a significant impact on their activities as youths, and raised certain problems concerning their schooling and the course of their early careers.

In industrialized societies, it has long been normal for men, except for farmers, to work outside the home. Until recently, however, the great bulk of women in America have spent the major portion of their adult lives inside the home. It is true that it was common for unmarried girls to seek outside employment during the period between the end of their schooling and their marriage. And it is also true that widows, as well as married women in the lowest income groups, were forced to seek employment to help support themselves and their families. By and large, however, the great bulk of married women occupied themselves with household duties. In 1890, women made up only some 16 percent of those gainfully employed, and married women were only 14 percent of the total number of women at work. By 1958, however, women constituted 32 percent of the labor force and over 50 percent of the women at work were married. The role of work in the lives of women has, therefore, changed considerably. In former decades, girls worked, if at all between end of school and marriage, and then confined themselves, as a rule, to household occupations. In recent years, however, they tend to remain in school longer and marry earlier, which restricts the frequency and length of premarital employment. On the other hand, as already noted, they have their children earlier, and they then enter the labor market in very large numbers as soon as the youngest of their children reach school age. And since the life-span of women is now longer than it used to be, many married women experience a long period of work outside the home.

This considerable transformation in the working life of women reflects the combined impact of a number of economic causes directly and indirectly. In the first place, there is the change in the character of work from manual labor to office work of various kinds, which has created a large number of jobs deemed suitable for women in our society. In addition, the early foundation and completion of families leaves women with reduced household duties at a time of life when they are still active and vigorous. Next, the wider spread of middle-class standards of living imposes on women the need to help their families sustain such standards both in ordinary consumption and in the education of their children. It is, perhaps, not too much to say that in former

decades children left school early to make money to help
support their parents at working-class standards. More recently, however, mothers feel impelled to leave their homes
to make money to help provide consumption goods and
schooling for their children at middle-class standards. We
must add finally that the entrance of women, especially married women, into work has been substantially eased by the
fact that hours of work are now shorter, leaving them a larger
amount of time to devote to children and household duties
than was previously available to a working woman, and that
homes are now easier to manage, thanks to the improvements
in household equipment and the transfer of many household
tasks to the commercial economy.

The fact that many women now feel impelled to enter
gainful employment for a substantial portion of their married
lives and that opportunities to do so now exist has already
had some effect on the upbringing and education of girls and
presumably should have still more. We note, first, that the
great bulk of girls now attend and finish high school and
that a considerable fraction of them continue their education
in college and beyond. Not only is secondary and higher
education for young women more widespread, it is now conducted with an eye somewhat more intent on the occupational and professional implications of such education. It is
by no means clear, however, that the process of modifying
the upbringing and education of girls has as yet gone as far
as it might in view of the working life which is now in prospect for a considerable fraction of women. At least two areas
of possible action need to be studied. First, curricula for

women both in high school and college which used to have
dominantly nonoccupational aims need to be reconsidered
to achieve a proper balance between the contribution they
can make to the work careers of women and to the other
objectives of education. Secondly, young girls and women
need to be made more aware than they already are about
the career choices now open to them, about the kinds of
training they can obtain, and about the way in which premarital work experience can help fit them for the much
longer period of work many of them will desire after their
children have entered school.

The New Standards of Consumption and Leisure

We have so far been concerned chiefly with the economic
development of the country upon the lives of our youth as
this has acted through the changes in work patterns and in
preparation for work. But the great rise in income, of course,
has accomplished a change not only in the working lives of
the bulk of our families, but also in their lives outside of
work. Two aspects of this change seem especially noteworthy.
In the first place, the great majority of families now enjoy
an income which provides a substantial surplus with which
they can buy goods and services yielding pleasure, as contrasted with commodities required to meet the necessities of
nourishment, clothing, and shelter. In the second place, we
have chosen to transform our enormous rise in productivity
only partly into higher incomes. In good part, we have chosen
to substitute fewer hours of work and more hours of leisure
for the still higher incomes we might otherwise have. Thus,

in 1890, a representative worker in a nonagricultural job would have worked an average of some fifty-eight hours per week. Today, he works only some thirty-nine hours per week, a change which has approximately doubled the effective leisure time at the disposal of employed persons. By contrast with the situation two or three generations ago, adults now have more goods to enjoy and more leisure time in which to enjoy them. Pleasure, play, community affairs, and non-work activities in general, it may be said, have now become, perhaps for the first time, substantial parts of the daily lives of the ordinary run of men and women.

The full implications of this striking, almost revolutionary change in the character of ordinary life are still far from clear. Two aspects of the matter, however, are quite closely tied to the themes already sounded. One is that fathers, like mothers, can now be with their families for a considerable portion of each day and week. The result has been a quickening and intensification of family life, and the family is again the center of youth's activities to a degree not experienced in urban communities for several generations. The return of the father to the family, however, has been in a rather new role —not as breadwinner, but as participant in the leisure-time activities of the family. One may categorize the change, somewhat too strongly perhaps, by saying that it was characteristic of an earlier and poorer generation that a major concern of family life was the effort of fathers to stimulate and govern the early stages of their sons' work activities. It is characteristic of our own more abundantly provided generation that a major concern of family life is the effort by sons—and daughters—to stimulate and govern the leisure-time activities of their fathers. However this may be, there is little doubt that fathers now share much more fully in the daily lives of their families and that family activities are now more largely concerned with things other than work than ever before. It may well be worth thinking whether this change in the pattern of family life is not connected in a significant way with the recent trend toward early courtship and marriage and with the tendency of young couples to have larger families earlier in their married life.

The new patterns of consumption and leisure may also be playing an important part in forming the goals and ambitions of youth as they look toward their careers in business. A long series of students from de Tocqueville in the 1820s to Andre Seigfried in the 1920s concurred in the finding that an intense and wholehearted dedication to the life of business and the goal of making (more) money was a distinctive characteristic of the American middle class. More recently, however, a new shade has been detected in the outlook of middle-class youth. Determined as ever to win a place in the world of work and to invest a major effort in this sphere, their dedication to the notion that their own goal, like America's, is success in business is no longer unqualified. They still look forward to careers that will win for them a secure status at a level perhaps better in most cases than their parents enjoyed. But more frequently, they seek to do so in jobs that will not demand from them the same intense application that their fathers and grandfathers were willing, and even eager, to accept. They are concerned, rather, to achieve a more even balance between the portion of their lives devoted to business or professional work and that which they are free to devote to their families, to the leisure-time activities in which their wives and children share, and to the affairs of the communities in which they live. We are challenged to consider how this more balanced, but less intensely pursued, round of activities will alter the quality of the satisfactions yielded by their lives. And we must also think how this more qualified devotion of our energies to business may influence the further economic development of the country.

"The child is the father of the man." For better or worse, the attitudes towards work, leisure, and consumption which will give tone to American civilization during the next generations are now being formed in our children. Their values and aspirations are emerging from the experience they now share with their parents and peers as we all learn to enjoy—to use or dissipate—our still new-won prosperity. Our own lives, private and public, will tell whether the affluence we now enjoy and the still more abounding productive powers which our children will control will be worthily used or most thoughtlessly squandered.

THE IMPACT OF URBANIZATION

by JEAN GOTTMANN

URBANIZATION today is a powerful trend, deeply modifying both the environmental conditions and the inner structure of modern society. Its impact on the majority of the people in Western countries cannot be too carefully studied. It is a particularly strong force in the United States because of the tremendous number of people involved.

The younger generation, most of whom today are born and grow up away from the farm, feels this impact in two ways: first, the environment of their childhood and adolescence is urban; second, the system to which they will eventually have to adapt their adult life is urban. This is no longer simply a steady flow from the farms to the towns. Urbanization today is one of the more striking expressions of the sweeping and profound changes now developing in the organization of society, and American-style urban growth is being reproduced increasingly in many other lands. Its impact carries the need for reassessing many of the values held and the

Jean Gottmann is Research Director, Study of Megalopolis, Twentieth Century Fund, and Professor, Ecole des Hautes Etudes, University of Paris.

measures adopted for the welfare and education of children and youth.

Momentum and New Forms of Urbanization

Urban growth is no more a phenomenon affecting only a small fraction of the total population and several isolated spots over a vast country. In the United States the population in urban territory rose from 45.7 percent of the total in 1910 to 64 percent in 1950. The farm population meanwhile declined to 15.3 percent in 1950 and probably to 11.7 percent by April, 1956. Farming is now the occupation of less than 1 out of 10 Americans; more than 90 percent of the nation live from and by activities of an urban type. Similar percentages are being achieved or forecast for many countries in Western Europe advanced in industrialization. The trend is worldwide and appears irreversible: the progress of agricultural techniques and farm mechanization make it possible to produce more agricultural goods with less and less hands. Thus a migration from farm to city goes on and must be accelerated as large numbers come of age in farming areas.

For years the terms urban and rural have represented the major dichotomy in the division of human labor and in the classification of landscapes. On one hand the green countryside was the locale of agricultural production. On the other hand the built-up, crowded, urbanized areas were the sites of manufacturing, trade, government, worship, and recreation. The rural territory extended over almost the whole land and rural life was reputed simple, natural, and healthy. Cities occupied small parcels of land surrounded with walls or boulevards, isolated spots amid rural territory, and were usually criticized as offering an artificial, unhealthy, complicated way of life. These old contrasts still exist in underdeveloped parts of the world. They are a tale of bygone days in the more advanced countries and especially in the United States.

Since more than 90 percent of the population now live by pursuits other than farming, i.e., by activities within the categories of industry, trade, services, and government, usually located in cities, urban territory cannot be expected to remain limited to a few small spots on the map. Urbanization has taken on a size and a momentum that has reversed old concepts of simple contrasts between urban and rural. Cities have broken out of old bounds and scattered buildings of urban aspect and functions all over the countryside, thus coming to occupy vast regions. The U.S. Census has had a hard time trying to keep up with these trends. As suburbs mushroomed around the old urban centers defined as *cities*, the Census established first the notion of *urbanized areas*, which consisted mainly of densely built-up territory. Then, in 1940, there was introduced the *metropolitan area*, a wider concept encompassing entire counties whose economy appears tightly dependent on a central city.[1] By 1950 the area of many of these standard metropolitan areas had to be extended and the population of the 174 areas in the continental United States totalled 85.5 million or 57 percent of the nation. In 1950 the majority of Americans lived in metropolitan regions; this does not mean they all lived in densely built-up

[1] See definitions and statistical data in *County and City Data Book 1956* (Washington, D.C.: U.S. Bureau of the Census, 1957).

districts, for a metropolitan area may well include green, rural looking sections, but its inhabitants engage in little agricultural activity and are primarily dependent for their livelihood on the connection with a central city of more than 50,000 people.

From 1940 to 1950, while the total population of the United States increased by 14.5 percent, the population of metropolitan areas grew by 22.2 percent. Since 1950 this latter rate of growth has accelerated. The Bureau of the Census estimated the growth of the country's civilian population between 1950 and 1956 to be 9.8 percent and that of the metropolitan areas to be 14.8 percent; but in many cases the peripheral growth has spilled over these limits into territory classified as non-metropolitan in 1950. There is no doubt that the 1960 Census will have to add many new counties to the list of those classified as metropolitan and it will then be recognized that the rate of increase of metropolitan population is more than 50 percent faster than the nation's growth. Thus we see that modern urbanization takes on original forms which scatter the urban functions and population around the countryside. While the old migration from farms towards towns goes on, the towns spread out in irregular fashion back into the formerly rural countryside.

For some time now the Census has distinguished between rural farm and rural nonfarm population. In any agricultural region some nonfarm activities are needed to service the farms. In an area of large and highly mechanized farms the nonfarm population may become more numerous than the farm population which it services; in such cases however a good part of it will be concentrated in towns of some size, and counted as urban rather than rural nonfarm. In any case it seems obvious that when the rural nonfarm element of a rural territory of a small region reaches a large majority, and in some cases it goes over 75 percent, the region depends on means of sustenance other than local agriculture.

A map of the United States showing the proportion of rural nonfarm population in rural territory by county demonstrates such a process of gradual de-ruralization over vast stretches. The map (fig. 1), giving the situation in 1950, well illustrates one stage of a trend which has progressed since then and will undoubtedly continue in the next decades. Farming will hardly need more lands; an increased consumption of farm products may be satisfied by reducing the surpluses and increasing, if need be, the yields over much of the major agricultural regions. The "de-ruralization" ought to gain in the Northeast (where it was already quite advanced in 1950), in the Southeast, some parts of the West, and even of the Midwest.

Modern urbanization has invaded so widely the regions formerly held as rural but without densely building them up, that the distinction between urban and rural in the old sense calls for revision. Unofficial proposals have suggested new terms such as "outer-suburbia," "exurbia," "interurbia," and recently sociologists offered to call these scattered populations "rurban." All such terms include some hint at the urban nature of the new areas and as they develop beside officially urban territory we may well speak of a degree of suburbanization (as fig. 1 indicates) pending new official definitions.

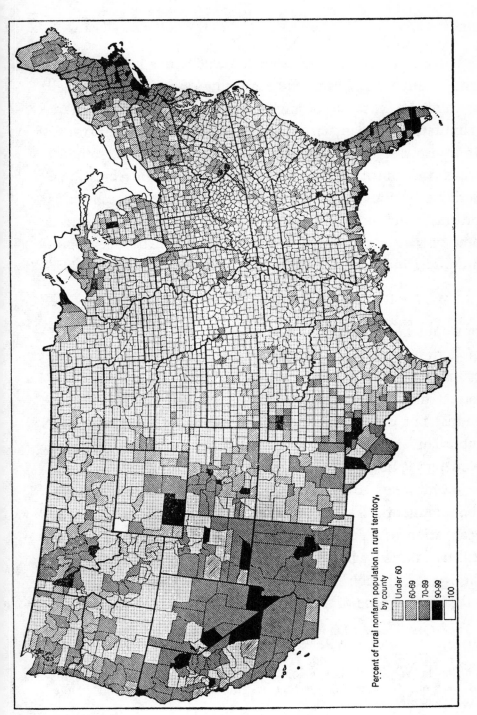

Percent of rural nonfarm population in rural territory, by county

Under 60
60-69
70-89
90-99
100

Figure 1. Suburbanization in the United States, 1950
Courtesy of the Twentieth Century Fund

Urbanization has taken on a new, nebulous kind of structure.[2] This results from the scattering of residences as well as from the centering of large shopping centers or important manufacturing plants at rural crossroads and in small towns.[3] It is also due to the development of rural regions, some of which were until recently being depopulated, for recreational activities in the mountains or at the seashore. Altogether this process of urbanization causes new forms of land use and a new system of relations within a community, between communities, and between individuals and their environment.

The Revolution in Land Use

It would be far too simple to sum up the major effects of modern urbanization by stressing the sprawl of suburban or metropolitan patterns over vast areas against farming's retreat to more limited, specialized regions. The two trends coexist but do not conflict on a large scale. True, in some suburban areas such as central Long Island and much of New Jersey, new developments have crowded out many farms in recent years. But on the whole and for many years the abandonment of tilled land has proceeded faster than the occupation of land for urban and interurban uses. This was still true on the whole throughout the United States even in the 1950s although land has been devoured for urban use at an estimated pace of a million acres per year. Total cropland

[2] See Otis Dudley Duncan and Albert J. Reiss, Jr., *Social Characteristics of Urban and Rural Communities, 1950* (New York: Wiley, 1956), especially part II, pp. 117–79.

[3] The latter pattern is spreading especially in the Southeast; see for instance Jean Gottmann, *Virginia at Mid-Century* (New York: Holt, 1955), chapter 7.

shrank from 1950 to 1954 by 10 million acres and total pasture and grazing area by 20 million acres. Woodland and forest land not used for grazing increased in the same four years by 28 million acres. The result of the present urbanization of the American population and economy is that the land is becoming greener and the country is reverting to a more natural condition.[4]

Whoever has recently traveled through or flown over the forested East has seen patches of land reoccupied by brush and young woods all over the countryside. In New England the increase of the wooded area since the beginning of the century and even in the last ten years has been substantial. This has happened not only in Maine and Vermont but also in the "suburbanized" states of Massachusetts, Rhode Island, and Connecticut. Similar trends can be observed over much of New York, Pennsylvania, Maryland and Virginia. It is interesting that woods are still increasing in and around the highly metropolitanized section on the northeastern seaboard which we call *Megalopolis* (from southern New Hampshire to northern Virginia, see fig. 2). This most impressive and continued chain of metropolitan regions contains one-fifth of the population of the United States on less than 2 percent of its land area.

Thus, even in the vicinity of the most crowded region in America, there still are more green spaces, and curiously enough more wildlife, than some fifty to sixty years ago.

[4] The above figures are based on the *Statistical Abstract of the United States* 1958 (Washington, D.C.: U.S. Bureau of the Census, 1958), Table No. 791, p. 612. See also on what follows Jean Gottmann, "The Revolution in Land Use," in *Landscape*, Santa Fe, New Mexico, Vol. 8, No. 2 (Winter, 1959), pp. 15–21.

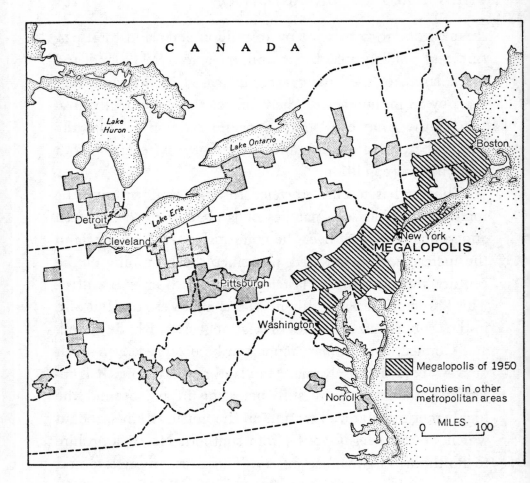

Figure 2. Megalopolis

Megalopolis is the continuous chain of counties of metropolitan economy as
defined for 1950 by the U. S. Bureau of the Census (in *State Economic Areas*).
It stretches from southern New Hampshire to northern Virginia, the greatest
such area in the United States, encompassing about one-fifth of the total
population.

Courtesy of the Twentieth Century Fund

These areas have great potential for educational and recreational opportunity. Of course such areas, almost suburban by their location, are not turning wild. The woods and brush are divided up by major highways along which ribbons of suburbs develop, while residences scatter along "rural" roads. In certain areas such residences may be occupied only for a season in the year, but increasingly they are year-round homes. In these same areas some agricultural production, yielding high profits, may take place. Lancaster county, Pennsylvania, for example, classified as a "standard metropolitan region," is also one of the richest counties in North America by virtue of its farm production. It has developed a most interesting interpenetration of urban and rural life; its farms specialize in the production of milk, meat, and poultry, i.e., in a processing stage of the agricultural cycle. The basic materials (grain, feed, and hay) are imported from afar. Indeed the new process of urbanization has created suburbs that look like farming areas used to look, and agricultural centers that look like suburbs because of the concentration of buildings. Certain types of farms, which are extremely well maintained, are actually in suburban territory because they are "estate" or "part-time" farms. A new way of life, properly suburban, has developed, for gentleman farmers are not, as in days of yore, gentlemen because they are big farmers, they are farmers because they are gentlemen with large enough incomes in the city to permit them to farm avocationally.

The rapid shifts in the land use do not affect only the rural-looking outer suburbs; they have at least as much impact on land use in the urbanized areas. In the old urban cores, the residential population is still increasing [5] but slowly, at a lower rate than in the nation as a whole, (4.7 percent increase in the central cities of standard metropolitan areas from 1950 to 1956, while the nation's increase was estimated at 9.8 percent); the metropolitan areas outside the central cities increased much faster (about 29.3 percent); and within the metropolitan areas the rural parts grew fastest (55.8 percent, adding 6 million people in six years!).

These figures concern places of residence. Much of the population in rural areas commutes to work in urban territory; and there is substantial commuting from city to city. Thus in the early 1950s close to 1,600,000 people residing elsewhere came to Manhattan to work; close to 450,000 went to Newark, N.J., to work, a figure slightly above the resident population of Newark as recorded by the Census. In most other large cities the numbers of commuters on weekdays reach hundreds of thousands. Despite endeavors at decentralization in the most crowded urban hubs, the numbers of people commuting to work have been on the increase through the 1940s and the 1950s. The Bureau of the Census, recognizing the inadequacy of recording population figures by place of residence, intends to introduce a new question about the place of work in the 1960 count.

Urbanization, in the modern sense, creates a growing dichotomy between daytime and nighttime populations in large cities. This is reinforced by the housing picture: as the trend of moving out to the periphery accelerates, the old urban core harbors age and decay. The houses emptied by

[5] No more in New York City where a 1957 census showed a decrease since 1950.

middle-income occupants who prefer to move out to the suburbs or further are taken over by tenants in the lower-income brackets who cannot afford to commute far and who often cannot for reasons of social discrimination find lodging in the highly suburban communities. Negroes and Puerto Ricans are so crowded into the large central cities that some among them commute to jobs in the suburbs. The colored population is increasing faster than the total resident population in Manhattan and Brooklyn, Washington, D.C., Baltimore, Chicago, and Philadelphia. The same trend is notable in smaller cities, especially in the highly urbanized northeast, such as Trenton or Hartford. All these cities have active business districts; but the kinds of people who walk the central city streets in daytime are increasingly different from those who are abroad at night. As urban renewal proceeds in such cities contrasts may sharpen for some of their central districts attract only affluent residents who can afford the higher costs. Even if they do not decay as residential areas,[6] central cities become sites of great contrasts between opposite extremes of the income scale. This is especially and spectacularly so in New York City and Washington, D.C. In Washington, the urban renewal of Georgetown sharpened the contrast. These growing differences between residents and daytime population are not conducive to social happiness and relaxation of tension.

Another set of contrasting patterns has developed between the different parts of a metropolitan region: in addition to the differences between the population by night and by day

[6] Raymond Vernon, *The Changing Economic Function of the Central City* (New York: Committee for Economic Development, 1959).

and the range of income levels, the suburbs have a different set of economic activities (besides the dormitory function) and an age and educational level substantially at variance with the central cities. The suburban population today as a whole is better educated, and has better housing and more recreational facilities within easy reach than the population in the urban core. With the exception of a few very large cities, the downtown areas of old urban cores are losing a good deal of their special functions as the center of the retail and entertainment trades. The present revolution in land-use results from many factors, among which perfected automobile transportation, the rising standard of living for the average family, and constantly increasing specialization of labor are probably the three main agents. This revolution in land-use ought to bring much improvement to American modes of living, learning, working, and relaxing. Whether the progress of urbanization can be made to serve such improvement is a major responsibility of our time.

Children and Youth in Urbanized Environment

The 1950 Census showed the suburban population to be slightly younger than the central city population. In all urbanized areas combined, the median age was 32.7 in central cities and 30.9 in the suburbs. It was observed that "the smaller the urbanized area, the greater is the difference in median age between central city and suburbs." [7] The age pyramid reveals a larger than average number of persons less

---

[7] Duncan and Reiss, *Social Characteristics of Urban and Rural Communities*, p. 120.

than twenty years of age in the suburbs. If similar statistics were available for the rural nonfarm population living within metropolitan areas, such differences would be even sharper. The quoted remark about the size of the "urbanized area" is significant: the larger the central city the further away extends its maximum commuting range. Many more people working in New York or Chicago can afford a residence for their families beyond the officially defined "urbanized area" than would be possible for people who work in Cincinnati or Albuquerque.

During the 1950s the migration to a metropolitan periphery of urban families with small children has probably been massive, especially from the larger cities, and the suburban areas ought to be "younger than ever" in the early 1960s. The usual reason a head of household gives for moving out is: "I am doing it for the children." It is also usual that the return from the suburbs to a central city is made by parents when the children, grown up, have left home. The same move also brings back to urban cores widows and widowers and even retired couples. From 1930 to 1950, the proportion of persons aged sixty-five and over in the nation went up from 5.5 percent to 8.1 percent; but it more than doubled in New York City. Nevertheless, the great metropolis was still below the national average, with the exception of Manhattan where it stood at 8.7 percent. Queens with 7.1 percent, the Bronx with 7.3 percent, and Brooklyn with 7.4 percent already reflected semi-suburban rates. New York City was surrounded with suburban counties where the proportion of aged people was below 8 percent, with the excep-

tion of the counties of Westchester and Rockland, N.Y.
A similar situation was observed around Philadelphia, Baltimore, and Washington, but Boston, and New England as
a whole, showed rather higher proportions of aged people.

The distribution of children less than fifteen years old in
1950 followed a somewhat different pattern in the highly
urbanized Northeastern seaboard from that in the rest of the
country. On the whole New York City had a low concentration; the proportion in the various counties of the metropolitan region varied between 17 and 24 percent, while the national average stood at 26.9 percent. Three states of southern New England showed slightly higher figures than did
New York City but the average was still below 26 percent in
all counties but one, and the same was true of rather suburbanized New Jersey and eastern Pennsylvania. The ratio of
children picked up quickly in the Pennsylvanian Appalachians to the west, and south from Maryland and Virginia.
The South has always had a higher birth rate than the Northeast; urbanization is not the only major factor in the distribution of children through the United States. It remains
however quite clear on the map of Megalopolis that suburban districts have a higher ratio of children than the central
urban cores. In 1950 this was the case around Manhattan,
Boston, Philadelphia, Baltimore, and Washington. By 1960
the suburbs may well have a higher ratio than the nation as
a whole.

The distribution of the youth, i.e., of persons aged fifteen
to twenty-four in 1950 was not very different from the general
pattern of children, but one significant difference may be

noted. The old urban cores often showed higher rates than the outlying suburbs. This was true of Boston, Philadelphia, Baltimore, and New York City as a whole, though not of Manhattan alone. The presence of colleges in these cities and the greater opportunity offered to young job-seekers are probably the main reasons for the attraction of youngsters, especially in the ages between nineteen and twenty-four, towards the urban hubs.

The local variations of the age pyramid confirm that children are being born and reared in the United States largely away from the main urban centers but increasingly not very far away. These statistics result partly from the inheritance of a traditional geographic distribution little related to modern urbanization trends, but partly also from the choice of the parents to move towards the metropolitan periphery. As the youngsters grow closer to coming of age they are increasingly drawn towards the urban centers not only by their work but also for residence. Finally, as the old urban cores have ratios of old and young people below the national average, they have a higher than average ratio of the adult and mature population (i.e., in the ages of twenty-five to sixty-four). This is true even of nighttime residents; the ratio is of course much higher for the daytime population as the commuters into the urban hubs are predominantly in these age brackets. Thus, although children today spend most of their time away from the cities (in the more crowded, densely occupied and built-up sense of the term "city"), they will usually spend at least part of their lives in a highly urbanized environment.

The whole evolution of the labor force indicates the growth of typically urban employment in nonagricultural and nonindustrial types of activities, or, according to a slightly different classification, the expansion of the white-collar labor force over the blue-collar. The vast majority of today's children will spend their later lives in urban or suburban work and residence. The education of most youngsters should therefore be definitely urban-oriented; it should also be more advanced for a larger proportion of the upcoming generation, as an increasing proportion of all jobs require more training, more skill, and involve more responsibility.

The isolated farm and the tightly knit and relatively isolated community of the small town in a truly rural region produce only a small minority of the younger generation. Does the present type of urban and suburban growth benefit the younger strata of the nation? For a long time it was traditionally held that boys from the farms or agricultural areas in general were a "better quality" of men, had more basic virtues—in brief were better prepared for life than city boys. This belief was not only American. It was also generally held in Europe. This writer grew up and went to school in the very crowded and large metropolis of Paris; he was taught, until he became a graduate student, that the farm population was the main strength, the backbone of France. However, he also knew, from everything he heard, that the leadership of the country, the policy makers in every field came from the schools located in the center of Paris to which he and his neighbors went. These two concepts did not seem to him contradictory but rather complementary: the countryside supplied the good solid rank and file; the leadership, predominantly urban, became strong through its rank and file following. But it seemed better taste not to insist on the latter proposition and simply to stress the virtues of rural education in which rural populations eagerly believed.

Systematic sociological studies of the early schooling and adult behavior of farm boys and city boys have exploded the old myth of the superiority of rural origin. A scholarly analysis of the records of the U.S. Armed Forces has recently shown in convincing fashion that the recruits from farming areas were on the whole less prepared for modern life than urban recruits.[8] The advantages of an urban environment for children and youth, especially in the industrialized nations of the West, were to be expected. The better organized and more strictly controlled system of supply of the large urban consuming markets has led to better nutrition. Even today in New York City it is difficult to find children (unless recently arrived there) with serious nutritional deficiencies. Water and milk have been made safer to drink in the large cities, precisely because of the dangers of infection and contamination inherent in the crowding in urban environment. Modern police forces are made necessary by the problems of crowded metropolises; and despite the merited outcry against criminality and juvenile delinquency, it ought to be recognized that people in the great urbanized areas of today are much safer by virtue of the policing and the legislation in

[8] Eli Ginzberg et al., *The Ineffective Soldier* (New York: Columbia University Press, 1959), 3 vols. See also to the same effect the results of an analysis of civilian statistics in Eleanor H. Bernert, *America's Children* (New York: Wiley, 1958).

force than their ancestors used to be in a rural environment.

The general progress of civilization has brought about improvements in nutrition, health, and security at the same time as it brought about urbanization. There is no direct relationship between, say, urban growth on one hand and better health conditions on the other. The latter could be achieved without the former and vice versa. It has happened at times. However it has been mankind's, and particularly America's experience that in the long run the two proceeded hand in hand. Similarly such modern trends as the rise of juvenile delinquency and of nervous disorders in modern society ought not to be associated too closely, as they often are, with urban growth. The latter is, like the trends, a simultaneous product of the modern evolution of society; it does not determine them. The evil in society is of course concentrated wherever society itself is gathered. Crowding especially in its beginnings may cause the worst trends to intensify, but it also compensates this effect by working out legal and social antidotes. If it does not the people involved are at fault rather than the impersonal process. In the early nineteenth century, the first stages of the industrial revolution caused crowding of ill-paid industrial workers in slums in many cities. But social evolution has established today in American cities conditions of living and working for youngsters quite different from those denounced by Charles Dickens a century ago.

Today urban areas can confidently claim better organized health and educational services than rural areas. Charities, hospitals, welfare organizations can function better in a large community than in rural areas and the urban communities can afford these services more easily in terms of both adequate financing and competent personnel. If they are lacking, it is not because of the density of population or of the size of the community, but because of the spirit of the people. In India, as a noted sociologist observed, sacred cows flock into the large cities because they know they will find food and care more readily available there! Urbanization, properly managed, should benefit children and adolescents as well as other sections of the population needing help and care. Modern urbanization, however, with its differentiations between place of work and place of residence on one hand, between central city, suburbs, and outer suburbia on the other, requires that more thought and study be given to the new problems and opportunities it has helped to create.

Assets and Liabilities of Urban and Suburban Areas

As the central parts of cities continue to specialize in the functions traditionally concentrated in the "downtown" areas, children residing there may lose some of the advantages previously associated with cities of large size. The financial burden on the city government may become too great for it to maintain adequate services for residents who cannot offer a strong and expanding tax base. The city, having to provide adequate facilities for the noontime tide of business activities finds increasing difficulty in also meeting the welfare, health, educational, and recreation needs of a poorer resident population.

In the suburbs, meanwhile, because of the momentum of the metropolitan sprawl, local government is faced with such a rapid rise in the needs for facilities of all kinds that resources can seldom keep pace with the demand. Many suburban towns have trouble in providing adequate sewage for their rapidly expanding population. The schools are crowded and not always staffed with as qualified teaching personnel as the pupils' parents wish for.

The case of the schools is a constant issue because of the present trends of urbanization. Urban areas normally offer better schools and have a better educated population than the rural regions.

This latter proposition is true today of the suburban towns and of the daytime population of central cities rather than for the residents of old urban cores. A map of the percentage of the adult population on the Northeastern seaboard having completed high school or more in 1950 (see fig. 3) shows in clear fashion that the larger cities in Megalopolis have a lower ratio than their immediate suburbs. Otherwise the metropolitan areas show up better than the rural countryside and that contrast is especially sharp south of Washington, D.C. This map, based on the 1950 census, shows considerable progress all over this section when compared with a similar map for 1940. The 1960 census will undoubtedly testify to much higher ratios, and probably to greater contrasts between city and suburbs in the Northeast, and possibly between city and rural areas in the South.

As the many stages of production, agricultural as well as industrial, are being mechanized, employers are growing more

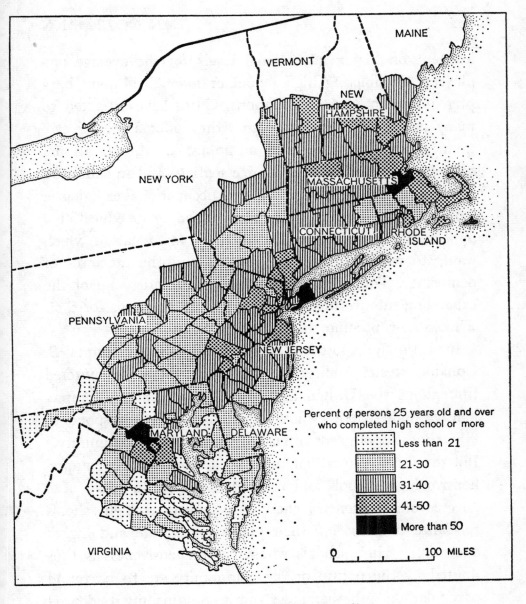

Figure 3. Education in Megalopolis, 1950
Courtesy of the Twentieth Century Fund

Percent of persons 25 years old and over
who completed high school or more

Less than 21
21-30
31-40
41-50
More than 50

0   100 MILES

insistent on higher educational levels for the average employee. "Completing high school or more" will soon be a prerequisite for most occupations. Cities have attracted so many people for decades because they offered greater economic opportunity; to take advantage of it, educational achievement daily becomes more essential—and an education that can seldom be replaced by early occupational experience. To provide the younger generation with adequate educational opportunity is an imperative necessity for a nation which wants to maintain national progress and the processes of democracy. The difficulties of the central cities and of the expanding suburbs in providing adequate programs for their schools now become disturbing concerns.

In a timely report on the high schools, Dr. James B. Conant stresses the great variety of these encountered throughout the United States. He speaks for a "comprehensive high school" whose programs would correspond to "the educational needs of *all* the youth of the community." But the survey shows that there are seldom entirely comprehensive high schools and the report prefers to speak of a "degree of comprehensiveness." In some cases high schools specialize in preparing their pupils for college and higher education. "High schools whose comprehensiveness is thus limited by the nature of the community are to be found particularly in suburban areas and in high income residential sections of large cities." There are suburban high schools which may not have the same problems in supplying an adequate degree of "comprehensiveness" as the large city high school. Selective academic high schools, designed for the academically talented youth, are found "in many of the Eastern cities of considerable size and in a few of the medium-sized cities." Such specialization of one or a few high schools among many more in that city seems to favor the comprehensiveness of the system as a whole. The small high school presents more complicated problems: "The enrollment of many American public high schools is too small to allow a diversified curriculum except at exorbitant expense. The prevalence of such high schools—those with graduating classes of less than one hundred students—constitutes one of the serious obstacles to good secondary education throughout most of the United States." [9]

These remarks indicate that the long-range educational consequences of urbanization will be favorable. The report leaves aside however the question of adequate financing in the forthcoming years, when the number of high-school students in the medium-sized cities and the suburbs will rapidly swell. The conclusions concerning the small high schools make one wonder about the results of the partitioning of the mushrooming suburbs into smaller communities. Will the less affluent suburban towns find the resources for adequately comprehensive high schools? Moreover, this suburban partitioning may affect the children's education in other ways and before the high-school age.

Years ago, the variety of urban life and the city's activities, its location at a crossroads, even its crowding, offered a picture of the world's variety and of society's problems which was

[9] James B. Conant, *The American High School Today: A First Report to Interested Citizens* (New York: McGraw-Hill, 1959), Section IV, pp. 77–95.

stimulating and often provided the children with enriching experiences. Although it is possible to spend a long life in a metropolis without seeing anything beyond a closed local circle, urban life offers many incentives to learn how to feel the pulse of a wide, complicated, striving world. This is an important aspect of educational opportunity at a time of rapid change, of growing interregional and international exchanges and interdependence. Here is an advantage available to youngsters who fully profit from the urban environment. Some of them will of course react negatively to the challenge and early build up an attitude of blasé sophistication, hoping to thus protect themselves from the on-rushing outside world.

As one reads the many volumes recently published on suburban life, one is impressed with the frequent endeavor of the new communities to remain homogeneous, tightly organized, and somewhat isolated from the surrounding areas. Such hints can easily be gathered from works such as: A. C. Spectorsky's *The Exurbanites*, John Keats' *The Crack in the Picture Window*, William H. Whyte's *The Organization Man*, etc. Such homogeneity may help solve many local problems and avoid others characteristic of more diversified groups. It may also take away from the youngsters' education and experience many valuable assets provided by the usual urban conditions, for the sheltered environment of such suburban towns does not always prepare children for real life in the outside world. The size of the town is not significant in this respect. Such closed-in communities have existed in large cities. The multiplication of such compartments in the suburbs does not necessarily entail an isolated education as the town is within easy reach of some bustling business district and of several very different towns. The fashion for such homogeneous suburbs appears indicative however of a psychological attitude favoring social isolation which may well be going against society's present trends.

As one wishes to see today the complexities of the urbanized areas put to better use, with an aim of familiarizing youth with the variety and complexity of the world, one also wonders whether cities and suburbs take full advantage of the educational and recreational assets offered by the expanding woods in their vicinity and by the growing interpenetration of suburban residential, manufacturing, and specialized farming areas. The variety of neighborhoods within a metropolitan region is often astonishing. The proximity to existing green belts is generally greater than usually expected. The access to these green belts and to this wide gamut of economic institutions is worth many theoretical lessons to children reared in built-up residential neighborhoods. Such educational assets can well be used with much profit for youngsters who would otherwise have little contact with nature and with the diverse activities of modern industry—but who ought to know about it all and would love it. These contacts can well be organized in a way that would not become a nuisance to the management of the woods, farms, or plants involved.

The impact of urbanization in its present form on American society is full of opportunities which could be beneficial in terms of the education and recreation of children and youth. It is however also full of dangerous pitfalls if some of the technical consequences of urban living are allowed to run wild. The street traffic needs and gets strict regulation, especially in neighborhoods densely populated with children. A number of other safety devices and rules have to be adopted and applied since adults cannot expect from children more knowledge and responsibility than they have had the time to acquire. The time left to teen-agers for leisure has been on the increase as the school programs have been lightened in many cases and as fewer of them work full time; this leisure time needs direction and opportunity to use it properly. Failure to provide these may cause more trouble on city streets than on scattered farms. In short, urbanization may be held as one of the factors which create need for more and more care and planning by parents. Technological progress may simplify in some ways the adults' tasks but adds new burdens to their responsibilities.

The New Frontier

It may well be claimed that urbanization has created for today and for some time ahead a new frontier for the American people to explore and to manage. This new frontier is not simply one of civilization advancing against the wilderness, a struggle with an environment of an unknown nature, but rather the reconstruction and continuous improvement of the areas overrun by modern urban growth. It is the urban renewal in the heart of old cities, the revitalizing of the declining suburbs in the "gray zone," the building of new suburbs, the management of the green areas left in the vicinity of the metropolises. Cities age as they grow, and the task seems one of almost constantly rejuvenating the vast urban regions in which congregate most of the population. This is a frontier left by the past, which the present must not misuse; it is an essential modern aspect of the permanent struggle of mankind for a better and brighter world to live in. A nation engaged upon it can hardly stop on the way without serious prejudice to the next generation; the frontier must be pushed ahead with the needs of the younger section of the population in mind. The sooner the youth can be associated with this great task, the better it will be, for it is a consuming endeavor but one yielding great rewards.

In this great work of expanding and rejuvenating vast urban regions, the United States is today more advanced than any of the other countries in the world. All these countries, with the exception of very few backward lands, feel the impact of on-rushing urbanization. It is a major concern in the U.S.S.R. and Canada, in Britain and Germany, the Netherlands and France, Italy and Denmark, Mexico and Brazil— even the government of Southern Rhodesia has found it necessary to appoint a Commission on Urban Affairs. Many experts and authorities throughout the world are deeply interested in this new facet of the American experiment. They may well look at the impact urban growth will have on the children and youth of America, and especially those in the large metropolitan areas of the Northeast, as a laboratory from which to learn.

Although such attention will be, and is already focused on these areas it does not follow that local solutions or ex-

periments will be easily copied or duplicated. Every student
of urban affairs knows how different is every urban area in
the practical handling of its problems, and in the possible
attempts at solution. Within the United States alone these
differences have already proven great. What is true of New
York does not necessarily apply to Philadelphia, certainly
not to Washington, and even less to Los Angeles. San Francisco and New Orleans are deeply different in almost every
aspect of their urban and metropolitan problems, and so
are Houston and Kansas City. Each can and must learn from
the experience of the others but it must always put the
knowledge thus acquired into the local or regional mold before any consequences can be deduced.

Just because urban growth multiplies along a street houses
which look alike on the outside does not mean that it stand-
ardizes the people who live in them. Urbanization in fact
probably brings more variety, movement, and turmoil to
society than was ever expected. These processes must be
recognized, their great variety respected and turned into a
better system of cooperation and comfort among people. It
seems important at this stage that the youth of today be
given a hopeful outlook about the city of tomorrow.

THE PLACE OF RELIGION IN AMERICAN LIFE

by MSGR. RAYMOND J.
GALLAGHER
RABBI MARC H. TANENBAUM
and the
REV. DR. WILLIAM J.
VILLAUME

FROM the very beginning of our nation's existence religion has occupied a central place. Belief in the Deity was more than a profession of faith. It found its place in the living experience of Americans. It was not a metaphysical principle that needed demonstration or proving. It was generally accepted as the ground of moral decision for facing all of life's affairs. Belief in God and its consequent responsibilities formed the keystone upholding the arch of national existence. The agenda of goals adopted by the Founding Fathers bears out convincingly their belief in God. Their

The Very Rev. Msgr. Raymond J. Gallagher is Assistant Director, Catholic Charities, Cleveland Diocese. Rabbi Marc H. Tanenbaum is Executive Director of the Synagogue Council of America. The Rev. Dr. William J. Villaume is Executive Director, Department of Social Welfare, Division of Christian Life and Work, National Council of Churches of Christ in the United States of America.

greatest hope for success in the bold ventures they contemplated was derived from their belief in His existence and their confidence that under His providence man could develop in honor and in dignity. Society, it seemed to them, was intimately dependent upon religion.

While revolutionary movements on the continent of Europe were threatening to destroy the influence of religion on public life, our Founding Fathers based their own revolutionary action on the rights inherent in man as a creature of God and placed their trust in His divine providence. The concept of man which they set forth in the Declaration of Independence was essentially a religious concept. Human equality stemmed from the fact that all men had been created by God who endowed them equally with rights.

Freedom, too, is essentially bound up with the religious concept of man. There can be no genuine or lasting freedom in any context that separates men from the creative and sustaining God. The enjoyment of all human rights is possible only in a society which acknowledges the supreme and omnipotent God. Government dedicated to the general welfare is derived from the religious concepts of man and society grounded in the Judeo-Christian tradition.

The early colonists treasured the convictions which they had salvaged from their previous experiences. Through the many upheavals of governments which marked the growth of European nations from the Judeo-Christian traditions, the basic belief in God had survived. While different governments rose and fell, while significant events left their impression on history, the basic relationships between man and God endured and proved their lasting value.

The Founding Fathers believed that the lineage of man could be traced back to a creative act of God. From this fact stem the rights and the duties of man. They understood that the essential worth of the human being is based upon his creation in the image of God. Man was considered a living reproduction capable of improving and sharpening the likeness through a life of prayer and godly works, words and deeds. They believed that the essential relationships in life are fashioned after the primary relationship of man to God. This conception set the high level of responsibility between government and the governed. The seriousness of the task and the sacredness of responsible programs are apparent to one who is aware that he is performing a task as a representative of the authority of God. Loyalty, responsibility, and dedication characterize his performance. The commerce and the national economy of such a people is necessarily based upon fairness, honesty, and reliability because both parties to a bargain understand their common identity as creatures of God. Every man's word can be accepted as his bond and his testimony as truthful when citizens acknowledge the fatherhood of God which all enjoy.

In brief summary of these paragraphs about our country's origin, it can be said that part of the bone and sinew of early America was its firm belief in God. Undoubtedly our readers are aware of instances when this simple statement of truth was not a matter of fact. We recognize that exceptions have existed. However, there is no doubt but that the United States is essentially a nation which grew out of convictions as to man's individual honor, freedom, and dignity, and these convictions were based on religion.

Children of God

The development of family life in early American tradition reflected the strong and positive influences that flowed from the biblical tradition. Respectful acceptance of the role of parent by the child and the reverent acceptance of the task of protecting and guiding children constituted the pillars upon which strong and closely knit family life developed. As set forth in the Scriptures the natural primacy of the father in the family was delicately delineated. His role as the good provider, protector, and mentor became the hallmark of a solid American family. Complementary to this position was the sincere honor and respect in which the mother was held. Duties and responsibilities, rights and privileges, meshed into a workable plan for the family.

Based on the traditions of religion whereon single and common lives were lived, marriage was considered to be a sanctified state, not simply a matter of natural instinct and desirability. Marriage offered an opportunity for the happiness of life and for the fulfillment of one's being as a parent, but more than that it offered an opportunity to share in the awesome privilege of creation. Parent and child relationships took their form and fiber from the fact that they were in a natural sequence whereby God placed under the care of parents this living image of their sanctified love.

Familiarity with the Scriptures supported parents in their determination to provide a proper setting for the whole being—body, mind, and spirit. Thus parents so acted as to prepare their children for the worship of God, constructive service to humanity, and individual fulfillment through a godly way of life.

A notable early American attitude toward children was the common conviction that each child had a responsibility for the future. Children were considered as more than mere links in a genealogy. If traditions were to be transmitted from one generation to the next, children had to become familiar with them and imbued with their importance. In the Jewish and Christian traditions, children and youth were considered the guarantors of tomorrow. Today's ideals and goals were not milestones upon which man could rest satisfied. Today's ideals would become tomorrow's achievements through the children who were pathways through a series of tomorrows.

The first born male child, whose uniqueness is clearly set forth in the biblical writings, occupied a position of prominence, importance, and responsibility. His conception of future responsibility would be the measure of family progress. In the early American family the eldest son was faced with the harsh realities of life at a very early early age so that the fearlessness and determination necessary to overcome obstacles would be thoroughly developed within him.

In the early stages of our country's history there was a close partnership between family practices and religious services in church and synagogue. Religious observances in the family began with morning prayer. Grace before meals was standard practice. Bible reading, participated in by the entire family, took place every evening. And on Sabbath and the religious holidays the family engaged in special worship. The table was an altar, the home a sanctuary in which God's presence was felt.

Progress and Change under God

The import of our words until now has been to the effect that religion played a vital role in the formation of our nation and in the generation of our families. A fair appraisal of circumstances as they now exist would indicate that considerable change has taken place. In the progress which we have enjoyed as a nation new interpretations have been placed upon the role of religion in American life. These have resulted in slightly changed and varied approaches but they have left unaltered the essence of the problem. It is probably true to say that America is coming of age and in the process is consolidating within its national identity many new, as well as traditional, ideas. Generally, America today enjoys a great deal more freedom, particularly intellectual freedom. Personal freedom has always been a mark of American society and with the extension of our frontiers and the development of many new areas of activity, intellectual freedom has become more widespread. All aspects of life are studied and analyzed. The communication of news has enjoyed a phenomenal development so that opportunity for analysis and comparison of ideas is now considerably advanced. Religion, among other foundations of the individual's life, must now face openly the test of competition from other values and other plans of life.

People feel they have a right to know the facts and a right to make a decision privately before they are expected to give a statement of their personal position. This democratic approach to knowledge is extended in the field of religion so that many individuals take an inquiring point of view in contemplating the application of religious principles to their private lives.

There is a fringe of extremism present in many of these judgmental activities. It is truthful to say that with regard to religion there is a minor segment of our population which is unbelieving. The place of religion is in no way threatened by them. It is logical to conclude that just as religion endured the upheaval of the world's history until now, it will continue to present a stable way of life to those who take the time to study it thoroughly and apply it in detail to their own life situations.

Another phenomenon in American life which has affected the role of religion is the mobility of individuals and the quickness of the life which they lead. The process of change is so accelerated as to discourage man from the meditative consideration of human existence. In the case of those who have judged it to be essential and who have provided sufficient time to consider the matter, the sound and practical role of religion in their lives has continued.

Educational opportunities have been offered to the broadest segment of the population. These, too, have a broadening effect on the horizons of life and have produced a more knowing appraisal of the institutions and symbolisms of life. Many who have thrilled to the exhilaration of intellectual freedom have misjudged the swing of the pendulum of credibility. Because the gaining of knowledge has had the effect of disproving many false notions, some have rejected those traditional institutions, such as religion, when they could find little in the pragmatic sciences to support religious forms and creeds. True knowledge finds its foundation in a variety of sources, and the mature student of religion has been able to maintain his religious convictions in the face of new scientific data.

In view of the developmental change which we have noted above, it is valid to raise questions at this point. Since many Americans are expressing their concern for the stability of the future, is it not reasonable to say that America is at another crucial point of decision?

America has succeeded in its struggle for identity. Our people were consumed by the fervor of forging a nation in the shortest possible time. They experienced the fever of conquest which led them to challenge the power of mountains, forests, and rivers to stay the hand of their progress. The United States has enjoyed a singular victory over ignorance and has upheld the right of man to know the truth and to enjoy the freedom of applying the truth. The United States has tested its right to endure. Militarily, we have engaged in battles from skirmishes to global conflicts. We have suffered through days of minimal material provisions, through days of sufficiency, regressing through depressions, then moving on to a point of national affluence. The

United States has emerged from diplomatic infancy to the stature of world leadership sworn to achieve the betterment of all peoples. It would not be an inappropriate description to say that America considers itself as having a mission to the world—ideals, goals, standards of living, and standards of performing which we hold so dear and which we agree are based upon religious foundations.

Now we stand on the threshold of the future where things basic to our nation are being challenged. An opposing philosophy of society is poised on the other side of the globe, challenging the worth and the endurance of the spiritual, cultural, and political essence of America. Perhaps more seriously, we are faced with the prospect of moving out of the comfortable limits of our globe into the uncharted universe. Will the present, current version of traditional American attitudes toward God, religious convictions, and value systems be sufficient to meet these tests?

In progressing into the unknown the United States might well formulate its plan in terms of tried and tested truths. As the United States stands at the beginning of another decade, it also faces the beginning of another era. It will aid us substantially if we seek an opportunity to assess the traditional religious concepts in American life and affirm their place in the foundation of American life for the future.

God as Our Goal

People of religious convictions believe that the quest for God and knowledge of His Kingdom are the main purposes of life. Material things, important as they are toward the perfecting of life, are but means to an end. Reaffirmation of belief in authentic spiritual values deserves a priority on the agenda of Americans at this crucial moment in history. The time would seem to be most propitious. Membership rolls of the three major faiths in America are larger than ever before in our history. However casual or superficial the commitment of this membership might be in some instances, it is at least an indication of the concern which families have for insuring a religious component in their lives. They wish to be identified with religious ideals and activities. Churches and synagogues would be derelict in their duty if they did not respond to the promise and opportunity for spiritual greatness which this phenomenon presents.

Religious institutions should be their own severest critics as to the manner and technique in which they present their spiritual message and promote their religious programs. Outmoded, ingrown, unrealistic methodologies should give way to those modern techniques which will keep pace with the phenomenal development of other areas of communication, new information, and knowledge. The closest cooperation among major faiths and sects should be developed. Pointless differences which now dissipate the strength of religious influence in our community should be analyzed and eliminated when their true identity becomes known. It is possible to give substantial emphasis to those basic considerations upon which all agree. Churches and synagogues standing together publicly on fundamental issues can multiply their effectiveness by combating the inroads of irreligion. Cooperation without concession or compromise is clearly possible for the major religious groups in the United States. Too long have we been concerned with protecting what we have, thus blinding ourselves to the advances we could make together.

If the church is to become a genuine force for good in the community, it must harken back to the example given by the best experience of the churches and synagogues in colonial days. These houses of worship were not only the centers of religious and social life but were also the places of leadership and community action. A similar need exists today. A community should look to its qualified leaders for advice and counsel in the decisive areas of life. The manner in which churches and synagogues act in concert to take on the leadership role in community life permits them to contribute greatly to the welfare of all of the nation's citizens. Moral standards, religious practices, delineations of value systems, these are their chief responsibility. Keeping aflame the love of God and fellowmen, inspiring community service, and upholding concepts and ideals which have a spiritual foundation—these are the responsibility of dynamic and fearless leadership on the part of men and women of religious convictions. It is the least the institutions of religion can contribute to a nation which has made possible the unprecedented blessings of religious freedom and toleration. It is the most essential contribution they can make to America as it faces the uncertainty of the future.

Many aspects of community life affecting children and youth can benefit from the introduction, rebirth, or perfecting of existing principles of religion. The degrees in which religion exists in the following facets of community life is at best inaccurately known and consequently no broad indictment or endorsement can be given.

In labor, the place of religion is fundamental. Churches and synagogues must look to the development of a sense of community responsibility so that the common good will be held above personal gains of either labor or management. According to the best religious traditions labor has dignity in itself. The spiritual satisfactions of honest labor and management are ofttimes lost sight of by reason of greed for success, money, and power. Honesty in the use of time, tools, materials, and capital by employers and employees is an application of religious principles to a practical purpose. Religious principles of justice, fairness in a day's pay and a day's work must stand as countervailing influences against those forces which would demean the high calling and purpose of labor.

The application of law to the lives of individual citizens is most acceptable when it involves principles drawn from religion. The law of the land is considered a sharing of the dominion of God over all mankind. As God's laws are made for the benefit of the governed, so present day legislators and other elected officials must be reminded of the attributes of justice tempered by mercy, which are of the Divine Lawgiver. Honesty, prudence, fairness and justice are but a few of the moral virtues which describe the true servant of the law. Service for the sake of others and not for self-aggrandizement is the qualification of those who would serve their community and their Creator through the practice of the law.

Government currently takes many roles in fulfilling responsibility to the governed. Maintenance of justice and order, leadership in meeting common problems, balance between collective and individual interests and needs are appropriate examples. When the concept of authority is being applied government acts out the role of the father of the greater community. All the noble qualities which apply to the ideal father in the family are pertinent here. Courage of conviction, leadership, judicious use of authority, bravery and dedication, self-sacrifice in the interest of others are all characteristic of the spiritual foundation which must be the basis of the government's service to the governed.

The contribution which love makes to the life of every individual is conditioned by the virtue and godliness which accompanies it. Every aspect of love, whether it be regard, respect, affection, or emotional and physical attraction exemplifies a fundamental virtue. By recognizing and turning to the religious sources of this human experience the community and the individual citizen will be sustained through the sanctity of this basic treasure. The preservation of the religious concept of love thy neighbor as thyself can help overcome indifference, blighting cynicism, or outright baseness of life in society, both governmental and familial.

In the field of education the goal is to prepare our children and youth to live full and creative lives. Careful consideration must be given to building sound moral character as well as to competency in the skills. Both public and private schools have a vital role to play in strengthening the life of the children and youth of America.

Another area where the application of traditional religious principles would serve the nation is that of amusement and recreation. We speak here in behalf of self-imposed standards of excellence. Within the ranks of those who promote amusement, recreation, and entertainment there are large numbers of nobly motivated, morally concerned people. Within these same ranks are a few who seek to profit by the use of subterfuge and legal deceptions. If the industry itself would identify those who, with malice aforethought, propagate examples of low moral conduct through theatrical presentations, through motion pictures, and through printed pages and pornographic magazines, a great service would be done the industry and the nation. Discipline from within would restore confidence in good motives and high moral purposes and would identify the profiteers for what they are, those who would capitalize upon protections available to them.

Parents and families have a distinct role to play in the re-establishing or the perfecting of moral standards, religious convictions, and ideals. Reconstituting themselves as the primary teaching unit and basing their instruction on the eternal verities which have withstood the test of time, parents can contribute to favorable circumstances wherein their children can realize their greatest potential. If there is no concerted and unified effort by parents to close ranks against the disorganizing force of modern urban society, they are menacing their children by handicapping them as well as creating an antagonistic society. It is true that the absence of citizen attention ofttimes permits the development of negative characteristics in the society in which their children move and live. The most direct contribution which they can make to the development of ideal circumstances for their children is to create and live by those standards of conduct, those value systems and ideals which lead to an improved citizenry. Once having accepted a code of behavior they should abide by it with great resolution. Once having made a decision about the practical value of this way of life, let them avoid those instances of self-exemption which only serve to confuse the child who watches the performance.

Taking a page from the practice of pioneer families, parents are urged to return to the observance of family religious practices. Family prayer has been promoted widely in the United States in recent years with encouraging results. It is not sufficiently promoted, however, to have a telling result on the spiritual climate of our society. The reading of the Scriptures by the members of the family presents a doubly favorable impression. Presenting the counsel of God through the pages of Scripture will not be lost on the minds of children who are looking for a way of life with authoritative endorsement. Worshiping as a family unit in churches and synagogues contributes to the integrity of the family. This, in turn, enables its children to withstand those forces which are contrary to family standards because of the godly strength which accrues to family standards through family worship.

Respectful observance of religious seasons, feasts, and festivals is another method of incorporating religious convictions and value systems in American life. Incorporating in every such observance an appropriate expression and commentary on the sacredness of the event and its symbolism will add to the impression which the child carries into the future. Above all, those practices which will deepen the convictions for our belonging to this congregation or that organization are of paramount importance. So often we are perplexed by the fact that children of well-regulated families, families which belong to all of the "right" organizations, still succumb to the ways of delinquency. Possibly we are content with mere superficial belonging and do not graft or ingrain into ourselves the basic ideals for which the faith or the organization stands.

The child's role in making these ideals, values, and standards workable is most essential. His complete trust in the leadership of well-motivated parents will contribute in the largest measure to his own fulfillment as an adult and inheritor of the future. In his educational and avocational work his fidelity to honesty, industry, and ambition should be etched on his service record. In his membership in the community, respect for authority as administered by elected and appointed officials will easily be given when it is based on his understanding of their responsibility in the affairs of the community. In his neighborhood his respect for his neighbor's rights and property will be compatible with his drive for property of his own. Kindliness, courtesy and good manners, helpfulness, these are the marks of one who has triumphed over the smallness and narrowness which sometimes captures human beings. A charitable concern for each neighbor, his home and his family, a respectful acceptance of differences in race, creed, and national origin, these are the marks of a youth who has truly inherited the tradition of America.

In his family he should have respect for his parents and the authority vested in their office as well as respect for authority vested in those who take the parents' place. This constitutes the surest guarantee of his ability to assume responsibilities as he grows through the years. A reverence for the union which binds his parents together and a fervent hope that his future will be similarly blessed, this describes a youth who understands his responsibility as a guarantor of the future.

In his private life, that which the child alone forms, his communion with God and his generous attitude toward other people are the foundation stones upon which his personal integrity is based. With religious nurture and experience a child emerges to a point of adult responsibility with honesty, justice, mercy, patriotism, modesty, loyalty, courage, bravery, and a sense of service to his fellowman often beyond the mere call of duty. Such a youth, despite whatever faces him and his country, is well prepared to deal successfully with the challenges that are ahead.

Conclusion

The foregoing has attempted to describe the place of religion in American life. The foundation which religion gives the standards, value systems, and ideals we treasure has been set forth in simple narrative without any effort to deal with the subject as a theological or an historical treatise. The attempt has succeeded if it has reminded those who seek guidance for the decade of the 1960s that the golden thread of religion woven through the tapestry of American history has served the nation well.

Material values alone tend towards diminishing returns, total lifelessness, and decay. People who live by them only are trying to perpetuate things which of their very mundane nature cannot be perpetuated. They cling to objects and values which time destroys without mercy. They are bound up in a contingent and material order of things, customs, clothes, architecture, places, and personalities which inevitably change and give way to something else.

We cannot bequeath to our children that which will crumble in the very act of possessing. We must consider our responsibilities unmet until we have included in the blueprint of our current American life those lasting values which will endure beyond the inevitable changes which face our children and the universe in which they will live.

THE NEW LEISURE

by AUGUST HECKSCHER

THE CHANGES which have occurred in American life over the past decade are cumulative and interwoven, so that it is difficult to make any one of them predominant or to single one out as the principal cause of others. The increase in the size of families, the move away from the center of the cities, the decline of inter-urban transportation, the increased proportion of young people making college their goal—these are all part of one picture. For purposes of study or action we may isolate one aspect or another. But as observers of social change, we must accept these and other factors as closely interrelated. In ways which can often be discussed only generally, these various developments react upon each other. Each stimulates the total movement and gives an impetus to the direction in which the social order tends to move.

If we were to look for a single change underlying others, however, we would have to give close attention to leisure. Today's child is growing up in a period marked by an emphasis on the values of leisure and a growing amount of

August Heckscher is Director of the Twentieth Century Fund.

leisure time. In no other force making for change has there been involved so deep a transformation of values, of philosophy, and of ethics. The United States was founded under the inspiration of religious and secular codes which gave primary emphasis to the place of work in a man's life. A job was related to the Puritan concept of a "calling"; and a "calling" was related to man's destiny both in this world and the next. The result was a striking capacity to accomplish material goals, but this was accompanied by the danger that the sources of cultural life might dry up. At its best Puritanism infused work with spiritual quality. But when this failed, as it did in time, the husk of materialism was left, and people spent their lives in work which had less and less inner meaning.

For various reasons the emphasis on work declined as the twentieth century advanced. Hours on the job were steadily reduced from approximately sixty in 1900 to an average of forty in 1950. Often, this occurred as part of a movement to "share the work" or as a tactic for gaining more "overtime"—the former in the depression, the latter in periods of prosperity. But there has been a genuine desire for a shorter working day, and this has been accomplished and combined with lengthened vacations for everyone, as well as a longer span of retirement extended even further by the added years contributed by medical science. In the period ahead we shall undoubtedly see the work week further shortened. It should not be overlooked, however, that people expect a continually higher standard of living, which means that a good portion of the gains in productivity—roughly two-thirds over the past decades—tend to be assigned to the output of more goods rather than the enjoyment of more free time.

Whatever the forms or the precise amount of leisure time which may accrue over the next decade, the fact is plain that a revolution has occurred in American values. No longer does work hold undisputed sway at the center of life. It may be a matter of debate as to what rivals it, or has taken its place. Travel, the family, improvement of the home, civic and cultural activities—each of these and others could make their claim. For the moment it is enough to suggest that the energizing focus of the individual's life has altered or been diffused; and this has led to dramatic changes throughout the whole social system.

The move to the suburbs, for example, is related to the new values of a leisure civilization. Men and women are getting away physically from the scene of their labors to an environment where a host of new interests and problems preoccupy them. The growing predominance of the private car in place of the instruments of mass transportation is likewise part of the new approach. In automobiles men seek the freedom and independence that have traditionally been associated with leisure pursuits.

Now such trends often defeat their real purpose. The preoccupations of suburban life come to exert a tyranny of their own; the long journey to and from work eats into the supposedly free hours of the day; the automobile immobilized in traffic becomes a symbol of the futility of man's effort to escape into a realm of freedom. We need to evaluate critically many of the forms and methods the country has adopted as a consequence of the decline of a work-centered civilization. But despite many frustrations and dead ends we are witnessing a search for genuine leisure. In the process of that search our institutions and habits are being made over.

The Impact on Youth

The life of children and young people in such a period of social change is bound to be deeply affected. Children are sensitive to a surprising degree to shifts in the winds of doctrine about them. The family may like to think of itself as a watertight unit, maintaining its own standards regardless of the world outside. But this is an illusion. The society of which we are all a part exerts an extraordinarily pervasive force. Parents brought up amid the economies of a depression may try to maintain among their children the habits of austerity and self-help which were among the rewarding features of that era. They find this to be an almost impossible task. The children are of their own time; its standards and tendencies speak to them compellingly.

How alert children are to the forces of the time may be seen by observing those families which do not own television. Despite its absence in the home the children will have picked up the language, the familiar images, the whole flavor of the TV age. It is as if their minds were peculiarly sensitized to their own period and armed against whatever is carried over or imposed by authority.

It is natural, therefore, that so profound a change as is

represented by the growth of leisure values should have caught on among the younger generation. How it has affected them is not easy to determine. The first answer would be that it has made them, like their elders, "leisure-minded," or especially concerned with recreational activities. But that would be an oversimplification. The essential point about youth is that, while absorbing and being influenced by the world of their elders, they inhabit very largely a world of their own. The communications between these two worlds are direct and continuous, but the messages arrive at their destinations in a distorted and sometimes incomprehensible form. There seems to be no doubt, for instance, that many of the behavior patterns which we describe under the name of "delinquency" are an effort on the part of the young to communicate something important to the adult group. Similarly, the adult communications on the subject of leisure reach the mind of youth in a garbled form.

The reason for this is that work and leisure have meanings of their own for children, often significantly at variance with those held by the rest of the population. In its most dramatic form this difference can be pointed out by the fact that the Greek word for leisure, *scola*, is essentially the same as our word for school. "What!" we can hear some young student exclaiming, "You mix up a word meaning fun and freedom and recreation with this word which speaks to us of toil and bondage. You have the audacity to suggest that when we're at school we're not working—that we're actually resting and enjoying ourselves!" Without stopping to ask how this strange derivation arose, we make for the moment the simple point that a child's concept of work, like a child's concept of leisure, is not the same as the philosopher's. It is by no means identical with the activities which the adult would place under these categories. (It should be added, incidentally, that not all adults agree as to what they consider leisure as opposed to work.)

Much of what we call "play" for children is undertaken seriously, in an entirely workmanlike manner. When children play they are preparing for the roles they will be called on to assume in later life. They imitate what they cannot yet comprehend, they play at "mothers" or "shopkeepers" or "soldiers" as the spirit moves them and as the fashions of the grown-up world suggest. In childhood the difference between work and play is not marked; even when they do something which their parents consider useful, such as setting the table or raking leaves, they still see themselves engaged in an imitation of adult behavior. If they grumble under what they affect to be a tyrannical imposition, that is also part of the game. They assume that such a reaction is expected of them. Have they not observed their elders giving vent to just such emotions?

The significant change which may be expected in these early years is not, therefore, more "leisure." It is play built around somewhat different patterns and preoccupations. The decline in the relative importance of the job as the adult criterion of status and prestige will mean that the children shift the objects of their imitation. The types of toys put on the market and their degrees of popularity should provide to the researcher an interesting test of the hypothesis presented here. Do the children organize their group around the image of a country club, instead of the image of an army? Do they put more emphasis on the simulated family than the simulated shop?

The Teen-Ager

In older children we begin to see more clearly the effect of a leisure oriented society upon youth. In the early teens, or perhaps before, the young person begins to make a very sharp distinction between work and play. We would expect, therefore, to see the element of play stressed to a degree that would have surprised earlier generations. This appears to be the case. The parents cannot but become more permissive toward their children as they relax for themselves the rigorous standards of an older code. The children cannot but become more inclined to take things easy. It may be difficult to document the change, but the fact seems to be that in terms of foot-pounds of energy the present generation of young people does not make the same expenditure as its predecessors. They do not walk as far; it is impossible to imagine them undertaking regularly a trip of even a few miles on foot to school. It is questionable whether they devote themselves with the same degree of application to intellectual tasks and studies. Memory exercises have gone out of fashion. As the emphasis on work diminishes, the young people turn to play and recreation with an avidity patterned on the behavior of their elders.

A shift in the school curriculum away from the classical and general studies toward more vocational subjects may be seen as one of the results of the leisure-minded society. The classical studies almost always require a high level of concentration as well as a dedication to work for its own sake. They deal with matters outside the immediate interests of the student. Their relevance is not evident at first glance and their best rewards are often deferred. In contrast, the vocational studies are easily assimilated and bring direct benefits.

The shift away from the classics in the school curriculum has, however, its paradoxical side. A society oriented toward leisure—at least toward leisure as it has been understood by past societies—would be expected to shun vocationalism. It would teach young people the values and pursuits which make it possible for a man or woman in later life to draw for enjoyment upon inner resources. The more practical emphasis in the curriculum has usually been associated with a life given over early and exclusively to a job. Actually, however, the vocational courses of today are frequently leisure-oriented. Not only do they require relatively little effort; they are bent to what are called "leisure skills." Thus automobile driving and automobile care are directly related to the aim of every high-school student to own a car at the earliest possible moment. One cannot help asking whether leisure skills can or should be isolated from the broader aims of education. And if they are to be the goal, is not the most important of them all a capacity to read with concentration and understanding?

In our society, in brief, vocationalism in education is often not associated with work, but with recreation. General studies, which should form the basis of a leisure-minded education, are neglected, in part because of the toil and sweat which their pursuit requires.

The curriculum is not the only part of school life affected by the trend toward leisure. The whole atmosphere of the school, its official and nonofficial extra-curricular activities, are influenced by what is going on in the life of the community around it. The architecture of the newer schools, which has certainly made them bright and cheerful, reflects the standards of the modern shopping center, or even of the modern place of work. The gymnasium and auditorium stand out prominently; wide corridors, courtyards, sheltered areas combine to impress upon the student a feeling that what goes on outside the classroom—the conversations, the friendly contacts, the periods of relaxation—are as important as what goes on within the classroom itself.

Beyond the high school, education also derives its atmosphere in large part from the same standards. College work has certainly become more demanding as a result of the heightened competition and the press of numbers; it may well be that a new seriousness is today setting the tone. But it is the seriousness, not of the traditional higher learning, but of the modern community—the modern suburban community. It is interesting to note to what degree the college campus has actually adopted the values and behavior patterns of the suburb. Coeducation and student marriages create interests which are oriented toward the personal and subjective, rather than toward that objective truth which was the aim of older education. The extra-curricular activities tend to become social in nature, rather than to be patterned on the battle field or the political forum. The curriculum is infused with the same values. History, for example, is viewed less as the actions of strong men, the creation of human will, than the result of impersonal trends and processes. Even the manner of teaching is affected. Wherever possible the old lecture course is abandoned in favor of the small group or seminar. The professor, instead of standing forth as a public figure, is like the leader of a congenial group of conversationalists during the coffee hour.

The fear once was that the college, instead of being a place apart, would become infected by the standards of the market place. The market place has declined in its appeal in an age of leisure. The new danger is that the college will be infected by the standards of suburban living.

Leisure and Consumption

The standards of a leisure society have further influenced young people by making them conscious of their role as consumers. Leisure as we understand it in the United States has little to do with the contemplative or passive mood. Reading may be a part of leisure, yet it is generally reading for self-improvement or reading which personally involves the individual, permitting him to escape from his normal circumstances into a realm of action or romance. Movies and television seem to be watched as a means to vicarious experience, not with a critical and disinterested spirit. In short, even those activities which on the surface appear passive are really a substitute for action, while action in palpable and vigorous forms provides the content of most leisure hours. Men and women boat, golf, ski, garden, bowl—and in innumerable other ways prove that they are devotees of what the advertisers like to call "active leisure."

As a result, leisure in the United States is an expensive commodity. It is not simply that people stop earning money when they leave the factory or office; they begin spending it at an increased rate. Common sense would tell us that this leads to a painful dilemma: if men want to enjoy their free time they must work more in order to make more money —but if they work more, then they do not have the free time. Fortunately certain economic factors come into play to rescue the leisure-minded individual from so impossible a situation. The process is something like this: The goods, services, and equipment which are consumed by the population in their free time create a vast demand which can only be met by the introduction of more efficient machines. These machines permit the production of constantly greater amounts in a given period—so much so that the worker, through the blessings of advanced technology, can earn more and have both his goods and his leisure. It is a beneficent process, but if it is to work it means that the population must live up to its role of consumers. It could not, even if it wished, content itself with the role of observers or philosophers.

The social ethic of consumerism puts its mark on younger people. Brought up in a period of prosperity and abundance they would be ready in any case to demand what they conceive to be their share of material goods. The large amount of uncommitted time which naturally falls to them increases this disposition. The "teen-age market" is a rich target for the merchant and advertiser. Even the younger children, whose material desires do not extend beyond the possession of a few toys, are sought as agents to influence the parents. Thus from the beginning leisure is colored by the tendency to link it with the buying of gadgets and the spending of money.

There is, of course, another quality of leisure; indeed the word has been associated in other periods with a passive rather than an active mood. The leisured aristocrat might have estates and costly ceremonies as the background against which his days of idleness were lived. But within this elaborate frame his pursuits were simple. Often, as in hunting or yachting, he deliberately recreated the conditions of a simpler, less mechanized existence. For the rest, his major delights were conversation, love-making, gossip, dancing, visiting, theater-going, and reading.

When leisure is of this kind an affinity exists between the way children and grown-ups spend their free time. For children in their natural state are also wanderers and gossipers, and pass the hours of the day without need for specific occupations or elaborate equipment. The play of younger children is not, it is true, as unstructured as it may appear to the outsider. What gives the impression of being endless and undifferentiated in the activities of an afternoon may involve for the participants a series of more or less definite periods, each with its own form and content. Yet in general children behave not unlike their elders in an idle and aristocratic age: when they go somewhere their major destination is "out," and when they do something they feel the best way to describe it is "nothing."

Today the standards of the adult world reach back into the world of children making them less "idle" but also more dependent for their pleasures on the output of the machine technology. These same children will, as they grow up, make the leisure of the future even more "active" and gadget-ridden. In other periods—even today when so much of an older ethic persists—the tendency toward a materialistic use of leisure is softened by habits natural to childhood. Amid the glittering temptations of worldliness the instincts of play remain. Long, unbounded summer days, with their expanses of delicious emptiness, linger in the memory and make it never quite possible to equate leisure with the doing of something formalized and expensive. But in the next generation this pool of simplicity may have been drained dry. Those whose childhood has been surrounded by an avalanche of consumer goods will accept, without saving inhibitions or doubts, the duty of consumption as the price of prosperity and increasing free time.

The Two Worlds

If leisure in the period ahead is to be meaningful, a new relationship must be established between the youthful and adult worlds. It is clear that a new relationship is in fact in the making: leisure has brought parents and children into a state of "togetherness" which is not the mere invention of the phrase-makers. What is not so clear is whether the interaction of these two worlds as it is at present developing will be of benefit to society as a whole. Children may well thrive on a certain degree of salutary neglect—or at least of independence; and as for parents, they certainly do better when they are not tied down completely to the care and entertainment of their offspring. It may be that the adult and youthful groups of the family, each maintaining its own separateness and identity, not only create a happier family life but also a better social order.

It may be asked at this point why "togetherness" and leisure necessarily accompany each other. It would be quite possible to conceive of a state of society in which the husband, released from his work, regularly passed several hours at his club, at sports, at a cafe or bar. This happens, of course. But in American life the normal pattern is for the man to move as rapidly as the commuting facilities allow between the two spheres of home and office. The more free time he has, the more time at home; and the more time at home, the greater the responsibilities he is inevitably compelled to take in the management of the household and the care of the children. The same happens in regard to vacations. The annual paid vacation is equivalent to a guaranteed period of close family life. Travel means travel with all the children.

One of the complicating factors in the growth of free time is, indeed, the necessity of keeping the work week of industry and that of the school geared to each other. Where a four-day week has been tried, a major factor against it has been the inability of the parents to undertake trips or excursions because the children did not share the extra day.

This awkwardness of scheduling is bound to be troublesome, especially if the development of the weekend house becomes as prevalent in the next decade as now seems likely. Of course the children might ask why their hours of work should not be reduced to the same extent as their parents'. Unfortunately increased productivity has not affected the schoolroom as it has the factory; learning, like art accomplishment, is still long. Another way out would be for school to move toward the four-day week in step with industry, making up for the lost time by shortening the summer vacation. This solution, however, would raise problems of its own.

The four-day week does not, as a matter of fact, appear to be in the offing. The labor unions prefer to put the emphasis on longer paid vacations, well aware that many workers would take second jobs during the three-day weekend, thus undermining union loyalty and discipline. Male workers (the women are in a somewhat different position) make this form of additional free time their first choice. The problem of coordinating the leisure of children and grown-ups will nevertheless become a real one in the future; there are many reasons of necessity for keeping family schedules meshed. But there is something to be said also, at least in theory, for keeping them independent of each other, with the parents and the children having at least some free time to themselves.

The arguments against having the father become too intricately involved in the chores of household and child-raising have been persuasively set forth by Margaret Mead and others. With the father so much of the time at home, and so busy helping the mother in her tasks, the sense of a distinct quality of maleness is dimmed; the role of the two sexes is confused, and the basis of paternal authority is undermined. As for the mother, she has, of course, a primary responsibility in this field. But even here the contacts with the children can be too close and continuous, without periods for refreshment, appraisal, or the cultivation of new interests.

The case for the independence of children, in at least a part of their leisure pursuits, can be made with equal weight. If it is necessary, in St. Paul's phrase, "to put away childish things," it is also necessary to have been thoroughly at home among such things in youth. We have already spoken of the quality of play and its importance in the life of the child. What needs to be stressed is how important it is in the life of society as a whole. *Homo Ludens*—Man Playing—is the title of one of the most subtle and profound of all books on leisure. Where the adult world loses the spirit of play there vanishes with it a capacity for disinterestedness, a sense of the meanings that underlie the outward forms of life, a delight in ceremonies and festivals and all the symbolic manifestations which can give to a civilization such color as it has. The instinct for play is deep in the child; but it is stifled or overlaid where grown-up standards are imposed too early. And if it is stifled, society loses one of the vitally important educative forces within it.

It would seem therefore, that as free time increases in our society, that we are going to have to devise means of keeping various elements—and particularly the worlds of young people and of grown-ups—from coalescing. Within the American culture, leisure has tended to mean a coming together, a homogenizing of elements which had once maintained a certain individual character and distinctness. Conformity and leisure have seemed to accompany each other. To counteract this trend our society could well give attention to means for giving young people opportunities for vacations apart from their parents, so that both—parents and children—could find in recreation a fulfillment of their own interests. It could make sure that alternative forms of enjoyment are not neglected under the influence of forces which draw everything tightly toward the home circle—toward the family room, the patio, the barbecue pit, and the private swimming pool. I would suggest that organizations which encourage scouting, skiing groups, wilderness trips, and youthful tourism could be especially useful in the time ahead. They emphasize a kind of recreation not primarily dependent on consumer purchases; they draw young people toward vigorous physical exercise, and remind them of the values which youth holds in common across the world.

The emphasis in this section has been on the necessity for youth to have its own forms of leisure. These forms would be different in many ways from those of adults in a consumer society where individuals, having attained a high degree of equality with each other, seem more than ever concerned with differentiating themselves from others on the basis of this consumption. In stressing this side of the coin I do not want, however, to undervalue the importance of recreational activities undertaken by the family group, or by father and son together. Indeed it is when the older and younger generations have each been allowed a certain measure of freedom and have enjoyed themselves in their own way that they can come together for the truest delights. Togetherness implies a degree of separateness as its base; this is particularly true in the context of American leisure.

The Role of Work

To speak of leisure without speaking of it in relation to work is to give only part of the picture. The simplest definition of leisure time is that part of a man's waking hours which are not given to the job. Even this implies a relationship; for what a man does in his free time is inevitably affected by what he does at his job. Jobs that ask nothing but routine efforts and those that are physically or mentally exhausting are more likely to lead to hours off the job spent purposelessly.

There are elements of a man's work—if the work be not wholly unrewarding—which have in them the qualities of leisure: the sense of voluntary effort, of satisfaction in the accomplishment of a manageable task. The place of work, moreover, is often deliberately designed so as to underline the modern relationship between work and leisure. Some of the newer office buildings, set handsomely in the country, surrounded by gardens and facilities for recreation, are obviously aimed to strike a note of relaxation.

As we think of youth today, we must be a little troubled by the realization of how slightly the image of work impinges on his mind. All around him in the most dramatic and tempting forms are the visible allurements of leisure. He knows his father is away during certain hours of the day, but he has little idea of what he does. A visit to the office may actually increase the wonderment, particularly as the surroundings can appear so agreeable. Meanwhile the more physical forms of man's toil, which in older generations were much in evidence, are hidden behind walls and rarely visited. Under these circumstances it is difficult for the young person to know or feel much about the world of work.

School and college are work of a kind, but they are not the same as a job seriously undertaken by a young person during vacations or during his education and sustained with growing responsibility. A boy's recreation is empty if it is not a contrast to real work; what should be leisure is mere boredom. As already suggested, juvenile delinquency is in part a protest, subconscious and inarticulate, against a society which gives to the rising generation no role which absorbs its energies and focuses its aims.

It is not only the weight of visible and obvious factors in the environment which draws youth away from work; it is the whole sentiment against "child labor," embodied in laws which had once a terrible justification as well as in the mores of a society which looks to a steadily decreasing work load. The tendency for everyone to go through high school, and now for increasing numbers to go through college, is part of this same picture. May it not be, however, that when we come to grapple effectively with the problems of the new leisure we shall retrace some of the steps we have taken in this century. We may well expect youth to enter earlier into the work force and to use the machine's gift of free time for the completion of his training and for liberal studies in subsequent years. Adult education may not only be the answer to the emptiness of so much of the free time which falls to men and women in later life; it may also be the key to restoring to youth an early sense of being part of the world's work.

If youth should thus recapture a sense of work, it would be carried over naturally into the adult years, and the way is opened for a more healthy balance between work and recreation in the whole social order. Here is a final example of what may be described as the central argument of this analysis: that there is a constant interaction between the leisure of the child and the leisure of the grown-up world. The child's play, imaginatively encouraged, creates a spirit which can give to all of his later life a leisurely and humane aspect; it permits the full maturing of the personality, the development of a detached, humorous, and worldly-wise attitude. The grown-up's recreation, on the other hand, can reach backward into the stage of adolescence. If it is a form of recreation dependent on status symbols and the purchase of material objects its effects will inevitably be debasing and narrowing. The adolescents of today, moreover, will be teaching their own children tomorrow, by example and precept, the then accepted patterns of recreation and entertainment.

To a greater degree than in other areas of life, the child teaches the adult as much as the adult teaches the child.

Therefore it is of the utmost importance that the natural disposition of each be developed along sound and creative lines. What may be considered healthy recreation for adults is a large question; but for young people, as we have suggested here, recreation must certainly involve a whole range of activities divorced from the highly organized and materialistic aspects of an industrialized age. They must be activities which keep alive the imagination, or delight in symbols and ceremonies, a love of nature, and a feeling for the endless variety and mystery of human relationships.

SUGGESTED READING

FROM FRONTIER TO SUBURBIA by FOSTER RHEA DULLES

Allen, Frederick Lewis. *The Big Change*. New York, Harper, 1952.

Hofstadter, Richard. *The Age of Reform*. New York, Knopf, 1955.

Knoles, George Harmon. *The New United States*. New York, Holt, 1959.

Lerner, Max. *America As a Civilization*. New York, Simon & Schuster, 1958.

Link, Arthur S. *American Epoch*. New York, Knopf, 1955.

DEMOGRAPHIC TRENDS AND IMPLICATIONS by ELEANOR H. BERNERT

Bernert, Eleanor H. *America's Children*. New York, Wiley, 1958.

Glick, Paul C. *American Families*. New York, Wiley, 1957.

Taeuber, Conrad and Irene B. Taeuber. *The Changing Population of the United States*. New York, Wiley, 1958.

THE AMERICAN FAMILY IN THE PERSPECTIVE OF OTHER CULTURES by CONRAD M. ARENSBERG

Chapple, E. D. and C. S. Coon. *Principles of Anthropology*. New York, Holt, 1942.

LePlay, Frédéric. *Les Ouvriers europeéns*. Paris, 1885.

Lowie, Robert E. *Social Organization*. New York, Rinehart, 1948.

Murdock, George P. *Social Structure*. Toronto, Macmillian, 1949.

Thomas, W. B., ed. *Man's Role in Changing the Face of the Earth*. Chicago, University of Chicago Press, 1955.

THE AMERICAN FAMILY TODAY *by* REUBEN HILL

Duvall, Evelyn M. *Family Development*. Chicago, Lippincott, 1957.

LeMasters, E. E. *Modern Courtship and Marriage*. New York, Macmillan, 1957.

Mead, Margaret. *Male and Female: A Study of the Sexes in a Changing World*. New York, Morrow, 1949.

Miller, Daniel R., and Guy E. Swanson. *The Changing American Parent*. New York, Wiley, 1958.

Sirjamaki, John. *The American Family in the 20th Century*. Cambridge, Harvard University Press, 1953.

THE CHANGING NEGRO FAMILY *by* HYLAN LEWIS

Frazier, E. Franklin. *Black Bourgeoisie*. Glencoe, Ill., Free Press, 1957.

Ginzberg, Eli. *The Negro Potential*. New York, Columbia University Press, 1956.

Merton, Robert K. *Social Theory and Social Structure*. Revised and enlarged edition. Glencoe, Ill., Free Press, 1957.

A HEALTHIER WORLD *by* GEORGE ROSEN, M.D.

Baker, S. J. *Fighting for Life*. New York, Macmillan, 1939.

Bradbury, D. E. *Four Decades of Action for Children: A Short History of the Children's Bureau*. Washington, D.C., Government Printing Office, 1956.

Duffus, R. L. and L. Emmett Holt, Jr. *L. Emmett Holt: Pioneer of a Children's Century*. New York, Appleton-Century, 1940.

Oliver, W. W. *The Man Who Lived for Tomorrow: A Biography of William Hallock Park, M.D.* New York, E. P. Dutton, 1941.
Rosen, George. *A History of Public Health.* New York, MD Publications, 1958.
Smillie, W. G. *Public Health: Its Promise for the Future.* New York, Macmillan, 1955.

GROWING UP IN AN AFFLUENT SOCIETY by MOSES ABRAMOVITZ

Galbraith, John Kenneth. *The Affluent Society.* New York, Houghton, 1958.
de Tocqueville, Alexis. *Democracy in America.* Corrected and revised by Philips Bradley. New York, Knopf, 1945.
Veblen, Thorstein. *The Theory of the Leisure Class.* 1899.

THE IMPACT OF URBANIZATION by JEAN GOTTMANN

Conant, James B. *The American High School Today: A First Report to Interested Citizens.* New York, McGraw-Hill, 1959.
Duncan, Otis Dudley and Albert J. Reiss, Jr. *Social Characteristics of Urban and Rural Communities.* New York, Wiley, 1950.
Ginzberg, Eli et al. *The Ineffective Soldier,* 3 vols. New York, Columbia University Press, 1959.
Gottmann, Jean. *Virginia at Mid-Century.* New York, Holt, 1955.

THE PLACE OF RELIGION IN AMERICAN LIFE by RAYMOND J. GALLAGHER, MARC H. TANENBAUM, and WILLIAM J. VILLAUME

Bryson, Lyman. *The New America.* New York, Harpers, 1956.
Cohen, Morris Raphael. *American Thought.* Glencoe, Free Press, 1954.

Cousins, Norman. *In God We Trust.* New York, Harpers, 1958.

Gabriel, R. Henry (ed.). *The Pageant of America.* Volume 10. New Haven, Yale University Press, 1928.

Garrison, Winfred. *March of Faith.* New York, Harpers, 1933.

Herberg, Will. *Protestant—Catholic—Jew.* New York, Doubleday, 1955.

Lerner, Max. *America As a Civilization.* New York, Simon and Schuster, 1958.

National Council of Churches of Christ in America, Social Welfare Department. *The Church and Juvenile Delinquency,* by Robert and Muriel Webb. New York, Association Press, 1957.

THE NEW LEISURE *by* AUGUST HECKSCHER

Arendt, Hannah. *The Human Condition.* Chicago, Chicago University Press, 1958.

Bell, Daniel. *Work and Its Discontent.* Boston, Beacon Press, 1958.

Huizinga, Johan. *Homo Ludens.* Boston, Beacon Press, 1955.

Larrabee, Eric and Rolf Meyersohn, eds. *Mass Leisure.* Glencoe, Free Press, 1958.

Veblen, Thorstein. *The Theory of the Leisure Class.* 1899.

Williams, Wayne R. *Recreation Places.* New York, Reinhold, 1958.

2: DEVELOPMENT AND EDUCATION

CONTENTS

CONTENTS

INTRODUCTION

by ELI GINZBERG

NO SOCIETY can afford to be indifferent to the way in which its young people grow up and are educated. For education, in the broadest sense of the term, is the means by which a society transmits, from one generation to the next, the values, knowledge, and skills which alone can insure its survival.

The attitudes a society has toward problems of development and education are as important as—and perhaps even more important than—the institutions that have specific responsibility for developing and educating the young. For many decades, two attitudes have been firmly ensconced in our culture—a belief in the importance of a happy childhood for the development of a sound adult, and a faith in the extension of educational opportunities as a social cure-all.

Each tenet has much to commend it. During this century both Western Europe and the United States have been greatly influenced by dynamic psychology—perhaps even

Eli Ginzberg is Director of the Conservation of Human Resources Project, Director of Staff Studies of the National Manpower Council, and Professor of Economics at Columbia University.

more than by quantum physics. The romantic enthrallment with the idea of the perfectibility of mankind through the establishment of a proper social environment has never been more enthusiastically underwritten than by this country's conviction that all of its problems can be solved by the school.

The unending flow of articles and books on child rearing practices, particularly on the emotional aspects of development, and the ever larger numbers of people who spend ever longer periods of their lives in school are two indices— if indices are needed—of the potency of these national convictions.

But science is dynamic and the tempo of the modern world is not conducive to complacency. Hence, no established belief is long immune from criticism or revision. We are a pragmatic as well as a romantic people, and when evidence from the laboratory or from life itself challenges our beliefs, even our most cherished ones, they will not be granted immunity. They must stand the test and be proved or they will be discarded and replaced.

The past several years have witnessed an intensified reappraisal of our theories of education in response to a growing awareness of a discrepancy between the nation's situation at home and abroad. The gap between the image of ourselves as we are (or at least as we hope to be) and the reality of our circumstances present and potential has become increasingly clear, and with increasing clarity has come increasing uneasiness.

"Development and Education," the second volume of

INTRODUCTION

The Nation's Children, presents a series of contributions from three vantage points that are focused on the analysis of the gap between our aspirations and our accomplishments in preparing young people for life: how the gap came to be, what can be done to narrow it, and the extent to which it will probably persist. Each contributor offers his own special knowledge and experience in his discussion of development and education.

Dr. Neel reminds us that important as environment is in human development, heredity sets severe limitations. Only a fraction of the population, certainly less than 10 percent, is inherently capable of making significant contributions to the fields on which our national well-being depends. His analysis further considers the negative impact of heredity: many physical malformations are congenital, and only a few of them are as yet remediable.

Professor Garn, directing his attention to the problems of physical growth and development, makes a series of startling observations: the loss of human life between conception and birth may well be 70 percent; we do not really know why children grow; there is no physiological reason why adolescence should be a period of stress and strain; the only measure of maturity from childhood through adolescence which is truly useful is a hand-wrist x-ray; over-nutrition is a major hazard because, among other reasons, overweight children become overweight adults. While fully aware of the gains which we have made while tinkering with human growth and development, Professor Garn warns us to take stock of the new hazards around us.

In reviewing the state of our knowledge about behavior and personality, Professor Anderson suggests that we consider the growing person as a system—a living organism with a high intake and output of transactions, and with the feedback from the environment playing an important role. Of crucial importance is the child's development of control over his appetites, emotions, and feelings. Professor Anderson states that from a developmental point of view the major aim would be to provide all children with appropriate instruction at appropriate points in time, but in order to do this we need more and better longitudinal studies.

These three essays, rich as they are in information and insight, are even richer in the critique which they provide, both directly and indirectly, of many current dogmas of human development. Their major contribution is to separate the sound from the ephemeral and thereby to lay a firmer basis for schools and other key institutions concerned with development to perform their tasks more effectively.

Dr. Tyler addresses himself directly to the heart of the educational controversy by considering the subject of educational objectives. He reminds us that the very success of the schools has been responsible for much of their present difficulty. The schools today find themselves with so many responsibilities entrusted to them by the American public that they are no longer able to concentrate on their primary task of developing and maintaining the intellectual interests and skills of their students. Dr. Tyler emphasizes the need in a democracy, where the people control the schools, for the public to appreciate the problems that the schools face and the possibilities that exist for the solution of such problems.

In the concluding essay, Dr. Gardner draws attention to the dynamic interplay between public attitudes and educational methods and goals by stressing the fact that Americans will tolerate certain policies directed toward the pursuit of excellence and will reject others. He explains that until the American public clarifies the nature of its commitment to equality there is little prospect of its acting effectively to nurture excellence. Equality does not mean treating all people as if they were exactly alike, but rather providing equality of opportunity for all. Individual differences exist and we must not deny them. Dr. Gardner suggests, however, that even in the face of great differences in ability, including the ability to profit from education, it is not only possible but necessary for the United States to nurture the talents of every citizen—since there are many kinds and levels of excellence —and our dynamic society has need for all of them.

There are four contributions that bear directly on the points of view advanced by Drs. Tyler and Gardner, contributions that help build a bridge from the theoretical to the concrete, from ideology to reality.

In his discussion of the age of science, Professor Zacharias calls attention to our society's increasing need for large numbers of well-trained scientists and suggests that they will emerge because of the strong pressures and incentives that exist to encourage their development. But he goes on to say that the permeation of the whole of contemporary life by science requires that every citizen have some appreciation of its nature and functioning. It is here that the schools face one of their greatest challenges, one that they will be able to meet only if they receive substantial help from the leaders of the scientific community.

In his exploration of the interplay between education and employment, Dr. Wolfbein presents evidence that the age of science has already brought about significant changes in the composition of the labor force, and that the future will see an acceleration of this trend. He quotes a recent advertisement in the Help Wanted section of the New York *Times* through which a large corporation was seeking personnel in eight specialties, but the names of these specialties would not even be recognized by the average college graduate! This is only an extreme example of a general trend in the economy that is resulting in a significant increase in the number and proportion of jobs requiring a high level of training and education. The more the schools can fulfill their basic purpose of training their students to cope with complex intellectual problems, the more they will also be contributing to their students' future occupational adjustment.

During the past two decades the nation's educational structure has undergone two significant extensions through industry and the Armed Services. Mr. Wool gives us an analysis of the extent to which the Armed Services have become a major training institution. Among his major points are these: about 7 out of every 10 men in their middle twenties have had a tour of military duty; the Armed Services today depend on the "soldier-technician"—they have twice as many mechanics as ground combat troops; the Services find it difficult to use men with limited educational background because such men are unable to absorb technical training; during the three years of the Korean conflict, 1.3 million servicemen received training in civilian-type specialties.

Dean Bond, in his analysis of "wasted talent," starts by assuming what Professor Zacharias, Dr. Wolfbein, and Mr. Wool have demonstrated, namely, that ours is a society that requires an increasing number of highly trained persons. It is therefore inefficient as well as inequitable not to encourage the development of young people with high potential. Yet Dean Bond presents some startling evidence of the scale of manpower waste, pointing out that the groups at the upper and lower end of the occupational scale though equal in size produce "talented" children in a ratio of 235 to 1, which reflects primarily the inferior education available to the latter.

Dr. Landis discusses the all-important question of religion and youth and presents a wealth of data about youth membership in church and synagogue as well as attendance figures for different types of religious schools. The figures are large, in fact, impressive. But, as Dr. Landis is quick to point out, those who have delved into the religious commitment of American youth are by no means confident as to what these figures really mean. Undoubtedly religion continues to play a significant role in the lives of large numbers of American youth, but serious questions remain about the extent to which it exercises a fundamental influence on their character formation and behavior.

In their consideration of the child as potential, the Murphys return to a theme that was noted but not elaborated on by several other contributors—that the illumination of the basic issues in educational development is seriously handicapped by the state of our knowledge. The Murphys suggest that the development of potential can best be encouraged by "letting the child choose," for children differ in potential and at different times have different developmental needs. Despite this individual-centered approach, the Murphys not only recognize but stress the reciprocity of the individual and the social world. They end with a plea for national and international unity of human effort without coercion of the individual.

This plea is perhaps only a contemporary translation of the vision of Micah:

Nations shall not lift up sword against nation,
Neither shall they learn war any more.
But they shall sit every man under his vine and his fig tree,
And none shall make them afraid.

THE GENETIC POTENTIAL

by J A M E S   V .   N E E L ,   M . D .

AS WE KNOW, each of us represents the outcome of an interplay between two sets of factors, labeled "heredity" and "environment." In man the interaction between these factors is generally complicated and sometimes extremely subtle. The present article, devoted to the question of realizing the genetic potential of our youth, will for obvious reasons deal primarily with "heredity," with the knowledge that other contributors to these volumes will adequately treat the very important "environmental" factors.

The determiners of inherited characteristics are known as genes. They are, with few exceptions, found in every cell of the body, physically located in the chromosomes of the cell nucleus. Genes occur in pairs, one member derived from the father and one from the mother. There are perhaps 50,000 gene pairs in man. Our present information suggests that so diverse are the kinds of genes which the human species possesses that no two individuals, with the

James V. Neel, M.D., is Professor of Human Genetics at the University of Michigan Medical School.

exception of identical twins, are genetically completely alike.

Since a child receives his genetic endowment from his parents, it is only natural that he resemble them in many respects. Since, on the other hand, each child probably represents a unique combination of genes, and since it is not only the kinds of genes present but the combinations in which they occur that determine a child's attributes, each child would from the genetic standpoint be something different from a simple blending of parental characteristics —even if this difference were not already assured by the fact that the environment is never precisely the same for two children.

Because some genes tend to express themselves no matter what the combination in which they occur, i.e., are dominant genes, we often see obvious similarities between a parent and a child. But the genetic redeployment which occurs each generation also permits wide divergences between parents and their offspring. It is possible to demonstrate parent-offspring correlations for a host of traits in a variety of animals, including man. Parents with a superior genetic endowment will tend to transmit this to their offspring. But the process of redeployment referred to above readily permits the birth of defective or inferior children to such superior parents. It also permits the converse: the appearance of superior children from dubious backgrounds.

To the geneticist, the fundamental challenge of a democracy is simple and clear: to permit each child, regardless of background, to realize to the full his innate genetic endowment, mindful always of the rights of others. Much has been achieved in this direction in the United States. Much remains to be done.

The Genetic Extremes

In the United States, existing social and educational facilities are characteristically geared to the average. The individual who falls outside the range for which the system has been developed thus creates a problem for the system. More specifically, while the existing social and educational structure of this country offers as much to the average child as can be found any place in the world today, it may be questioned whether the effort being devoted to the extremes—the exceptionally gifted children and the exceptionally handicapped—is adequate and properly directed.

THE GIFTED. Far more than ever in the past, the present is, and the future will be, characterized by rapid scientific and technological advances. The strength of any country, large or small, lies in its ability to keep abreast or even to lead in these advances.

Not all of us are born with the intellectual endowment which permits us to master higher mathematics, nuclear physics, electronics, advanced chemistry, or certain aspects of economics, sociology, or medicine. The fraction of individuals in our population inherently capable of making the really original contributions in these fields on which our continued national well-being depends is certainly less than

10 percent. It is an inescapable fact that in these rapidly moving days, these individuals constitute our greatest national resource.

In any culture, in any country, at any time, the handicapped, be it for physical or intellectual reasons, tend to come to public attention. Given in this country the added factors of our predominantly Christian and Jewish religious heritage, with its emphasis on compassion, and the American sense of fair play, and there has evolved a system of services for the handicapped in which we may take great pride. None of these services should in any way be weakened. Indeed, many must be strengthened. But it is high time that we faced the proposition that the gifted on whom we unknowingly rely to such an extent deserve from this democracy far more than they have been given in the past. It is high time we faced the fact that by gearing our educational effort to the average, and putting the great bulk of our special efforts into facilities for the handicapped, we have been giving our very able children less than the equal opportunity to which they are entitled.

Concern for the gifted child is by no means unique to the geneticist. However, to the geneticist it has a special significance. To the extent that these special gifts are genetically determined—let us say 50 percent—they tend to be transmitted to the next generation. As has already been brought out, this statement, while correct in a statistical sense, is subject to numerous individual exceptions. Nevertheless, "like begets like." While considerations of this nature may be transgressing the bounds set for this conference, the fact should be borne in mind that our present system not only fails to give the gifted child the same attention in developing his potentialities as the handicapped, but from the standpoint of our species as a whole, places him at an added disadvantage: if he is able to arrange the prolonged training necessary to the full realization of his talents, this often results in deferred marriage and a lower net fertility. To the geneticist this argues strongly for a series of merit scholarships with stipends adequate for marriage at the usual age.

THE HANDICAPPED. Let us turn now to the other end of the spectrum of human variation, to the question of physical and mental handicap. That which is environmentally determined—be it by accidents involving the child during his early years or by accidents during his intra-uterine existence (viral disease of the mother, prolonged lack of oxygen during a difficult delivery)—is essentially preventable. That which is genetic is not so readily preventable.

Genetically determined physical handicap presents a rather different problem from mental handicap. To a growing extent, genetically determined physical handicap is subject to remedial measures. Thus, congenital cataract or harelip, of the genetic type, may be greatly improved by surgical intervention. The outlook in cystic fibrosis of the pancreas, although still leaving a great deal to be desired, is certainly much better now than before the availability of pancreatic extracts and antibiotics.

Moreover, only in its extreme forms is physical handicap a barrier to a rich, useful, and rewarding life. History is replete with individuals who surmounted physical defects, and with our increasingly understanding treatment of such handicaps, the outlook for individuals so afflicted can only improve.

Not so for the mentally handicapped. With the increasing complexity of our social organization, their outlook can only become more perplexing. Children whose limited intellectual endowment would permit them to meet the day to day developments of a simple agrarian community, and even function in a useful capacity, would not be able to so function in New York City.

In considering the problem of the mentally defective individual, it is important from the genetic standpoint to bear in mind constantly certain differences between children with extreme degrees of mental defect (idiots and imbeciles) and those in whom the defect is less pronounced (morons or feebleminded children).[1] By and large, children with an extreme degree of mental defect (idiot or imbecile level) tend to be born of essentially normal parents. The brothers and sisters of such children, if mentally defective, tend to exhibit the same degree of mental defect. On the other hand, children at the moron level tend—on the average— to be born of parents themselves dull. Their siblings, when mentally subnormal, are more often morons than idiots or imbeciles.

These facts may most readily be explained by the following

[1] See J. A. Fraser Roberts, 1952. "The Genetics of Mental Deficiency," *Eugenics Review* (1952), 44:71–83.

assumptions: The extreme degrees of mental defect, when not due to environmental accidents, are often due to the fact that the child in question possesses a double dose of (is homozygous for) a particular recessive gene which has been carried in hidden form by his parents. Since children with extreme degrees of mental defect seldom reproduce, this type of genetically determined defect continues to find expression each generation only because, in each generation, normal carriers of the recessive genes by chance marry one another and unknowingly set the biological stage for the birth of a child who has received the defective gene from both his parents. The more moderate degrees of mental defect, on the other hand, would appear, on the basis of the evidence just presented plus some too technical to consider here, to be due to the action of multiple genes, both dominant and recessive. Paradoxically, then, the more extreme types of mental defect tend to have a simpler genetic etiology.

Now, then, it is an axiom of modern genetics that in the final analysis most genes exert their influence on the final form and function of the individual through controlling one (or more) of the multitude of complex chemical reactions on which our development and continued functioning depends. Otherwise stated, on the basis of our present knowledge, the ultimate cause of a condition determined by a single gene will be simpler than of a condition determined by many genes. It should thus be relatively easier to determine the precise nature of the basic defect in the more simply

inherited (and severer) types of mental defect than in the
more complex (less severe) types. Once the cause of a disease
is well understood, the way lies open for its cure.

Extreme Types of Mental Defect

Three examples of our expanding knowledge concerning the
cause and cure of the more extreme types of mental defect
will suffice to make this point. All of these examples are
numerically relatively insignificant, i.e., small numbers of
children are involved. But the principle has far-reaching implications.

CRETINISM. This disease is due to a deficiency of thyroid
hormone, in consequence of which there is retarded physical
and intellectual development. In many parts of the world
the most common cause of cretinism is an absence of iodine
in the diet, both of mother and child. Since iodine is an essential building block in the synthesis of thyroid hormone,
this iodine lack prevents formation of the hormone in normal
amounts. With the widespread introduction of iodized salt
all over the world, this cause of cretinism is decreasing in importance. However, even after iodized salt becomes freely
available in iodine deficient areas, cretinism will not be
abolished. Children with cretinism—fortunately few in number—will still be born, not only in iodine deficient areas but
elsewhere as well, in whom the cause of the hormone lack is
not an exogenous factor, i.e., lack of iodine, but in whom
the primary fault is in the thyroid gland itself. In the United
States, this latter type of cretinism has always been relatively much more common than the former; indeed, some

authorities question whether true iodine-lack cretinism has ever been seen in the United States.

These children in whom cretinism is due to a defect in the thyroid gland itself are of two types. In one group, the thyroid gland appears to be totally absent. These children may in many respects be thought of as children with a congenital malformation. In the second group, the thyroid gland is present, but for genetic reasons unable to function properly. The synthesis of thyroid hormone involves a complicated sequence of chemical reactions. In this latter group, certain of the steps in this sequence are blocked because of genetic deficiencies. These metabolic blocks have now been shown in a number of instances to depend on simple recessive inheritance.

Whether the lack of thyroid hormone is due to the complete absence of a thyroid gland or to the malfunctioning of a genetically defective gland, early recognition of this lack and the administration of adequate amounts of thyroid hormone will prevent the tragedy of cretinism. For the development of the child to be completely normal, recognition of the deficiency and treatment must come during the early months of the child's existence, the earlier the better. If recognition is delayed until, say, one year of age, irreversible damage has usually occurred to the nervous system. Although improvement will result from the initiation of therapy at this age, the child will not, as a rule, completely revert to normal.

Here, then, is an example of a disease, often genetically determined, in which early recognition and adequate treatment will result in a normal development. However, the fundamental defect will remain present throughout life, so that treatment must be continued as long as the individual lives.

PHENYLKETONURIA. This is a type of mental defect, usually severe, first recognized because affected individuals excrete in their urine large amounts of a chemical substance usually present only in trace amounts. The origin of this substance is as follows: The proteins of which our bodies are composed are made up of building blocks termed amino acids. The average protein is a complex substance composed of a thousand or more amino acids. Some of these amino acids can be synthesized by our bodies, but others, known as "essential" amino acids, cannot be so synthesized and we are dependent for normal development on an adequate supply of these latter in the diet. Whenever we take in more amino acids than we need, the body breaks them down into simpler compounds, thereby deriving energy for its various functions. One of the essential amino acids commonly encountered in dietary protein is phenylalanine. Normally, most of the phenylalanine excess to the body's needs is converted into another amino acid, tyrosine, and thence to a series of simpler components. In phenylketonuria, the body is unable to make this conversion, and there accumulate relatively large amounts of other by-products of the breakdown of phenylalanine, by-products which would normally be present only in trace amounts. One of these is phenylpyruvic acid, a phenylketone, which, spilling over into the urine, gives the disease its name. Some of these by-products in large quantities are toxic to the development and functioning of the brain. The inability to make the conversion from phenylalanine to tyrosine seems due to simple recessive inheritance.

In the past several years, there have appeared in the medical literature repeated reports of the results of detecting children with this type of defect at an early age and placing them on a diet very low in phenylalanine. Such a diet must contain enough phenylalanine to meet the body's needs, but still be low enough in this substance to prevent the accumulation of phenylpyruvic acid and related substances. It now appears that the early institution of such a diet may forestall the development of mental defect. The crux of the therapeutic problem is, as in the case of cretinism, early detection. On the basis of the present limited information, it appears that detection at the age of one or two years is too late for maximal benefits: only limited improvement in behavior results, and little or no increase in the I.Q. Since the presence of mental defect is often not suspected before the age of six months, even in a child under close pediatric supervision, the early detection of these children presents a difficult challenge. In this connection, it should be noted that because of the recessive inheritance of this defect it tends to affect multiple children in a family. The group in which careful examination for the presence of this disease is mandatory is composed of the newborn, younger siblings of children in whom the defect has already been diagnosed. Tests of the urine should be carried out as early as possible, but because the telltale phenylpyruvic acid may not appear before three to six weeks of age, a single negative test of the urine at age one month is not sufficient to exclude the disease. Tests of the blood may yield positive results when tests of the urine are negative.

The parents of affected children of course themselves carry in single dose the gene which has such devastating effects when present in double dose in their offspring. It is an interesting and theoretically important fact that frequently, by suitable laboratory tests, these parents can be shown to have defects similar to those in their children, but very much milder in nature, so mild as to cause no symptoms. This observation is theoretically important because it indicates that even so-called recessive genes may have effects when present in single dose. The finding is also important because with further refinements of this test it could become possible to anticipate which marriages were apt to produce defective children. While it would scarcely be practical to apply these tests to all marriages, it would be possible to apply the tests to marriages for which there was a high index of suspicion, such as the marriages of the siblings of a known affected individual. We will return to this possibility later, when we discuss genetic counseling.

GALACTOSEMIA. The principal source of energy in the newborn child is milk sugar, technically known as lactose. Lactose is composed of two simpler sugars, galactose and glucose. In normal digestion, lactose is first broken down into these two constituent sugars and then the galactose is converted to glucose. In galactosemia, the child is unable to change galactose into glucose, a step necessary to the ultimate release of the energy in galactose. The affected child thus literally starves in the midst of plenty. At the same time, the accumulation in the blood and tissues of the galactose which the child cannot utilize appears to have a variety of untoward effects, involving the eyes, the kidney, the liver, and the brain. Mental development may be profoundly retarded. The inability to utilize galactose is inherited as a simple recessive trait.

All of the ill-effects of this inherited defect disappear if the child is placed on a diet free of milk sugar. Again, however, early detection is of the utmost importance, since after two or three months of uncontrolled disease, irreversible changes may have taken place. Fortunately, detection in this case is not so difficult as in the case of phenylketonuria. The affected child is obviously ill shortly after birth, which should bring him to a physician's attention; examination of the urine will reveal the presence of a sugar, which by suitable tests can be shown to be galactose.

Here, too, it is possible to show that the parents of affected children have a minor abnormality, similar to that in the children but not so severe. Thus, the basis of the defect in affected children is the apparent absence of an enzyme whose technical name is P-gal-uridyl-transferase. It has now been shown that in the parents of affected children, this enzyme occurs in approximately half-normal concentration. Because there is a large safety factor in most of the body's functions, even a reduction of as much as 50 percent in the amount of an enzyme may have no obvious ill-effects. The regular reduction in the amount of this enzyme present in the carriers of the defective gene has the same implications for genetic counseling as the defect in phenylketonuria and will be returned to shortly.

Turning now to the problem of borderline mental defect, we do not see the same bright therapeutic possibilities. The prospects of identifying relatively simple and remediable defects are, for reasons stated earlier, less hopeful. For many years to come, the bulk of the effort in this field will probably be directed towards educating the child up to the limits of his capabilities.

Protecting Our Genetic Potential

If, now, it is man's genetic endowment and the culture it has enabled him to create which more than anything else distinguishes man from the other animals which inhabit the earth, it is obviously in the best interests of our species to protect that endowment in so far as possible. Paradoxically, the very type of medical developments discussed in the foregoing pages, which now permit children with serious genetic defects to live normal lives, creates genetic problems for the species, since these children, who would normally not reproduce, now can pass their defective genes on to future generations. The result is inescapably an increase, generation by generation, in the pool of defective genes, with a growing dependence of members of the species on the availability of certain types of medical care. Fortunately, these increases take place at very slow rates indeed; there is no emergency.

In the past, efforts to protect and improve our genetic endowment have gone under the term "eugenics." The eugenics movement has a long and complex background, much of which reflects enthusiasms and strong personal convictions rather than scientific knowledge. Contemporary eugenics has two aspects, a positive and a negative. On the positive side, eugenics is concerned to encourage the reproduction of the fit. While few would quarrel with the thesis that the human species would be well off replacing itself, generation by generation, with its more able and gifted members, practical difficulties at once arise when one attempts to define fitness. We will not essay here the solution of a problem which has eluded so many. However, in the present context we can perhaps agree that a meritorious step in the right direction would be the initiation of measures to obtund, if not relieve completely, the penalty on reproduction now imposed on the poor but able advanced student who must so often defer for a considerable period marriage and a family.

On the negative side, eugenics has been concerned with measures designed to discourage the reproduction of the unfit. Again, problems of definition quickly arise. While there are some few genetic unfortunates whose combination of undesirable inherited traits is such that the world would undoubtedly be better off were these not passed on to the next generation, one quickly moves from a relatively few clear decisions to a great many ambiguous situations. It has been the position of the author that so little do we understand of the forces that have shaped the human species, so limited is our knowledge of human genetics, that organized attempts to influence the reproductive behavior of segments of the human race are for the present most unwise. In passing, attention should be called to the genetically indefensible nature of the so-called eugenic laws of many of our states.

Genetic Counseling

But while organized attempts to influence groups of individuals in their reproductive behavior appear unwise, the fact remains that family planning is an established aspect of our reproductive pattern, and one element in planning is the probable nature of the children. Many families into which there have been born one or more children with genetically determined disease are deeply concerned over the likelihood of subsequent recurrences. The reproductive patterns of such families will often be influenced by their understanding of this likelihood. Recent years have seen the development over the country of clinics devoted to attempting to explain real or fancied genetic situations to concerned parents. The genetic counseling of such clinics is an accepted facet of modern medical practice.

Genetic counseling embraces a variety of activities. The most common type of problem with which heredity clinics have to deal is the probability of recurrence of a particular disease or defect, once an affected child has appeared in a family. A somewhat different type of problem arises when prospective marital partners, conscious of a genetic problem in the family background, request advice concerning the genetic risks for their children. As has already been brought out, there are available an increasing number of laboratory tests useful in the detection of the carriers of inherited disease, which can assist in meeting the particular problems of such individuals. The advisability of cousin marriage is a perennial problem at heredity clinics. Finally, some clinics have the resources to deal with problems of paternity exclusion and racial ancestry, especially in relation to adoption.

It is a social paradox that often it is the parents with the most to offer children, both from the standpoint of genetics and sociology, who are most concerned about the possibility of abnormality in their offspring. It is part of the responsibility of the individual engaged in genetic counseling to lead parents to a rounded and balanced picture of both their positive and negative potential contributions to a child.

Avoidance of Agents Producing Mutations

There exist at the present time widely divergent viewpoints concerning many aspects of eugenics. But concerning a related topic, which also involves the genetic well-being of future generations, there is a remarkable unanimity of opinion. Geneticists in general agree that the human species should certainly avoid exposure to noxious agents likely to harm our genetic endowment. This brings us to a consideration of attitudes towards ionizing radiation and other agents capable of bringing about inherited changes in the properties of the genes, changes termed mutations.

The demonstration that x-rays and related types of ionizing radiation could produce mutations in exposed animals goes back only a little over thirty years. Concern over the possible genetic consequences of our exposure to increasing amounts of ionizing radiation stems from the following considerations: A certain number of "spontaneous" mutations occur in our germ cells and are transmitted to our offspring each generation. The ultimate causes of these mutations are poorly understood. The majority of mutations appear to have undesirable effects. In a state of nature, natural selection would tend to eliminate the undesirable mutations and conserve those advantageous to the species. For each animal species, including our own, there is thought to be an optimum mutation rate. If the mutation rate is too low, then the species will not have a sufficient store of variability to draw on in meeting changing conditions, and the species is in danger of being left behind in the competitions of life, especially if the environment changes radically (as seems to be the case for man today). On the other hand, if mutation rates are too high, then the rate of introduction of new mutations into our germ plasm may exceed the rate with which the undesirable majority of mutations can be eliminated. While, because of improved socioeconomic circumstances and advancing levels of medical care, the species can undoubtedly tolerate some increase in mutation rates, there must be a limit. X-rays, which produce mutations very like those occurring spontaneously, create a problem because they threaten to upset the natural balance between the occurrence of spontaneous mutations and natural selection.

The unit of measurement of x-ray dose is the *roentgen* or *r* unit. The early genetic work with x-rays involved relatively large doses of radiation, of the order of 1,000 or more *r*. More recent work has involved much lower doses, some as low as 25 or 50 *r*. Over this entire dose range, the number of mutations produced by a given treatment has been proportional to the amount of radiation delivered to the germ cells. Although thus far, because of their extremely laborious nature, experiments have not been carried out at very low dose levels, say 5 or 10 r, it would seem to be on the side of caution to assume that even at these low doses x-rays will produce mutations.

Much of the experimental work has involved the delivery of the radiation dose to the germ cells over a very short time interval. Recent investigations suggest that if a given dose of radiation is spread out over a considerable period of time, it may have a lesser effect than if all were delivered within a few minutes. This is an observation of considerable practical importance, since most human exposures involve repeated, very small doses rather than a single or several large doses. Again, in facing the unknown, it seems best to proceed cautiously and assume that no matter how low-level and protracted the radiation exposure, genetic effects will ensue.

What, now, are the facts of radiation exposure in the twentieth century? A study in 1957 sponsored by the Committee on Radiation Genetics of the National Academy of Sciences brought out a number of interesting points. To the geneticist, the important radiation is that delivered to the germ cells. The study showed that in the United States, by the time the average citizen reaches the age of thirty, he or she has received from natural sources a total (cumulative) dose to the germ cells of approximately 3 r. This dose results from the natural radioactivity of the atmosphere, the earth, and the body itself. From man-made sources, the average individual receives another 4.5 r. The bulk of this radiation

comes from the medical uses of x-rays. A small fraction—
perhaps .1 to .2 *r* will result from fall-out due to the testing of atomic weapons, assuming testing continues at more
or less the same rate as during 1951–1955, and current estimates concerning the rate with which atmospheric contamination is deposited are essentially correct.

At these low levels of radiation, and with the many uncon-
trollable variables in human populations, it almost certainly
will be impossible to demonstrate genetic effects from these
additional, man-made exposures to radiation. Even in the
children born to the survivors of the atomic bombings of
Hiroshima and Nagasaki, where the radiation doses were far
greater, it was only with great difficulty that a small effect
on the sex ratio could be demonstrated, while no effect on
the frequency of congenital malformations was seen. Nevertheless, it seems an inescapable conclusion that some additional mutations will result from these increased exposures.
It follows from this that efforts to minimize our exposure
to radiation are in order.

To what lengths one should go to minimize radiation exposures is one of the hotly debated topics among scientists today.
The decisions to be made involve striking difficult balances
between gain and loss. With respect to medical exposure, the
gain is relatively easy to visualize. It is difficult to conceive
of the practice of modern medicine without recourse to x-rays,
and no responsible student of the problem has yet suggested
any curtailment of procedures for which there are sound
medical indications. On the other hand, there are sometimes

elective procedures involving the use of x-rays, with respect to which increasing medical caution will undoubtedly be apparent in the future.

In passing, the point should be made that technical improvements in radiology promise to reduce to perhaps one-half the amount of radiation delivered by a variety of standard x-ray practices. Many of these improvements, which involve both the machines and the types of film they employ, are already being put into effect—some are still in the developmental stage.

Also in passing, attention should be directed towards the importance of the public's attitude towards x-ray exposure in determining our cumulative dose. One concrete example will suffice. Recent years have witnessed an increasingly critical attitude of the general public towards the medical profession, an attitude reflected in the growing frequency of malpractice suits. Now, of 1,000 persons who consult a physician because of an apparently minor accident, there may be one or two who have a cracked or chipped bone, a type of injury not so obvious as the usual break. Many such fractures may be suspected on the basis of a persistence of soreness beyond the usual time, i.e., they would be recognized and treated properly a relatively few days after the accident, with the patient none the worse for the delay. Unfortunately, the physician who delays taking an immediate x-ray runs the risk of a malpractice suit in the very rare case in which an unsuspected fracture is found later. These circumstances foster the unnecessary use of x-rays.

The problem of gain and loss is more complex when we turn to the consequences of nuclear weapons testing. Doubtless, every responsible citizen would welcome an end to continued testing, a testing which is, after all, only a symptom of a much more basic problem, East-West tensions. But until satisfactory agreements can be reached, the alternative to continued testing would seem to be unilateral action which might not only jeopardize our position and that of our allies, but also open the way to a far greater loss of life than will ever result from the testing program.

Thus far in this aspect of the discussion, we have referred to x-rays as if they were the only agent capable of accelerating mutation rates to which the human species was exposed. The fact is that the same expanding and wonderful medical armamentarium which provides the physician with effective approaches to so many diseases contains numerous agents known to influence mutation rates in experimental organisms. The mutations produced by these agents are quite similar to those produced by x-rays. A partial list of these drugs includes ether, chloral hydrate, codeine, benzedrine, cortisone, urethane, colchicine, peroxides, and chelating agents. Even caffein has been found to be a weak producer of mutations in the fruit fly, that favorite subject of the experimental geneticist. As in the case of x-rays, the use of these drugs certainly creates no acute genetic problems. But the genetic potentialities involved must be mentioned if we are to have an overall approach to the problems created by man's increasing mastery over self and environment.

Conclusion

Only in relatively recent years have we come to some realization of the full complexity of our genetic heritage, and the complicated and subtle fashion in which its expression is shaped by environmental factors. The present century in retrospect may well be characterized as the century in which man assumed responsibility for creating his own environment. From fleeing storm and pestilence, dreading droughts and crop failures, man has emerged possessed of what as recently as a few hundred years ago would have seemed almost supernatural control over the world about him. With this new control over environment comes awesome responsibilities, and to the geneticist the greatest of all these is the creation of the circumstances in which human evolution may continue and the genetic potentiality of each individual be realized to the fullest extent possible.

GROWTH AND DEVELOPMENT

by STANLEY M. GARN

FROM the moment of conception and for more than twenty years the human organism both grows and develops. Shortly after fertilization, when one venturesome sperm successfully penetrates an ovum, there is an increase in the number of cells; that is *growth*, and growth continues well into the third decade. By the time the number of divided cells in the cell-mass reaches sixteen or so, *development* (differential growth) truly begins. Development continues throughout the growing period, and is heightened at the time of sexual maturity.

However many ages William Shakespeare penned for man, there are five distinct stages of growth and development. Each of these stages is unique, self-limiting, and has its own problems both practical and investigative. No one scientist is equipped intellectually or instrumentally to study them all. Few individuals not concerned with growth research are aware of all of the complications. The practical

Stanley M. Garn is Chairman of the Physical Growth Department of the Fels Research Institute and Associate Professor of Anthropology at Antioch College.

problems of one stage of development often refer back to investigative problems at an earlier stage.

Consider the first trimester, the first three months of gestation, the period during which the embryo comes to look obviously and unquestionably human. This is a period of enormous wastage: at least 3 out of every 10 known conceptions never get beyond the first trimester. Since very early embryonic losses commonly go unnoticed, the true wastage before birth may well be 70 percent of all conceptions! The first trimester, moreover, is a time of tremendous danger to the embryo: though tiny, its rapidly developing cells are highly susceptible to oxygen-deprivation, toxins, and viral agents. It is during the first trimester that almost all developmental defects—the cleft palates, missing limbs, blindnesses, and monstrosities—we see at birth occur. Possibly a single virus affecting susceptible tissue at a critical horizon results in the association between Mongolism and leukemia. The one bright side of the picture of embryonic wastage and prenatal loss is that the grossest of the defects and the most lethal of the genes never get beyond the first trimester. Thus we are spared untoward numbers of defective individuals and our genetic makeup constantly purifies itself by prenatal attrition.

From the sixth through the ninth month of pregnancy, hazards are fewer and the completion of major stages of development makes the fetus less vulnerable to injury. Yet it is in this time period when neural growth may be set back by environmental insults too mild to yield gross anatomical defects. Nutritional deficiencies during later pregnancy may lead to unsound teeth, jaw-face defects, and disturbances of behavior and personality observable in later life. Extreme prematurity, one of the hazards we have not yet learned to cope with successfully, may in part represent veritable rejects from the maternal womb. Many problems of growth and development during later pregnancy remain to be solved including the causes of physiologic "giantism" of diabetic progeny. As we save the majority of adult diabetics, and carry more and more of them successfully through pregnancy, we see with increasing frequency the peculiar explosive growth of many of their progeny.

Growth during infancy and growth during childhood are facts of life we all know something about. Although we know that children grow, we do not really know why they grow. We do not fully understand the implications of fatness (fat infants do not grow faster, but fat children do). We know a tremendous amount about bone growth, yet we do not know the exact sites of action of many of the hormones and enzymes we have isolated. We know next to nothing about the growth and development of the teeth, indeed, the commonly quoted standards for tooth formation are based on only 25 infant cadavers! While we can measure size and calculate the rate of growth, and compare both to norms, the protein requirements of infants are still to be worked out.

The child moves toward maturity with the secretion of several pituitary hormones that stimulate the gonads to secrete steroid hormones that build muscle, that accelerate and then terminate bone growth, and that bring about the production of mature germ cells. Some of the obvious changes during puberty we all know. In the male, less commonly in the female, there is a period of accelerated growth, sometimes exceeding four inches a year, when the cuffs of the pants shoot upward from the shoelaces to above the ankles, and great quantities of foodstuffs move through the alimentary canal.

Traditionally, in our culture, adolescence is a period of stress and strain but there is no physiological reason for it. Twenty milligrams of testosterone is not unsettling except to a few dozen sebaceous glands. "Adolescent rebellion" occurs in the hypogonadal lad as well as in the normal boy. Growth, itself, does not result in awkwardness. Despite a raft of elementary textbooks, an overnight increase of two-hundredths of an inch hardly unsettles the balance of Joe, or Pete, or Tom, or Dick. We cannot blame undesirable adolescent behavior on growth, genes, or glands, but only on a culture that has no meaningful place for the adolescent. This however, does not lessen the vicissitudes of adolescent growth and its effect on the adult-to-be. The fat adolescent is unhappy in a lean milieu. Six chances out of ten she or he will eat a broad path directly into fat adulthood. At the other end of the plate, fad diets and self-directed starvation lead to nutritional deficiencies. In our mammocentric culture the bosomy lass may enjoy temporary popularity at the expense of her lithe-figured peers. In the sports-oriented school the lean or nonmuscular boy may gravitate into an intellectual corner, or into a mischievous group. Lacking muscular outlets the muscular lad is more likely to find prestige in an antisocial gang. Differences in growth rate, physique, and fat-patterning may have tremendous repercussions on the adolescents themselves. Yet we "democratically" believe in one school, one curriculum, and one set of social expectations for a variety of growing human organisms of different shapes and sizes.

Sooner or later growth-cessation is reached, that is "young adulthood," and "early maturity." At this time growth is no longer easily measured en masse, and development becomes more subtle to detect. By fifteen or so the majority of girls are prospective mothers and by seventeen almost all boys can become fathers. Except in the lowest social groups we try to forestall both possibilities with monastic institutions and by ritualized group activities. For military purposes an eighteen-year-old is an adult, regardless of the extent of epiphyseal union, yet we now know that muscle mass increases through the twenties. Stature can increase at least through age twenty-five. Some of the more sex-specific characteristics continue to develop even after the irrevocable declines in performance have made their appearance. The period of growth, the period of maturity, and the period of aging are not discrete. Aging begins in some tissues long before growth is completed in others. From conception on, the rate of cell-growth declines and by the time measurable growth is completed, the human organism already shows demonstrable decreases in performance.

Physical growth is an inseparable part of physical aging. Research on growth, while directed primarily at the "growing" period, has obvious bearings on gerontological research and the whole problem of decreased physical performance in the later years.

The Adequacy of Growth

Quite often a major aim of growth research is to provide norms, standards, charts, and techniques for appraising the adequacy of growth. In many nations where science must be immediately "useful" to command funds, this is too frequently the only task allowed to growth research. Even here, where the pure research of today becomes the applied science of tomorrow, growth research is often construed simply as a search for yardsticks. In a nation dedicated to its children, sincerely interested in offering them every material and psychological advantage, such an attitude is understandable. Who of us does not wish for our children the opportunities for optimum growth? Yet what is "optimum" growth? Poor growth is commonly associated with small size. This is true in under-nutrition, in protein-deficiency states, in vitamin deficiencies, and as the result of a variety of emotional disturbances. Size, moreover, is easily measured, and can be compared to tables of averages and percentiles for boys and girls of various ages from birth through statural maturity. The big question is *which* table of averages and percentiles?

Children have been getting bigger. The Bowditch tables of a hundred years ago are now historical mementoes. The Baldwin-Wood tables, once the model of their kind, are now hopelessly obsolete (though still furnished gratis by enterprising manufacturers). While up-to-date tables of size-for-age are obviously necessary, and continuing revision of such data justified, there is a tarnished cloud on the silver lining. Since today's norms will be obsolete a decade hence, since they will be uniformly too small like last-year's jeans, is average size-for-age really an indication of the adequacy of growth of a particular child?

As is commonly known, there is a fair relationship between family wealth and children's size. This relationship is a complicated one beginning in prenatal life, and is not just a matter of calories consumed or vitamin pills eaten. On the average, doctors, lawyers, and managers are taller and they have taller children: day-laborers, itinerant workers, and migratory laborers have smaller offspring. Here in America the socio-economic span in children's stature is far less than in Eastern and Middle-Eastern countries. Still, it poses a particular problem—that of which norms to use. In the Middle East this relationship between size and wealth holds potential political dynamite. In our own country, is the "optimum" average the national average, the collegiate average, the lower-class average, or what? If we are to set down norms for Americans, norms to use in growth appraisal, what norms and whose norms ought we to use? Should we use the larger Los Angeles norms, the smaller Boston norms, or compromise on Iowa norms? For the Puerto Rican children in New York, and for other recent immigrants or genetically distinct groups, what are the appropriate norms to employ?

Stature, that is length or height, has the dual advantage of being easily taken, and of being relatively simple to comprehend. However, problems arise with long-legged populations, such as many American colored groups, or with the short-legged Eskimo and Aleut: for such groups "tallness" or "shortness" must be separately interpreted. Weight, moreover, is an excessively complicated measure, and therefore any attempt to utilize weight or to relate weight to height brings in unforeseen variables. As we know now some of the young men rejected from the draft as being "overweight" were actually less fat than the average. They had exceptionally high fat-free weights. There are fat "underweight" children and lean "overweight" children. Without such additional measures as fat-folds, or radiographic measurements of outer fat, the very information we want from weight is too easily lost in the numbers. Overweight or underweight are realistic measures of fatness only at the extremes. In between there is no substitute for measuring fat itself.

One further variable must be added to this section on growth appraisal, and that is maturity status. Neither height nor weight nor amount of stored fat can be adequately interpreted until maturity status is taken into account. At 39 inches tall Johnny may be hopelessly behind in maturity, and Willy surprisingly ahead. At present, the only measure of maturity truly useful from childhood through adolescence is a hand-wrist x-ray. Properly taken the gonadal exposure from such an x-ray is under 0.001 mr, equivalent to a few minutes natural background radiation, that is the amount absorbed in a few minutes of normal living! The information from such a radiograph is not equalled by any other measure we know of now.

It is possible to say that a child is tall or short, in reference to reasonably appropriate norms. It is also possible to say whether the child is fat or lean, or average, below average or above average in maturity status. The meaning of all of this, however, is quite unknown except at the extremes where the clinician must take charge. Without question, growth can be speeded by stuffing the child, and growth can be slowed by withholding food. Periods of exceptionally slow growth are suspect but beyond this can we actually appraise the adequacy of growth?

With the techniques now at hand, and using the well-to-do as a baseline or reference, it is indeed possible to make growth appraisals in individual children or in populations where growth adequacy is a problem. But for the bulk of American childhood, for the children of tall parents or the taller children of short parents, neat and precise growth appraisals (using charts and graphs) are less effective than the nonmetrical but skilled appraisal of a pediatrician or family doctor who knows both the child and his parents.

The major growth studies of America, at Berkeley, at Denver, at the Fels Research Institute, and at Harvard, and the newer programs in Philadelphia and now Louisville, have accumulated and are accumulating irreplaceable, detailed lifetime growth curves of several thousand children. Numerous patterns of growth can be documented in each of these series. By careful analysis and painstaking reference to the health histories and to the dietary records, these analyses will help us to know just how much growth-appraising we reasonably can do. Until then the evaluation of growth adequacy by measurement, by chart, and by graph remains macroscopic. We can pick out the small child, the thin child, the late-maturing child, and the child who simply fails to grow. The meaning and practical importance of the minor deviations, the statistically atypical growth patterns of apparently still-normal children—these we still have to discover. To succeed, more than a yardstick and a weighing-scale will have to be used, and no copyrighted way of putting height and weight together will make up for the limitations of these two useful, traditional, but still limited measures.

The Problem of Overnutrition

The White House Conference in 1930 coincided with the great depression. The major concern then was with inadequate nutrition. Millions of American children were on short rations both calorie-wise and nutrient-wise. Moreover, as their parents economized on coal, and their clothing became threadbare and thin, caloric expenditures of the body were viciously raised while caloric intake unfortunately diminished.

Today the situation is vastly different. Caloric intake is at an all-time high. Vitamin supplementation is inevitable and unavoidable, even in candy bars and all-day suckers. Homes are hotter, clothing is warm though light. Moreover, many old avenues for caloric expenditure are closed. Two pervasive problems of our decade, obesity and parking, involve the children even more than the adult population. To many pediatricians, overnutrition is a singular concern, and the symposium on overnutrition at the Ninth International

Congress of Pediatrics at Montreal in 1959 was packed to standing room.

Exactly what are the effects of overnutrition? Some we know. The fatter the child is, the faster he grows, the earlier he matures, and the sooner he achieves final stature. The fat child, therefore, particularly the fat girl, not only has the temporal disadvantage of being fat (with all of its psychological sequels) but the further disadvantage of being sexually mature in a peer-group of the sexually immature.

Fatness in childhood, moreover, is of more than transitory importance. A recent study has shown that 80 percent of overweight children in one community became overweight adults. A pattern possibly leading to cardio-vascular and renal diseases, and a reduced life expectancy, was thus traceable back to the formative years. Individuals who were fat in childhood are less susceptible to caloric control as adults. And, today, an increasing proportion of our juvenile population appears to be becoming fat. We should no longer exhibit American height-weight data with unalloyed pride, and we need not compliment ourselves on the earlier age of sexual maturity. This latter accomplishment is beginning to concern some of our school boards, who see a physiological reason for realigning the eighth grade with the high school, and diminishing the length of the junior-high school period.

The reasons for increasing fatness are at least partly comprehensible. The availability of food is one obvious cause. Food supplements, largely sugars, are being doled out to the children by their parents. Chocolate milk-amplifiers under any name are largely flavored corn syrup. Through the stimulation of advertising, tap water is being replaced by sugared juices, milk, and carbonated drinks. Snacks have become a ritualized part of the movies and are inseparably associated with television viewing. Avenues for caloric expenditure are gradually diminishing. In many of our great cities, safe opportunities for strenuous play now scarcely exist. There is room at the curb for father to lather the automobile, but precious little space for tag. As suburbia expands into the denuded suburbs, there are fewer trees to climb, fewer things to do. The car-pool and the school-bus reduce the energy expenditure and the ranch house no longer provides calorie-expending stairs to climb.

These strictures would be strictly academic, if the picture was only of rosy-cheeked and chubby cherubs, but there are dark clouds considerably bigger than a man's body. The general hazards of obesity in adulthood we already know. From mortality data "optimum" weight is already well below "average" weight. Moreover, there is increasing evidence that atherosclerosis, far from being an exclusively adult predisposition, actually begins in childhood. Does earlier maturity lead to earlier demise? Are we eating our way to the cemetery beginning in the perambulator?

Moreover, the American child's diet, once characterized as one big milkshake, comes perilously close to a dietary known to be atherogenic. If 35 percent of his calories come from fats, is junior being prepared starting in nursery school for a coronary occlusion? Reviewing the dietaries of some of our teen-agers, I am struck by the resemblance to the diet that Dr. Olaf Mickelsen uses to create obesity in rats. Frappes, fat-meat hamburgers, bacon-and-mayonnaise sandwiches, followed by ice cream may be good for the farmer, good for the undertaker, and bad for the populace.

Admittedly, we are at a crossroads. From an undernourished past we have succeeded in providing a dietary and a way of life for near-maximum growth. In so doing we may have passed the point of maximum health returns. Can we create a cultural climate in which calories are reduced? Can we make popular the kind of low-fat diet that Irvin Page is developing? And, in fact, is it not our purpose to see beyond childhood? Should we not keep the six-year-old from eating his way into a premature grave at sixty even if it means making life less joyous in the childhood period? Again is it our purpose to emulate Banta's starved water-fleas, and McCance's undernourished rats? They lived longer, but is longevity the primary aim?

Newer Hazards to Growth and Development

In the past forty years much has been accomplished to reduce prenatal wastage, to decrease the proportion of the prematurely born, to pull feeble infants through the hazardous first weeks, and to promote sound bone growth during infancy and childhood. Hormonal therapy and bed rest are both employed in the event of threatened abortion, and a variety of approaches are now used to prevent later but still precipitous entrance into the world. The smallest of the "premies" are boxed, warmed, humidified, and oxygenated. Children of all ages are liberally vitaminized with a well-advertised hand.

Many of the results have been heart-warming indeed. The mortality of the larger "premies" has been so much reduced that the birth of a four-pound or even a three-pound infant is no longer a calamity. Since the days of cod-liver oil, D-deficiency rickets has practically disappeared. However, reduced prenatal human wastage, the disappearance of many vitamin deficiencies, and sound bone growth have not been achieved without certain new hazards. Some of these hazards are currently a real source of concern.

In the event of threatened abortion, certain steroid hormones, namely progesterone and progesterone-like substances are used. Such substances may be routinely prescribed for women with a history of abortion. Related steroids have also been utilized in later pregnancy. There is now mounting evidence that in some proportion of cases, partial sex reversal does result from hormonal therapy. Girl babies have become masculinized *in utero* and some boy babies have become feminized. The whole course of normal postnatal physical and emotional growth has thus been altered by prenatal treatment. The small proportion of cases of sex reversals that occur may be a small danger in comparison to the number of pregnancies that would otherwise have terminated prematurely. But here is one example of a modern measure that returns some portion of evil in return for demonstrable good.

As a result of improved clinical care, including much more prenatal attention, it is now safe for the older woman to bear children. If otherwise healthy, she faces scarcely more danger than a twenty-year-old. Yet no medical care has yet been able to minimize the chances of her bearing a

Mongolian imbecile. With mounting age the probability of Mongoloid offspring markedly increases. In this year of celebration for Charles Darwin, it is pertinent to remember that Emma Wedgwood Darwin was delivered of a Mongolian imbecile in her fiftieth year. Making it safe to have children later increases the probability of Mongolism. Again we must learn to calculate the risks.

Many authorities are beginning to cast a jaundiced eye at elaborate attempts to retain conceptuses that threaten to abort. They point to the much higher incidence of abnormalities in the early adventurers right up to the seventh and eighth months. A very high proportion of the very prematurely born exhibit malformations. The smaller of the still-viable premies commonly exhibit symptoms of neural damage: evidently their prematurity stems from multiple developmental problems. At what cost does the increased probability of defective development outweigh the desirability of saving the infant? In this instance is there a special danger of telling nature she does not know her own business?

As an example of the influence of technology on normal growth and development, let us consider the incubator. Long used for chickens, the incubator came to be employed for the human infant just about forty years ago. As time progressed, simple boxes heated with hot water bottles became more complex, more automatic, and more efficient. It was possible to provide a high oxygen atmosphere in tightly sealed isolettes and this, as we now know, too often resulted in *retrolental fibroplasia*, a developing blindness resulting from overly high oxygen levels at a critical period in the smallest of the prematures. Obviously, technology outstripped knowledge of developmental anatomy. We are paying now in special schools, and special programs for children who had retrolental fibroplasia a decade and more ago for yet another hazard to normal growth development.

When one thinks of vitamins one does not ordinarily think of possible dangers. In most cases dangerous doses of vitamins are far in excess of the physiological (i.e., useful) dosage. Yet hypervitaminosis-D and hypervitaminosis-A are recurring concerns. Marked abnormalities in bone formation and in growth occur in infants who eat large amounts of fortified butter or oleomargerine a day and in children who are overly indulged by parents engaged in their own private practice of pseudo-medicine. This is not a transient danger, moreover, for some of the self-styled food authorities and prophets of Health-Through-Eating consider vitamins to be cold remedies, intelligence improvers, and food substitutes. With parents who leave insecticides, carbon tetrachloride, arsenic, or strychnine about, health education is a good remedy, but it may also have dangers. Hypervitaminosis, even though resulting from good intentions, is probably an increasing hazard to normal growth and development.

In the past, most of the hazards faced by the child led to retarded growth and delayed development. Today, the availability of synthetic and natural hormones poses a real threat, one frequently resulting in abnormally accelerated sexual development. Children have got hold of stilbesterol intended for animal feeding. They have swallowed their mother's bust-improving pills; they have greased themselves with estrogenic creams. Since sex hormones are increasingly used in the veterinarian's management of pet disorders, the opportunities of eating Fido's pills and kitty's capsules abound. There are reports in the veterinary literature of premature sexual development resulting from ingestion of such substances. The common tendency to use steroid-thyroid "cocktails" in the management of the aged pet pose a further threat. While foods containing residual amounts of stilbesterol do not pose hazards for children, the average home increasingly holds dangers and the possibility of abnormally accelerated development.

While the appearance of antibiotic-resistant strains of bacteria and secondary manifestations of antibiotic sensitivity in children are outside of the scope of this essay, the question of continued antibiotic therapy must be considered in relation to growth development. Pigs, geese, sheep, and cattle grow bigger on antibiotic-supplemented feed. It is questionable however, whether such supplementation is appropriate to the human child. While aureomycin has been used with alleged success in "improving" the growth of children with certain bone disorders, the overall value of such a program remains doubtful. We know that the growth of hogs is improved if tranquilizers are added to their diet, pigs being more skittish and erratic eaters than their reputation has led us to believe. Yet this success at the animal level does not make it safe to use tranquilizers routinely in improving the dietary practices of finicky eaters among our boys and girls.

X-radiation is a much talked about hazard with too little

distinction made between a 1000 roentgen local therapeutic dose, a 500 roentgen total-body lethal dose, a 0.1 roentgen localized diagnostic dose or the 0.001 milliroentgen (0.00001 roentgen) gonadal dose from a properly shielded diagnostic radiograph. The normal *daily* background radiation is large in comparison to the gonadal radiation for many properly taken diagnostic x-rays.

Nevertheless, dental x-rays often repeated in children constitute a present area of concern, not so much from the standpoint of gonadal dosages but in view of the rather large total dosages that can accrue from a number of series of full-mouth radiograms. While cumulative small dosages apparently have less biological effect than single large doses of the same order of magnitude, the effect of 100 roentgens or more of x-radiation to the developing teeth and jaws is of current concern.

At the same time, the advantages of careful dental radiography are considerable and should not be neglected. One cannot ask a pedodontist to exert every possible skill in treating a child's teeth without affording the dentist the opportunity to make whatever diagnostic x-rays necessary. Here is one area where technological advances in radiography have fallen well behind. Even with present techniques, it is possible to obtain adequate radiographs of the posterior teeth with a much lower total dosage of x-radiation. But the films, which have been speeded up by 100 percent in the last three years, need to be ten times faster before repeated full-mouth x-rays cease to be a source of immediate concern.

Progress in any area of human achievement consists of

many steps forward and a few steps back. Progress can be measured in terms of the proportion of the newborn that live to maturity. As compared to groups where 2 out of 3 children never reach maturity, the extent of progress in our own country is notable indeed. Our ability to minimize prenatal and neonatal wastage is considerable. It is improving and will improve still further. Yet we must be aware that each step of progress holds with it the possibility of inherent danger, that some proportion of the children saved will ultimately be lost because of the measures used to save them. Moreover, some proportion of the children so saved, though not lost, will be blind or deaf; they will grow abnormally or they will attain sexual development prematurely or even in the wrong direction.

We are now at the point where we can tinker with human growth and development from the very moment of conception right on to early maturity. It would be folly to decry progress or to demand a return to the cruder days when a newborn infant had less than a 50-50 chance of living for one year, and where the probabilities of his growing adequately and well were far smaller than that. We need not be pessimistic. Nevertheless we are building up hazards, and it is an appropriate time to take stock of the hazards that exist.

THE DEVELOPMENT OF BEHAVIOR AND PERSONALITY

by J O H N E . A N D E R S O N

THE MOST obvious fact of growth and development is progress from infancy to adult life. All of us have known infants and adults. So common and universal are growth and development that we take them for granted without realizing how complex and wonderful they are.

The baby is already nine months along the course of development when he is born. He moves through infancy into childhood; then after puberty, into adolescence. After growth ceases he, as an adult, has a long period of maturity with full power, after which come the declines of senescence. Death ends the life cycle. All living beings go through this course, unless it is terminated prematurely by disease or accident. Children cannot be kept as babies; nor can adolescents be treated as children. With growth children and adolescents assert their independence and take their places in life as adults.

Growth and development are not merely changes in phys-

John E. Anderson is Director of the Institute of Child Development and Welfare and Professor of Psychology at the University of Minnesota.

ical size or bodily proportions. Changes occur in almost every relation within and without the human being. For our present purposes, we may call attention to the increased range of objects and experiences to which the growing person responds; to his increased strength, speed and motor skill; to his growing intellectual and problem solving capacity; to his greater ease in using language and communicating with others; to his enriched social life with its web of interrelations; and to his changing interests, activities, and values. From the dependence of infancy the person moves to the maturity and responsibility of adult life.

What Is a Child?

Before describing growth and development, we ask in very general terms, what is a child? He is, first, a complex physical chemical system for converting food into energy; and second, a system of sense organs, nerves, and muscles which, by responding to stimulation, directs energy into the channels we know as behavior or action. Thus there are two aspects of life.

The first aspect is that of impulse, drive, emotion, and feeling. It furnishes the impulsion or motivation which, through the operations of the nervous system, makes adjustment possible. In the world of impulse, the person seeks to meet biological needs. He takes in food, eliminates waste, breathes in air, reproduces his kind. These are the appetites which make existence and reproduction possible. Next come the emergency reactions, which under appropriate conditions move the person to anger, to fear, or to exciting love. These exciting emotions mobilize resources for short periods, heighten the energy output, and produce the more varied, more intense, and more rapid behavior which makes it possible to meet an emergency. Then there are the attachments or likes and dislikes. These attitudes toward objects, persons, and relations affect all aspects of behavior.

Throughout infancy, childhood, and adolescence we can follow the modification of appetite, emotion, and feeling. Much of development centers in the building of controls and the direction of energy into activities that are personally and socially useful. As a result, in the older child we find learned ways of persisting in particular activities until a goal is reached. Tensions organize energy output to achieve various purposes.

The controls which appear, however, are in large part a function of the second aspect of the person. This aspect is concerned with sensing and perceiving objects, persons, and relations, and with reacting to them by means of the various motor and symbolic processes that center in skills, problem solving, and intellectual activity. Almost all phases of this domain show marked increases with age which are readily measured. Moreover, they are significantly related to the efficiency of the mature person. It is in this area that society by concentrating its formal educational procedures makes possible the accomplishment of the adult. Within limits, often determined by genetic factors, progress depends upon the amount and type of learning that is done.

As we view the growing person as a system, we may emphasize either biological needs or orientation toward stimulation. We are now swinging back to an emphasis upon the infant as stimulus-oriented, that is, as seeking more and more stimulation within moderate ranges of quality and intensity. In an earlier day psychologists referred to the curiosity and manipulation of the infant, to his positive reaction tendencies, and to the principle of ambience. These views see the infant not as a passive being concerned only with the satisfaction of biological needs, but as an active mobile person very much interested in the objects in his environment. Through this outward searching and the contacts with a wider environment, much of what we know as human, as distinct from animal, behavior evolves. Out of stimulus-orientation and spontaneous or play activity superimposed upon the need reduction of appetites the human being builds his complex life as a person. Involved is an elaboration of activity through perceptive and symbolic processes, reinforced by the ability to retain earlier experiences. In this elaboration communications and relations with other persons play a great role. As the infant is transformed into the free moving and communicative child, life with all its manifold possibilities of interest, activity, and social life opens up. And biological needs are channeled. Free locomotion, the agile hand with thumb opposition, the flexible throat with its variety of sound, added to the child's curiosity and manipulation, lead to a search and exploration of the environment that creates a new world for him and for other children.

The Environment of the Child

Naively we think of an environment as consisting of specific stimuli which occur once and produce immediate response. But when observations of children in their natural habitat were made by Barker and Wright, by following children and recording their behavior from early morning until late at night, a different picture was obtained. In the small Kansas town, there were some 2,030 different settings made up of behavior objects to which children were called upon to react. By various sampling techniques Barker and Wright estimated the total number of behavior objects to which the normal eight-year-old child can react and came out with a figure of 1,200,000. This figure should give us pause, as it indicates the tremendous number of differential responses already built up out of the high intake and high outgo at a comparatively early age. Some 2,200 distinct transactions involving some 660 different behavior objects occur during a 24-hour period. The child is in about 150 different learning situations during a waking day, many of which are outside of the formal school situation. Moreover, experience has a marked repetitive quality when observed from day to day. Children when told to do a thing once do not proceed to do it, but rather arrive at organized behavior through iteration and reiteration: in other words, through time and practice. Multiplying these daily figures by seven for a week or 30 for a month or 365 for a year will give an idea of the flow of transactions through the child as a system.

Some attention should go to the recent work of Hebb and

his associates. On restricting the amount of stimulation received by humans and animals to minimal levels, they found quick deterioration in behavior and activity. They believe that a certain amount of stimulation, which they call arousal stimulation, is necessary to keep the organism functioning, and that above this level there is the stimulation from specific cues which enables us to perceive objects, persons, and relations, and thus respond effectively to them. This is a kind of psychological tonus, not too different in conception from physiological tonus.

In any event, it is clear that in the living organism there is a high intake and high output of transactions in quantitative terms and that the atmosphere in which the child develops is made up of recurring experiences, attitudes, and emotional episodes which reinforce or extinguish various behaviors. Some recurring situations have a standing or lasting quality in time, while others have a fluid quality or brief existence in time.

Comparable studies of discipline indicate that the behavior of children over time varies with the proportion of permissive versus nonpermissive, or of positive and negative suggestions made by the parent or teacher. This also is a flow concept that leads us to conceive of an atmosphere of iteration. Such observations raise the question as to whether the world of control is a black and white one with a sharp separation between categories, or one of reinforcements and inhibitions which vary in amount over time. The question is also raised whether behavior is as stable as it seems to be;

rather it seems to involve an equilibrium maintained by the relation between input and outgo.

Another school of thought thinks of the child's experiences as made up of episodes which are traumatic and which, therefore, affect behavior over long periods. Sometimes attempts are made to trace later behavior back to such episodes in the early years. But others regard the events that impinge on the child at one period as a sample of the events which are likely to occur throughout development. Thus emphasis goes to the consistency of the parents' reactions over time. This view holds that a good mother does not suddenly become a poor one, but rather shows the same quality as a mother when her children are in infancy, childhood, or adolescence. There are unexplored problems in this area, especially when we move away from the stimulation of the moment to the effect of atmospheres and practices over time.

An important aspect of stimulation concerns the feedback received by the child from his environment. The child has eyes and ears. He not only senses what happens directly around him, but he also observes the effects of his actions upon others and modifies his behavior accordingly. Success elicits favorable responses and failure negative responses from others. If the child is continually frustrated, he will in time react not only to the same stimuli as are received by other children from objects and persons, but also to the manner in which others reject him. Thus the delinquent child reacts not only to the objects which he steals or destroys, but also to the fact that other people knowing of his delinquency expect him to be so. Similarly, the child interested in a particular activity builds up skill which by attracting the attention of other children or of adults leads him to build up more skill. Thus there is a dynamic series of relations with a social overlay in which expectancies of various types modify and change behavior. Many of these relations are circular and reverberating. Therefore the child and the environment cannot be conceived as two sharply separated and distinct entities, but as parts of a field in which there is continuous interaction. Improving the behavior of children may involve modifying the behavior of their parents, their associates, and their teachers quite as much as it involves changing the behavior of the child himself. Thus we seek knowledge about positive and negative feedback from the environment.

Out of studies of infants has come the view that the infant and young child need much stimulation and much affection during their early years in order to promote their mental growth and development. On the one hand this problem has been approached by asking how young children who are deprived of much or of particular types of stimulation develop, and by asking how enhancement of stimulation promotes development. In the former area much experimental work on animals is now going forward and there is still controversy. The problem here is one of separating the effects of sensory stimulation from those of affection and both of these from those of contact with a particular person, the mother. Early it was found that gentling or handling the animal infant improved his adult behavior. This was interpreted as satisfying an emotional need. Then experiments in which stimulation was given mechanically produced similar adult outcomes, suggesting that it was the sensory stimulation rather than emotion which produced the result. Recent work by Harlow and his associates demonstrates that infant monkeys given bodily contact with a satisfying surface show better development in most aspects of overt behavior and that such contact is more effective than the nursing of the animal, which would be expected to affect such outcomes. I have emphasized animal rather than human studies because they bring the controversy into sharper relief. But both are leading to a systematic exploration of the environment of the young.

At later age levels studies have shown the different effects of control procedures depending on the personality of the mother. A warm mother can maintain stricter discipline without harm to the child than can a cold mother; whereas with a cold mother, less discipline seems to be better. Thus an analysis of the effectiveness of techniques for nurturing children must consider both the procedures used for control and the emotional atmosphere in which the control is exerted. What seems, on the surface, to be a simple and direct relation, must in fact be analyzed as a complex of factors.

Suppose that we deal with children who have been exposed to very bad environments. What do we know about the types and amount of stimulation which, given later, will repair or compensate for deficiencies in early stimulation? Some data indicate that these children at later ages show under comparable conditions more rapid rates of learning and more effective learning. Studies of individual children exposed to incredible experiences during World War II, or who have met terrifying experiences in ordinary living, sometimes reveal amazing recoveries with competent and happy living at later age levels. Other studies do not show such effects. What is the nature of the "self-repair mechanisms" which operate when external stress is removed and how can the environment be given an appropriate stimulating quality? We know little about the mechanisms of recovery from psychological stress. Because effective self-repair mechanisms exist for many physical diseases, medicine often thinks that its function is to make it possible for the person to cure himself. For both theoretical and practical purposes, we need knowledge of how stability is re-established and how good adjustment emerges after stress. It is quite clear that the normal child has substantial capacity to withstand stress, that he recovers quickly from short term deprivations, and that he has great capacity for self-repair and adjustment.

Development and Age

After describing the child as an energy system, we return to development. Although changes with age are not striking when observed over very short periods of time, they are very great over a long period. A young child seems almost like a different person when we see him after a few months absence. As the child grows and interacts with objects and persons, it becomes difficult to separate out the results of maturing from those of learning and from the cumulated skills and knowledge in the repertoire for meeting life situations.

Studies of development show significant progress with age in perception, in skills, and in knowledge no matter where we dip into them. In emotional traits and in motivation age changes are not as great. This suggests that there may be age-bound and age-free traits and that there is some separation between the energy, motive power, or drive of the organism and the manner in which the energy available to him is manifested in activities.

Development is not uniform throughout all phases of mental life. For each process there are differences in rate, in the age at which acceleration occurs, and in the age at which the terminal point is reached. Nor is development merely a matter of adding inches to stature, or ability to ability; instead it is a complex process of integrating many structures and functions. In some areas the person grows rapidly in infancy, slowly in childhood, and little in adolescence; in others he grows slowly in childhood and rapidly in adolescence; whereas in others the rate is fairly constant throughout childhood and youth. But overall, the rate of change tends to be greatest in infancy and early childhood and least as the person approaches adulthood.

Examination of the interrelations found between the various aspects of growth indicates that at any level the child, both physically and mentally, exists in his own right and is, therefore, to be understood in terms of the developmental level he has reached rather than as a miniature adult. A common error in the popular and scientific literature on children involves projecting adult processes or states backward and assuming that children possess the characteristics of the mature person. For example, care should be taken in projecting the anxiety or aggression typical of adults backward and assuming that children's behavior, which superficially resembles it, has the same origin or character. Similarly, we cannot assume for scientific and practical purposes that the intelligence of the child is precisely the same as that of the adult. This adultomorphic fallacy often leads to grave error.

As we study the development of children, we find that virtually every process changes in some degree and remains stable in some degree. The extent of change and of stability has to be determined by appropriate studies. The growing person is not a static creature with much fixed behavior, but an adaptable system that acquires many skills and much knowledge with which to move into adult life. Moreover, in the absence of pathology, he retains his learning capacity throughout adult life and well into old age.

In a discussion of age changes a word of caution should be inserted. Although all persons develop along much the same course, there are, nevertheless, marked differences between individuals in their capacities and in the rates and manner in which they develop. Some have more resources, some have fewer; some develop faster, some more slowly. But all move toward maturity. In practical programs we need to know not only where the child is in the age progression, but also the level of his capacities and skills.

DEVELOPMENTAL TASKS. As the child grows, he encounters

a series of tasks of which some are put to him by his environment and some by his internal growth processes. There are events which by changing the relation of the child to his environment acquire significance. The first such event is birth, when the child emerges from an environment in the mother's womb that is quite constant and of low stimulating value, to the variable and highly stimulating external world. A little later when the child begins to walk, he changes from a person tied to a particular spot to which stimulation must come, into an active, free-moving organism that can explore his environment and create his own stimulation. Although walking is internally initiated and appears universally within a narrow age span, the child who walks faces the problem of adapting himself to a new world of space and of developing a large repertoire of new perceptual and motor skills. This will take many years.

Similarly, the appearance of speech changes the child from an animallike person who can respond only to signals into a person who, with symbols at his command, can condense and symbolize experience, store memories, and influence other people. While the transition to symbolization takes place quickly, the development of competence in verbal and communication skills takes many years and affects many areas of living. Still later a great transformation takes place at puberty when the child moves into adolescence and becomes sexually mature. This transition gives the child new interests and powers and radically changes his orientation to life.

But there is another developmental phenomenon which

is geared to the demands of society. At six society requires the child to attend school, to learn to read, and to manipulate numbers. For a number of years thereafter he will be acquiring competence in these and related skills. While the acquisition of these skills is slow and the demand comes from outside, nevertheless, there is a transition into a new area of competence and a substantial enlargement of the life space. Many later skills depend upon reading ability and upon numbers in much the same sense that many motor skills depend upon locomotion. We should also point out that within each of the broad areas of development, whether orginating in internal impulse or social demand, similar transformations occur. For example, within intellectual development there is a transition from concern with the concrete to concern with the abstract.

Paralleling these transitions to new levels of competence is a somewhat similar developmental course with respect to appetite control. In early life the child learns to control his appetites by acquiring various habits of eating, eliminating, and sleeping. In acquiring these controls, the basic problem is that of ordering internal impulses, which have their own natural cycles, to living in a society which sets its own cycles and determines much of the behavior through which the appetite is met or channeled. Present studies stress the importance of developing this behavior at an appropriate time in the life cycle under skillful training with good models and without too rigorous control. Since the demands of different appetite systems may be parallel, the child may be working on various control systems at the same time. At one time strictness in scheduling and training was emphasized; then came the period of self-demand and easy training; now we are in a period of consolidating the two approaches.

If we look at these phenomena for common features, we find a new and partially organized pattern of response, arising as a result either of internal process or of external demand. There follows a period in which the emerging process itself becomes organized. This involves the acquisition of new skills and orientations. Then competence or maturity with respect to the process in question is followed by a movement to new experiences with enlarged power and greater freedom.

In a sense the growing person is continuously achieving freedom to meet new zones of experience. After competence is obtained in one area, the situation, problem, or event loses its problem character and is met by routine or semi-automatic behavior. This process of automatization or ritualization is an important phase of development as it permits the growing person to push problems behind him as he advances. These phenomena become closely tied to age and can be readily plotted in our age-graded society. But there is also an hierarchy of level and content in the demands at various ages. The best example is the school curriculum which locates its subject-matter at particular age levels and expects the child to follow a normal course in acquiring skills and controls.

Because the children of any particular age level are moving along together, and because children differ among themselves, pressures develop among children to conform to the pattern. Children know each other as friends and rivals; their parents have expectancies and compare them with other children. To be accelerated is to receive acclaim; to be retarded is to receive blame and to develop feelings of guilt. The child who fails to make normal progress and who grows up among his fellows who are at the same age levels is put under unusual pressures. Thus we have thwarted, blocked, retarded, and handicapped children within each area who need special treatment to meet life's problems. The attack is twofold: first, to normalize their progress through the developmental course by special assistance at critical periods, and, if normal progress is not possible, to see that they attain as much competence as they can within the limits of their own nature. Involved in either type of adjustment is the problem of lessening the feedback from age peers and adults which has harmful effects in that the child reacts, as was pointed out earlier, not only to the situations presented to the normal child, but also to the knowledge of his own inadequacies among others. Thus children who are retarded or delayed in development live in a different psychological environment than do normal children. Although this is also true of the accelerated child, the feedback is not as bad as it is much more likely to be positive than negative.

To adapt the child to the demands of our life and to give him the skills necessary to meet them, we instruct him. From the developmental point of view, the major problem is to provide instruction at appropriate points in time. This is not only the point at which the child is ready for instruction, but also the point that will anticipate his need for the skill in the life situation. Since each child learns within the framework of his developmental level and capacities, it follows that the parent, teacher, or coach is guiding an internal process rather than imposing a pattern. In order that learning go forward, there must be opportunities for practice under high motivation with knowledge of the results.

The process of acquiring controls and skills is relatively slow; it is spread out in time and involves many errors on the part of the learner. It moves ahead best in an atmosphere of patience, forbearance, and understanding. The most important point to keep in mind is that out of the fumbling, inaccurate, and inadequate attempts of the beginner there comes the skill, competence, and mastery of the expert. In the early stages there are many reversals and difficulties. Hence, too early and too rigorous emphasis upon accuracy, error, or minute detail may cut the motivation of the child and limit the possibilities of learning. In the early stages of learning a good model of the behavior desired with primary emphasis upon the pattern and praise for successes is effective. As practice goes forward, more emphasis can go to smaller units, details, and criticism. In fact, many children reach a stage at which they voluntarily seek criticism as they come to understand its relation to performance.

In some respects the development and the learning resemble each other in that the child is in the process of becoming. Hence those responsible for children should be more interested in progress than in the status of the child at any particular moment. It is not so much perfection in the immediate moment as the likelihood that the child will respond better later on that should govern the actions of parents and teachers. If the child is moving ahead and is responsive to his own internal demands and to those of society, those responsible for him can have confidence in the outcomes.

Several other aspects of the course of development are important. One relates to the manner in which the person classifies and orders his experience in order to operate in the world of objects and persons. The external world is very complex in terms of the amount and variety of stimulation. Even though the child is positively oriented toward stimulation, he must simplify it in order to manipulate it. For example, he learns to call objects of certain shapes "chairs" by ignoring their color and reacting to their form and use. He learns to see a human figure at varying distances from his eye as of a constant height, irrespective of the fact that persons farther away subtend a smaller visual angle. He learns to hear spoken words clearly, even though they vary widely in pronunciation and inflection. In his motor behavior he moves toward economy by simplifying action. These processes not only facilitate his perception and reaction, but they also make it possible for him to react to a greater range and variety of stimulation. As a result, the adult lives in a structured and ordered world in terms of the interrelations of its parts.

A second principle relates to the selectivity of the person. When life begins, the person is a unique pattern of traits which have come down to him from his ancestors. He faces a complex environment in which his experiences and learning will differ from that of any other person. As he faces experience, he chooses activities that are congruent with his own make-up and his developmental level. With age and the organization of behavior, selection becomes apparent. Studies show that the child at eight or nine years has the widest range of interests and activities and that as he grows older his range of interests narrows. However, his concern with particular interests becomes greater. Thus life in its early stages becomes literally an exploration in which various activities are tried and some are selected. Studies also show that children select their chums and companions in terms of the presence of abilities and interests that resemble their own. For example, brighter children select older and duller children select younger ones as companions. As children develop, these tendencies become more marked. As a result, social groupings of all types show more homogeneity at later than at earlier ages. Vocations and recreational activities, with their hurdles and training requirements, carry the selective process still further.

Our information on selection suggests that we should set up environments that permit a wide range of activities in the earlier years. There are two reasons for this. Since traits and abilities show low correlations with one another, it follows that the person needs to explore himself and his environment in order to determine his potentialities. Next, since the process of development is one of organization in which simple units are put together into more complex patterns, it follows that a broad base of experience will facilitate higher levels of final organization. A rich and varied environment offers better possibilities for selection than does a limited and narrow one and permits the person to move from breadth of concern to depth of concern.

The Concept of Maturity

From the analysis of the developmental course there emerges a concept of maturity. Although maturity is defined in various ways, there is a common basis of agreement, despite the fact that adults, even when very well adjusted, are not equally mature in all respects. For example, some adults are primitive in their thinking in one area while quite advanced in another, and persons who are competent in some phases of life may be emotionally immature in others.

A mature person is one who, having met many problems, has developed a range of competencies which enable him to meet those of adult life. From his experiences he has acquired some capacity for independent action, for making his own decisions, and for controlling his emotions. He subordinates the satisfaction of some impulses in order to accomplish more worthy purposes. Because he tends to be task-oriented rather than self-oriented, he can work with and feel with others in spite of their inadequacies and imperfections. He meets problems, solves them, and moves on without prolonged emotional disturbance. Thus an ability to bounce back and to repair oneself, added to the capacity to remain stable and wholesome in the face of the complexities of living, marks a well-adjusted and mature person. The goal of development is then the orderly, persistent, and responsible behavior out of which comes efficiency and power. It is assumed that if the emerging life pattern is coordinated with the capacities and goals of the person, happiness will become an aspect of maturity.

Questions of maturity can be raised about all persons, adults or children. Is the child advanced or retarded in comparison with others of his age level in meeting particular problems? In the areas in which he is immature, what experiences and opportunities can help him to eliminate or reduce his immaturity? Does the environment give the child opportunities to acquire competence? Or is it of such a nature that the child is in constant difficulty? Some environments are continuously frustrating in the sense that no matter what the child does, he cannot move forward. Other environments are facilitating, even though they present difficult problems. To be facilitating there must be a way through the difficulty by learning appropriate skills. For example, a frustrating environment for the adolescent with respect to social life would be one in which every attempt on his part to mingle with his fellows on his own is discouraged, either by direct command or by an attitude such as viewing sociability as abnormal, not as normal. On the other hand, a facilitating environment would be one in which high values were placed on cooperation with one's fellows, in which social relations were taken as a matter of course, and in which facilities for relations with others were available.

Progress toward maturity then, depends in some degree

upon the freedom given children or youth for growing. But it also depends on the availability of support for growing. In an appropriately designed environment the child's efforts to develop will be encouraged. Those about him will not be quite so much concerned with his occasional failures or inadequacies as with his successes and triumphs. They will give him feelings of accomplishment as he meets problems and builds skills. It will not be so demanding or so emphasize perfection that no matter what he does it will be wrong, nor so easy and slip-shod that anything goes. It will be facilitating rather than frustrating and thus give freedom for growth.

The Self-Concept and Personality

In discussing the manner in which an environment that will facilitate development can be conceived, we must not forget the person's own conception of his relationship to life. From the tenor of our discussion it is clear that development within our society is thought of as a transition from external to internal controls. The outcome of socialization, or our way of adapting the impulses of the child to the demands of society, is an internalization of motive in which self-control largely replaces external control. In such a view, emphasis goes to attitudes, goals, and value systems as revealed in the person's concept of himself.

Through his experience the child comes to conceive of himself as a particular kind of person. He gains some awareness of his own competence and of his skill patterns. He develops sensitivity to the values others place upon his efforts. He reacts to the values in the atmospheres of his home, his school, his community, and his country. He responds to group pressures. He develops aspirations and ideals.

There are three major aspects of his personality: his skill and competence as shown in his accomplishments, the effect produced by his behavior on other persons, sometimes referred to as his social stimulus value, and his conception of himself. While these aspects are interrelated, they are far from perfectly correlated. When we try to trace the origins of the elements in the personality of the mature person, we have difficulty, whether we concern ourselves with skills and knowledges or with attitudes and value systems. Much attention in our society goes to the formal instruction centered in our schools. Some goes to informal instruction given in the home, where children observe the reactions of the mother, father, and the other children to and among themselves, see and hear how the parents act toward the neighbors, and are present when guests selected by the parents are entertained. The child is also a member of a family which lives in a particular neighborhood, belongs to a particular church, has a political viewpoint, subscribes to particular magazines, and so on and on. From these sources material comes down to the child through informal discussions and osmosis rather than formal instruction. It is within this framework that many attitudes and beliefs are formed.

If, however, within this framework, the child becomes more attached to one parent than to the other, to one teacher more than another, or if in his reading or in his viewing of television he selects particular characters as his heroes, attachments develop that are likely to increase the effect of stimulation from a particular source. Thus what psychologists call identification makes both formal and informal instruction more effective. Children need heroes with whom they can identify. They need persons who by giving them a pat on the back from time to time give them emotional reinforcement. They also need people with whom they can talk freely. Some of the factors which lead to sex typing, to occupational choice, and to the development of long-time interest patterns reside in this area.

What may be emphasized, however, in considering these phenomena is a continuing contact over time. If a single experience is to be effective, it must in some way modify the stream of practice or affect the current of social relations. Even where single and sudden experiences reorganize behavior, it is possible that the person has been prepared in advance by his previous experience. What we seek then is knowledge of how to eliminate destructive components and to reduce negative components, while we increase the positive stimulation given the child.

In the past research has been much concerned with limited environments operating over short periods. Now that we are making longitudinal studies of children, the effects of longer lasting environments are emerging. We now write descriptions of what to do for children less in terms of stimuli that operate for a short term and more in terms of those that operate over long periods. We now look forward to being able to describe in some detail atmospheres and the sources of stimulation that will affect the later behavior of children and youth. Much study now goes to deprived and restricted environments. Many are concerned with the education of retarded, normal, and bright children by enriching the environment. Thus we attack from converging angles.

Conformity and Independence

But lurking in the background is the central problem of the modern world. Obviously, as we know more and more about patterns of stimulation, we increase our control over outcomes. What are the political and social outcomes if such controls are exercised for poor purposes? This problem was put in striking fashion by Aldous Huxley in *Brave New World* and by George Orwell in 1984. It is discussed in many popular books and has received professional attention. No immediate and easy solution appears.

But two basic assumptions become clear if we approach this controversy from our American ideals. The first is that we are not primarily concerned with imposed patterns, but with establishing environments that will make it possible for the individual to preserve his identity as a person by freedom to establish his own patterns. Thus we seek personality development and enhancement rather than conformity to a prescribed pattern. But even in a modern democratic society this takes some doing since every person is surrounded by masses of informal stipulation which move him toward conformity. Second, it is clear that in the design of our training program we need to foster self-reliance, responsibility, and independence, while at the same time we encourage cooperative relations with others.

But because society as a system needs a continuing stream of new ideas, we must also encourage unusual personality types—the "other" types of mind. From the long-time point of view we seek fertility of ideas and a continuing new look at experience, even while we are engaged in preparing persons to meet the specific roles upon which a complex and interlocking society depends. Emphasis goes, then, to freedom and responsibility rather than to conformity and dependence upon a central figure.

In conclusion, we may return again to the movement from the dependence of infancy to the independence of adult life, with which we began. A living organism is a very complex system maturing within a complex environment. Whatever may be our views about the genetic limits within which development occurs, the fact remains that it is the environment in and with which we work in order to improve the well-being of children and the adjustment of adults.

How then can we, in the broadest sense, characterize a desirable environment in relation to the early years? In our terms, it is one that is rich in the sense of stimulation, and supporting in the sense of affection. It is one that permits identification with models of desirable behavior. It is one that gives the child an opportunity to develop stable behavior patterns by not being erratic and inconsistent. It is one that enhances rather than degrades personality. In a phase, it is one in which the primary concern is building up the child's confidence in his environment.

Then comes puberty with its marked changes in orientation toward life. The child, now an adolescent, begins to move away from the home. Within a few years he will be on his own and take on the responsibility for his own family. Our task with adolescents is to facilitate the movement from the security of childhood to the responsibility of adult life. If the early home environment is concerned primarily with building up the child's confidence in his environment, the essential task of the home environment of the adolescent is that of building up his confidence in himself. Self-reliance does not develop in a vacuum, but comes through opportunities for making decisions and for participating on one's own in meaningful activities. Opportunities should come first in small degree, later in large degree.

What we have here described as two types of environment, one for children and one for adolescents, is not as bipolar as our language suggests. Throughout development we are concerned with transformations in time. These sometimes occur in a short period, sometimes in a long one. These transformations vary with age level and with individual differences. Hence, we emphasize insight into and understanding of the child's capacities, and of his level of development. Our goal is to transform the child's confidence in the environment gradually into the confidence in himself that enables the adult to meet life with zest and vigor.

EDUCATIONAL OBJECTIVES OF AMERICAN DEMOCRACY

by R A L P H   W .   T Y L E R

IN THE EARLY days of our nation free public education was strongly advocated and eventually established. In the debates over this step two primary purposes of education were emphasized. For the individual child education was to provide the opportunity to realize his potential and to become a constructive and happy person in the station of life which he would occupy because of his birth and ability. For the nation, the education of each child was essential to provide a literate citizenry. Since the new nation was ruled by its people, ignorance among the people threatened the survival of the country.

Today, these remain two of the educational objectives of our schools, recognized by the public generally and firmly embedded in the thinking of educators. But since 1870 we have added three other objectives. As the tide of immigration from Europe reached massive proportions in the latter part of the century and as the children of immigrants be-

Ralph W. Tyler is Director of the Center for Advanced Study in the Behavioral Sciences.

came a considerable proportion of the school population in several of the states, many of the new citizens began to perceive the American schools as a means by which their children might have a fuller life than they had had. Their children could get a chance through education to get better jobs and to enjoy other benefits of American life which they had been unable to do. Hence, in addition to providing opportunities for individual self-realization and educating for intelligent citizenship, the American schools have become a major avenue for social mobility, the means by which the American dream has been achieved by many thousands of families, and new strains of vigorous leadership have been injected into our maturing society.

The expectation that public elementary and secondary schools would prepare the workers needed in our expanding economy was not commonly held until the close of World War I. Farm laborers, construction workers for railroads and highways, domestic servants and unskilled "helpers" comprised the majority of the labor force. Skilled tradesmen came from Europe or were trained through apprenticeship in this country. But the rapid rate of industrialization and business development since 1910 required many workers with higher levels of skills and understanding such as mechanics, stenographers, clerks, and salespeople. The level of education required came to be expressed increasingly in terms of a high-school diploma. Furthermore, specific vocational education was introduced in many high schools with grants-in-aid provided by the federal government. By 1925, the public generally and the schools as well were including

as one of the objectives of American education the preparation of young people for the world of work.

Since 1925, and particularly since World War II, the rapid
rate of technological development in industry and agriculture has so changed the occupational distribution of the
total labor force that the chance for a youth or young adult
without high-school education to obtain employment is less
and less. Farmers and farm laborers who made up 38 percent of the labor force at the turn of the century now comprise about one-tenth and the Bureau of Labor Statistics pre-
dicts a further reduction of nearly 20 percent of the present
figure during the next ten years. Similarly, opportunities for
employment in unskilled occupations have dropped sharply
and are continuing to diminish. The percentage of the labor
force employed in skilled trades is not likely to increase.
But there are large increases in the percentage of people
employed in science, engineering, health services, recreation, administration, accounting, and controlling, and the
changes are accelerating. The Bureau of Labor Statistics estimates that during the next ten years the labor force will
grow dramatically, increasing by 13.5 million, and during this
period, 26 million new workers will enter the labor force,
37 percent more than during the 1950s. Not only is high-
school education essential for most employment but the
percentage of jobs requiring college education is increasing
at a rapid rate. Education as preparation for employment is
more important than ever before.

To maintain and to increase the productivity of the American economy require not only an ample supply of workers

at higher levels of competence but also consumers who want and are willing to pay for the wide range of consumer goods and services which the economy can produce. If the American people wanted only food, clothing, and shelter, a major fraction would be unemployed because these goods can be produced by a small part of our labor force. The desire and the willingness to pay for health, education, recreation, and other services create the demand which enables the economy to shift its patterns of production to take advantage of the greater efficiency of technology, without stagnation. This sets a fifth major objective of American education, namely, to develop in students understanding and appreciation of the wide range of experiences, services, and goods which can contribute much to their health and satisfactions. Only through education can people learn to make wise economic choices as well as wise choices in the personal, social, and political fields.

This increase in the number of objectives which the American schools are expected to attain is the natural result of the changes in our whole society. In the nearly 200 years since this country was founded, society has increased enormously in complexity. Yet today, the human individual at birth does not differ appreciably from the babies born at the time of the American Revolution. All of the knowledge, skills, and attitudes required to live in modern society must be acquired by each individual after birth. Since society is continuing to increase in complexity and scope, the development of youth for effective modern life increases in difficulty and in magnitude with each generation.

The Basic Tasks of the School

Up to the present, the American schools have been amazingly effective in assuming these increased responsibilities but their spectacular success is a major source of present difficulty. Whatever the educational demand of the moment—driver education, elimination of juvenile delinquency, "air age" education, swimming and other sports, specific vocational skills—the American public views their schools as not only capable of assuming successfully almost any conceivable task of education or training but also as the proper agency to undertake any such job that seems important to some group. No clear basis which the schools can use in selecting among the tasks is commonly recognized in America.

Discussions of this problem are frequently confused by arguments regarding the values of learning to drive safely, of wholesome recreation, of appreciating the contributions of aviation, of learning to swim and to participate in other sports, and of acquiring specific occupational skills. These are not the primary issues facing American education. Many of the jobs the schools are urged to do are worthwhile and many of them the schools can do effectively. The essential point here is that the total educational task involved in inducting youth into responsible adulthood is far too great for any one of our social institutions to undertake effectively. Only by the fullest utilization of the potential educational efforts of home, church, school, recreational agencies, youth-serving organizations, the library, the press, motion pictures, radio, television, and other formal and informal activities can this nation meet its educational needs. The educational task is a tremendous one which can only be met by the enlistment of all relevant resources. Failure to encourage and to help other institutions to bear part of the responsibility inevitably weakens our total social structure and reduces the effectiveness of our total educational achievements.

Yet this is what we do when we in the schools assume responsibilities which can be discharged by others. Reduced working hours give many adults time to teach driving, swimming, and the like. Churches and other institutions are seeking channels through which to serve youth. Many industries are able to provide on-the-job training. Few, if any, communities adequately utilize the educational potential available outside the school. Instead, they waste the precious resources of the school on jobs which others can do. It is clear that two things are necessary: We need to organize community understanding and leadership for a wide attack upon the total educational job, and we must clearly differentiate the educational responsibilities of the school from those of other agencies.

In identifying the tasks which are particularly appropriate for the school, its special characteristics need to be carefully considered. One major feature is the fact that its teachers have been educated in the arts and sciences. Frequently this characteristic is played down or overlooked because subject matter has often been viewed as dead material—a collection of items to be remembered but not a vital ingredient in life itself. Too frequently we have failed to identify the constructive role of the arts and sciences in education. Properly understood, the subject matter of these fields is not dead but can be the source of a variety of understandings, values, abilities, and the like which aid the student in living more effectively and more happily. The school should be drawing upon these resources to enrich the lives of the students.

This viewpoint emphasizes college and university education in the arts and sciences as a primary resource for the high school to use, but this is a valid position only in so far as the contributions of the arts and sciences are used as vital means of learning and not as dead items to recall. This can be done and often is. All of us can think of illustrations of the way in which each of the major fields of science and scholarship can provide things that open up avenues for living. In science, for example, the kinds of problems with which the scientist deals in seeking to understand natural phenomena and to gain some control over them, the methods that scientists use for studying problems, the concepts they have developed for helping to understand the phenomena with which they deal, the data they are obtaining about various natural phenomena, and the generalizations which they have developed for relating factors and for explaining phenomena, all give us tools for understanding our natural world and for seeking to gain more control over it. They also give us a basis for continuing our own study and learning about natural phenomena long after high school.

In history, to take another example, we find bases for understanding developments which take place over periods of time. History gives us methods for studying problems which involve the time dimension and the interrelations of political, economic, social, and intellectual life. History gives us concepts with which to think about and to understand social change. It gives us data and some generalizations. It can help the high-school student to be at home in a world of change and development and to take an active understanding role in this world.

The other subject fields can furnish similar examples of problems, methods, concepts, and generalizations so important in finding meaning and effectiveness in life. In building the high-school curriculum, the arts and sciences need to be treated as vital means of learning. They must be examined carefully for their possible contributions rather than viewed as matters of rote memorization. Furthermore, the education of teachers in these fields should be effectively utilized. All too often we have employed teachers in jobs that do not draw upon their education. The task of the school is partly defined by this important characteristic: the employment of teachers who are educated in the arts and sciences.

A second significant characteristic is the skill of the school staff in facilitating the learning of students. By and large, teachers are effective in teaching. Their training and experience have been largely focused on it. In addition to these characteristics of the teaching staff, there are three other features of the school to be considered in selecting appropriate educational tasks. The school has special types of equipment and facilities, such as libraries and laboratories. The arrangements of enrollment and attendance in the school permit the organization of learning experiences over a considerable period of time. The school has built a tradition commonly recognized and respected in the community. This tradition includes such elements as impartiality, objectivity, and concern for human values. These are very important characteristics not possessed in equal degree by other social institutions. The kinds of jobs the school undertakes should primarily be those which depend upon these characteristics, since they provide for unique contributions.

Considering these features of the school, several kinds of educational tasks are recognized as particularly appropriate. One of these has already been mentioned, namely, learning which is based substantially upon the arts and sciences. A second is the learning of complex and difficult things that require organization of experience and distribution of practice over considerable periods of time. A number of illustrations will quickly come to mind. Probably reading and mathematics are most commonly recognized as fields in which the basic concepts and skills require careful organization, beginning with simple materials and moving gradually to more complex matters over the years of elementary and secondary school. Clearly, this kind of learning is uniquely possible in the school rather than in the less well-organized conditions of other agencies.

A third kind of educational task appropriate for the school is to provide learning where the essential factors are not obvious to one observing the phenomenon and where the principals, concepts, and meanings must be brought specially to the attention of the learner. Thus the scientific concepts and principles which explain the growth and development of plants are not obvious to the observer of plants or even to an uneducated farm hand. The school can more effectively provide for this learning than can the home or job.

A fourth kind of learning appropriate for the school is where the experiences required cannot be provided directly in the ordinary activities of daily life. Geography and history are excellent illustrations of fields where daily life experience alone is not likely to provide sufficient insight into historic matters and matters relating to places far removed. If young people are to develop an understanding of history, it will require the attention of a specialized agency able to provide materials serving to give vicarious experiences and to organize them effectively. The same is true for geography. We cannot depend entirely upon the informal experiences of daily life to provide these kinds of learning.

A fifth kind of learning particularly appropriate for the school is that which requires more "purified experience" than is commonly available in life outside the school. Students may learn something of art, music, literature, or human relations from the examples commonly found in the community, but where these fall far short of the best, the students have no chance to set high standards for themselves. The school can provide examples for study and enjoyment which represent the best available.

A sixth kind of learning particularly appropriate to the school is that in which re-examination and interpretation of experience are very essential. Our basic ethical values are commonly involved in the daily experiences of youth. Questions of justice, fairness, goodness arise again and again on the playground, in the marketplace, and elsewhere. It is not likely, however, that sheer contact with these ideas will be enough to help the individual youth to develop values that are clearly understood and effectively utilized. The school can provide opportunity from time to time to recall these experiences, to examine them, and seek to interpret them, thus clarifying the meaning of values as well as helping youth to appreciate them more adequately. In the realm of ethical values this type of responsibility will be shared by the home, the Church, and youth organizations, but in the realm of esthetic values it is probably true that only the school is likely to provide the opportunity systematically.

These six kinds of learning which are peculiarly appropriate for the school ought to be strongly emphasized in its program in contrast to other learnings which can be provided by other agencies. There are, of course, educational jobs which are good in themselves but do not require the particular conditions that the school provides. When the school undertakes these tasks, it must either neglect other important things or attempt more than it can do well, spreading itself too thin, and not achieving as effective educational results as it should. Concentrating its efforts upon the educational job which the school is uniquely fitted to undertake and encouraging other community agencies in their responsibilities will greatly raise the educational level of the nation.

Research and Experimentation

The more adequate attainment of the purposes of American education demands not only the concentration of attention of the school upon its core tasks and the strengthening of the educational contribution of the home, the Church, and other community agencies, but it also requires increasing effort to find and devise more effective and efficient means of teaching. The phenomenal growth and increased efficiency of American industry, agriculture, and medicine are due largely to the continued search and research for new materials, new techniques, new ways of organizing and managing the enterprises, and a favorable and receptive attitude to new ideas and to experimentation.

There is sufficient indication in the experiments in military training and education and in the scattered investigations in schools and colleges that search, research, and experimentation can produce significant improvements in the effectiveness of education in the schools. But the public attitude toward research and experimentation in education is very different from the attitude of business, agriculture, and medicine toward these activities in their fields. Hence, only a fraction of 1 percent of educational expenditures is devoted to research and experimentation, and changes in materials, methods of learning and teaching, and organization within the schools are commonly greeted with strong opposition. Educational procedures change slowly and even those which have been shown in a number of schools to be more effective are not likely to be adopted by even half of our schools in less than twenty-five years. For example, educational motion pictures, pupil projects which provide concrete applications of school learning, and work experience tied in with the school program have all been in use more than a quarter of a century and have contributed to the effectiveness of teaching in the schools where they are used, but they are still not used in more than half of America's schools. To achieve the level of educational effectiveness required today, we must find new and better materials, techniques and means of organizing education. The public needs to support and encourage research, experimentation and the adoption of new and improved methods.

Equality of Educational Opportunity

Another essential step to attain more adequately the objectives of American education is to attack more vigorously the problem of equality of educational opportunity in our schools. Mention has already been made of the increasing need to maximize the educational achievements of all children to meet the national demands for educated people as well as to decrease individual frustration and failure. In a society where only a small fraction of educated people are needed, single standards can be enforced without great social loss resulting from the failure of large numbers of children to meet the standard. The individuals who fail can be used as unskilled labor, and the possibility of salvage is a matter of humane concern but is not critical to the maintenance of that society. But our society can follow such wasteful practices only at the cost of the breakdown of our dynamic economy and the onset of political demagoguery. Studies in child development clearly indicate that a great deal of learning is possible for almost all children if means can be found to motivate and encourage them, to arrange tasks that each can accomplish, and to provide other adaptations for the variety of individual differences found among school children.

Not only in the elementary schools but also in the high schools, all youth do not have equal educational opportunity. Success in most high-school courses requires a fairly high level of verbal facility and a background of middle-class experience with books and language. Those youth who do not have this background usually find it difficult to pursue the normal high-school program. Instead of recognizing this situation as a challenge to try to work out ways of helping young people of different backgrounds to achieve the basic objectives of education, the school more commonly guides these students into vocational or other nonverbal programs, not as a means of attaining the liberal objectives of the high school but as a substitute for these objectives. To learn to run a lathe, helpful as that is as a means for earning a living as a skilled laborer, is no substitute for gaining a deeper understanding of what life is about, what science, history, literature, art, and other fields have to offer in helping us to understand our world and gain greater command over it. Probably there has never been a time when it was so important for all citizens to gain intelligent understanding and this need is not met by shifting some students into programs that deal primarily with technical skills and manual facility. Even though it is difficult to reach students whose backgrounds have been limited, this is a responsibility which must be met.

Public Attitudes Toward Education

Since the public schools are controlled by people and the school pupils are the children of the people, public attitudes have a tremendous influence on the quality and amount of public education and upon the direction and amount of effort which youth put into their school work. In general, the American public attitude is highly favorable to education. The great growth in school enrollments and the great increases in the public funds provided for schools and colleges are evidences of the public regard for education. However, this favorable opinion of the importance of education and the common desire to have every youth obtain at least a high-school diploma are mixed with other public attitudes which fail to give the most effective support to the attainment of the objectives of American education.

In most American communities, youth see greater public interest and appreciation for athletic performance and bathing beauty contests than for educational achievements. The attitudes which are expressed by the adults in a community are quite commonly acquired by the children and youth and serve to direct their attention and efforts. If the maximum educational achievements are to be obtained, the attitudes expressed by the words and actions of adults and by television, radio, magazines, newspapers, and movies must serve to reinforce these educational objectives. Otherwise, the distraction of attention and the lessened effort which youth put into their studies will reduce their achievements.

Another inadequacy of public attitudes toward education lies in its superficial vacillations from one emphasis to another. During World War II there was great public expression of concern for the physical fitness of youth and in some states laws were passed specifying the amount of time the public schools must devote to physical education. Since Sputnik an even stronger cry has arisen for more science and mathematics. Each fluctuation of public opinion is capitalized by some "pressure group" to influence the schools to shift their emphasis to the special interests of this group.

Of course, new conditions require new study of the educational program to see that the schools are focusing upon the proper objectives in an intelligent fashion, but the need for more scientists and engineers does not require a neglect of other educational fields. Increasing the amount of time the schools are required to devote to physical education is not necessarily a means of improving physical fitness of youth, and it is certainly not an intelligent means of deciding what educational tasks the schools can best undertake and what tasks are more properly the responsibility of other agencies. Furthermore, each new shift of public concern is commonly associated with attacks upon the adequacy of the schools and these are more likely to reduce the morale of teachers and students than they are to increase the schools' effectiveness. Continuing, intelligent criticism of American education and the schools by the public is a good thing when it takes on the quality of a statesmanlike debate in which consideration is given to the several objectives of the school and to the proper balance among them and among the fields of study.

Another matter on which public opinion periodically vacillates is the emphasis upon "toughness" in school work. A few years age the common parental attitude toward mathematics and foreign languages was one of concern that these subjects were too hard for young people and especially too demanding for girls. Currently the attitude expressed is that school work is too easy and that more difficult subjects and hard work should be required by the schools. What the public fails to recognize is that effective learning requires a task which for each pupil is difficult but one which he can accomplish. On the one hand, the thing to be learned needs to be challenging, something beyond the pupil's present knowledge or skill which demands real effort for him to master. On the other hand, for the pupil to put forth his energy and work hard at the task he needs to feel that he can accomplish it and have confidence in his ability to achieve. Because in every school the children represent a wide range of abilities and backgrounds, a task which challenges a less able student is likely to be too easy for the more able one, and a task which is difficult enough to demand real effort from the more able ones will appear to be beyond possibility of achievement by the less able. What is required is the development of a variety of learning tasks so that every student can push his own achievement beyond his previous performance and so that there is a real possibility for every student to gain confidence in his ability to learn things which are difficult for him.

The effect of the present vacillating attitude toward toughness is to influence the schools at some times to develop educational programs that challenge no one and at other times to develop programs which challenge some of the more able but seem so hard for others that their learning is reduced. A realistic recognition of this situation by the public would help to stabilize intelligent efforts to improve the curriculum and instruction in the schools.

The foregoing illustrations are intended to suggest the importance of public attitudes toward education in increasing the effectiveness of the schools in attaining the objectives of American democracy and to illustrate some of the respects in which the current attitudes hinder rather than help. The generally favorable attitudes of the public toward the importance of education can be strengthened by continuing intelligent criticism based on thoughtful study rather than vacillating expressions of conflicting concerns.

The Role of the Teaching Profession in the Community

Public attitudes toward education are in some degree dependent upon the information provided by the teachers and administrators in the schools or the lack of it. It is fair to say that many schools have not clarified their objectives for themselves and still more of them have not explained to their publics in simple fashion what they are trying to do, that is, what their objectives are and how these objectives are being attained. Without these simple, clear-cut explanations many lay people will have only their own memory of school in their minds and will not understand the great socioeconomic changes that are taking place to which the schools must respond. Hence, the teaching profession has a responsibility to explain to the community the basic purposes of the school and its ways of working and why these are important and necessary. What is required is straightforward reporting and discussion rather than glamor stories about matters peripheral to the schools' main job.

The teaching profession also has a responsibility in relation to the other educational institutions in the community. The most important of these is the home. Its function in providing the basic physical and emotional needs of the child is unique. In addition, the home can give encouragement to the child's curiosity in a way that greatly facilitates school learning, or the home may greatly inhibit learning in the school by discouraging or punishing the child's efforts to ask questions, to seek in countless ways to satisfy his curiosity, and to express his active interest in learning. A positive attitude in the home toward problem-solving and the interest shown by parents in seeking new light on questions facilitate the efforts of the school in this direction, whereas the attitude that persons in authority have the answers retards the active learning of the child. The provision in the home of means to explore new areas and to carry on inquiries, such as making available appropriate books, music, pictures, a simple shop, is another important contribution of the home to attaining the objectives which are the school's central task.

The interrelation of home and school in the education of children has long been recognized, and the development of the parent-teacher association is one of the important efforts to share responsibility and to coordinate activities. In some communities where homes fail to meet their educational responsibilities, a two-pronged attack is undertaken.

On the one hand, religious and social agencies are employed to counsel and encourage parents to assume proper educational roles, and, on the other hand, socially minded adults are recruited to serve as parent substitutes so that some of the basic emotional and educational conditions may be provided for children whose homes are grossly inadequate.

In addition to the home, there are other institutions in the community which educate, or miseducate, children. For example, the Payne Fund Study of Motion Pictures and Youth demonstrated conclusively that children get from motion pictures ideas about the world and about life which they retain more vividly than many ideas obtained in school. The effect of motion pictures on attitudes and on conduct is also striking and greater than many school influences. If the ideas that the children obtain from movies are untrue or misleading, if the attitudes and conduct engendered by motion pictures are opposed to those sought by the schools, then our educational efforts will be nullified at those points, and the school's goals will not be realized.

A similar condition exists with reference to many other aspects of the child's environment. An effective and thoroughgoing job of education demands more careful study of the total environment of the children and more effort to control the environment so that it will provide an atmosphere and conditions conducive to the growth and development we are seeking to achieve. In this sense, the school cannot sit idly by, unconcerned with the nature of the community in which its children grow up. It is obvious to many of us that we are derelict in our duty when we permit safety hazards and health hazards to exist in the school neighborhood; but in some respects the psychological, the social, and emotional hazards and conflicts surrounding our young people have more disastrous effects upon them than the health and safety hazards.

The school staff must take a stand on matters which affect the opportunities for the education of the children in the community. The school has responsibility for helping to create and maintain an educative social environment. School people should take leadership in initiating those reforms necessary to provide opportunities for education. In many cases, failure to take leadership in these reforms has meant that, within certain sections of the community, education has largely been nullified.

The particular conditions which limit or deny education to many children in a given community are so varied and subject to such changes that they require continuous study and eternal vigilance. In some cases, it may be the poisoned propaganda of a partisan newspaper that so blinds the vision of young people as to warp their conception of social reality and to dry up the springs of social idealism. In others, it may be the lack of any beauty—trees, parks, music, and art—that sterilizes taste and makes life commonplace. In still others, it may be the overprotection of parents, who fail to give children opportunities for the all-important experiences of self-direction and assumption of responsibility.

Because these limiting conditions are so numerous and are not always easy to recognize, they are not likely to be eliminated or improved unless school people take active leadership. This requires knowledge of education and of child development in order to recognize factors in the environment that are not likely to be recognized by the layman until their devastating effects have become obvious. School people as school people have no more responsibility than have any other citizens for seeking the general reform of social institutions, but school people, by the very nature of their task, do have responsibility for seeking those reforms necessary to improve the opportunities for the education and development of children.

Summary

In this chapter several major points have been presented. With the profound changes taking place in our society since our educational system was established, the objectives of American education have expanded. With this enlargement of purposes the schools have also assumed many tasks which are not central to their role, and they are in danger of spreading themselves too thin. The core task is to arouse and maintain interest and skill in learning those things which involve deeper understanding and the solution of new problems. Having defined this central role, the schools must be encouraged to conduct research and experimentation to find new ways to improve their effectiveness. Particularly, new efforts are needed to achieve equality of educational opportunity and to salvage the wasted abilities and talents of children with limited backgrounds. In this effort to achieve more nearly our educational objectives intelligent constructive public attitudes can exercise important influence and the teaching profession can provide further assistance in its

cooperation with the rest of the community. Only by
strengthening and coordinating the work of other educational institutions as well as the school can our total educational resources be made adequate to the difficult but essential job ahead.

THE AGE OF SCIENCE

by JERROLD R. ZACHARIAS

WE HAVE ALL been hearing and reading—perhaps more often than any of us finds absolutely necessary—such phrases as "The Age of Science," "The Scientific Revolution," "The Dominance of Science." According to the tempers of our own minds we may find them irritating, or arrogant, or naive. What we rarely do with such phrases, or indeed with any catch-phrases, is to think about what they are intended to mean.

I am a scientist and the word "science" has a certain real meaning for me. To a surprisingly large extent it is the expression of an attitude, and as such it is remarkably hard to define. But the attitude stems from a body of practice and a body of procedures, and these at least can be described and considered.

Let me describe the practice of science as the careful preparation of questions to be put to Nature (or the Universe, or the Real World, or whatever you wish to call it), followed by the strict recording of the replies that Nature appears to

Jerrold R. Zacharias is Professor of Physics at the Massachusetts Institute of Technology.

give to such questions, and the attempt to find order and pattern in those replies. I do not pretend for a moment that I have given here an exhaustive definition of science. It is clear at once that it does not include such activities as those of the astronomer or of the taxonomist, both of whom are undeniably scientists. But it does cover most of the activities I would be willing to call science and with a good deal more trouble than it would be worth in the present context it could be extended to cover the rest.

Now, the very existence of an extensive pursuit of such activities presumes the wide existence of two distinct faiths. The first of these is the faith that there is indeed some sort of orderliness and pattern in Nature and that with the exercise of human intelligence and human ingenuity it can be discovered. The second of these is the faith that out of this kind of pursuit and discovery will come something of value to humanity—something we humans desire and from which we can profit. (There is, I suppose, a third faith—the faith that the Universe or the Real World actually exists but I am quite willing to leave that question to the systematic philosophers and much good it may do them!)

You will notice that these two faiths stand at completely different levels. The faith in order applies primarily to the scientist himself, and makes his work possible. The faith in the value of science applies to society in general; it constitutes the basis of the support that society (knowingly or not) is willing to tender the scientist. And at this moment, in the middle of the twentieth century, both these faiths are widely and generally held.

This may not be particularly surprising, but it is certainly new. In the long history of mankind neither of these faiths has deep roots. The second of them is so recent that we can not yet be certain that it is firmly established; the Scientific Revolution no less than the Industrial Revolution has its Luddites, and it is conceivable that this time they will prevail.

It is not much more than three hundred years since the idea of an orderliness in nature began to dominate men's minds. The Greeks had more than a glimpse of it but the Greeks somehow never managed to learn how to catch hold of it; they did what they could with the intellectual tools they possessed and came quickly to a dead end. After that it was not until the time of Galileo and of Newton that the concept was born again. This time, through the genius of these men and their fellows, to the faith in orderliness there was added a technique of eliciting that orderliness by posing perspicacious questions; since Galileo that has been the method of science and its effectiveness cannot sensibly be challenged.

But if Galileo and his descendants created science, they did little to provide fertile ground for its cultivation. For centuries science remained almost an aesthetic pursuit carried on by the sons of the wealthy and a few others whom the general public regarded as eccentrics. The scientists occupied the status, more or less, that the poet holds today.

In our own country, there was simply no general belief that benefits were likely to accrue from the practice of science. Between Franklin and Gibbs—a lapse of well over a century—America was unable to produce a scientist of even modest stature. Into the early years of this century, this country was incapable of providing an education for a man of scientific bent, or of making use of his services when they became available. When General Electric became involved in the intricacies of alternating current, they were forced to send to Germany for a man who could do the mathematics and even if there had been an American Steinmetz he probably would have made his home abroad.

All this has changed. The methods of Galileo and Newton are no longer novel. They have become so deeply embedded in our modes of thinking that we see them pushed beyond their proper boundaries; they are applied to problems to which they are clearly not appropriate. We take the orderliness of Nature for granted, and we are disappointed when we do not find an equal orderliness in, say, language. We consider it a truism that one finds out about the atom, or electricity, or chemical reactions, by doing experiments and there are some who press ahead anxiously to find out about the Soul in the same manner.

And except for moments of disquiet when it appears likely that science will destroy every one of us, the public usually believes that science provides us with things we want. To the scientist himself this belief seems frequently to rest upon a misunderstanding of exactly what it is the scientist does, but what is most important to the scientist is the fact that the support does indeed exist.

To put the matter in its crudest form, there are more

scientists than poets in the United States today because the people of the United States believe they require, for the satisfaction of their needs, more of the one than of the other. They may be totally mistaken but they believe it, and the community of scientists grows in response to that belief. A hundred years ago the belief did not exist, and a hundred years ago there were a good many more poets than scientists in the United States.

It is for these reasons, and for no others, that I think it is meaningful to say that we do indeed live in an Age of Science. I trust, although I am by no means certain, that there will be found neither arrogance nor naivete in the statement as I have attempted to put it forward. Lest I be charged with an immodesty I do not possess, let me make it clear that I am by no means certain that the Age of Science is the best of all possible worlds. All I insist upon is that it is with us, or we are with it, and we cannot wish it away.

The Scientist

Let me now turn from the Age to the individual and allow me to select the individual of whom I should know the most: myself.

A large part of my life has been spent in learning physics, doing physics, teaching physics and discussing physics; I have been fortunate enough to be able to do this at progressively higher levels. I have done experiments, published my results, and seen them incorporated in the corpus of knowledge within my field of effort. With the passage of time I have been awarded the privilege of putting certain distinctive letters before my name and others after it. In short I am called a scientist, and I believe I am one.

What does all this amount to? What do I possess, or what am I doing, that a person who is not a scientist does not possess or does not do; what sets me off?

To begin with I possess a body of skills and a body of knowledge. I am capable of combining familiar materials into an unfamiliar configuration, to predict with some assurance how this new configuration will in general behave, to recognize particular aspects of the new configuration with which I am unfamiliar, and to find out something about these particular aspects. I have done this sort of thing so often, and studied with such attention similar work that has been done by others, that I am a living storehouse of information about such things, and I can call upon that information either for my own use or for the instruction of others.

All this is very satisfying, but it is scarcely distinctive in itself. Change a word or two here and there, and much the same could be said by any practicing poet, bricklayer, or baseball player. And whatever in my heart I may believe, I am not prepared to say that what I do is more edifying, more noble, or more beneficial than what a poet, a bricklayer, or a baseball player does. If I did so, I am convinced that all poets, many bricklayers, and even a few baseball players would be eager to debate the point with me, and the outcome of any such debate is irrelevant to what I wish to establish. I can afford to concede that they are all more worthwhile than I am without prejudicing my argument.

What I can maintain is that society considers my activities more important, more useful. Among the more influential members of society, this is hardly disputable: government and business incorporate scientists into their councils; colleges and universities give them pride of place. And even in the wider range of the whole democracy it remains so: the average scientist is honored far more widely than the average baseball player or the average poet or the average bricklayer. I do not wish to be crass but I might also point out that he is generally paid better, lives better, and enjoys better credit.

I have my skills, then, and a certain position as a consequence. But I derive something more from my particular set of skills. They are part of a family of skills, and I enter into the life of that family.

As a physicist, I have found it necessary to know something of chemistry, astronomy, and a few other sciences that are directly allied to physics or have been spun off from physics. There are other sciences about which I know less, and some about which I know nothing at all—at least in the sense that I could not give an account of them or pass a respectable examination in them. But in another sense, I am familiar with all sciences. I know how they work. I know what a practitioner of any science is up to. I know the sort of thing he must do to advance his knowledge. I know the criteria he uses to judge whether an act of his has indeed advanced his knowledge, or has merely been a false start or a deception.

Now once again, I have by this established no advantage

over the poet, the bricklayer, or the baseball player. The poet, given a block of marble and a chisel, might well be at a complete loss. But the poet knows fairly well what is on the sculptor's mind when he stands before the rough slab of stone, and the poet will look knowingly upon the finished statue. The baseball player may have no competence before the high-jump bar, but he knows about muscle and sinew and concentration, and he has a far deeper appreciation than the rest of us when he watches a seven-foot leap. All skills come in families, mine no more than theirs.

But my family is the family that is relevant to the Age of Science. What this means is simply that the poet and his skills almost never impinge upon the bricklayer or the baseball player and their skills. These are families that can afford to ignore one another. None of them, today, can ignore science. It affects their daily living and the way the fruits of their labor are distributed. It affects them in the practices of their own skills. Most of all, since they are as deeply embedded in the Age of Science as I am, science affects the very manner in which they think, and reason, and come to conclusions. The poet, whether he knows it or not, has borrowed from science both in the manner in which he makes his poems and in the manner in which he judges them. This does not necessarily make them better poems—I, for one, suspect it makes them somewhat worse—but he is as helpless as I in the matter.

I must repeat that I am not attempting to set up a hierarchy of values. I am writing of the world as it is, and we are all free to wish it otherwise. In the world as it is, my family is more relevant than theirs; I mean nothing more than that.

So far I have tried to be specific. But now I must speak of the delight that I derive from science, and I am not sure that I can make that delight completely clear to someone who has not himself experienced it.

I spend my life looking for the orderliness that I believe is to be found in Nature. Nature herself is not hostile to this business of poking and pushing in which I am engaged, although there are certainly times when an experimental physicist is tempted to believe that natural events are engaged in an immense conspiracy against him. But Nature is neither wily, nor tricky, nor antagonistic. She is something that is much worse: she is passive. And it is exactly that which makes science such an enormously exciting challenge.

The answers are all there—perhaps not the answers to the questions that I am asking, but the answers to the questions I should be wise enough to ask. And the pattern is there. All I have to do is find it. No one and nothing prevents me, or makes it difficult for me. It is entirely, unmistakably, and inescapably up to me. If I am capable, I will make progress. If I am very capable, I will make great progress. If I am inadequate, I will fail, and it is entirely because of my own inadequacies that I will fail.

And because the challenge is so great, the rewards are tremendously satisfying. Every step forward is a triumph of mankind. I can glory not only in my own successes (if I am fortunate enough to enjoy successes), I can glory as well in the successes of my colleagues, and derive excitement merely from an account of them. More than that, I can read accounts of the triumphs of Galileo, or Kepler, or Darwin, and glory in them. I know the challenge they faced, I can feel in my bones and my liver and my intestines their tribulations as they faced the challenge, and at the end of the account I shout "Eureka" as enthusiastically as Archimedes ever shouted it.

This is not a response that is peculiar to me or to scientists. Every human being who has ever faced a problem has experienced the delight, the splendor, of the moment when all the disparate elements suddenly fall into place, when the key is revealed, when the insoluble is solved. The scientist and the mathematician live with such problems, all the more pleasurable, as they are the more subtle and the more resistent to solution. It is their business to meet them and attack them. It is their great reward occasionally to solve them.

I do not deny the existence of other delights—those experienced by the poet, the bricklayer, or the baseball player. The happy man is the man who is aware of them all, and who makes an honest effort to taste them all. I might well propose that the delights of the scientist are richer than some of the others because they are harder to come by—they demand more of the man who would share them. The mountain is a good deal more challenging to climb than the foothill. Perhaps I might go further and express a willingness to believe that the peaks occasionally scaled by the poet, the musician, the mystic are even higher than the highest reached by the scientist. But my own greatest pleasures are the ones I know best, and I would like to share them.

Finally, I must speak of one more characteristic of the scientist's career. The young scientist, more than the young practitioner of any other activity, can expect with some confidence that his work will survive him. It may not be a spectacular survival. He is guaranteed inclusion in no Hall of Fame, however parochial. But some of his work is likely to endure and be useful.

This does not arise out of the nature of the scientist, but out of the nature of science. It is, to begin with, an accumulative process. Every poet, every musician, every athlete, every statesman must begin, to a large extent, anew. He can learn, perhaps, from his predecessors, but the edifice he erects must be his own. The scientist, on the contrary, works within a structure that has been in being for centuries. Foundations have been laid, some rooms have almost been completed (they are never quite completed), and new wings are started in each generation. The new workman may add, or alter, or even help design a whole section, but there is no reason whatsoever that he should attempt to begin afresh, and he is rarely tempted to do so.

And so the man who puts in a single humble nail has contributed to the building, and that nail will continue to be part of the building as long as the building survives. On the man who drove it, it confers a kind of immortality—at least as much as anything can.

The chance of an aspiring scientist to make such a contribution, or more, is a good one. He works with extraordinarily sharp tools, themselves the result of an accumulative process. Setting out to accomplish something, the scientist has all the skills and all the insights of his predecessors upon which to draw. If he needs the calculus, Newton and Leibnitz invented it for him, and generations of mathematicians have given it a cutting edge; it is his to employ. Science is an immensely efficient method for gathering certain sorts of knowledge, and all the power of that method is within reach of the young experimenter or the young theoretician.

These are advantages that are peculiarly the scientist's. The musician who does not write great music is quickly forgotten—and great music is not easily written. The second-rate entrepreneur leaves no mark on the world of affairs. But the second-rate scientist who plods away at an honest experiment, and sets down his results for others to study and build upon, will leave an ineradicable mark upon physics, even if all he has achieved has been to make it possible for a better man to do the same experiment more profitably. I do not set this forth as a particularly laudable ambition, but it can certainly be a comfort.

Education

I have spoken of the Age of Science and of the scientist, perhaps at inordinate length and perhaps not always pertinently so far as my real topic is concerned. What I wish now to discuss is the matter of education in this Age of Science.

Education, I believe, is designed in part to accommodate

the child to the world in which he is to live, and in part to make it possible for that child to make a better world. I have set these down as if they were two distinct purposes, but they are actually one and the same, for the child who does not understand and participate in his world is surely not likely to alter it for the better.

The education which we commonly offer our children today is dominated, for the most part, by the considerations of another era. The Age of Science has affected education both as to method and as to substance. But the effects for the most part have been peripheral: the young student studies a little more science and a little less Greek; he is more likely to reach calculus during his high school years, and less likely to reach Horace. These changes, for whatever they are worth, are a concession to the changing times, but little more. The general educational posture today is very little more than the consequence of what it set out to be fifty years ago; our schools seek to conceal intellectual disparities among their students by giving the intellect as little as possible to feed upon, and at the same time proliferate their playing fields and gymnasiums to the end that physical disparities may be made as obvious as possible.

I do not quite know how and why education shifted from the production of mental competence to the encouragement of baton-twirling. In any case, I am content to leave the work of analysis to others, and to speak only of what I, as a scientist, would like to require of an educational system.

Certainly, an educational system should not be designed

to drop its other concerns in favor of converting all its students into scientists. Nothing the schools could do—not even what they are doing now—would be less desirable. Fortunately, it is also impossible. Science requires a certain temper of mind, and most people would be incompetent and unhappy as scientists, just as most scientists would be incompetent and unhappy as business men, authors, or attorneys.

There is no great need to impress young people into careers in science. The nature of the times in which we live is already assuring us that we will have as many candidates for science degrees as we could possibly use. It may be that they are wildly misused after they have been graduated, but that is certainly a problem distinct from the ones that concern us here.

What I would ask from the schools, however, is an honest effort to convey to all their students some reasonable awareness of what science is, what it does, why it does it, and how it does it. I ask, in other words, nothing more than the poets ask, and have been in some degree getting. An appreciation of poetry is instilled into children from the earliest moment that they are capable of responding to it—at least, this is the intention. It continues through the grade schools, through the high schools, and through college. It is certainly not done with any intention of turning out whole generations of poets and essayists and critics; it is done because of a belief that an appreciation of literature, and a knowledge of literature, are part of the intellectual baggage of any educated man—a belief that a man who has never read Shakespeare is very likely not to have anything worthwhile to say. In this Age of Science, I am equally uneasy about the man who has not read Einstein or Bohr.

But it must be made clear that this "appreciation of science" is possible only to those who have "done" science. Physics, biology, chemistry are, above all, methods of coming into touch with Nature, and they can be comprehended only in the doing. It is not enough to read about them, or hear about them—one must participate.

Let me introduce an analogy that is surprisingly apt. I know the rules of baseball, and I know the rules of cricket; I know something about the history of both games. When I watch a baseball game, I watch it with all my being. My muscles twitch when the batter lets a curve slide over the corner of the plate; I feel the ball burrow into the webbing of the glove when the third baseman lunges for a smash down the line. But when I watch a cricket match, I am merely watching grown men hit hard balls with sticks.

The difference? I played baseball when I was young. I played it badly, and I played it with no great devotion, but from time to time I was out on the field running and fielding and batting, and I therefore have a knowledge of baseball— a visceral knowledge—that is entirely different in kind from the knowledge I have of cricket.

That is the only kind of knowledge of science that is worth having. It comes from working at experiments; from setting out to elicit new knowledge from nature. In this context, I mean by "new" only that it must be new to the seeker. He must honestly be looking for the answers to questions that are truly questions; there is certainly no point at all in what passes for "laboratory work" in most of our schools today where the student, having previously been drilled in the fact that the latent heat of vaporization of water is so many calories, sets about grimly making his data come out to exactly that figure. This is not only not science; it is a total perversion of science. The latent heat of vaporization of water is not very important, and in any case can be found in any reference book. It *is* important that a student learn that data never come out "exactly" to anything, and that all knowledge is approximate knowledge—this is a very useful thing to know and may prevent him from doing foolish things several times in later life.

This in itself would be a net gain, but an honest education in science will profit the student far more widely. He can, to begin with, make himself capable of understanding the world in which he lives—a world upon which science impinges at every moment and in every aspect. But beyond that, he will be in a position to participate in science in exactly the sense that he participates in the World Series. He will be able to follow science intelligently, have at least a glimmer of comprehension of moves that he himself could not possibly have made, and share in the intense satisfaction of achievement and progress.

I find it impossible to put this as strongly as I would like to. The next few years are going to be as exciting for a scientist as any era could possibly be. I believe, for example, that the biochemists and the biophysicists are on the very verge of creating life in test-tubes; that within a handful of years they will be able to combine ordinary substances—atoms of this and atoms of that and atoms of the other—in such a way that the product will be alive. As a consequence, they will begin to gather knowledge about the greatest of all our unsolved mysteries—life itself.

I am neither a biochemist nor a biophysicist. I possess neither the store of knowledge, nor the skills, nor even the overwhelming urge to do the things they do. But because I know what science is and how it works, I shall follow their work with a sense of excitement, of participation—let me say it, a sense of glory—that is forever forbidden to those among us who have never come into real contact with science. And I am ashamed of an educational system that denies this participation to 90 percent or more of our citizens.

I find it equally shameful that these statements I have just made about the production of life in the laboratory can be confused—and will be confused by many who read this—with statements about establishing colonies upon Venus. There is a possibility that some day both statements, in one form or another, will appear upon the front page of the New York *Times*; one will be the statement of a scientist reasoning carefully from his data, prepared to lead another scientist step-by-step through the chain of experiment and conclusion that has led him to his goal; the other will be a statement by a man who, out of ignorance or lust for political power or sheer incompetence, wishes people to believe in the wisdom of appropriating large sums of money for studying space travel. No person with the most meager acquaint-

ance with science could fail to distinguish between the va-
lidity of the two statements. But judging from the hard facts
of experience, the editors of the New York *Times* will be
unable to make the distinction, nor will most of the people
who read the New York *Times*.

Considered in terms of dollars and cents, we cannot afford this kind of ignorance among our citizens any more
than the Age of the Industrial Revolution could afford illiteracy. We have already paid heavily for it. During the war
it was frequently pointed out that the most valuable discovery that science could contribute to the war effort would
be a device that would enable generals and admirals to
distinguish between scientists and people who merely said
they were scientists. There was no such device available, and
for the lack of it we wasted billions of dollars and I do not
know how many lives. And worst of all, the device exists: it
is called education.

We have failed to provide an education in science for our
children, and a large part of the blame for this must fall
squarely upon the scientist.

The complex of education is made up of the teacher, and
the tools with which the teacher works, and the atmosphere
in which he works. I am not concerned about the first of
these. It would be good to pay teachers at least according to
the scale of skilled laborers, and I believe that soon they will
rise to that eminence. Meanwhile, we have them—devoted,
earnest men and women who are teaching the young because they love to teach the young, and are doing it every

bit as well as they are permitted to, and often a little bit better. As for the atmosphere in which a teacher works, I have said something about that and will say more about it later.

The tools with which the teacher works—the textbooks, the collateral reading, the films, his own continuing education, and (in the sciences at least) the laboratory materials—all these must be supplied by the professional scholar. And in the sciences, the professional scholar until a few years ago has simply turned his back on the problem; in many of the sciences he continues to do so.

Let me say this very clearly: a high-school textbook on biology can be written only by a man who does biology. Laboratory experiments in chemistry can be created only by an experimental chemist. Films about physics must be made by physicists. A science teacher who wishes to teach science more effectively must be educated in science, and not educated simply in education.

And when I write that the professional scientist must assume the responsibility for these things, I mean every word of it. I do not mean that a committee of scientists should meet and make recommendations about the textbook that must be written; I mean that one or two or six of those scientists must sit down and write the textbook, and follow it in the schools, and revise it where it does not do what they want it to do, and follow it again through the schools, and, when they have emerged with a product that satisfies them, must be prepared to do it all over again in a few years.

Unless this is done we condemn ourselves to the situation

that now exists: physics, chemistry, biology, and mathematics (and for all that, geography, history, and economics) as they are taught in the schools bear no relation whatsoever to physics, chemistry, biology, or mathematics (or geography, history, or economics) as they are practiced. They are irrelevant to the concerns or the environment of the student just as they are irrelevant to the concerns and the environment of the scholar. They can neither inspire the student nor excite him; they bore and repel him because they are boring and repellent.

And once the proper substance has been provided the teacher, it must be buttressed by every aid to learning that the ingenuity of man can devise. Learning is hard, desperately hard. Learning a hard subject is hardest of all, and science, if it is to be worth its salt, is a hard subject. The teacher needs films and slides and optical projectors; he needs someone to help him with disciplinary and administrative details so he can concentrate on teaching; he needs the psychologists of learning to help him chart his course.

This takes money, but the sums are pitifully small. A few million dollars—say the money that is spent annually to buy costumes and batons for drum-majorettes—will do the job in any one subject. For the national expenditure on driver-training, library science, and coed cooking I would expect that the job could be done for every subject that a high school should offer, sciences and humanities alike.

Perhaps I am an optimist, but I am inclined to believe that the restoration of intellectual substance in education would of itself go a long way toward recreating an atmosphere in which teaching will be possible. If there is a contempt for intellectual achievement in our schools today, it comes at least in part from the fact that shamefully little is demanded in the way of intellectual achievement. The football player is constantly challenged to run faster, hit harder, and react more expeditiously than his followers: as a result not only he but those who cheer him on learn to respect running and hitting and reacting. The student who drones away at the extraction of square roots is never urged to try calculus; he is compelled instead to extract square roots at exactly the pace of the slowest arithmetician in his class and he becomes an object of suspicion if he tries cube roots.

I have been dealing for more than three years with the revivification of high-school physics, and the most heartening aspect of the work has been our growing realization that the students themselves are far wiser than their elders normally suspect. We have given them a difficult course, and one that is designed to strain their abilities to the utmost— to strain the bright student as well as the dull one. We have had our troubles. But the students, on the whole, have taken it in stride.

Let me quote from a report from a teacher in Iowa, and I quote this because it is typical: "I conducted a survey following the completion of the course to see what the kids really thought about it after all the grades were in. Practically all said it was the hardest course they had ever taken, and the same number said it was the best. One girl who received 3 A's and 1 C this year (the C in physics) said that she had worked harder and learned more from the C work in physics than she had ever done in getting an A. She felt that her previous study habits had let her down and her background in math had been shallow since she was able to do A work without really understanding what she was doing."

That girl, I am pleased to say, has learned something from her physics course: she has learned that her community has cheated her out of a knowledge of mathematics, not because she could not do mathematics but because she was never given the chance.

Our children must be given the chance. It is not enough to offer them something called "life sciences" (whatever they may be), or "earth science" (whatever that may be); or to provide for some 10 percent or 15 percent of our students unrecognizable melanges of dull facts and bad technology under the name of physics or chemistry. At the very least, they should be given mathematics as fast as their minds can take it—and right now mathematicians are proving that children can take mathematics with bewildering facility. (Let me digress: quite recently Mr. David Page of the University of Illinois Arithmetic Project was showing me exactly how a certain mathematical concept was presented to fifth-grade students. As he concluded, he said, "Of course, with the children I actually go much faster." He was not being entirely facetious.)

Children should be given, in the grade schools, some general acquaintance with science. In high school, they should have at least one course a year in science; perhaps an introductory course followed by courses in biology, chemistry, and physics. And all these courses should be prepared by first rate scientists and mathematicians, presented with all the rigor of true scholarship, supported by every teaching device our society can bring to bear. This much is a minimum program for the Age of Science—the least we can offer if we intend to create for all of us, and for our children, a better, happier and more satisfying world.

WASTED TALENT

by HORACE MANN BOND

IN THE MANNER of all institutionalized ideas, the current interest in "wasted talent" carries old concepts over into a situation presumed to present a new challenge, and to require new attitudes and devices. The older concept was that either through the infinite wisdom of God, or the only slightly less miraculous workings of the genes, there were to be found in the totality of humanity a very small number of exceptionally gifted persons. There was little curiosity about the fact that most of these "talented" persons were the children of persons in the upper brackets of the social order; indeed, this was regarded as a matter-of-fact consequence of the nature of their "gifts," and of the mechanism by which social orders existed, whereby special abilities were transmitted and rose to the top. Everyone knew that cream would rise in fresh milk, and everyone knew that high intellectual capacity in human society had the same ingredient of self-rising fat globules. Less attention was given to the fact that once risen, the cream stayed on top, even unto

Horace Mann Bond is Dean of the School of Education at Atlanta University.

the third and subsequent generations. When the fact, and its reverse, was noted, the harsh but inevitable dispensations of God—or of the genes—furnished a final answer. Who would question either the mysterious ways of God, or the mathematical certainties of eugenics?

Consequently the wastage of "talent" has led us principally to deplore the circumstances that side-track the "gifted" on their otherwise certain road to academic glory. Obliged by the vast numbers involved to quantify our knowledge of the nature and extent of ability, we have elaborated short-cut testing instruments in which we repose increasing confidence as revealers of capacity. On the basis of these findings we have projected numerous ways and means to avoid wasting the "talent" so disclosed. We provide scholarships designed to keep the specially able but struggling student in high school and college, and are only slightly dismayed when we discover that most of our prospects for rescue already are well equipped with the financial buoyancy of their economic and social upper class origin. Increasingly we turn to studies of motivation and personality, or to devices such as guidance and counseling. Be it noted that in all of this we are still ringing the changes on the old refrain: that "talent" is a matter of divine or genetic endowment; and that what most needs to be done is to begin with the fact that "talent" is a scarce and limited commodity, and the nation's sake demands the best thought and action calculated to refine methods for discovering and nourishing this very special rarity.

The purpose of this paper is to present some opposite

views. This is a nation founded by intellectuals who infused eighteenth-century deistic equalitarianism into the documents they framed to declare the national aspiration. The founders, and the people they represented in the Continental Congress, were also the products of a Bible-believing age. While holding that "All men are created equal," they interpreted individual differences around them in terms of the parable of the talents. We do no differently. Reinforced by nineteenth-century evolutionary and genetic theories, the theory of unequal creation is in our generation inspired by religion and science. As is the way of all true believers, to offer even a mild dissent is to provoke, from the faithful, enraged response. In a recent parlor conversation with two highly intelligent persons—one a cultivated New Englander, a member of the family of a world-famous physicist; the other, an equally cultivated Zulu professor—I was obliged to desist from a further, however timid, defense of the theory of absolute equalitarianism, for fear of precipitating a scene. Both of my companions became increasingly indignant—almost apoplectic—that anyone should dare explain high intellectual competence, including their own, on any other basis than that of the magic of the highly superior genes they carried within their own bodies.

One is tempted to conclude that practically no one in the United States actually believes that "All men are created equal," or ever were. The public, like my Zulu professor and my physicist's-kin, has as solid a faith in genetic inequality as Calvin and Torquemada had in their credal varieties.

I have no ambition to become a martyr, but I must never-

theless introduce this paper with a confession of faith—
faith in the equal creation of all men. This faith I am quite
prepared to adulterate, to the extent that certain rare prenatal accidents *do* occur; and, even, to include those equally
rare genetic deficits and surpluses and other aberrations that
are the delight of pathologists. The word "talent" is here
used in quotation marks. The etymologists say that we are
receding from the old meaning of the word. Instead of being
thought of, almost exclusively, as a "gift of God," the word
is now being used in the sense of "will or inclination," derived from the Middle English figure of the "inclination or
tilting of a balance."

I agree with Wechsler, who says that while "individual
differences are real and important, they are not nearly so
great as has commonly been supposed"; and with Pressey,
that "Superior abilities are now generally considered so
predominantly a product of innate constitution that certain
'educational' factors, possibly of very great importance in the
growth of such abilities, are overlooked. . . . This paper
. . . presumes to suggest that there may be ways by which
many more 'geniuses' might not only be discovered but even,
to a substantial degree, *made* and brought to fruition."

In short, I believe that potentially high intellectual ability is not rare, nor to be found only in a select, and limited,
group of human beings; on the contrary, I believe that
there is an enormous reservoir of high potential abilities in
our population, that now, for all practical purposes, goes to
waste. The reasons for this wastage, and possible means for
its recovery, are ancillary themes.

The Gene on a Pedestal

The great majority of evidence published on the subject has been used to substantiate the theory that the historic concentration of high ability in very small segments of the population is of genetic origin. The writings of Sir Francis Galton, cousin to Charles Darwin, appearing from 1865 to 1905, came easily to the conclusion that eminent "Men of Science" and of other fields derived from relatively few family lines. Added to the old Biblical parable, the conclusion became irresistible, that the development of more and abler thinkers depended on better breeding.

Numerous similar investigations, inspired by Galton's pioneer work, have since been made in all of the Western countries, and have pointed to the same conclusions reached by him. The voices taking at least a moderate view have not been lacking in stridence; it has been almost fifty years since W. I. Thomas dared suggest that man never inherited culture; he had always to learn it. Nor can John B. Watson be remembered as a shrinking academician; yet all of his icon-breaking could not prevail against the religio-scientific creed of genetically induced inequalitarianism.

It will be recalled that Galton took the fact of occupational superiority to be causally associated with demonstrated genetic superiority. Of his 107 British men of science, 2 were sons of farmers, 1 of a laborer, 43 of business men, 18 of public officials; 34 of professionals, 9 of the nobility; and, to narrow even further the field of choice, the interwoven "blood" lines were numerous. In the stratified British class system of his time, and even of our own, Galton was a bright and shining example of his own theory. The one child of a laborer represented in his scientific galaxy became an argument for biological inheritance; it was scarcely to be thought of that this rarity might as well have been used to prove the weighty influence of the culture.

This is so with the great number of studies of the origins of other men of distinction undertaken and reported by Pitirim Sorokin. These studies of high ability originated in the hypothesis that outstanding performance resulted from genetic combinations. It is an ironic commentary on the nature of bio-social research that precisely the same material can be useful in defending the opposite hypothesis.

Let us review some of these studies. Philiptschenko studied the origin of Russian scholars, scientists, men of letters, and members of the Russian Academy in the eighty years preceding 1910. His findings were that scholars came from "agriculture" (not differentiated among owners, tenants, and serfs) in 7.9 percent and from labor (all kinds) in 2.7 percent of the cases. Men of letters came from each class in 9.6 percent of the cases. Outstanding contemporary scientists came from agriculture in 14.1 percent of the cases and from laborers (including peasants, not further defined) in 3.5 percent. All of the rest came from the upper classes that comprised less than 5 percent of the Russian population during the period studied. Not more than one-fifth of these outstanding Russians came from rural areas, in a time when more than 85 percent of the population lived in rural areas.

Fritz Maas made a similar analysis of the social origins of

German scientists born after 1700 and dying before 1910. Less than a quarter of these scientists came from the "lower classes"; by our contemporary American definitions, a large portion of those so classified would now be regarded as "middle class." Dividing the scientific group into "exact" and "natural" scientists, Maas reported that only 6.1 percent of the "exact," and 1.3 percent of the "natural" scientists, came from what we would now call the true "lower" classes—peasants and proletarians. Maas concluded that, "This can only be explained through the influence of natural endowment," and citing the fact that the comparatively large number of famous statesmen derived from peasant farmers showed the genetic transmission of the "slyness and craftiness of the peasant, which is a characteristic very advantageous for diplomats."

The biographies of outstanding mathematicians assembled by E. T. Bell contain frequent references to "good intellectual heredity." If this list is taken as a fair distillation of the very highest mathematical genius ("talent") produced in man's recorded history up to the beginning of the twentieth century, it provides an interesting index to the differential social sources of "talent" in the ages preceding our own, rough though such an estimate has to be. In the table that follows, we have tried to place these "geniuses" in contemporary occupational classifications, as used by the United States Census; realizing, of course, that the enormous changes wrought by the machine age within the last century have created new social classes, and new distributions of populations within those classes, analogous to the past only by wide and generous estimates of relative status. For comparative purposes, we have also made a rough estimate of the average occupational distribution of the male labor force in pre-industrial Western societies.

We then arrive at the distributions shown in Table I.

From this table, it appears that upwards of 85 percent of mathematical geniuses were derived from what was, at most, not more than the 10 percent of the population that were in the upper social and economic classes. It is here freely admitted that such a distribution can be—as it has been—used to support the case for the genetic explanation of these abilities.

But our subject is "Wasted Talent." National origins are of interest in this distribution. Western Europe, particularly England, France, and Germany, was prolific in the development of notable mathematicians during the seventeenth and eighteenth centuries; but it was not until the nineteenth century that Eastern Europe—particularly Poland and Russia—began to contribute. Whatever genetic explanations come to mind, the delayed appearance of mathematical genius in Eastern Europe indicates that an enormous amount of "talent" was wasted prior to the nineteenth century.

To these studies, let us add a piquant hint of what might be one of the more perverse investigations of our times, could it be fully conducted. On October 16, 1957, shortly after the prideful announcement of the launching of Sputnik I, *Pravda* published a list of the thirty-four Soviet "heroes of Science" to whom the chief credit was due for this world-shaking achievement. The list was reprinted in the

TABLE I. Thirty-Seven Mathematicians Classified According to Father's Occupational Class

Occupational Class	Mathematicians			Estimated Percentage Distribution of Male Labor Force
	Name	Number	Percent	
I. Aristocrats and professional, technical workers, etc.	Descartes, Hermite, Pascal, Cauchy, Cayley, Galois, Hamilton, Lobachevski, Abel, Euler, Kummer, Poincaré, Riemann, 8 members of Bernoulli family, Dedekind, Leibniz, Weierstrass	24	65	1
II. Directors, officials, proprietors	Boole, Fermat, Jacobi, Kovalevski, Kronecker, Sylvester, Lagrange	7	19	2
III. Farm owners, managers	Newton	1	3	5
IV. Sales workers	——	0	0	1
V. Clerical workers, etc.	——	0	0	5
VI. Craftsmen, foremen, etc.	Gauss, Monge, Fourier *	3	8	5
VII. Operatives, etc.	——	0	0	1
VIII. Service workers	——	0	0	5
IX. Farm laborers	Laplace, † Zeno of Elea ‡	2	5	60
X. Other laborers	——	0	0	15
Totals		37	100	100

* Fourier, the son of a tailor, was adopted by a wealthy woman when he was eight years old.
† Laplace was reared in a religious orphanage.
‡ Zeno is reported to have been a "self-taught country boy"; after 2,000 years, his family status is understandably vague!

New York *Times* on the following day. It must be admitted that research into the social origins of these men is extremely difficult; the Russian system is not one where either pride in social or biological descent is fashionable. Yet, from the *Soviet Encyclopaedia,* and Western sources, one finds out enough about this select list to justify the suspicion that its social origins are precisely those of the British Men of Science described by Galton in 1865, and of the American scientists studied by Cattell five decades ago.

Most of these men were born long enough before the October Revolution of 1917 so that their academic careers were fixed well before the Revolution, and certainly before the Soviet educational system began to take its present form in the early 1930s. Kapitsa, perhaps the most important, is the son of a general in the Engineering Corps of the Czarist army, and was educated in the aristocratic polytechnic school at Kronstadt, at the Petersburg Polytechnic, and at Cambridge. Lavrentyev, mathematician, described socially as the "son of a scientific worker," is in fact the son of a professor of mechanics at the University of Moscow. M. A. Leontovich, physicist, is the son of A. V. Leontovich, late head of the Department of Normal Physiology at Kiev. V. G. Khlopin, whose contributions to optics are noteworthy, carried on his first scientific activities in the laboratory of his father, G. V. Khlopin, a professor of physics at the University of Moscow. Another great name in optics is that of A. A. Lebedev, son of Professor P. N. Lebedev, also lately of the University of Moscow. B. A. Kazansky, chemist, is also the "son of a scientific worker."

In short, the "heroes of Soviet Science," at least to a most recent date, are likely to be, in the first instance, the products of a Czarist education; they come from precisely that "professional, technical, and kindred workers" class from which the great mathematicians of the Western world, the British and American scientists, and the scholarship winners of the National Merit Scholarship competitions come. The Russians are acutely conscious of the problem; the new dispensation in education announced by Khrushchev in the fall of 1958 is an example. The device of requiring students to intersperse their university and technical studies with labor among the masses was admittedly to be instituted because of the growing estrangement of the intellectuals—presumably, now, "scientific workers"—from the proletariat. Mr. Khrushchev has himself revealed a sensitivity to the problem during his recent American tour; he told his September 16th dinner audience that the schism hoped for by the enemies of the Communist system would not in fact take place.

Despite Mr. Khrushchev's disclaimers, and since there is no Soviet social science that would enable us to know the facts, one can only suspect that in this problem Soviet communism, like American democracy, faces its greatest challenge to the survival of an equalitarian credo. *If* the high abilities of mathematicians and physicists are genetic, the dream of absolute equalitarianism to come must vanish, as the dream of "All men are created equal" has been tarnished in our country. On the contrary, there is much reason to believe that even in Soviet Russia today, high ability has been transmitted by a social milieu at least as powerful as the influence of the genes.

It will be recalled that Peter the Great, seeking to westernize Russia, imported numbers of German and other scholars; and that Catherine the Great followed Peter in giving especial attention to the Academy and the University of Moscow. The academic immigrants to Russia stipulated as one condition of their accepting employment the establishment of good schools for their own children, to be connected with the higher institutions where they labored, and to be supervised by them. In the remarkable reappearance in successive generations of notable scientists in the same family, that was paralleled in many Western families but nowhere to the same degree as in Russian institutions, the strength of societal influences even stronger than biological inheritance may be glimpsed.

The Prevalence of "Talent"

As suggested earlier, studies of demonstrated ability in the United States point to the same class pattern characteristic of the European past and present. Investigations by Schneider and by Cattell show a heavy concentration of American scientists derived from the upper middle classes. There were also, said Cattell, qualitative as well as quantitative differences: "A larger proportion of the scientists born on farms were of low distinction and a small proportion of higher distinction. However, no home of a person engaged in domestic service or in day labor even of the highest grades produced an eminent scientist."

Every study employing tests on a national scale has shown the coincidence of the "talented" with social and occupational class, geographic regions, and ethnic and national origin. Among these endeavors, all in a manner devices for "talent searching," have been Army Alpha of World War I, the Army GCT of World War II, and the current National Merit Scholarship competitions. One would judge, from the findings of these endeavors, that "talent" is to be found most frequently among descendants of the North European stocks (excepting, only, the "pure" English and Scotch-descended Southern mountaineers) than among South Europeans and Negroes; among urban and suburban dwellers than in the country; and among Protestants (excepting, again, those of the South) and Jews than among Catholics.

The results of the National Merit Scholarship selections for 1956 are particularly useful for enabling one to estimate how many "talented" youngsters there are in the United States, for finding out the social and economic classes from which they come, and for estimating how much "talent" is being wasted.

To make such an estimate, let us assume the convenient "upper 2 percent" formula so frequently taken as the boundary within which our highest potential is found. In itself, this sharp delimitation is an unconscious revelation of the genetic obsession. James Bryant Conant, among others, has notably expanded the borders so far as to include the "upper 30 percent". For our purposes, let us meet the problem at its severest limits by assuming that the "talented" are limited to the upper 2 percent of high-school graduates.

In 1959 the number of high-school graduates was 1,400,-000. Using the upper 2 percent rate, 28,000 of these were "talented" youngsters. For various reasons—perhaps genetic, perhaps environmental—on examination we find, by extension of the National Merit data, that the 28,000 residual "talented"—the upper 2 percent—are concentrated in the upper social and economic classes of the population. We owe to the National Merit Scholarship competitions a fairly precise demonstration of this fact, set forth in Table II.

How much "talent" are we wasting?

The answer, of course, will depend on how strong is one's belief in the genetic nature of "talent." If one agrees with Sir Francis Galton, or Pitirim Sorokin, the answer would be: "Very little!" This school of thought would hold that the existence of "natural" ability is reflected in the National Merit Scholarship findings, as it is in Galton's studies of British Men of Science, and in the other numerous studies of "genius" quoted earlier.

On the other hand, a confirmed environmentalist might argue that the vast majority of children, granted superior environment and education, are potential candidates for the ranks of the "talented." We should then be wasting the talents of closer to 2 million children annually: most of the 1,400,000 high-school graduates, plus many of their approximately 900,000 fellow students who do not graduate from high school.

Forsaking this extreme, it may appear reasonable to believe that the potential of "talent" in the American population is better suggested, not by the 54 "talented" children

TABLE II. Distribution of "Talented" Children
by Occupational Class of Fathers

Occupational Class	Percentage Distribution of Male Labor Force *	Talented Children Number	Percent
I. Professional, technical workers etc.	8.5	12,649	45.2
II. Managers, officials, and proprietors	12.2	6,216	22.2
III. Sales workers	5.6	1,838	6.6
IV. Clerical workers, etc.	6.5	1,514	5.4
V. Craftsmen, foremen, etc.	19.1	3,027	10.8
VI. Operatives, etc.	21.4	1,459	5.2
VII. Service workers †	6.4	378	1.3
VIII. Farmers, farm managers, farm laborers, and foremen †	11.8	865	3.1
IX. Laborers, except farm and mine	8.5	54	.2
Totals	100.0	28,000	100.0

* In 1956, the same year as the scholarship data.

† This list of nine basic occupational classes is derived from the census list of eleven. For lack of precise data in the National Merit Scholarship Reports, we have been obliged to combine in "Service workers" the two separate census classifications, "Private household workers" and "Service workers except private"; and into Class VIII of "Farmers, etc.," "Farmers and farm managers," and "Farm laborers and foremen." The "Service workers" class combination does not greatly affect the results; however, if "Farmers and farm managers" could be separated from "Farm laborers and foremen," "Farmers (owners) and farm managers" would then be shown to have a much higher productive ratio, while "farm laborers and foremen" would fall at, or very near, the bottom of the list.

of laborers, but by the 12,649 "talented" children of professional, technical, and kindred workers. If we assume that the nation's children are distributed, by occupation of father, in the same proportions as the occupational distribution of the male labor force, then our estimates show that 1 out of every 3,600 children of the laboring classes is classified as a "talented" person; while 1 in every 15 children of the professionals will earn that title. Those who believe that 3,900,000 male lawyers, college professors, physicians, and other professionals, and an equal number of laborers, as tallied by the United States Census in 1956, were cast in their respective roles because of their genes, will also believe in the continued persistence of a biologically hereditary class of "talented" persons.

In this essay we may be permitted to take a leaf from the book of the students of population, and develop a range of estimates, under the severe limitation of an "upper 2 percent" for the "talented," of the potential number of such children in this country. But note that the "2 percent" limitation is arbitrary and if we admit that educational and other environmental influences can enlarge the ability scope of the child the boundaries of the potential talent pool must be widened. If we believe that heredity is all that matters, the number of the "talented" (currently 28,000) will total 2 percent of each year-class, and we must reconcile ourselves to the fact that about 45 percent of this number—12,649— will come from the most-favored occupational classes in our population. Each of the other occupational classes will, under this theory, have the same ratio of the 28,000 total developed earlier, and we can visualize few, if any, "wasted talents." This becomes our low estimate.

In our medium and high estimates, we keep constant the number of "talented" (12,649) to be derived from the highest class—the professionals; this can serve as the standard to which children of other occupational groups might conform. In our highest estimate-level, every occupational class is producing "talented" youngsters in the same proportion as the professionals: or, in a ratio of 1 "talented" child to every 15 children in the year-class population. Our medium estimates are arbitrarily set at half of the high.

TABLE III. *Range of Estimated Numbers of "Talented" Children by Occupational Class of Fathers*

Occupational Class	Low Estimate	Medium Estimate	High Estimate
I. Professional, technical workers, etc. (standard)	12,649	12,649	12,649
II. Managers, officials, and proprietors	6,216	9,077	18,155
III. Sales workers	1,838	4,167	8,333
IV. Clerical workers, etc.	1,514	4,836	9,673
V. Craftsmen, foremen, etc.	3,027	14,212	28,423
VI. Operatives, etc.	1,459	15,922	31,845
VII. Service workers	378	4,762	9,524
VIII. Farmers, farm managers, farm laborers, and foremen	865	8,780	17,560
IX. Laborers, except farm and mine	54	6,325	12,649
Totals	28,000	80,730	148,811

In brief: our argument is that, could we but give to every child in the land the same opportunities for intellectual stimulation now enjoyed by the children of professional, technical, and kindred workers, we could increase our "talent pool" fivefold. Even if we could move but part-way in this direction, as suggested by our medium estimate, we could have available more than 80,000 "talents" in place of our presently estimated 28,000. The measure of future potential would be even greater; for the elevation of the entire community would inevitably raise the standard, by increasing the proportion of "talented" to be derived from the top class.

As far short as we are of realizing the goal of equal opportunity in our public schools, there are few who would argue against the possibility of at least doubling our present potential of very able persons. Judgments about the academic ability now being produced by different classes and groups, and estimates as to their potential, assume a degree of equality of opportunity far greater than presently exists, in family, in community, in school.

On the floor of Congress, in 1837, the dedicated spokesman for states' rights, John C. Calhoun, argued for the continued enslavement of the Negro on the basis of his inherent racial inability to attain to the higher mental processes. He declared himself willing to grant the intellectual capacity of the race when he found a Negro who could parse a Greek sentence, or do an exercise in higher mathematics. The great South Carolinian was misinformed, even in his own generation, for these high tests of capacity invoked by Calhoun had already then been surpassed by Africans and American Negroes in European and American universities.

This writer is presently conducting a study of American Negroes holding the academic doctorate, with the aim of determining, if possible, the central factors involved in the emergence of unusual academic ability in this minority population. Although the study is far from completion, preliminary findings suggest an enormous untapped potential in this population—one whose representatives now infrequently qualify for National Merit Scholarships. Similarly, few if any white children native to the Southern Appalachians qualify for these grants, and, genetically, this latter population, composed principally of what Berea's late President Frost called "our contemporary Elizabethans," must be acknowledged to be the "purest Anglo-Saxon stock" in the United States.

The sample for this study, which is limited to Negroes who have achieved the doctorate, shows, among other features, one fascinating ancestral fact. When the birthplaces of parents and grandparents are "spotted" on a county map of the United States, a pattern of concentration appears. Among the counties showing a high concentration of ancestors are: Dinwiddie county, Virginia; Richland county, South Carolina; Madison county, Kentucky; and, most prolific of all, Perry county, in Alabama.

One searches in vain for any factors that would differentiate these particular counties from dozens of others among the South's 1,200 counties—that is, until one lays the map showing the birthplaces of the grandparents of Negroes who have won the highest American academic degree over a map published by Thomas Jesse Jones in 1915, as a part of a study of Negro education sponsored by the Phelps-Stokes Fund and the United States Office of Education. The Jones' map shows the location of every school offering education on the secondary school level for Negroes in the South at that time; they were principally privately controlled and supported institutions, as even so recently there existed few publicly supported secondary schools for Negroes in the South.

In the text accompanying the maps, Jones had given meticulous histories of their service, and estimates of their worth at the time of his inspections. Reading the text, examining the two maps, one begins to suspect that there is more than a coincidental relationship between them. Most of these mission schools were founded immediately after the Civil War; they had been the joyous recourse of most of the grandparents of these contemporary academic doctors.

The inspection tells one that Dinwiddie county, Virginia, was the location of the Dinwiddie County Training School, a mission-founded private school in the 1870s, that shortly before its inspection in 1916 had begun to receive state support. One of its first Negro principals was James Colson, a graduate, Phi Beta Kappa, of Dartmouth College. Also located in the county, in its seat at Petersburg, was the Virginia Normal and Industrial Institute (now, the Virginia State College), staffed from its inception in 1882 by the best trained Negro personnel available in the nation.

Madison county, Kentucky, is the seat of Berea College; this college, founded by the redoubtable Kentucky-bred abolitionist, John G. Fee, admitted Negroes freely to all of its grades, from elementary school through college, until the United States Supreme Court, in 1907, upheld the segregating Kentucky Day Law of 1904.

In Columbia, in Richland county, South Carolina, were Benedict College and Allen University, two institutions that liberally scattered their graduates throughout the surrounding countryside, to teach in the log cabins and shacks that passed for schools so long a time ago, but with a devotion beyond present imagining.

And Perry county, Alabama, was the seat, at Marion, of the Lincoln Normal School—to very recent years a Yankee-staffed grade and high school that was founded immediately after the Civil War. Viewing on this map the bare spaces in the surrounding "black belt" counties of Alabama, where the percentage of Negro illiteracy, of farm tenancy, and of other indices of deprivation, scarcely varies from those ratios in Perry county, the viewer can scarcely doubt that the very superior educational institution that was the Lincoln Normal School accounts for much of the difference. Undeniably, Negro "talent" of highest quality has had its ancestral roots in Perry county, which has given us a federal judge, distinguished physicians, as well as research scientists and other scholars with doctoral degrees from America's great universities.

Was there a particular variety of intellectual Negro genes in Perry county? I think it unlikely.

More likely, I think it, that the happiest of circumstances conspired in Perry county to contribute "talent" to America —the circumstance of a first-class school, even for plantation ex-slaves. By this and other tokens, I take it that in every depressed racial group, in every "lower class" occupational group in the country, in every culturally deprived geographical region, there are today potentially "talented" youngsters of every economic or racial or religious persuasion. Indeed, the surface has scarcely been tapped.

The specifics of saving this now-wasted talent are scarcely within the scope of this paper. Clearly, it involves an enterprise more heroic—and costly—than that of providing subsidies for ten or twenty or even a hundred thousand individual youngsters.

The waste calls for the improvement of education in the large for every child in America; for the children of 4 million laborers, of more than 4.5 million farmers and farm laborers, of 9 million operatives, among a present total of some 48,000,000 male workers in the land. Beyond the schools are the other improvements in the level of life to which this nation is already committed; for that relatively brief historical moment through which the nation's destiny now passes, the school must remain our last, best hope, for the utilization of the highest capacities of all of our people to the full, and for the elimination of waste of high human ability.

EDUCATION AND EMPLOYMENT

by SEYMOUR L. WOLFBEIN

ON THE masthead of a major journal in the field of vocational guidance there appeared for a long time the following inscription: "Vocational guidance is the process of assisting the individual to choose an occupation, prepare for it, enter upon, and progress in it."

To those who are now attempting to assess the problems and opportunities of the 1960s, this maxim must have a nostalgic ring indeed. It conjures up a rather neatly packaged world where goals may be firmly and early set, pathways to those goals clearly defined, and where, in spite of life's many pitfalls the established pathways can be followed to their expected ends, with the proper help from properly trained professional personnel.

Not so in the 1960s—just as it had not been so for many decades before.

Education and guidance seek to relate and orient the individual child and youth to the forces of his environment—and one of the major forces involved is that of work. And

Seymour L. Wolfbein is Deputy Assistant Secretary of Labor, Washington, D.C.

one of the major features of the world of work is *change*. The goal of education and guidance in this regard might therefore be more aptly put: To help the individual withstand the onslaughts and, in fact, take advantage of the inevitable changes which will take place in the world of work.

These two conceptions of the orientation process of young people to their economic environment are meaningfully different in a number of important respects. At the very least, they create different expectations for the educational system itself (how and what to teach and guide), which is now engaged in a major reevaluation of methods and goals; and for the young person himself, who must view the occupational world not as a great array of fixed job slots with ready accommodations for those with different talents, aptitudes, and interests, but as a constantly changing structure with a constantly changing set of educational and training prerequisites and functions and responsibilities.

It is against this background of change in the work world and the significant emphasis it gives to the need for flexibility on the part of education and training, educators and trainers, and the educated and trained that this brief essay discusses some of the major dimensions of our manpower future.

Youth in the Work Force of the 1960s

According to most recent Labor Department estimates, we can expect the American labor force to increase from about 73.5 million persons in 1960 to about 87 million persons in

1970. Because of the historically almost unique kind of population changes we will experience during this decade, young people will play a critically important role in the 13.5 million or almost 20 percent increase in the number of workers during the 1960s. These changes are detailed in Table I.

TABLE I. Expected Labor Force Changes
By Age and Sex: 1960–1970

	In the Labor Force		Change: 1960–70	
	In 1960	In 1970	Number	Percent
	(in millions)		(in millions)	
All persons 14 years and older	73,550	87,092	13,542	18.4
Males	49,971	57,443	7,472	15.0
14–24	8,963	13,121	4,158	46.4
25–34	10,913	12,173	1,260	11.5
35–44	11,367	10,999	−368	−3.2
45–54	9,681	10,725	1,044	10.8
55–64	6,484	7,721	1,237	19.1
65 and over	2,563	2,704	141	5.5
Females	23,579	29,649	6,070	25.7
14–24	4,822	7,046	2,224	46.1
25–34	4,364	4,905	541	12.4
35–44	5,268	5,470	202	3.8
45–54	5,141	6,555	1,414	27.5
55–64	3,031	4,313	1,282	42.3
65 and over	953	1,360	407	42.7

Source: U.S. Department of Labor, Bureau of Labor Statistics

There are at least three major points which this kind of labor force change underscores in terms of the role of youth.

In the first place, the sheer numbers of young people participating as economically active members of the population will reach an historic high. In total, a little over 20 million persons fourteen to twenty-four years of age will be in the labor force in 1970—an increase of almost 6.5 million over 1960.

This is the age cohort, of course, which was born in the high birth rate years of the immediate postwar decade 1946 through 1956 and who will reach labor force age (by definition age fourteen) during the 1960s. The numbers of workers in this age group in 1970 will be only a little short of the total number of people in that age group in 1930. It will be two and a half times as large as at the turn of this century, 60 percent higher than at the middle of this century.

Second, the relative increase in these young workers will be just as significant. The rate of increase among young male workers during the 1960s will be five times as large as the corresponding rate among male workers of all other ages; the rate of increase among young female workers during the same period of time will be more than double the corresponding rate among female workers of all other ages. As a result, the proportion of the total labor force made up of youth (fourteen to twenty-four years of age) will rise to the point where they will account for almost one out of every four workers in the United States in 1970.

Since the beginning of this century, the proportion of the working population made up of persons in the younger age groups has declined steadily because of the significant and substantial drop in labor market participation among youth. This trend, in turn has been due to a wide variety of factors, among which legislation and regulations concerning youth employment and increased school enrollments were most important. This long-term trend is now being reversed, despite the expected continuation of the decline in labor market participation rates among the young. Again, the sheer volume of young persons coming into the labor force will raise the proportion they make up of the total work force throughout the decade of the '60s.

The strategic role of the younger person in the labor force of the '60s receives additional emphasis, in the third place, when viewed against the trends for other groups in the working population. The following brief summary makes the point:

The labor force increase of 13.5 million during the 1960s will come from the following groups:

Age	Percent
14–24	47
25–34	13
35–44	−1
45–64	37
65 and over	4
Total	100

Thus, just about one out of every two new additions to the labor supply in the '60s will come from the younger age groups. In fact the two groups most often dubbed as "problems"—the younger and older—will account for the preponderant majority of our additional workers during the decade. The key part these persons will have in the labor force of the immediate future is underscored by the fact that, in the face of increases practically across the board, the prime working age group thirty-five to forty-four years old will actually decline by 1970, as the low-birth depression years of the 1930s continue to affect our population and manpower posture.

There are many other significant aspects of overall manpower change during the '60s which the reader may want to see by examining Table 1. One in particular may be mentioned at this point. It will be noted that a little over 6 million, or 45 percent, of the total labor force increase of this decade will be made up of women. More than 1 out of every 3 in this 6 million increase will be accounted for by the young women fourteen to twenty-four, whose relative rise over the decade will exactly match the increase among the males in the same young age cohort. The number of young women in the work force in 1970 will be triple the number at the beginning of this century, about 50 percent higher than at the middle of this century.

Thus, the numbers and proportions of younger workers—both male and female—are going to reach historic levels, emphasized all the more by the accompanying differential trends among the rest of the age groups in the working population.

Industrial and Occupational Change

A recent New York *Times* advertisement by a long established multibranch company calls for applications from persons with experience in:

Transistorized circuitry   Ferret Reconnaissance
Inertial guidance—missiles   Human factors science

| Gyrodynamics-supersonic aircraft | Micro-miniaturization |
| Shielding design-atomic power | Data telemetry |

This "help wanted ad" contains occupations which were hardly even known just a few years ago. Dealing as they do with some of the frontiers of current work in the physical sciences they are representative of the great forces of change in the world of work. How many persons are there in the United States today who carefully chose, prepared for, and entered these occupations?

This brief listing of occupations is also symptomatic of a basic and overridingly important shift in the very industrial and occupational structure of the United States—a shift which took place slowly but almost inexorably throughout this century, reached an historic turning point during the '50s and will continue to be a major force to be reckoned with during the '60s.

In a recent month during 1959, persons who work for a wage or salary (but including farmers as well as farm hands) were distributed as follows among the major industries of the United States:

(in millions)

Manufacturing	16.1	Transportation and public	3.9
Construction	2.8	utilities	
Mining	.7	Trade	11.2
Agriculture	6.4	Finance, insurance	2.4
		Service	6.6
		Government	8.2
	26.0		32.3

On the left we have the workers who produce "goods": all of the items literally manufactured—autos, steel, rubber, apparel, furniture, chemicals, etc.; everything built—the millions of homes every year, bridges, highways, factories, office buildings, etc.; everything mined from the ground—coal, lead, zinc, gold, uranium, etc.; all the food, feed and fiber produced by the agricultural sector of the American economy.

On the right we have the workers who produce "services" —who buy and sell, finance and service, teach, work for the government as firemen, policemen, economists or clerks, etc., etc. They now outnumber the "goods" producers by 6 millions. Had we, in addition to the wage and salary workers, included persons earning their livelihood by owning their own business off the farm, the difference would have been even much greater in favor of the service sector, since most self-employed persons are in such sectors as trade.

Throughout this century, workers in the service producing industries have been gaining on those producing goods; they overtook them in the early part of the '50s, have moved steadily ahead since then, and there is nothing in the offing which will change this trend as we move into the '60s.

Inevitably, this kind of change in industrial structure has brought a corresponding change in the occupations we follow as workers. Here again is a brief recapitulation of past, present, and expected future developments:

	1910	1959	1970
	(in percent)		
All workers	100	100	100
White-collar	22	42	45
Professional and technical	5	11	13
Proprietary and managerial	7	11	11
Clerical and sales	10	20	21

Blue-collar	37	37	36
Skilled	12	13	13
Semiskilled	14	18	18
Unskilled	11	6	5
Service	10	12	13
Farm	31	9	6

In a real way this brief table reflects some of the major social and economic changes of the twentieth century in this country:

1. The almost complete turn-around from a rural to urban economy: in 1910 almost one out of every three workers was on the farm; today the ratio is below one in ten and still going down.

2. The emergence to a majority position of the white-collar group in the late 1950s: in 1910, more than one in three employed persons was a blue-collar worker and only about one in five a white-collar worker; now the white-collar worker outnumbers his blue-collar counterpart and is scheduled to increase his numerical and proportionate advantage during the '60s.

3. The great growth in the professional and clerical and sales groups, which have doubled their standings in the occupational hierarchy over the past fifty odd years.

4. The stable (but key) position of the skilled craftsman.

5. And the enormous decline in unskilled jobs in the United States.

As can be seen from the summary figures, these occupational trends are expected to continue into the '60s, highlighted particularly by the persistent growth in white-collar jobs. This growth, it may be added, is expected to affect the goods-producing as well as the service-producing sectors of the economy, as indeed it already has.

For example: In 1948 there were among manufacturing (factory) employees a little short of 13 million production workers and about 2.5 million nonproduction workers. The former represent workers in and around the factory production line; the latter include largely the clerical, managerial, and professional personnel in the offices of factory plants. Ten years later (1958) production workers had fallen by a million under the impact of the business downturn of that year; nonproduction workers had increased by 1.25 million over the same period of time.

These expected trends should not be taken to denigrate the continued importance of at least one major group among the blue-collar workers—the skilled craftsmen, for whom the demand is expected to be substantial in the decade to come. The situation in this field, in fact, illustrates one of the points we are coming to in the following section—the role of training.

For example: The U.S. Bureau of Apprenticeship reports that the number of new building trades craftsmen emerging from apprenticeship training programs between 1950 and 1958 was less than the number of journeymen lost to the trade because of death and retirement.

All in all, then, the '60s are expected to witness a significant increase in the skill level of the labor force across the occupational structure.

Some Implications

It is when we juxtapose the findings of the two preceding substantive sections that some of the major issues of the '60s with regard to employment of youth come into focus. The conjunction of the size and composition of labor force growth and the kind of industrial and occupational changes we have described so far poses some of the major problems —as well as opportunities—of the coming ten years.

On the one hand, the expectations are for a significant increase in the number and proportion of jobs demanding increased education and training in both the white-collar and blue-collar occupations. On the other hand, the preponderant increase in available manpower will come from the young, some of whom will still be in the process of obtaining their education and training, practically all of whom will be at the beginnings of their career development. In the age group from which we normally draw a substantial proportion of our higher level personnel, we face a deficit of experienced workers.

Thus once again is underscored the truth of the axiom "what is past is prologue" in the field we are discussing. The very low birth rates of the '30s, succeeded by the huge upturn in births in the '40s have given us a unique configuration in our population and manpower distribution. When related to the kind of industrial and occupational changes we can expect, we can at least anticipate the uneven kind of problem posed by the necessity to provide employment opportunities for a substantially increased number of young men and women, while engaged in the task of filling an increasing number of professional, technical, and skilled jobs in the face of a shortage in one of the prime working-age groups.

In a free and democratic society the pathways available for meeting such a set of problems are essentially twofold: the provision of the best kind of education and guidance to all, consonant with the principle of free choice and based on the individual's talents, interests, and aptitudes; and the best kinds of selection, utilization, and organizational procedures on the part of employers, be they government, industry, or business.

All of this, of course, can take place only in the context of continued economic growth with high levels of employment. All of the estimates and projections, as well as reflections, presented here are predicated on a continuation of the kind of economic growth we have had since the end of World War II. Granting these assumptions, there are at least five points that may be made briefly concerning the relationships between education and employment:

1. As we already have indicated, education and training represent the major catalyst for bringing together and meshing the occupational demands of the future with the resources available to meet them. This, of course, is one of the traditional jobs of education; it may be more difficult, it certainly will be much more extensive in the decade ahead. The discussions by John Gardner and Ralph Tyler in these volumes point up some of the perspectives and issues in this field.

2. The impact of the labor market upon education in the '60s will be highlighted by higher educational and training prerequisites for employment. The almost perfect match between level of educational attainment and the growth areas of the occupational structure can be seen from the following brief summary of the amount of schooling by members of different occupational groupings.

Occupation	Average Years of School Completed
White-Collar	
Professional and technical	16+
Clerical	12.5
Proprietary and managerial	12.4
Sales	12.4
Blue-Collar	
Skilled	10.5
Semiskilled	9.5
Unskilled	8.5
Service	9.6
Farmers	8.6
Farm Workers	8.2

Thus, it is the occupations which require higher educational attainment that represent the growth areas of the future. And, even in these occupations the educational requirements continue to rise. Witness the increasing time required for an engineering degree; the recent increase from four to five years for a baccalaureate in pharmacy and architecture; the increasing demand for teachers with master's degrees, the rising demand for secretaries and clerical personnel with some post high-school work, etc.

3. At the same time, there is every indication that young people in ever-increasing numbers and proportions will be going after the increased education and training which our changing job structure will apparently call for. Back in 1940, only 26 percent of the population fifteen years of age and over were high-school graduates; the Census Bureau projects a figure of 45 percent for 1970. Similarly, only 3.8 million in our population twenty years of age and over were college graduates in 1940; the Census projects a tripling of that figure for 1970.

4. The education—occupation—employment links which we have emphasized so much in this discussion have and will prove themselves out in the acid test of the labor market. One of the more persevering labor force trends in this country is the inverse relationship between educational attainment and occupational status on the one hand and the rate of unemployment on the other. Here was the situation in the spring of 1959; the numbers may change with alterations in the business cycle, but the relationships among the different occupational groups stay on:

Occupational Level	Rate of Unemployment (in percent)
Unskilled	11.8
Semiskilled	7.5
Skilled	5.4
Sales	4.1
Clerical	3.3
Proprietors, managerial	1.4
Professional and technical	1.3

5. The various changes described so far emphasize once again a long standing problem which fits squarely within

the context of our discussion on the relationship between education and employment—the school dropout. Studied extensively for many years by both public and private groups, the young person who ends his educational career before high-school graduation still represents one of the more intractable problems.

According to recent investigations about 1 out of every 3 dropouts from the school system leaves during the eighth grade or before; 2 out of 3 never get to senior high school, i.e., they drop out before the tenth grade. Thus, a huge proportion of these persons not only do not get the high-school education which is becoming a minimum requirement for more and more jobs; they leave before those grades in which most kinds of formal guidance and occupational information programs begin to take place.

In terms of labor market adjustment, the dropouts do very poorly indeed. For example, a study of the contrasting experience between girl dropouts and girl high-school graduates who did not go on to college showed that two out of every three of the graduates obtained jobs in the white-collar clerical fields, while two-thirds of the dropouts found jobs in the unskilled ranks as waitresses, etc. But by far the sharpest difference among both boys and girls (dropouts vs. high school graduates not going on to college) was in the unemployment they experienced. On all scores—in terms of rates of unemployment, spells of unemployment, and total time since leaving school spent as unemployed workers, the dropouts had a much worse record than the graduates.

The changing labor force, industrial, and occupational pictures for the 1960s with their emphasis on stiffer competition at higher skill levels and higher skill development make the prognosis for these young persons even more negative. Others in these volumes discuss the quantitative and qualitative dimensions of the problems in education for the '60s. At this point, however, two relevant matters warrant consideration.

The first is the necessity—since a large proportion of dropouts are retarded in the early grades and actually leave well before the completion of high school—to consider the development of programs of guidance and counseling at the elementary school level. The second relates to the possibility of increasing the "holding power" of the schools through the design of courses of instruction which can both hold the interest of and be of substantive value to some of the young people who do not make any progress within existing curricula. Is it possible to offer earlier a broader choice of educational avenues along which this kind of student can move with profit and dignity?

Conclusions

We have alluded to the kinds of expectations which will be generated by the changing manpower picture of the 1960s. We conclude with a somewhat closer and more concrete indication of what some of these expectations are likely to be—for the three broad areas which together are going to make the difference in how successfully we manage our affairs during the decade.

As to the educational process itself and those who will be responsible for its operation and sense of direction, perhaps the best way to underline again the overriding importance of this sector to our manpower future is as follows: we have indicated that about 20 million persons fourteen to twenty-four years of age will be in the American labor force in 1970. Simple arithmetic shows that this group is now (1960) four to fourteen years of age—it is, or will shortly be, the elementary school population of the United States, which will move through the grades, through secondary school and college as the decade advances. In other words, just about all of the 20 millions of young people who are going to be such an important part of the work force are right now within the purview of our educational and training institutions. What we do and plan to do right now will have a really determining effect on the knowledge and skills, the arts and sciences, the attitudes and motivations toward work with which this critical part of our manpower is endowed.

This, perhaps, is at the core of what we expect from education in its relationship to employment—in concert, of course, with the other responsible agents in this field, i.e., the parents and other community organizations.

For education, the expectations include some major problems of a quantitative and qualitative dimension. Not only will the numbers with whom the educational institutions have to cope increase, but so will the demand for quality of curriculum geared to the higher training and skill development requirements of the world of work of the '60s. These considerations underscore, at the same time, the critical importance of guidance and counseling of young people in their career planning as part of the educational process.

Advances in education and training are, or course, by no means the entire answer to our manpower problems. They can never, by themselves, guarantee successful performance and utilization of the labor force. Side by side with an adequate preparation of the new labor supply has to come some very careful manpower planning on the part of employing institutions themselves.

We did not have to call upon the talents of a prophet or seer to anticipate some of the critical manpower problems of the '6os—the tremendous inflow of younger workers seeking their first job, the emerging shortage group in the ages thirty-five to forty-four years, etc. In very much the same way organizations, for example, can obtain a substantial amount of information concerning their manpower problems by a simple replacement schedule indicating the exits from their labor force to be expected simply on the basis of retirements to come—and set themselves up to meet the needs these exits will inevitably generate.

This is why the role of organizational and managerial policy—not only in terms of selection, training, utilization and setting standards of work but in careful and creative manpower planning—is so important. In fact, it is a most necessary complement to the points we raised on education and training. We call upon the educational system and the student for a maximum effort and investment in training and skill development. We should follow up with the maximum effort and investment in looking ahead in the manpower field by employers as well.

As in the arena of education, much is still left to be discovered in the field of organizational programs and planning. We close this part of our discussion with the following quotation from the significant work on *The Ineffective Soldier* by Eli Ginzberg and his associates which is very much to this point:

Much is known about the way in which these several approaches can contribute to effective performance, but much remains to be learned. For instance, the proper balancing of the rate of technological improvement with additional efforts to raise the skill level of those who must manage, operate, and maintain the increasingly complex structures warrants further study. So too does the problem of work motivation. We are only at the beginning of understanding the marked differences between the strongly and poorly motivated in the world of work. We also need new knowledge about how the individual, his immediate work group, and the larger organization can be more effectively integrated so that performance can be improved.[1]

These then, are some of the expectations from management in relation to the manpower future of the '6os.

Finally, we come to the youth themselves.

Their expectations also have both a quantitative and qualitative dimension. With regard to their role as workers they will find, first, more competition simply because of the numbers of their colleagues searching for employment. And, as we already have indicated, more and more of their competition will be better and better educated and trained.

Yet, in the face of a significantly changing occupational and industrial structure, they will have a major advantage, in view of the expected deficit in the number of their older

[1] Eli Ginzberg et al., *Patterns of Performance* (Vol. III of *The Ineffective Soldier*, New York: Columbia University Press, 1959), p. 303.

counterparts, in the competition to fill the higher level jobs. Given a continuation of relatively high levels of economic activity and employment, many may have the opportunity to move ahead in their careers at an accelerated pace.

To achieve these goals youth will have to be adaptable, flexible, and mobile. Every study, incidentally, that has been made shows that mobility varies directly with the amount of education and training a person has—underscoring again the pivotal relationship between education and employment. And this makes sense—after all, the more education and skill an individual has, the better he will be able to respond to new opportunities and new settings in different places and different jobs. This will be all the more important in the '60s when we have to face up to significant changes in our very manpower, industrial, and occupational structure.

THE ARMED SERVICES AS A
TRAINING INSTITUTION

by H A R O L D   W O O L

DURING the 1950s, military service obligation became an accepted fact of life for young American males approaching adulthood. A post-World War II draft law, enacted in 1948, remained continuously on the statute books throughout the decade and in 1959 was extended by the Congress until 1963. Partly as a result of their military service liability under the law, and partly in voluntary response to the opportunities offered by military careers, over 7 million youths entered active military service. By the end of the decade, fully 70 percent of the men aged twenty-five to twenty-six had entered or completed a tour of active military duty; the remainder consisted almost entirely of those deferred or disqualified for service.

In contrast to earlier periods of full mobilization, when the Armed Services had drawn upon a broad range of adult manpower, the new entrants into military service in recent years

Harold Wool is Staff Director of the Analysis Division, Office of the Assistant Secretary of Defense (Manpower, Personnel, and Reserves).

were mainly in their late teens or early twenties. Relatively few had acquired substantial vocational skills. To most, military service initiated their first departure from home, school, and community. As a result, the Military Establishment which, except in crisis, had been historically relegated to a relatively minor role in the American pattern of life, suddenly emerged as an institution with tremendous significance in the molding of American youth.

An appreciation of the role of the Armed Services as a training and educational institution and as an initial vocational experience for a large segment of our youth requires at the outset some understanding of the nature of the military structure. Military training programs are designed, necesarily, to meet the special needs of the Armed Services for skilled manpower. These needs overlap in some ways, but contrast in other respects, with those of civilian industry. As in the civilian work force, changes in technology have resulted in significant changes in military skill requirements in recent years. These changes, in turn, have had a direct impact on the numbers and kinds of men required for military service and on the nature of military training programs.

In the following sections we shall review, in turn, the military skill structure, major skill trends, changes in the number and characteristics of personnel entering service, the nature and scope of military training programs, and some of the implications of this training for youth in relation to civilian work careers.

The Military Skill Structure

Although some small degree of specialization has always been required of military personnel, the concept of military personnel as "specialists" with widely differing duties, skills, and training is of recent origin. Until a few decades ago, most personnel in our military forces were classified simply as commissioned officers, noncommissioned officers, and privates. The commissioned officers provided the executive and professional leadership; the noncommissioned officers, the direct supervision; and the privates, the mass of combat manpower. As general-duty soldiers or seamen, they also performed a wide range of support duties of an unskilled or semiskilled nature. In those limited instances where more skilled or technical work was required, the lack of occupational specialization and of in-service training systems required resort to special recruitment programs for skilled craftsmen, or to use of auxiliary civilian contract personnel.[1]

This crude military division of labor, although suited to the needs of infantry or cavalry troops in frontier America, proved wholly inadequate to cope with the vastly more complex array of equipment and functions required in our twentieth century military forces, as became painfully evident during the early phases of mobilization in World War

[1] The Navy, we should note, constituted a limited exception to this pattern. The shipboard "rating" structure for enlisted personnel, under which its petty officers are identified in terms of their specialized shipboard duties and skills, traces back to Revolutionary times. These ratings, however, were originally taken over from the civilian merchant fleet, which, until the closing years of the nineteenth century, was also the Navy's principal source of skilled personnel.

I, when shortages of skilled specialists proved to be serious bottlenecks in the organization, equipping, and movement of our troops overseas. It was not until World War II, however, that comprehensive systems for occupational classification of military jobs and personnel were established in each of the Armed Services.

These military occupational classifications have been subject to periodical overhaul since World War II, in response to changing job requirements and training concepts. The number of specialized skills required in each of the Armed Services today provides in itself a striking measure of the wide range and complexity of the military job structure. For enlisted personnel, the number of specialties ranges from about 400 in the Navy and Marine Corps to more than 900 in the Army. These specialties are grouped into a series of occupational ladders, each providing a systematic progression from the entry or apprentice level to journeyman and, finally, to the senior supervisory ranks. Descriptions of these enlisted occupational fields are published by the Armed Services in occupational handbooks for use by counselors, school officials, and individuals interested in Service careers.

A similar pattern of occupational specialization has also emerged for the officer ranks. The pattern of officer-career management, however, is generally designed to provide progressive broadening of professional experience and responsibilities, rather than narrow technical specialization.

The scope and variety of military jobs, and the extent to which they now parallel civilian-type skills, is suggested by the accompanying distribution of enlisted personnel by occupational group. (Table I) These occupational groups are designed generally to match broadly analogous groupings for the civilian labor force, with the obvious exception of "ground combat" skills, which have no civilian counterpart.

TABLE I. *Percentage Distribution of Assigned Enlisted Personnel by Occupational Group, 31 December 1958* *

Group	Percentage of Total Assigned Enlisted Personnel
Total	100.0
Ground combat	12.9
Infantry	6.9
Artillery	3.0
Armored vehicle crews	1.6
Combat engineering	1.4
Electronics	13.5
Electronics equipment maintenance	7.0
Electronics equipment operators, excluding radio	3.2
Radio operators	2.7
Air traffic control	.7
Other technical	7.4
Medical and dental	4.3
Intelligence	1.0
Surveyors and draftsmen	.6
Photography	.5
Weather	.4
Other	.6
Administrative and clerical	20.6
General administration and clerical	6.9
Supply	6.8

Group	Percentage of Total Assigned Enlisted Personnel
Communications	2.4
Personnel	1.7
Disbursing and finance	.8
Machine accounting and statistics	.6
Other	.9
Mechanics and repairmen	25.8
Aircraft and engine, including parts	11.0
Shipboard machinery	4.5
Electrical and wire communications	3.9
Automotive	3.6
Munitions and weapons	2.6
Other	.2
Crafts	7.6
Construction and utilities	3.3
Naval operating crafts	1.3
Metal working	.9
Firefighting	.8
Fabric, rubber, and leather	.5
Other	.7
Services	11.8
Food service	4.7
Security	3.2
Motor transport	2.7
Other	1.2
Miscellaneous (e.g., musicians)	.4

Source: *Department of Defense.*

* Based on total of approximately 1,890,000 enlisted personnel assigned to units, for whom military occupational specialties were reported. Excludes about 340,000 enlisted personnel not assigned to units, and those with unidentifiable skill, e.g., recruits, trainees, transients, and Navy general duty personnel (seamen, airmen).

This table highlights in a striking way the extent to which the Armed Services now rely on the "soldier-technician." Much has been written about the increased "technicality" of military skills. However, for those whose military service exposure was in World War II or earlier, it may still come as a shock to realize that, for all Services combined, our modern enlisted force now requires twice as many mechanics as it does ground combat specialists; or that the number of electronics equipment maintenance technicians now exceeds the number of infantrymen.

In comparing the military occupational categories with their civilian counterparts, certain unique features of the military job structure should be noted:

First, the very nature of the military mission requires that military personnel be capable of fulfilling a variety of functions, particularly under the stress of combat conditions. Throughout their careers, personnel assigned to specialized tasks may, at the same time, he expected to perform additional duties, such as guard duty or details, commensurate with their rank and supervisory level. This pattern of multiple assignments is particularly characteristic of the Navy job structure where, because of shipboard space limitations, each enlisted man has watch, quarter, and battle station assignments, in addition to strictly technical duties.

Second, unlike the civilian labor force, there is very little provision in the present military occupational structure for the "unskilled laborer" as such. The unskilled and semi-skilled duties of all types, including the "fatigue" details, are in fact mainly performed by junior personnel—recent recruits and trainees—who are, at the same time, serving their apprenticeship or acquiring on-the-job training in a particular military specialty.

Finally, it will be apparent that there is no precise correspondence in job content between the large majority of military and civilian occupations, even though the title may be similar. Many jobs for enlisted men, particularly in the more technical fields, are necessarily more specialized than their civilian counterparts in view of the limited time available for training and utilizing the average recruit. Many other differences in equipment, organization, and function also prevent any precise matching of civilian and military jobs. These are, however, merely an extension of the differences in occupational job content among different civilian industries or even among different employers in the same industry.

Major Skill Trends

The military occupational structure, far from being static, has been in a continuing state of flux and evolution in the post-World War II period. Comparison of the present major occupational groups with those in 1945 and in the early 1950s reveals an unmistakable trend: the sharp relative expansion of the technical-mechanical skill groups at the expense of the more conventional ground combat, crafts, and services occupations. (Table II) The most dramatic increase has been in the electronics group which has more than doubled in relative size since the end of World War II. Over the same period, the percentage of enlisted jobs in ground combat dropped sharply, from nearly 24 percent to less than 13 percent of total strength.

TABLE II. *Percentage Distribution of Enlisted Jobs by Major Occupational Group: End of World War II, During Korean Conflict, and 31 December 1958*

Major Occupational Group	End of World War II	During Korean Conflict	31 Dec. 1958
Electronics	6.2	9.6	13.5
Other technical	6.9	6.9	7.4
Mechanics and repairmen	21.3	22.6	25.8
Administrative and clerical	15.3	20.8	20.6
Crafts and services	26.7	22.7	19.4
Ground combat	23.6	17.4	12.9
Total	100.0	100.0	100.0

Source: Department of Defense.

These sharp shifts are traceable in part to fundamental differences in force requirements over the period. The changes in force composition are partially illustrated by the shift in relative strengths among the Services. At the end of World War II, the Army Air Force accounted for 19 percent of total military strength and increased steadily to 33.5 percent, by June, 1959. In contrast, the percentage of active duty strength allocated to the Army dropped sharply from 49 percent at the end of World War II to 34 percent in 1959. These shifts in manpower allocations *among* the military services have been paralleled by equally sharp shifts *within* the Services, with increased emphasis consistently on those branches and elements relying on the newer military technology.

Equally important, and closely related to these shifts in force structure, has been the far-flung impact of the revolution of military technology upon all components of the military services during the past decade. Sustained by a massive research and development effort, and by the many new scientific "break throughs" during and after World War II, the rate of technological advance in military equipment has been unparalleled in our peacetime history. Some of its most sensational impacts have been in the field of electronic equipment, suggested by the fact that the number of electron tubes in the equipment of a Navy destroyer rose from less than 200 in 1940 to as many as 5,400 at present.

The trend towards new and continually more complex equipment is illustrated, too, by the contrast between World War II military aircraft and their recent counterparts. The modern jet bomber includes items of equipment such as speed brakes, cabin pressurization, air conditioning systems, seat ejection, air refueling, anti-fogging, flight control systems, and many others not in existence in World War II bombers. Similar comparisons can readily be made between the World War II submarine and the present nuclear submarine and for a vast array of other military weapons, equipment, and techniques, ranging from atomic artillery to data processing equipment.

The rapid pace of technological advance, in turn, has served to accelerate the long-term trend towards skill specialization. New weapons systems have created the need for completely new types of skills in such fields as guided missiles, rocket propulsion and nuclear weapons assembly. Addition of new and more complex items of equipment in other areas has also resulted in a multiplication of specialized skills in previously established fields, such as radar and aircraft engine maintenance.

The trend has, of course, not been all one-sided. Automation has simplified some operator skills, and stress has been placed upon designing military equipment in a way which will facilitate maintenance. These factors have, however, simply checked what would otherwise have been an even more rapid increase in total technical personnel needs.

Characteristics of Personnel Entering Service

In meeting their formidable requirements for trained specialists, the Armed Services have been confronted by a unique set of conditions, quite unlike those faced by most civilian employers. These stem from the characteristics of the new recruits entering military service in recent years: their youth and lack of working experience, their relatively brief tours of duty, and their heterogeneous backgrounds, interests, and capabilities. Let us review some of these factors briefly.

As shown in Table III, the total number of personnel entering and leaving service each year has gradually declined during the course of the past decade, following the extremely heavy inflow during the Korean conflict. In contrast to these earlier years when heavy reliance was necessarily placed on inductees and on involuntary reserve call-ups, most of the new entrants into military service since 1953 have been voluntary enlistees. With limited exceptions, the Army has been the only Service requiring inductees; and draft calls into that

TABLE III. Active-Duty Military Strength and Net Gains and Losses* 1951 to 1959 (in thousands)

Fiscal Year	Strength Beginning of Year	Total Gains	Officer Gains †	Enlisted Gains Total	First Enlistments	Reserves to Active Duty ‡	Inductions	Total Losses
1951	1,460	1,964	138	1,826	630	609	587	175
1952	3,249	1,052	61	991	510	102	379	665
1953	3,636	1,008	47	961	343	54	564	1,089
1954	3,555	685	38	647	329	53	265	938
1955	3,302	730	35	695	440	40	215	1,097
1956	2,935	614	31	583	371	75	137	743
1957	2,806	606	30	576	303	93	180	616
1958	2,796	479	25	454	271	56	127	674
1959	2,601 §	474	22	452	310	31	111	577

Source: Department of Defense.

* Excludes reenlistments in the same Service and intra-Service transfers.

† Includes R.O.T.C. graduates, aviation cadets, Service academy graduates, direct appointments, and various specialized officer procurement programs, as well as Reserve recalls. Reserves accounted for a major portion of officer gains in 1951–52.

‡ Of total enlisted Reservists entering active duty, personnel with prior active service totaled about 430,000 in 1951 and about 30,000 in 1952. Since 1953, over 90 percent have been personnel without prior active service.

§ Preliminary.

Service have dropped substantially, from over 200,000 in 1954 and 1955 to slightly over 100,000 in 1959.

The primary reliance of the Armed Services on voluntary enlistees, has, in turn, directly influenced the age distribution of new personnel. The median age of new enlistees in each year since 1954 has consistently been eighteen and a half years; about 85 percent have been in the age group of seventeen to nineteen years. It thus appears that the large majority of young men have entered military service either immediately after leaving school or after only limited periods of work experience. This, in turn, has compelled the Armed Services to rely very heavily upon in-service training programs to develop their needed skills.

The type and length of skill training programs offered to new entrants into military service have necessarily been influenced by the length of their tours of duty and by the prospects of their retention in service as career personnel. Initial tours of enlisted service in recent years have ranged from two years for inductees to three or four years for regular enlistments. Very few of the inductees—less than 5 percent —continue in the service beyond their obligated two-year tours. The Services, therefore, have relied mainly upon the regular enlistees to meet their requirements for career noncommissioned officers and skilled technicians, and have given preferential treatment to "regulars" in selection for specialized training courses.

In the years immediately following the end of Korean hostilities, reenlistment rates for regulars completing initial tours of duty proved to be disappointingly low, averaging less than 15 percent in 1954–55. This was due, in part, to the fact that many young men not normally on the "recruitment market," had enlisted in the Air Force or Navy during the Korean period in preference to being drafted in the ground combat arms. The high rates of personnel turnover resulting from these losses prompted the initiation of a wide range of programs designed to increase retention of qualified personnel. These included increased reenlistment bonuses in 1954; two major military pay laws, in 1955 and 1958; improvements in "fringe benefits" and military housing facilities; and a variety of administrative measures designed to enhance the career attractiveness of military service. These measures, as well as the gradual change in the composition of the enlistee groups, resulted in a significant increase in the "first-termer" reenlistment rate, to an average of 30 percent in 1959. This improvement has also been reflected in a steady increase in the size of the career enlisted force from about 530,000 in June, 1950, to 750,000 in December, 1954, and to about 1.0 million in December, 1958.[2]

Despite such improvement, the Armed Services have continued to be faced with the probability that the majority of their new trainees will leave military service after completing initial tours of duty. The difficulty has been intensified, moreover, by a persistent inverse relationship between technicality of skill and reenlistment rates. Since 1955, when occupational reenlistment rates were first reported, first-term reenlistment

[2] The "career" force is defined as consisting of personnel on second, or subsequent, terms of active duty. It is estimated on the basis of the number of personnel who have completed four or more years of military service.

rates have been consistently lowest among men in electronics and certain other highly technical skills, and highest in non-technical occupational groups such as food service and military police. This differential pattern has been related, in large part, to the fact that the Services have tended to select their best-educated recruits for training in the more technical skills; and that these personnel for various economic and socio-logical reasons have been least responsive to enlisted careers.

The training problem faced by the Armed Services, stemming from high rates of personnel turnover, can perhaps best be summarized by this comparison: The average working life expectancy of the eighteen-year-old civilian male worker has been estimated at 44.8 years by the Bureau of Labor Statistics, based on 1955 data. In contrast, on the basis of recent re-enlistment and attrition experience, we have estimated that the average active military service expectancy of the new enlistee, at the time of his entry into Service, is less than five years. The potential "return" on training investment is thus nearly ten times greater in the civilian economy than in the military.

A third and equally important set of considerations influencing military training programs relates to the mental aptitudes and educational level of the trainees. In civilian life, hiring standards are governed by job requirements and by practical labor market considerations. In the case of the Armed Services, however, public policy has dictated that broad considerations of equity also be recognized in establishing standards of selection for military service. Thus, in order to assure that the obligation of military service be shared as widely as possible, the Congress in 1951 set the minimum mental standard for induction at roughly the equivalent of a fourth-grade level of educational attainment. It was recognized at the time as undesirably low since it required acceptance of many individuals in the lowest acceptable mental category (Group IV) with little or no capability for specialized training.

The problem of low mental standards of acceptability was intensified by the cutbacks of total military strength following the end of Korean hostilities, and by the relatively high replacement needs of the Services for personnel with aptitudes for specialized training. Faced with a growing "qualitative gap" between job requirements and quality of personnel, the Department of Defense, beginning in 1955, authorized higher standards of acceptability for regular enlistees and encouraged large-scale programs for screening out personnel with limited training potential. In addition, under an amendment to the draft law enacted in 1958, mental standards for inductees were also raised by a requirement that registrants in Mental Group IV attain passing scores in a supplementary aptitude test battery before being accepted for induction.

A trend towards increased selectivity is evident in the altered distribution of new enlisted personnel by Mental Group since 1954. There was a sharp reduction in the acceptance of men in Mental Group IV, from 29 percent to 12 percent, and an increased concentration in Mental Group

III (or "average" category) from nearly 37 percent to 47 percent.

A similar improvement is indicated by trends in the over-all educational level of the enlisted force. In the Army, the percentage of enlisted men who were high-school graduates rose from 48 percent in December, 1952, to 61 percent in December, 1958. In the Air Force, the increase over the same period was from 64 percent to 75 percent. Comparable data are not at present available for the Navy or Marine Corps, but the trend has undoubtedly been in the same direction.

Although much of this increase in educational level was due to higher mental standards of selection and retention, the wide range of voluntary off-duty education programs for servicemen, supported by the Department of Defense, con-tributed to these gains. These include an extensive cor-respondence course program offered through the U.S. Armed Forces Institute, a Resident Center Program providing for college-level classroom courses at military posts or in nearby institutions, and Group Study Programs designed to fill a need for classroom education at sea or in areas where regular college facilities are not available. A total of about 240,000 servicemen were enrolled in these three programs in 1959.

Despite the very substantial improvement, it would be un-realistic to infer that the quality and educational level of personnel recently entering Service has reached an optimum level. The percentage of recruits who have enlisted before completing high school is still undesirably large. Moreover, the fact that the Services draw personnel from all sections of the nation, with widely divergent educational systems and standards, compels them to gear their training programs to a relative low "common denominator," which is probably much too elementary for some, while difficult for others.

Military Skill Training Programs

Faced with steady expansion of technical military skills and with high rates of personnel turnover, the Armed Services have in recent years been compelled to devote a sizable portion of their resources to in-service training programs. The task of transforming new recruits into seasoned fighting men and technicians has, in fact, become one of the primary peacetime missions of the military establishment.

Until recent decades, the limited needs of the Armed Services for trained specialists, which were not filled by direct recruitment of skilled workers from civilian life, were mainly met through informal on-the-job or apprentice-type training in military units. These gradual apprenticeship methods proved wholly inadequate, by themselves, to meet the urgent and more exacting skill requirements of our modern mechanized forces, particularly under mobilization conditions. Experience in World War I and World War II demonstrated the need for large-scale formal training programs to provide more intensive skill training to new recruits. An extensive network of Service schools was established which, in combination with supplementary civilian facilities, was equipped to train personnel in the full range of military specialties. These Service schools now constitute the primary vehicle for initial skill training in the Armed Services, particularly in the more technical skills.

Some indication of the size of the formal school training program of the Armed Services in recent years is provided by a special Department of Defense study made in 1956.[3] During the three-year period of Korean hostilities, a total of nearly 1.3 million servicemen, or more than 400,000 per year, received training in civilian-type specialties. This total, moreover, excludes combat training in purely military-type skills, flying training, professional training of officers, correspondence courses, and numerous short courses conducted at Navy bases or in informal troop schools. In 1955, the last year for which comparable data are available, the total number of trainees was 430,000. Since 1955 there has been some reduction in the absolute number of trainees due to reduced personnel intake, but the percentage of new personnel receiving initial school training has tended to increase, as a result of the need to assign an increasing proportion of new personnel to the expanding technical skill fields.

Despite the magnitude of these formal school programs, on-the-job training has continued to play an essential role in the overall process of military skill development. As in the civilian economy, many skilled military crafts can only be effectively acquired on-the-job, under actual operating conditions. This is true, for example, of the Navy deck ratings, such as Boatswain's Mates and Quartermaster's Mates, where shipboard apprenticeship is still considered the only method of acquiring the needed experience and "know-how."

For the more technical maintenance skills, many practical

[3] From report by the President's Commission on Veterans' Pensions, *Veterans in Our Society*, June 1956, House Com. Print No. 261, 84th Cong., 2d Sess., p. 47.

considerations also militate against attempting to develop a full-fledged journeyman or technician in the formal school system: the great diversity in types of equipment and in actual operating situations; the need to rotate and reassign personnel at periodical intervals; and in particular the short period of effective service available from most recruits. As a result, most entry-level training courses have as their objective the development of personnel qualified at an apprentice or junior level of skill, and rely on job training to develop the more specific skills needed to fully qualify at the journeyman level. In addition, advanced training is offered in Service schools, in civilian institutions, and through correspondence courses, designed to provide specialized training in new equipment or procedures and a broader technical foundation in various skills. These advanced courses have increased in relative importance in recent years, with the gradual growth in the number of career personnel, but still account for a modest share of the overall school training program.

As shown in Table IV, the proportion of enlisted personnel initially trained in Service schools, rather than in units, and the average length of the training courses, tend to vary directly with the technicality of the skill. In highly technical specialties, such as electronics maintenance, virtually all personnel are sent initially to school for courses averaging about one-half year in length. In contrast, less than half of the personnel assigned to clerical, crafts, or Services occupations received initial school training, in courses averaging between two and four months in length.

These occupational differences in training methods are

TABLE IV. *Percentage of Enlisted Personnel Initially Trained in Service Schools and Average Length of Training Courses by Major Occupational Group, 1956*

Occupational Group	Percent Trained	Average Length of Course (weeks)
Electronics	86	21
Electronics maintenance	98	28
Electronics Equipment operation	78	25
Other technical	73	15
Mechanics and repairmen	74	15
Administrative and clerical	47	10
Crafts	42	15
Services	40	9

broadly paralleled in the civilian economy. In general, formal training courses are also a major source of initial training of civilians, in the case of the newer technician skills, which require more theoretical background and an understanding of complex equipment. Formal training has continued to be relatively unimportant, however, in the more traditional skilled crafts, where apprenticeship or informal on-the-job training methods predominate.

In other respects, however, the content and methods of military training programs have differed substantially from their civilian counterparts. The short period of effective military service available from most recruits has imposed practical upper limits on the length of entry-level skill training. The tendency has, therefore, been to curtail or eliminate theoretical course content and to concentrate on the more immediate and practical elements of a relatively narrow job specialty.

As a result, the scope of most military courses in mechanical or technician skills is necessarily much more restricted than courses offered in technical institutes or similar civilian schools. For example, a typical civilian institute course in aircraft maintenance lasts for two full years. The graduate of such a course is considered qualified to perform all levels of maintenance on a variety of aircraft types with little or no technical supervision. A typical Air Force counterpart, the Apprentice Aircraft Mechanic Course on reciprocating engine aircraft, lasts only eighteen weeks. However, this course qualifies a graduate only to perform the more routine types of maintenance work under the direct supervision of a skilled mechanic, generally on a specific type of aircraft. An additional period of on-the-job experience of one year or more may be required before the apprentice Air Force mechanic can qualify as a "journeyman" in his more restricted specialty. Beyond that, broader training in advanced technical courses will be available to him if he chooses to reenlist and make the Air Force a career.

Similar contrasts may readily be drawn between Service school training in skilled crafts and civilian apprenticeship programs. For example, the Air Force offers a basic electrician's course of fourteen weeks duration, designed to train airmen in fundamentals of electricity and in techniques of electrical installation and maintenance. This training may be comparable to a high-school level vocational course but scarcely to a four-year civilian apprenticeship.

The very necessity to develop competent mechanics and

other skilled workers in short time periods has caused the military services to pioneer in a wide range of advanced skill training techniques. These have included use of training films, simulators, and many other types of training aids, and more recently extensive use of classroom television. One measure of the contribution of the Armed Services towards advancement of skill training methods is provided by the fact that, in 1957, over 1,000 training publications used in the Department of Defense were made available for inclusion in Training Materials Centers established by the Department of Labor, as part of that Department's program to strengthen the skills of the nation's work force.

Vocational Implications of Military Skill Training

From the foregoing summary, it is apparent that military skill training programs are geared, necessarily, to meet a special pattern of military job requirements. From the standpoint of the Military Services, the "return" on their training investment must be gauged by the extent to which this training contributes to the overall combat readiness of the Armed Services. One measure of this "return" is the fact that the Active military forces, at the end of the decade, included more than one million fully trained career enlisted men and officers, or about twice the number at the beginning of the decade. Another measure is the increase in the strength of the Reserve Forces, not on active duty, from a total of 2.6 million in June, 1950, consisting mainly of World War II veterans, to 4.4 million in June, 1959, including a much larger proportion of recent separatees from Service.

At the same time, the Armed Services have clearly made a substantial contribution to the vocational equipment of American youth and to the sum total of skills of the nation's civilian work force. Between July, 1950, and July, 1959, a total of over 6 million servicemen returned to civilian life after completing periods of military training and service. And, as we have seen, the great majority of these personnel received training in skills which have their counterpart in the civilian economy.

We have, unfortunately, only limited evidence as to the extent to which this military skill training has been directly used in later civilian employment. From earlier experience, we know that pilots trained in the Armed Forces during or after World War I served as the prime source of airline pilots in the expanding aviation industry. Similarly, a Bureau of Labor Statistics study conducted in 1952 revealed that 34 percent of all electronics technicians employed in the civilian economy, had been trained—in whole or in part—in Armed Forces technical schools, mainly during World War II.[4] (This, however, probably represented less than one-tenth of the total number of military personnel trained in electronics maintenance during the war.)

A more recent study, conducted for the Air Force in 1955, provides more specific information on the post-Service work experience of a sample of 5,000 airmen who had originally enlisted in 1950 and separated from the Air Force in 1954. The survey was confined to personnel in seven Air Force

[4] U.S. Bureau of Labor Statistics, *The Mobility of Electronic Technicians*, 1940–52, Bulletin No. 1150, p. 46.

career fields, ranging from highly technical skills, such as radio and radar maintenance, to nontechnical fields, such as supply and food service. On the basis of information obtained mainly from field interviews, the airmen were classified as to the relationship between their Air Force specialty and current occupation.

Some 17 percent in all seven fields had succeeded in getting a job considered to be related to their Air Force experience. The percentages varied widely among career fields, from 36 percent for radio and radar maintenance to only 4 percent in communications and 2 percent in air traffic control and warning. The low percentages in the latter skills are explained in large part by the limited availability of jobs such as air traffic control or radio operators in the civilian economy. The study also indicated a limited interest on the part of many youth in continuing in their military skills as a lifelong career. For example, two-thirds of those employed in food service jobs in the service did not attempt to get similar work in civilian life.[5]

The comparatively high percentage of former Air Force maintenance technicians who were reported working in related jobs in civilian life tended to confirm the observations of many military personnel officials that competition from civilian industry was a major factor in their high technician loss rates. These percentages, however, require some qualification. It is apparent from the survey report that a rather broad interpretation was placed on relationship between mili-

[5] Robert L. Thorndike and Elizabeth P. Hagen, *Attitudes, Educational Programs, and Job Experiences of Airmen Who Did Not Reenlist* (Air Force Personnel Training and Research Center, June, 1957).

tary and civilian jobs. For example, Air Force personnel trained in military electronic equipment maintenance (radio, radar, fire control equipment) were classified as working in the "same" or "closely related" jobs if they were subsequently engaged in a wide range of electrical repair jobs. In a much more restricted sense, the report notes that "a qualitative examination of the records does not indicate that many of these men are working in a civilian capacity on Air Force equipment supplied to the Air Force by civilian contractors. The men have scattered widely into a large number of companies and jobs, and are using their Air Force experience in many ways and in many settings." [6]

Despite the limitations in scope and timing of the statistics cited above, certain generalizations are indicated.

First, it is clear that a major contribution has been made by the Armed Services towards the training of men in electronics and in those other mechanical and technical skills which are most closely allied to the new military technology. It is probable, too, that many personnel trained in other older military skills which have civilian counterparts have also applied their training successfully in civilian life; however, statistical evidence on this score is lacking. In any event, they have accounted for a relatively smaller share of the trained labor force.

Secondly, there are broad contrasts between the military and civilian skill structures which militate against the ready transferability of skills. Many military skills, such as Army infantry or artillery crews, or Navy sonar operators, have no

[6] Thorndike and Hagen, *Attitudes, Programs, Experiences of Airmen*, p. 56.

civilian counterpart. Others, such as aircraft mechanics and electronics maintenance technicians, are required in much higher proportions in the Services than in the civilian economy. However, a rapidly expanding demand in some fields— such as electronics—may partly offset the disparity in total employment. In contrast, the Armed Services do not have occupational specialties directly comparable to those of farmers, sales workers, or manufacturing operatives.

Finally, the jobs to which men have been assigned in military service do not necessarily correspond to the occupations which they may wish to follow as life-long careers. This was particularly true during periods of large-scale mobilization and to a more limited degree during the Korean conflict, when many mature men, with established civilian work careers, were brought into military service. In more recent years, the increased reliance on voluntary recruitment, and the opportunities available to qualified enlistees to choose their occupational field and type of training, have made it possible for the Services to more closely match the individual's interests and special capabilities with his military job assignment. In fact, the opportunities available in military service to obtain this specialized training for possible later use in civilian life have been an increasingly important inducement for enlistment into military service.

As in the case of the young civilian worker, however, there is a "trial and error" process associated with occupational choice. The very process of training and working in a particular skill while in military service probably has influenced many young men to transfer into other lines of work after leaving military service. In fact, one of the more obvious reasons for failure to reenlist has been a desire to shift to a different occupation in civilian life.

On balance, we believe it reasonable to conclude that military skill training has made a direct and important contribution to the occupational skills of a significant minority of the youth who have returned to civilian life. It has been a major source of trained personnel in selected industries and occupations closely allied with military technology. In the case of many other youth, training in military skills has probably contributed more generally to their total knowledge and capabilities—including their hobbies and "do-it-yourself" activities—but has not found a direct and closely identifiable application in their civilian employment.

RELIGION AND YOUTH

by BENSON Y. LANDIS

CHILDREN AND YOUTH today live in a society in which there is considerable ferment regarding religion. The discussions are widespread both within and outside of religious circles. There are frequent references to large sums being expended for construction of new buildings for religious purposes, including the religious education of children and youth. The U.S. Department of Commerce estimates that these expenditures by religious bodies of all faiths were $863,-000,000 in 1958, $474,000,000 in 1953, $251,000,000 in 1948, and, omitting the war years when construction was restricted by regulation, $51,000,000 in 1938. Membership of some 250 religious bodies, reported by the official statisticians of all faiths, was, in round figures, 109,500,000 persons in 1958, 94,850,000 in 1953, 79,400,000 in 1948, 68,500,000 in 1940. Since 1940 the membership officially reported has increased much more rapidly than population. Books by religious leaders are found often on best-seller lists, and the sales of one

Benson Y. Landis is Editor, Research Publications, Bureau of Research and Survey, National Council of Churches of Christ in the U. S. A.

edition of the Bible since 1950 have made high records in the history of religious publishing.

However, there appears to be more enthusiasm over these figures from journalists than from professional churchmen or social scientists. The religious bodies do not record or report attendance at their services; they do not know what proportion of their members contribute money year by year; they do not generally state other evidence of the involvement of their members. While contributions to churches advance, so does the national income. Organized religion, so far as is now known, receives regularly one half of all sums given to philanthropy each year; and this amount is apparently steadily at about 1 percent of the disposable income of the people. If there has been a revival of religion, as some allege, there appears to be no increase in generosity of support of religion.

Among both religious leaders and social scientists one notes sharply diverse opinions concerning the recent developments in organized religion. One of the nation's noted theologians says that the United States is now both the most secular and the most religious nation. It is most secular, he writes, in the sense that people's important decisions frequently seem to be made without the guidance of the teachings of the historic religious; it is the most religious, he contends, because there is evidence of wide participation of lay people in the affairs of the religious organizations. An experienced clergyman says that official reports of church statistics convey impressions at variance with the experience of himself and of his colleagues while working among people.

In a prominent pulpit a clergyman who does much personal counseling preaches a sermon on religious revival and moral decline.

Members of religious bodies are largely "religious illiterates," says a religious educator at a seminar of specialists, and no one dissents. A well-known sociologist, studying democratic institutions, publishes an article entitled, "What Religious Revival?," and states that his weighing of evidence leads him to the conclusion that in the United States no fundamental long-time changes in religious interest or activity have occurred.

The dual role of religion in society is often described by the students of society. Religion makes for establishment of close ties between human beings—it is also a force making for division. Religion makes for the integration of the human personality, it is often testified; religious differences have also been cited as responsible for some of the bitterest antagonisms. There are undoubtedly universal elements in the teachings of the great religions; there are also emphases on uniqueness or distinctiveness that result in the separation of religious group from religious group. In our own communities we may see or hear about efforts for cooperation under religious auspices; we may also note the opposite. And religious differences, in our complex society, are observed to be "compounded" with other differences, such as those over power, economic position, social policies, or aims of education. Joseph Fichter, in *Sociology*,[1] says that in the United States

---

[1] Joseph H. Fichter, *Sociology* (Chicago: University of Chicago Press, 1957).

religious affiliation "conserves social status for the individual."

The foregoing is only a short reference to the current debate concerning religion in the United States. It is meant as a setting for the consideration of information on religion and youth that follows. This chapter will briefly interpret a variety of studies in the following fields, which obviously overlap to some extent: 1) The general experience of childhood and youth with respect to religion; 2) Participation of youth in the institutions of religion, particularly in the organizations for religious education, such as Sunday or Sabbath schools, day schools in which religion is taught, etc.; 3) Expressions by youth concerning standards commonly called religious, and opinions relating to religion; 4) Social conditions that affect the participation or functioning of youth in religious organizations.

Childhood and Adolescent Experiences

Young children form their ideas regarding religion with frail capacity and slight experience, and they gradually approximate the concepts of their elders, Allport writes in *The Individual and His Religion*.[2] Childhood experience, he says, is marked by fantasies and egocentrism. Inquiries are frequently put by small children to others. The children not only ask many questions in the realm of religion, even of theology, but they also expect prompt and precise answers. The child takes the religious practices that he sees about him for granted. Learning about religion is a "very subtle process,"

[2] Gordon W. Allport, *The Individual and His Religion* (New York: Macmillan, 1950).

however. Many children are disappointed with their early
experience. Some drop references to religion at an early age,
in part because they seem to find it of no immediate or practical aid.

More critical experiences with religion come during adolescence. Now the young person has more firsthand experience
with the institutions of religion, assumes a more independent
attitude, and often rebels against it. There is testimony that
about two-thirds of adolescents assume some definite negative attitudes toward parental teachings of all kinds, including religion. Thus youth often change their earlier attitudes
toward religion. Although the general tendency is for youth
to enter the religious body of parents, there is some shifting
of religious affiliation away from that of parents. Often,
whether the young person shifts formal religion or not, doubts
appear and are taken seriously, and he may drift into indifferent or opportunistic attitudes regarding the problems and
issues of life. Opinions are frequently expressed to the effect
that "modern youth" particularly have assumed these attitudes.

The days of adolescence are "days of decision," many researchers generalize. It is also called the "age of religious
awakening" by Argyle in *Religious Behavior*.[3] This awakening, when it occurs, may be gradual or sudden. The sudden
awakening or reconstruction of experience is often labeled
"conversion." The frequency of conversion in our day, compared with earlier eras, cannot be definitely stated; frequency
undoubtedly varies by regions and by cultural experience,

[3] Michael Argyle, *Religious Behavior* (Glencoe, Ill.: Free Press, 1959).

and by the practices of religious bodies. Apparently conversions frequently take place at about age sixteen, possibly at fifteen for girls.

When young people try to tell about their own religious experience during adolescence the writing becomes very varied, Professor Allport says. In this connection one must note that religious opinions are strongly influenced by other opinions, for example, artistic sentiments. Studies consulted seem to indicate that, of youth who profess to adhere to religious values, about 70 percent state that their awakening in adolescence was gradual, while the others went through marked crises or reported unusual emotional stimulation. But not all the decisions are in favor of religion; an unknown proportion of youth also make definite decisions away from adherence to the faith of their fathers or from that of their early childhood.

Participation

The extensive statistics officially reported reveal relatively wide participation by youth compared with ten or fifteen years ago. Children—including infants—and youth are on many rolls of church members, but there is no precise reporting of age groups by the religious bodies. Some crude estimates indicate that at least 20 percent of the 109,500,000 members of religious bodies may be under thirteen years of age. In the bodies that do not include children as members the practice is to admit persons at about age thirteen. Hence children and youth are often listed in the churches as full members. These national reports, however, say nothing about the quality or extent of involvement. It is probable that many youth contacts with institutions of religion—like those of adults—are altogether superficial.

The Protestant Sunday Schools report over 90 percent of all Sunday or Sabbath School enrollment in the country. Over 200 Protestant bodies reported 37,861,531 pupils in 1958, compared with 24,609,808 in 1945 (there was no enumeration in 1948). An analysis by age groups in 1957 revealed that only about 65 percent of the pupils were less than twenty-four years of age. The Protestant churches also reported 4,794 elementary and secondary *day schools* with a total enrollment of 358,739 pupils in 1958. About 80 percent of the enrollment—281,897—was in elementary schools, compared with 187,000 pupils in 3,000 elementary schools in 1952. There was no earlier enumeration of Protestant secondary schools. These reports appear in the annual *Yearbook of American Churches*.

According to the *Official Catholic Directory* there were 3,933,167 elementary school pupils in the Roman Catholic parochial day schools in 1958, and 783,155 pupils in secondary Catholic day schools, a total of 4,716,322 persons. By contrast, in 1948 there were 2,289,420 elementary day school pupils, and 506,397 in secondary schools, a total of 2,795,817. The Roman Catholic enrollment in the day schools in 1958 was equal to about 12 percent of total elementary and secondary school enrollment (public and private). Roman Catholic parishes are also required to give religious instruction to children in the public (tax-supported) schools. According to the *Directory* quoted there was 2,725,582 pupils in 1958, and 2,452,595 in 1948.

The "first national study of Jewish education in the United States," concentrating on elementary education, revealed 553,600 pupils aged five through seventeen in the Jewish schools of all types, and it was estimated that about 80 percent of all Jewish children receive "some Jewish schooling at some time during school age." In weekday afternoon schools were reported 47.1 percent of the total enrollment; in one-day schools in session either Saturdays or Sundays, 45.1 percent; and in day schools, 7.8 percent. Of all persons enrolled, 88.5 percent were in congregational schools, compared with 82.7 percent in 1948. A majority of pupils attend Jewish schools for three or four years. A majority of Jewish high-school youth do not receive religious education, it was stated in the report, *Jewish Education in The United States.*[4] According to the *American Jewish Yearbook* (1950) there were 258,052 pupils in schools in session either Saturdays or Sundays; rapid development during and after World War II was reported in that book.

The literature of specialists studying Protestant and Jewish education particularly reveals wide variance in stated goals, even within the same denomination, and varying emphases on method. Probably there would be wide agreement with a generalization by an educator that much religious education is "like a shallow river, 'a mile wide and an inch deep.'"

[4] Alexander M. Dushkin and Uriah Z. Engelman, *Jewish Education* (New York: American Association for Jewish Education, 1959).

In a national sample of 1,925 adolescent girls in grades six to twelve, in a study made for the Girl Scouts, 52 percent reported that they belonged to "some church group." [5] Of girls over sixteen, 55 percent belonged to a church group, of those aged eleven and under, only 24 percent belonged to some church group or club.

Standards and Opinions

When youth are queried about religion they generally state their adherence to the traditional religious teachings in our society, but at the same time many who profess adherence are not actively expressing their religious convictions and a considerable proportion of these reveal themselves confused concerning the place of religion both in their own lives and in the communities in which they live. In this section "summaries of summaries" of various studies will be given.

Of a sample of 10,000 teen-agers in metropolitan Chicago it is reported that the majority professed adherence to the historic faiths. Those queried were a broad sample of the teen-agers of the metropolitan area, and thus included persons from every major religious group and persons with no affiliation. About one-third, however, felt confused in their religious beliefs. One-third agreed with the following statement: "Men working and thinking together can build a good society without any divine or supernatural help"; one-third were undecided; one-third disagreed. Seventy-three percent did not agree with this statement: "The more I learn about

[5] Survey Research Center, Institute for Social and Religious Research, *Adolescent Girls* (Ann Arbor, Mich.: University of Michigan, 1956).

science, the more I doubt my religious beliefs." Seventy-one percent said they would like to have more information about religion than they had. About 41 percent said they were still searching for beliefs that would "make sense to them." [6]

In "Elmtown," a Midwestern corn belt community, 735 adolescent boys and girls were reported by A. B. Hollingshead as usually accepting the religion of their parents.[7] Formal religious training begins in the Sunday school. However, only one-half of the high-school students actually participated in religious activities. To 90 percent of the boys and to 80 percent of the girls religion did not have a "compulsive quality." To these youth religion did not appear to have specific content or meaning. Adolescents were interested in their church groups or classes more for social than for religious purposes. Ministers were concerned about the "loss" of young people from church life. There were also open conflicts between the recreational practices of young people and the standards of some clergymen. Adolescents hid many of their activities from their parents, teachers, and clergymen.

When 2 percent of the homes in Kalamazoo, Mich. were visited by volunteer interviewers, it was found that over half the parents were members of various religious bodies, and about one-third of the total number of families reported that they had special problems with religious activities for their children and themselves during the summer. Low-income people reported the most problems. Church-goers had prob-

[6] Y.M.C.A. of Metropolitan Chicago, *The Youth of Chicagoland: A Study of Its Attitudes, Beliefs, Ideas, and Problems* (1958). Mimeographed.

[7] A. B. Hollingshead, *Elmtown's Youth* (New York: Wiley, 1949).

lems just as often as nonchurch goers, and the number who felt a need for guidance was not significantly lower among church affiliated families. The interviewers suggested that summer is becoming "increasingly a period of total family activity." People of all faiths and none were questioned.[8]

More than 1,000 boys and girls in junior and senior high schools in Oklahoma, when asked to state their "areas of concern and problems," rated "religious problems" below several others. Fifty-five percent of senior high-school youth interviewed attended church and 55 percent attended Sunday School. Those making the study reported that little interest was shown by youth in understanding democracy.[9]

The ability of 915 Roman Catholic girls in eleventh grade to apply the principles of the moral law to actual and hypothetical life situations was studied by Carmen V. Diaz.[10] Five hundred of the girls were in diocesan high schools and the remainder were in the public schools of New York and New Jersey. All the girls received religious training. Those in diocesan high schools received the regular instruction given there and those in public schools attended the instruction given in parishes for Catholics in public schools. Various tests were given. In general, it was concluded that

[8] Lauris Whitman, Helen F. Spaulding, and Alice Dimock, *A Study of the Summertime Activities of Children in Relation to the Summer Program of the Churches* (New York: National Council of Churches, 1959). Mimeographed.
[9] Lloyd Estes et al., *Teen-Age Frontiers Survey*, 1953. Unpublished. Summarized in Richard E. Hamlin, *Hi-Y Today* (New York: Association Press, 1955).
[10] Carmen V. Diaz, *A Study of the Ability of 11th Grade Girls to Apply the Principles of the Moral Law to Actual and Hypothetical Life Situations* (New York: Fordham University, 1952). Dissertation.

Catholic girls in eleventh grade possessed the ability to apply the principles of the moral law as taught by that church. However, no significant difference was found between the scores of those girls who had eleven years of religious training and those who had three to six years of training.

"Religion is at the center of the total function of the Roman Catholic parochial school," Joseph Fichter writes after a team of researchers studied St. Luke's elementary school in a Midwestern city. Many aspects of the life of the school and of the attitudes of the 632 pupils are interpreted, and some comparisons are made with 180 Catholic pupils in a public school. "The religious practices and groups of St. Luke's school are interwoven with the whole educational program. They are themselves educational since they are designed to assist in the promotion of the 'different kind' of education that parochial school children obtain. It would be unthinkable to the teaching staff of the school to separate religion from education, or to suggest either that religion interferes with the school or that the school interferes with religion." The public school pupils attended the weekly classes in religion provided by the parish for children not in the parochial school.

Catholic children in parochial and in public schools were found to have "quite similar" tastes and preferences. They nominated the "same great historical persons in the same order." There appeared to be "little difference between parochial and public school children" in standards of conduct as measured by a personality test that did not include reference to religious convictions or supernatural motivation, "the

area in which the parochial school pupils are at their best."
The Catholic children in both schools "accept and demonstrate, in about the same proportions, the virtues of honesty,
obedience, gratitude, self-control, and kindliness."

"The greatest difference between the two schools is the
fact that parochial school children explain their attitudes
most often with religious and supernatural reasons." Another
difference was that parochial school children expressed more
favorable opinions toward labor unions and the foreign aid
program of the United States. Parochial school children in
the community studied appeared to receive a broader social
education than the Catholic children in public school.

The parochial school is described as "the largest single
focus for cooperation" among the church members, and as
an "example of successful voluntary association." [11]

Polls of 11,000 children of elementary school grades receiving instruction in Jewish schools, recorded by Dushkin
and Engelman revealed the following results: 6 out of 10
of the children reported that they "liked their Jewish school
and would go if given free choice." Nine out of 10 children
"accept Jewish education as natural and desirable in the
American environment where, they say, all children should
receive some form of religious education." However, a poll
of 1,560 adult Jewish community leaders revealed that 75
percent were opposed to the full-time Jewish day school,
which enrolls only 7.8 percent of all Jewish pupils receiving
religious instruction.

[11] Joseph H. Fichter, *Parochial School* (Notre Dame, Ind.: University
of Notre Dame Press, 1958).

Protestant youth who are in senior high school and in older age brackets, and who are also in church youth organizations, rate their churches favorably but say that they have in their churches few opportunities to put into action the convictions and attitudes that they had acquired through religious activities. A broad sample of 1,667 youth in 188 local churches was studied by Helen F. Spaulding and Olga Haley.[12] Relatively few reported opportunities for meeting or working with youth of denominations other than their own. In general they thought that adults in the churches wanted youth to participate and valued the opinions of youth in the program of the local churches. The youth asked for adult leaders with more training than those they had. In many churches the youth program was reported to be "very limited."

The relation of youth's personal adjustment problems to ten teachings of the church of the Brethren, a Protestant denomination, were considered by A. Stauffer Curry.[13] He secured information from 505 Brethren youth and 388 in interchurch Protestant groups, all being fifteen to twenty-four years of age. The Church of the Brethren teaches its youth not to smoke, not to go to the movies, not to dance. The study indicated that 57 percent of the Brethren youth indicated that they had "problems" engendered by the church teaching against participation in dancing, 29 percent in con-

[12] Helen F. Spaulding and Olga Haley, A Study of Youth Work in Protestant Churches (New York: National Council of Churches, 1955). Mimeographed.

[13] A. Stauffer Curry, But To Understand: An Analysis of Youth's Personal Problems As They Relate to 10 Social Practices (Elgin, Ill.: Brethren Publishing House, 1953).

200 BENSON Y. LANDIS

nection with attending movies, and 18 percent with smoking. In most instances lower proportions of interchurch groups reported such problems.

"While young people in the Y.M.C.A. accept (or rather assent to) traditional religious beliefs, these beliefs exist on the whole as part of a vague set of ideas which are not incorporated into the lives of the large majority of young people. Few young people take these beliefs seriously enough so as to use them as the main directive for their lives. The major interest of youth seems to be focused on carving out a little area of life in which there is security for themselves and their families. Deep concern for the welfare of others and desire to participate vigorously in community development is shown only by a small minority." With these words Murray G. Ross sums up studies of 1,935 youth, constituents of city Y.M.C.A.s throughout the country,[14] of whom 80 percent were male and 50 percent had been to college. All were in the eighteen to twenty-nine year age group; 34 percent were Roman Catholics, 59.1 percent, Protestant, 3.5 percent, Jewish, and the remaining unclassified.

A marked increase in professed commitment to religious values is reported after comparing tests of groups of college students at Ohio State University over three decades, 1929 to 1958.[15] In 1958 there was much more severe moral judgment about the statement, "disbelieving in God," than in

[14] Murray G. Ross, *Religious Beliefs of Youth* (New York: Association Press, 1950).
[15] Solomon Rettig and Benjamin Pasamanick, "Changes in Moral Values Over Three Decades," *Social Problems*, VI (Spring, 1959).

1929, but only slightly more than in 1939 and 1949. The same tendency is noted in severe moral judgment about the statement, "not giving to support religion when able." Moral values do undergo change, the investigators conclude. In 1959 they report that there appears to be an increase in severity of moral standards in those matters "that may be associated with the sanctity of the individual life, and those that assure the basic democratic form of voting behavior."

"The Jewish [college] student sincerely believes that his home has been the major factor in influencing his Jewish attitudes." He thinks that Jewish students who participate in Jewish organizations "have been influenced in their Jewish thinking by such participation." "He does feel that his formal Jewish education has had much effect on him." "His college experience has weakened his religious interest." The student "grows more and more eager for social and cultural contact with the larger world, and seeks to broaden the local, narrow concerns of family and religion." Thus does Leon Feldman sum up for general readers many studies of the personal attitudes and values of Jewish college students.[16]

Some disaffection of college youth from formal religious life seems to occur in all faiths, Gordon W. Allport concludes. However, after years of rebellion against traditional forms many young people return to these same forms. But some of those returning show only vestiges of loyalty or main-

[16] Leon Feldman, "The Jewish College Student," *Jewish Spectator* (December, 1955). A more technical paper is his "The Personality of the Jewish College Student" presented before Yivo Social Science Circle, New York, June 6, 1956.

tain only nominal connections with religious organizations. He also records his opinion that college students are in the main ignorant of the writings of the great theologians and of those "brilliant minds" that have engaged in strenuous thinking as they have wrestled with the critical issues of life and "the attainment of religious maturity."

Social Conditions Affecting Participation

The functioning of youth in religious organizations is reported to be related to such factors as class, mobility, and the rise of the suburb.

Of Elmtown's youth, A. B. Hollingshead wrote: "Nonparticipation [in religious organizations] is very strongly associated with lower class, and participation with higher class position. The students who participate in religious organizations carry the class system into the church; consequently religious clubs are class biased." In Elmtown, 51 percent of the high-school students had no active connection with the town's religious bodies.

"The kind of religion to which one belongs both reflects the social status of the individual and contributes to his status," Joseph Fichter writes in Sociology. "The conservative and traditional churches which pursue their functions unobtrusively and do not put great demands upon their members are typical of high-status religions. They represent a kind of haven for the energetic and harassed American. They provide reassurance and comfort and satisfy the important American quest for security. It is as though everything else must change but these upper-class religions must remain stable. . . . Religion is the slowest-changing major institution in the American culture. The religious groups, especially those which have the highest aura of social prestige and respectability, tend to conform to, rather than to change, the secular milieu in which they exist."

The high mobility of Americans and the resulting "rootlessness" are often remarked. This mobility is of two kinds: horizontal or geographical, and vertical. The first type, involving frequent movement from community to community is thought by many to weaken the traditional family system, but the precise deleterious effects on the family, or youth specifically, are difficult to ascertain. Mobility, it is also stated, makes for affiliation with religious bodies—when people reach a new community they wish to have a few friends and one way to acquire them is to attend religious services.

Vertical mobility, movement up or down in the social scale, is also a marked characteristic in our modern life. This social mobility tends to disturb "family solidarity," Sidney Aronson writes.[17] Desire for success, according to American standards, is often cited as a force for changing social status. Change of social status makes for "social distance" between members of families. Mr. Aronson mentions a mother who said she felt comfortable only "in the home of the son who had not gone to college." Professor Fichter also considers the common desire for "upward social mobility." Our economy has offered varied opportunities to our people. Not only

[17] Sidney Aronson, *Religious Revival and Jewish Family Life* (New York: Synagogue Council of America, 1957). Mimeographed.

the immigrant but also the native American, he says, strives to "go as high as his competence will allow." He states that the opportunity for lay participation in religious institutions "also provides an avenue for upward social mobility." "A person may gain social recognition through these activities when he finds himself blocked and frustrated in the secular channels of mobility. Many of the functions thus performed are in essence secular but they are given an extra value in that they are being done 'for the church.'"

In the rapidly expanding suburbs many local religious organizations are growing rapidly and many new structures are being built; moreover, here is the focus of the interest of experienced churchmen who are concerned about the quality of local religious life. Speaking before the Synagogue Council of America, Rabbi Albert I. Gordon made generalizations about the suburbs which probably receive wide agreement from Jewish and other religious leaders.[18] Many activities are being carried on with the synagogue as the center. Great strides forward are being made in religious education. There are "superior" buildings for the teaching of religion to children. Women appear to have assumed new positions of leadership in families. But he says that evidence of commitment to the historic religion is such that "we are forced to admit the synagogue is far from witnessing a revival of religion." Writers belonging to other denominations mention many activities in suburban churches, strong local institu-

[18] Albert I. Gordon, *What Do We Know About American Jewish Life As It Affects the Jewish Religious Scene?* (New York: Synagogue Council of America, 1957). Mimeographed. See also this author's *Jews in Suburbia* (Boston: Beacon Press, 1959).

tions, much emphasis on buildings and organization, but little evidence of dedication to the historic standards of the religions.

There are "two worlds of church life in the United States," Glen W. Trimble writes; the metropolitan and the non-metropolitan.[19] A study of 114 religious bodies for 1953 reveals that 46 percent of the Protestants, 75 percent of the Roman Catholics, and 98 percent of the Jews, live in the standard metropolitan areas. In the metropolitan areas are 29 percent of the local Protestant churches and 50 percent of the local Roman Catholic churches. Protestant membership is highest, in relation to total population, in the South, and lowest in the Northeast, while the Roman Catholic situation is the reverse.

Summary

There is wide public discussion of religion, with sharply varying opinions among both laymen and social scientists with respect to the religious interest of people. The author agrees with the statement that probably no fundamental long-time changes have occurred. Religion is both a uniting and a divisive force in society.

Young children usually take for granted the religious practices they see around them and assume the beliefs of their elders. Adolescence is a time of awakening, of decision, and of significant rebellion against traditional religion. For many decades college experience has been resulting in weakening

[19] Glen W. Trimble, "Two Worlds of Church Life in the United States," Information Service, National Council of Churches, XXXVIII, No. 7. (March 28, 1959).

commitment to historic faiths in an undetermined proportion of students, but many of these later return to participation in religious organizations.

The numbers of pupils receiving religious education in the institutions of the three major faiths were much higher in 1958 than in 1948. Much of the education that goes on is superficial, however, and many contacts of children and youth with these schools are also superficial, according to the testimony presented here.

Most youth, when questioned or tested express accord with traditional beliefs or principles, but fewer of them participate in religious organizations and actively implement their ideals, according to reports here reviewed. One study of college students at a state university comparing present values with those of prior decades indicates that there is now more acceptance of religious values.

The functioning of youth in religious organizations is frequently along class lines. Much concern is stated by religious leaders about mobility, and "rootless" people. The growing suburbs are marked by many activities for all age groups in religious organizations, but experienced observers do not report a "revival" of commitment to historic religion there.

THE CHILD AS POTENTIAL

by GARDNER MURPHY
and LOIS BARCLAY MURPHY

THE CONCEPT of the child as potential is challenging—so challenging, indeed, that it is threatening, so limited are our resources to deal with the problem, potential for *what?* As a culture oriented toward universal education and the promotion of knowledge regarding health and growth, we have made progress in promoting the child's potential as a physical and intellectual being. In what terms are we to think ahead about the child's potential in a technological, atomic, space-expanding, and, from a military point of view, potentially explosive era?

Knowledge of nutrition, vitamins, and minerals, together with the achievements of miracle drugs, have saved lives of children, contributed to increased growth and physical strength in the last few generations. A parallel task for the next generations is that of making available resources to salvage and help to social usefulness thousands of children unnecessarily doomed by preventable retardation and emo-

Gardner Murphy is Director of Research and Lois Barclay Murphy is Research Psychologist at the Menninger Foundation, Topeka, Kansas.

tional disturbance. Many of these are highly sensitive children with potentials for a good life and important contributions. Today we have the paradox that expert knowledge has produced extraordinary results in salvaging the potentialities of *some* crippled, cerebral palsied, polio, and brain damaged children. But these technical resources are not yet available for all.

We are just beginning to learn that some psychogenically retarded, autistic and intellectually blocked children, can be helped to become the actively functioning sensitive people they are capable of being. We are learning that sensory deprivation in infancy, lack of adequate mothering, traumatic separation, or institutionalization can cripple the physical, mental, or emotional development of babies; but we have not yet achieved the professional resources or the institutional changes required to prevent such unnecessary losses. We need more research, concerning both prevention and therapy, on all groups of children whose development has been disturbed by inadequate nurturing, traumatic interruptions, or illnesses; we have much to learn about sensitivity and vulnerability and ways of strengthening and promoting growth in sensitive children. We are concerned, however, not only with the unusual child but with the everyday child whose individual pattern of weaknesses, strengths, talents, limitations, individual drives, and social belongingness requires equally skilled guidance and understanding.

Second, we may be concerned with his potential as a member of a community that may be very different from the one in which he is growing up. This includes his potential contribution to the solutions of the staggering problems which confront this rising generation, his potential as a clear, honest, courageous analyst of the issues which will confront him in domestic and international relations, and himself as a potential component and creative shaper of a democratic society gradually outgrowing injustices and self-contradictions and achieving a group life which is fulfilling to its members and capable of carrying itself forward through years of dynamic change.

Third, we are interested in his fulfillment as contributor to the destiny of American life—contributor in biological terms as parent, ultimately ancestor, with the personality riches of wide and freely emancipated potentialities which belong to each person, and free contributor toward the cultural trends which have long-range viability and promise in a maturing democratic society.

Who knows enough to tell how to realize such potentialities? The only realistic thing we can do is to suggest directions in which present research points, issues that cannot lightly be dismissed, areas in which one might look for more information, problems with which parents, educators, and community members must wrestle.

The Child Should Choose

Our first tentative reply is this: Since no one can tell us in full, let us begin by noting and studying what the child can tell us. Perhaps in many ways—through all his inarticulateness, his nonverbal communication, his gestures, tears, clenched fist, sleeplessness, or, on the other hand, radiant joy and deep relaxed absorption into himself—he can point the direction in which we might give him more of what he seems to need in order to grow in a balanced, resilient, creative way. The first answer then well might be: Let us give positive response to that which the child himself positively emphasizes. No answer is final: The child may in his anguish seem first of all to need self-justification or even revenge, a need which would be slight or nonexistent if somehow his life could be better structured. Our thesis is simply that it is better to let the child tell us what he positively craves; indeed, if we do not respond to his joys and resentments, if we do not take his feelings seriously, we have no full or clear picture. We must be alert to notice signs of his cravings for companionship, for social understanding, for skills, for an understanding of the physical world, the living world, the esthetic and scientific world, the social and personal world. If his mind is not free to reach out and immerse itself in the things which mean most to him, we are unlikely to be able to guide him well.

First of all, then, in answer to the question which of the child's potentials shall we accent at any given time, "Let the child choose." Let us learn from his choices where his interests and talents lie in terms of what he is ready for, can use for growth at a given time, what his pace, potential depth, and range are. He may need support and help in sustaining an interest, in developing the techniques he needs in order to carry it through. But if it is *his* interest, goal, longing, there will be an optimal chance for fullest growth of his potential capacity.

Many everyday questions may be involved here. Does the child need freedom or discipline? Since patently most children need some of both and, indeed, ask for both, and since the answer regarding the proportions and areas of each depends upon age level, temperament, previous development, and the subtleties of present-day personality interactions in family and community, we would say: Let the child, through his behavior, through his emotional responses, through his rigidities, apathies, gaiety, impulsive animal spirits, tension or relaxation, his tendency to function best in a given balance of external control and autonomy, tell us what doses of freedom and of discipline he may be able to use and where, and when.

Some children need more free time, free from adult coercion; some children need more supervision, guidance, and control. In both instances we would try to avoid the dangers of a casualness which seems to mean lack of interest and, on the other hand, the type of supervision which the child experiences as nagging and coercive. Again, there may be overstimulation and continuous pressure through excessive demands, or understimulation in which the child's struggle to take in the meaning of the world or to master it, his eagerness for contact with richer experience, is ignored to the point of "deprivation." The amount of freedom a child can use depends in part on his ability to grasp and to organize situations for himself; the amount of structure or formal organization he needs depends in part on the level of complexity, confusion, or tension which would exist without adult directives and the child's capacity to handle the complexity of confusion constructively. The work of Kurt Lewin and his associates showed that for many children both laissez-faire and autocratic methods produced tense, frustrated, hostile feelings, while democratic guidance produced the most co-operative attitudes and the best achievements. The degree of satisfaction, integration, and progress in achieving goals shown by the child will indicate whether the balance he has is good for him.

Differences in Potential

Again with reference to encouragement of and concentration upon the child's potential strengths rather than his weaknesses, experience with individual children's responses to adult ways of handling this problem can be profoundly helpful. When we speak of developing potentialities, we do not mean to advocate pushing individual talents to a degree that prevents healthy development of the whole personality. Many gifted people, like John Stuart Mill, Ruth Slenczynska, and Norbert Wiener, have regretted as adults the forced and excessively concentrated focus on specialized achievement which kept them from normal childhood, and either necessitated great adjustments as adults or impoverished their whole adult life. There has to be room for the growing period, with all its needs, for adequate opportunity for maturation and experience in each area of the personality, and for a chance to grow into the human family. The child may tell us that he needs music or science, or craftsmanship, as many a biography has made clear; but many a talented child also needs a range of social contacts and social acceptance, a range of normal experiences serving as context for the delight in a specialized gift.

Nor can we assume out of hand that every child has some one outstanding potential gift and proceed simply to emphasize that, or assume that all children have potentialities in every area. Some children show from early years a well-balanced capacity for growth at a healthy but moderate level, where other children show wide irregularities in development. With this second group there is always the question, how can the strengths of such children be developed without ignoring and therefore increasing their relative weaknesses? How can they be strengthened in the weak spots, without depriving the special abilities of a chance to mature?

These are not easy questions to answer. We cannot demand perfection, and may need to settle for compromises made with the best judgment available in reference to each particular child. The whole issue would be much less painful to children and ultimately to ourselves if we could modify our often bleak, rigid, mechanical concepts of normality (our concern with "the normal range") so that individuals would feel less self-conscious and embarrassed by relative weaknesses in one or more areas. Holding a child to high standards need not constrict his personality if the standards are within his reach—if his muscles, visual, and auditory equipment, maturity of differentiation, and capacity for integration are "ready" to meet the demands that are made. And the development of social strengths does not preclude full use of a child's talents, capacity for mastery, for creativity, for scientific achievement if the latter are not emphasized in an isolating way or conceived as special and differentiating the child from other children. We might, indeed, take a lesson from some other countries, such as India, where there seems to be more tolerance of individual variation, and where "norms" of development are certainly very much less coercive.

Such individual differences, together with the paucity of our knowledge, mean that some loss can be expected to accompany each gain. In some modern schools, where there is strong emphasis on intellectual curiosity, individuality in painting, storytelling, dramatic expression, and imagination in contriving and carrying out science experiments, the children do, indeed, appear to be more goal-minded and creative than children in group-oriented schools. But in some research studies these creative, goal-minded children appear to show considerable tension, and one could raise the question whether it is sound to put demands for originality on all of the children at seven or eight. At a period when children need to become aware of themselves, aware of the individualities of other children about them, aware of the nature of childish as contrasted with adult interests and modes of thought and feeling, some have a special need for fuller group participation. The development of potentials, then, means the study of the right time for different degrees of emphasis between individualized and socialized capacities in different children.

The question of providing for range as against narrow concentration is not simple. Hackneyed terms of this sort are misleading. There are children who need above all to discover their own potential in terms of depth, in terms perhaps of a single deep and overwhelming intellectual, esthetic, or social form of self-fulfillment, or the discovery of their powers. There can be danger in filling up such a child's life with a diversity of scheduled activities, with a succession of clubs, sports, and lessons to the point at which the child says, "The one thing that interests me now is just to paint and paint and paint." Or, as another child said, "There isn't any place for myself."

This does not mean that the child can always accurately assay the consequences of today's activity. His concentration on one activity may not be productive, but may be a substitute for other satisfactions he is afraid to pursue. He may drive himself beyond the safety point into hypertension and sleeplessness. He may fray the edge of his own margin to the point of exhaustion. This means only that we should try to receive *all* of the child's testimony and let it consolidate itself and become clear before we think of turning a deaf ear to it; that we always find eyes and ears for the testimony of the hidden potential as well as for the overt expression of the child who has learned so well what it is that we want to hear, what it is that meets the norms and requirements which in the long run are deemed appropriate for an age group or a community group. A flower or a tree cannot tell us articulately what it needs for growth, but can still tell us a great deal. We ask only that the child be watched as closely as a flower or a tree would be when new soils, new methods of handling are being considered. Indeed, the child would soon be telling us more articulately how we can help him to realize his potential and—what is often forgotten—how we can help organize or define the environment, the round of duties, the world of social give and take, so that it can be most fulfilling to him.

We can not only give him resoluteness in facing walls that are hard to scale; we may, when walls are being used only to butt his head against, find ways to help him get over or around the walls, or occasionally help him to blast through or rebuild the more fundamental architecture of his life. In the "inner-directed" world of David Riesman's pioneers, the aim was always to batter down the opposition. Today, along with such an emphasis, we realize that the demands of many a child's environment are sometimes too much for him, sometimes too little, and that hand-in-hand with the realization of inner potentials goes the rebuilding of the world in such a way that more children can more adequately realize what is inarticulate within them.

The Individual and the Group

This has been an "individual-centered" plea. Children's needs are complex and manifold. Children vary beyond all possibility of adequate description, and there is no likelihood that in our generation we shall know how to set free the potentials of each. The other chapters in this symposium will help us to grasp how scant our knowledge of genetics remains today and therefore how scant our understanding of the basic human biology of the growth potential; they will indicate how limited is our knowledge of the basic laws of social and cultural dynamics upon which individual fulfillment must depend. We must, however, do our best now as we shift to another primary emphasis of this brief discussion: Emphasis upon the reciprocity of individual and social world, shared feelings of belonging to family and group, the ways in which the individual can best be fulfilled by attending to a unit larger than the individual, namely, the parent-child or whole-family patterns and the family-family or community, national and international pattern upon which, in this inter-dependent world, each individual's fulfillment must necessarily depend.

It is not difficult to construct a bridge from our concern with individuality to our concern with group membership, for, as already hinted, many a child tells us that his greatest need, his greatest unfulfilled potential, lies in the area of "feelings of belonging." Just as he may want an opportunity to exercise free imagination with a chance for creative thought and experience, so he may want most of all the feeling of easy friendly interchange, the sense of knowing how to achieve normal acceptance. "Feelings of rejection" are very common not only among children brought to clinics for therapy but even in family circles in which it is taken for granted that "of course the child knows we love him"; and feelings of rejection in the elementary-school period and in adolescence are very widely reported in our culture, possibly intensified by conditions of individual competitiveness which have dominated the American cultural scene.

At any rate, to push the child into social interaction is a very different thing from studying his social hungers, the terms in which friendship and participation are possible for him, his troubles in achieving acceptance, his inability to accept the pushing which parents and teachers often regard as their duty. A social world dominated by technological progress runs the risk of losing the human insight and sensitivity needed to make social gains on this planet during the space age. The foundations for this sensitivity and insight have to be laid in the very beginnings of personality development through shared feeling and understanding—first between mother and small child, then through the whole family, and in school, and in the major settings of the child's life.

Margaret Fries' article on the relation between early personality development and the difficulty of international cooperation did not concern itself just with the occasional Hitler or McCarthy, but with the problem of hostility and aggression rooted in childhood, as it distorts or disturbs all levels of political action in adult life. Here we need to recognize individual differences in thresholds for frustration, in tendencies to respond to frustration by aggression, in tendencies to develop or to accumulate potentially explosive reservoirs of aggressive tensions, persistent overt or covert hostile attitudes, and differences in the ways in which the child's experiences channel these into constructive or destructive directions. Just as nuclear reactivity can be used to destroy civilization with hydrogen bombs or to provide new dimensions of constructive energy, so the energy generated in the interaction of personalities may destroy nations or lead to new levels of culture. We know that the will to attack can be directed against disease, slums, flood areas, or ignorance; it can save instead of destroying.

Some studies of children in contemporary families show that it is possible to keep warmth in family living, strong family loyalty, the father's sense of closeness to all the family, the mother's concern with each child's needs despite the pressures of modern technical and competitive patterns associated with high living standards, labor-saving devices, and community activities. There seems to be no doubt that the strong patterns of family life still evident in the United States, where family solidarity means at-homeness, an inner sense of "knowing who you are" and delight or pride in family membership, may often accomplish what cannot be accomplished by any amount of experience outside the family. It may be that the neighborhood and community experience can most effectively permit the extension of the first family experiences, the feeling of resonance to and capacity to identify with other human beings, and that the school years—if there is not too much moving from one neighborhood to another, with its often disturbing change of friendship patterns—gradually allow the first family warmth to suffuse other relationships.

There is a place for planned social experiences in the elementary-school years and in the high-school years. Such planning, however, is likely to be effective only in the context of the consolidation of the family experiences and community experiences which precede them, and only when care is taken not to demand the same vigorous pace, the same quick socialization and social reciprocity of all children without reference to backgrounds. Too much planned activity in an institutional setting may actually attenuate or jeopardize the family life which was and is still needed to feed the roots of warm relationships.

It has often been contended that commercial amusements may break up family living. It is equally true that shared commercial amusements may under certain conditions keep family members together, not only physically but personally. The important point is not what the leisure time activity is, but what it means to the child eager to share his interests and eager likewise to gain respect for those interests which may at the time transcend or overflow the group standard.

The Child and the Community

There is no "one-way street" for what the community can offer the child without reference to what the child can offer the community. Research has led us to see that the desire and the ability of the child to give is just as important as his ability to receive; that his generosities are far from artificial products of teaching or sheer desires to repay what has been received, to liquidate a debt or reduce a sense of guilt. The child may enjoy giving and sharing as intensely as he does anything in life. Family participation in community life can evoke this two-way sense and can make for joy in the child if he can contribute something to the joy of others. Informal opportunities to help other children or the more formal efforts through the teaching of geography and the social studies may help children to "feel with" the children of other communities or countries. It is not only at the time of a "drive," or Christmas gift campaign, or disaster relief or other community crises that we can accentuate the sense of being one with the group, being a contributing participant in its life as well as receiving from it.

In India and other developing countries children can sometimes participate in basic community tasks of construction and reconstruction—opportunities denied to children in our rich, advanced, country. Modern education seems at times to have forgotten the important distinction between individual mental hygiene and capacity for social participation. While it is assumed that the mastery of stress or the reduction of anxiety is a therapeutic problem independent of community organization, it is also sometimes assumed that socialization, in the sense of free interchange of ideas and feelings in the group, is an automatic guarantee against loneliness and insecurity. The problems are too intricate for such a summary. Children differ too much, communities differ too much, for such a cliché to be useful. We can, however, say that the problem of helping the child to give to the family, to the neighborhood, to the community, to the nation, and to the world, helping the child to find deep satisfaction in what he can contribute, is just as basic a need in this era as the need to free the individual from misunderstandings, rigidities, and tensions. There is just as great an unfulfilled potential in the matter of warm, generous membership in a community as there is in neglected science and art talents. There is as big a need to study, understand, and develop the child's potential for happy social living as there is a need for the child to develop and utilize special skills. Some children need a definite structure and organization to help consolidate feelings of belonging; letting such a child struggle by himself can reinforce his isolation. For others the structural requirements are slight, and the great need is simply to put no obstacles in their way. For all, however, humanness means basically a capacity for social relatedness in terms healthy for the individual child; a preoccupation with the individualistic can defeat the human potential just as fully as can the oversocialization which denies individuality its place.

The Child and the Future

Coming to our third and last major theme, the children of today as the progenitors of the people of future centuries, we can admit our ignorance of genetics and of cultural evolution and still see that the decisions we make in this era will start twigs bending in one direction rather than another, and that the personal mental health and well-being as well as the wise decisions of today's children will in considerable measure guide the generations and centuries which follow in achieving sounder and sounder decisions about human living. Decisions impetuously made today to correct or overcorrect the mistakes of yesterday are not necessarily the decisions which are the best guide to very long-range living in the culture which is to be. In the long, long range the answer is always to get more evidence through science and through exploration, through the arts and new modes of social living, rather than through dogmatic standardization.

The aim of discovering weaknesses and trying to correct them does not excuse us for neglecting the patient and steady emphasis on more research in human genetics and on cultural evolution.

Indeed, the more deeply one penetrates the mysteries surrounding the nuclear problems of the human potential, the more one realizes the urgency of the need for deeper, sounder, more extensive research, the tentativeness and downright error of the best that we can hope to do by way of advice, the need to listen to evidence from every quarter, and, above all, the need to listen to the child himself. We cannot afford to close our ears to any line of evidence as to the direction in which human nature is changing or can change. Human culture is enormously plastic and variable; so, too, is human biology. The social and biological changes effected in human nature through economic, political, military, and, today especially, scientific modes of thinking, cannot possibly be exaggerated. Hiroshima, polio, and concentration camp children have all taught us surprising things about childhood resilience and resourcefulness as well as childhood vulnerabilities, so have children of child-care programs in the Israeli Kibbutzim and in Soviet factory nurseries. Children of Japanese parents on the West Coast of the United States taught us new facts about growth. Anne Frank has given the post World War II generation a new concept of courage while the *Child of Our Time* tells us what can help a child to survive. If human potentials, individually and collectively, are to be enriched, if the potential of one man is not to jeopardize the potential of another, if the capacity for creative social interchange as well as individual achievement is to be realized, if some sort of conception of human nature is ultimately to be built in which both national and international unity of human effort can be achieved without coercion of the individual, we shall have moved a little toward fulfillment of the latent potential of today's children.

EXCELLENCE AND EQUALITY

by JOHN W. GARDNER

WILLIAM JAMES once said, "Democracy is on trial, and no one knows how it will stand the ordeal. . . . What its critics now affirm is that its preferences are inveterately for the inferior. Mediocrity enthroned and institutionalized, elbowing everything superior from the highway, this, they tell us, is our irremediable destiny."

William James was quoting the critics of democracy. He himself did not believe that mediocrity was our destiny. And I do not think that most people today believe it. Certainly I do not. But we would be very foolish indeed if we ignored the danger.

One might suppose that nothing could be less controversial than the relative merits of mediocrity and excellence. Yet people who set out to promote excellence often find that they have got themselves into a slugging match they cannot possibly win. The truth is that when it comes to the pursuit of excellence, there are some ways of going about it which Americans will accept and some ways which are offensive to them. Anyone who believes—as I do—that the en-

John W. Gardner is President of the Carnegie Corporation of New York.

couragement of excellence is about as important a goal as Americans could have today had better understand the hazards that line the course—and how to get around them. If anyone thinks that I am exaggerating the difficulties and wants to test this, let him launch a really vigorous campaign to promote excellence in his local school system—and see what happens.

In the first place, he will discover that there are people in the community who have very little fondness for democracy, and who never did believe in the widespread extension of educational opportunity. They will welcome his remarks in favor of excellence as an attack on democratic concepts of education and will promptly offer to join in on an attack on the school system. If he accumulates allies of that sort, his usefulness in the community will be at an end.

On the other side he will discover that there are some people in the community who believe that any reference to excellence is an attack upon American ideals of equality, and will accuse him of trying to create an elite.

At this point he will seriously consider going back to stamp-collecting, or bridge, or whatever that peaceful hobby was that he indulged in before becoming interesting in the schools. Unless one knows precisely what one believes in and what is meant by excellence, one is going to have a difficult time of it. But there is no greater service that can be done for a community than to help it to think clearly about these issues.

There are a good many Americans who have a genuine desire for excellence but have never really been clear in their own minds as to whether this was at odds with American ideals of equality. This is a question with which we had better deal head-on. What do we mean by equality? Do we mean any more or less than the Irishman when he said, "I'm as good as you are, and a great deal better, too"? Let us see what we do mean.

The eighteenth-century philosophers who made *equality* a central term in our political vocabulary never meant to imply that men are equal in all respects, in all dimensions, in all attributes of their persons and their lives. Nor do Americans today take such a view. It is possible to state in fairly simple terms the views concerning equality that would receive most widespread endorsement in our country today. The most fundamental of these views is simply that in the final matters of human existence all men are equally worthy of our care and concern. Further, we believe that men should be equal in the enjoyment of certain familiar legal, civil, and political rights. They should be, as the phrase goes, equal before the law.

But men are unequal in their native capacities and in their motivations, and therefore in their attainments. The most widely accepted means of dealing with this problem has been to emphasize *equality of opportunity*. The great advantage of the conception of equality of opportunity is that it candidly recognizes differences in native capacity and in willingness to work and accepts the certainty of differences in achievement. By allowing free play to these differences it preserves the freedom to excel, which counts for so much in terms of individual aspiration and has produced so much of mankind's greatness.

At the same time one must admit that the conception of equality has its limitations and ambiguities. In practice it means an equal chance to compete within the framework of rules established by the society in question; and this framework tends to favor certain kinds of people with certain kinds of gifts. This is unavoidable, but it is only proper that it be recognized. We must also recognize that in a society in which there are substantial differences from one family to another in wealth, learning, and concern for education, the formal equality of opportunity represented by free schooling may never erase the tremendous variations in opportunity represented by home background. In other words, we cannot assume that we have put our perplexities behind us when we assert our devotion to equality of opportunity.

So much for the conceptions of equality which would win almost universal acceptance in the United States today. But a good many Americans have gone considerably further in their equalitarian views. They have believed that no man should be regarded as better than another in any dimension.

People holding this view have tended to believe, for example, that men of great leadership capacities, great energies, or greatly superior aptitudes are more trouble to society than they are worth. Merle Curti reminds us that in the Jacksonian era in this country, equalitarianism reached such heights that trained personnel in the public service were considered unnecessary. "The democratic faith further held that no special group might mediate between the common man and the truth, even though trained competence might make the difference between life and death." Thus in the West, even licensing of physicians was lax, because not to be lax was thought to be undemocratic.

In such efforts to force a spurious equality, we can detect not only the hand of the generous man who honestly regrets that some must lose the foot race, but the hand of the envious man who resents achievement, who detests superiority in others, who will punish eminence at every opportunity.

Whether through the efforts of generous men or envious men, we have seen enough of this extreme equalitarianism to know what it implies. We have seen mediocrity breed mediocrity. We have seen the tyranny of the least common denominator.

In short, we now understand what Kierkegaard meant when he warned us of the danger of an equalitarianism so extreme as to be "unrelieved by even the smallest eminence." We now know what Flexner meant when he said, "We have to defend the country against mediocrity, mediocrity of souls, mediocrity of ideas, mediocrity of action. We must also fight against it in ourselves."

It is understandable that Americans should be cautious about excessive emphasis upon the difference in native capacity between one individual and another. Enemies of democracy have often cited the unequal capacities of men as justification for political and social philosophies which violate our most deeply held beliefs.

But we cannot escape the fact of individual differences

and we cannot escape the necessity of coping with them. Whether we like it or not, they are a central fact in any educational system—and indeed in any society. The good society is not one that ignores them but one that deals with them wisely and compassionately. This is the nub of the problem of excellence in a free society. It is the problem of dealing wisely and constructively with individual differences.

In education, for example, if we ignore individual differences we end up treating everyone alike—and one result is that we do not demand enough of our ablest youngsters. That is precisely the error we have made in recent decades. But if we toughen up the program and still ignore individual differences we only do an injustice to the average youngster who will have to drop by the wayside. The only solution is to admit that individuals differ and provide different treatment for different levels of ability. And never forget that we must do a good job at every level of ability. Our kind of society calls for the maximum development of individual potentialities at all levels.

But how does one provide different treatment for different levels of ability? That is where the arguments begin. Should we allow bright youngsters to skip grades, or should we observe the lockstep in which no one advances faster than anyone else? Should we have separate schools for the gifted as Admiral Rickover recommends, or comprehensive high schools as James B. Conant recommends?

I am not going to suggest specific solutions. I am going to lay down some principles to keep in mind if anything intelligent is to be done about this problem.

The first thing we must recognize if we are to deal wisely

with individual differences is that Americans are extremely reluctant to put labels on differences in general capacity. This is a deeply rooted national characteristic and anyone who ignores it does so at his peril. We do not like any arrangement which seems to suggest that some youngsters in our schools are first-class citizens and others second-class citizens.

An example of this is to be found in the broad interpretation which we give to the phrase "college education." When youngsters are graduated from high school we discuss those going on to college as though they were a homogeneous lot, all headed for a similar experience. Actually, a behind-the-scenes view of the process will reveal that they are quietly but fairly effectively sorted out.

At the key point in the sorting process is the high-school dean. The students need not listen to his advice but usually do. He sends his college-bound students out along widely diverging pathways—to colleges of the highest possible standards, to colleges of moderate difficulty, and so on down to colleges which may actually be lower academically than the high school from which the youngster is being graduated. But although the essence of his job is to arrive at clear appraisals of the relative standings of colleges and the relative capacities of students, the high-school dean will ordinarily take considerable care not to make these appraisals explicit in his talks with students and parents.

This reluctance makes some critics extremely impatient. But this is a point on which the American people insist—and for my part I am glad that they do.

One way of looking at this national reluctance to label individual differences is that it is nonsensical and that we have developed a ridiculous squeamishness about such matters. Critics trace it to our desire to make young people "happy," to our concern for psychological adjustment. But such critics are barking up the wrong tree. The reason we are reluctant to label individual differences in native capacity is that native capacity holds a uniquely important place in our scheme of things. It must never be forgotten that ours is one of the relatively few societies in the history of the world in which performance is a primary determinant of status. More than in any other society, in the United States the individual's standing is determined by his capacity to perform. In a stratified society—a class society—the individual's standing, his status, is determined by his family, by the class into which he was born. Performance is not an important factor in establishing the individual's status so he can afford to be less deeply concerned about his native capacity. In our society the individual's future depends to an unprecedented degree upon his native gifts.

Of course, we are oversimplifying matters greatly in using such general terms as "native capacity." There are all kinds of native capacity. That is a point to which we shall return later. But for complex reasons, Americans see appraisals of "intelligence," however defined, as total judgments on the individual and as central to his self-esteem.

Some critics note that we discriminate nicely between excellence and mediocrity in athletics, but refuse to be similarly precise about differences in intelligence; and they attribute this to the fact that we are more seriously concerned with athletic ability than with intelligence. Nothing could be further from the truth. We can afford, emotionally speaking, to be candid and coldly objective in judgments of athletic ability precisely because we do not take these as total judgments on the individual and as necessarily central to his self-esteem.

The second fundamental point which must be understood by everyone who wants to deal constructively with individual differences in our society is what might be termed the principle of multiple chances. The European system of education separates youngsters at ten or eleven years of age, on the basis of ability, into two radically different school systems, one college preparatory and the other not. This is, in many respects, an efficient procedure. It solves many problems which plague our comprehensive high schools. It would never work in America, chiefly because early separation of the very gifted and the less gifted violates our principle of multiple chances.

We believe that the youngster should have many successive opportunities to discover himself. We postpone as long as possible any final closing of the door on the individual's chances. It is a unique feature of our system that the "late bloomer" is given repeated opportunities to prove himself. I do not need to dwell on the fact that this can be overdone. If the late bloomer passes up too many opportunities he may turn out to be a wilted blossom. But any plan devised to deal with individual differences in our educational system must be a plan in which the individual may try again, and again, and again. It would be exceedingly foolish to imagine that the American people are going to change their views on this subject.

The final principle for dealing constructively with individual differences in our society is that our conception of excellence must embrace many kinds of achievement at many levels. We must not adopt a narrow or constricting view of excellence. There is excellence in abstract intellectual activity, in art, in music, in managerial activities, in craftsmanship, in human relations, in technical work. Some kinds of excellence can be fostered by the educational system and other kinds must be fostered outside the educational system. Some kinds of excellence will reflect themselves in good grades and other kinds will not. There are some kinds of excellence which involve doing something well, and others which involve being a certain kind of person.

It is easier to bear in mind that there are different kinds of excellence than to bear in mind that there are different levels at which excellence may be achieved. But the latter point is extremely important. Our society cannot achieve greatness unless individuals at many levels of ability accept the need for high standards of performance and strive to achieve those standards within the limits possible for them. Democracy must foster a conception of excellence which may be applied to every level of ability and to every socially acceptable activity. The missile may blow up on its launching pad because the designer was incompetent or because the mechanic who adjusted the last valve was incompetent. The same is true of everything else in our society. We need excellent physicists and excellent mechanics. We need excellent cabinet members and excellent first-grade teachers. The whole tone and fiber of our society depends upon a pervasive and almost universal striving for good performance.

And you are not going to have that kind of morale, that kind of striving, that kind of alert and proud attention to performance unless you can sell the whole society on a conception of excellence that leaves room for everybody who is willing to strive for it—a conception of excellence which means that whoever I am or whatever I am doing, if I am engaged in a socially acceptable activity, some kind of excellence is within my reach.

Those, then, are the three principles which I consider basic for dealing constructively with individual differences in education: First, to avoid arrangements which unnecessarily diminish the dignity of the less able youngster; second, to preserve the principle of multiple chances; and third, to recognize the many kinds and levels of excellence which we need and must nourish in a healthy society.

In applying these principles to the school system, the important thing is to keep the fundamental goal in mind: to deal wisely and constructively with individual differences, not to ignore them, not to brush them aside, not to pretend that they do not exist.

And when you have got yourself into a position to deal with each youngster in terms of his own potentialities and his own level of competence, then you can justly require that every youngster be *stretched* in terms of his own capacities; he must be expected to strive to the limit of performance of which he is capable. All high performance takes place with a framework of expectations, especially where young people are concerned. No expectations, no performance. We need not—indeed we must not—expect all of our youngsters to reach the same standard of performance. But we must expect that every youngster will strive to achieve the best that *he* is capable of achieving. If we do not expect it we are certain not to get it.

As to the down-to-earth practical arrangements which make it possible to deal with each youngster in terms of his ability, there are great differences of opinion among teachers. Many favor a certain amount of acceleration, that is, grade skipping, but others are opposed to it. Most educators now accept the need for grouping by ability, that is, putting youngsters of the same level of aptitude into the same classroom, but again, others are opposed to this. I happen to favor the system recommended by James Conant—a system called *sectioning by subject matter*. In this system the youngster might be in the advanced section in mathematics, but not in history. And youngsters of all levels of ability attend the same school and join in the same school activities. There are no distinctions between them outside the classroom.

But it is important not to be an inflexible advocate of any one system. Flexibility is the rule. The important thing is to keep the objective in mind. The means should be fitted to the situation, and in some cases to the individual. It may be that acceleration will be useful in some cases, but injurious in others. It may be that in some schools, one kind of grouping by ability is natural and workable and in other schools another kind is workable.

In some big cities, special high schools for unusually gifted youngsters have proven effective. It is foolish to be dogmatic about these matters. The important thing is to find solutions somehow.

What we want is a system in which youngsters at every level of ability are stretched to their best performance and get the maximum education of which they are capable. We do not want any youngster to feel that he is unworthy or lacking in human dignity because of limitations in aptitude, but we do want to see our ablest youngsters encouraged, stimulated, and inspired to reach the heights of performance of which they are capable. I like to think that we are now sufficiently mature as a people to keep both of those objectives in mind and not to slight either of them.

SUGGESTED READING

THE GENETIC POTENTIAL by JAMES V. NEEL, M.D.

Goodman, H. C. and C. N. Herndon. "Genetic Factors in the Etiology of Mental Retardation," *International Records of Medicine* (1959), vol. 172.

National Academy of Sciences: National Research Council. *The Biological Effects of Radiation*. Washington, D.C., 1956.

Neel, James V. and W. J. Schull. *Human Heredity*. Chicago, University of Chicago Press, 1954.

Penrose, L. S. *The Biology of Mental Defect*. New York, Grune and Stratton, 1949.

Scheinfeld, A. *The New You and Heredity*. Philadelphia, Lippincott, 1950.

Stern, C. *Principles of Human Genetics*. San Francisco, Freeman, 1949.

GROWTH AND DEVELOPMENT by STANLEY M. GARN

Garn, Stanley M. and Z. Shamir. *Methods for Research in Human Growth*. Springfield, Ill., Thomas, 1958.

Mintz, Beatrice, ed. *Environmental Influences on Prenatal Development*. Chicago, University of Chicago Press, 1958.

Tanner, J. M. *Growth at Adolescence*. Oxford, Oxford University Press, 1955; Springfield, Ill., Thomas, 1955.

Zubek, J. P. and P. A. Solberg. *Human Development*. New York, McGraw-Hill, 1954.

THE DEVELOPMENT OF BEHAVIOR AND PERSONALITY by JOHN E. ANDERSON

Anderson, John E. *The Psychology of Development and Personality Adjustment*. New York, Holt, 1949.

Blair, A. W. and W. H. Burton. *Growth and Development of the Preadolescent*. New York, Appleton Century Crofts, 1951.

Erikson, E. H. *Childhood and Society*. New York, Norton, 1953.

Havighurst, Robert J. *Human Development and Education*. New York, Longmans Green, 1953.

Stone, L. J. and J. Church. *Childhood and Adolescence*. New York, Random House, 1957.

EDUCATIONAL OBJECTIVES OF AMERICAN DEMOCRACY by RALPH W. TYLER

Alcorn, Marvin D. and James M. Linley, eds. *Issues in Curriculum Development*. Yonkers, World, 1959.

Chase, Francis S. and Harold A. Anderson, eds. *The High School in a New Era*. Chicago, University of Chicago Press, 1958.

Henry, Nelson B., ed. *Adapting Secondary Schools to the Needs of Youth*. National Society for the Study of Education, 52d Yearbook, Part I. Chicago, University of Chicago Press, 1953.

Hunnicutt, Clarence W., ed. *Education 2000 A.D.* Syracuse, University of Syracuse Press, 1956.

WASTED TALENT by HORACE MANN BOND

Bond, Horace Mann. *The Search for Talent*. Cambridge, Harvard University Press, 1959.

French, Joseph L., ed. *Educating the Gifted*. New York, Holt, 1959.

Ginzberg, Eli. *The Negro Potential*. New York, Columbia University Press, 1956.

Wechsler, D. *Range of Human Capacities*. Revised ed. Baltimore, Williams and Wilkins, 1952.

Wolfle, Dale. *America's Resources of Specialized Talent*. New York, Harper, 1954.

THE ARMED FORCES AS A TRAINING INSTITUTION
by HAROLD WOOL

Ginzberg, Eli et al. *The Ineffective Soldier*. 3 vols. Vol. 3, *Patterns of Performance*. New York, Columbia University Press, 1959.

National Manpower Council. *A Policy for Skilled Manpower*. New York, Columbia University Press, 1954.

President's Commission on Veterans' Pensions. *Veterans' Benefits in the United States*. 3 vols. Washington, D.C., Government Printing Office, 1956.

Thorndike, Robert L. and Elizabeth P. Hagen. *Attitudes, Educational Programs, and Job Experiences of Airmen Who Did Not Reenlist*. Air Force Personnel and Training Research Center, 1957.

U.S. Department of the Air Force. *United States Air Force Occupational Handbook, 1959–60*. Washington, D.C., Government Printing Office.

U.S. Department of the Army. *Army Occupations and You*. Revised edition. Washington, D.C., Government Printing Office, 1956.

U.S. Department of Defense. *The Military Service Outlook*. Washington, D.C., Government Printing Office, 1959.

———. Defense Advisory Committee on Professional and Technical Compensation. *A Modern Concept of Manpower Management and Compensation for Personnel of the Uniformed Services*. Vol. 2. Washington, D.C., Government Printing Office, 1957.

U.S. Department of the Navy. *United States Navy Occupational Handbook, 1959*. Washington, D.C., Government Printing Office.

U.S. Marine Corps. *A Guide to Occupational Training*. Revised ed. Washington, D.C., Government Printing Office, 1959.

RELIGION AND YOUTH *by* BENSON Y. LANDIS

Allport, Gordon W. *The Individual and His Religion*. New York, Macmillan, 1950.

Argyle, Michael. *Religious Behavior*. Glencoe, Ill., Free Press, 1959.

Aronson, Sidney. *Religious Revival and Jewish Family Life*. New York, Synagogue Council of America, 1957. Mimeographed.

Fichter, Joseph H. *Sociology*. Chicago, University of Chicago Press, 1957.

Hollingshead, A. B. *Elmtown's Youth*. New York, Wiley, 1949.

Rettig, Solomon and Benjamin Pasamanick. "Changes in Moral Values Over Three Decades," *Social Problems*, VI (Spring, 1959).

Ross, Murray G. *Religious Beliefs of Youth*. New York, Association Press, 1950.

THE CHILD AS POTENTIAL *by* GARDNER MURPHY *and* LOIS BARCLAY MURPHY

American Council on Education, Commission on Teacher Education. *Helping Teachers Understand Children*. New York, 1945.

Del Castillo, Michel. *Child of Our Time*. New York, Knopf, 1958.

Murphy, Gardner. *Human Potentialities*. New York, Basic Books, 1958.

Murphy, Lois Barclay. *Able to Cope*. New York, Basic Books, 1960.

———. *Colin: A Normal Child*. New York, Basic Books, 1956.

Stone, L. J. and J. Church. *Childhood and Adolescence*. New York, Random House, 1957.

3: PROBLEMS AND PROSPECTS

CONTENTS

CONTENTS

INTRODUCTION

by ELI GINZBERG

SOMEWHERE there may be a society where change is so slow that it cannot be observed, where there are neither general problems nor specific prospects. Such a society may be afflicted, and frequently is, by immediate scourges natural and man-made, but it may simply accept misfortune.

How different it is in our own society. We are always beset by problems and as soon as we solve one, two new ones take its place. This is true of our expectations: as soon as one objective is taken, we set ourselves two others. To paraphrase Samuel Gompers, the American people always want more.

The more dynamic a society is, the more it is likely to be beset by problems, for with change comes disturbance. But the more affluent a society is, the greater are its opportunities to solve the problems which change creates.

The third volume of *The Nation's Children*, as its title indicates, is focused on this point-counterpoint of "Problems

Eli Ginzberg is Director of the Conservation of Human Resources Project, Director of Staff Studies of the National Manpower Council, and Professor of Economics at Columbia University.

and Prospects." Among the problem groups singled out are rural youth, youth in minority groups, and youth in trouble with the law. These are important both because of the large numbers involved and because of the difficulties our society has experienced in handling their problems.

The volume also presents reviews of the voluntary and government mechanisms available to mitigate social mal-functioning and the extent to which we make use of these mechanisms. Finally, there are several contributions that assess the potential for adjustment in our basic institutions; we must control change if we are not to be overwhelmed by it.

In studying rural youth, Professor Kolb calls attention to the continuing large-scale migration from rural areas into urban communities and the difficulties that the migrants face as they seek to orient themselves to a new way of life and to new occupations, difficulties that are accentuated because so many of these youth have had an inferior education. Further, Professor Kolb indicates that those who remain behind must adapt themselves to "agribusiness," unless they belong to submerged farm families who do not even have the chance to adapt. Farm communities are further handicapped because they have lost their former cohesion and are increasingly buffeted by decisions made by leadership groups located in distant centers of power.

In his delineation of the major factors influencing Negro youth in the South, Dr. Lewis Jones emphasizes the order of change that has taken place during the past two decades on every front—legal, educational, and economic. He reminds us that segregation is a system of deliberate and systematic exploitation, a system that denies the Negro his basic civil rights as well as access to good schools and good jobs. Fortunately this oppressive system is crumbling and Negro youth are increasingly in the foreground of the struggle. Dr. Jones warns that some of these youth are so unsettled by the gap between their inalienable rights and the continuing exploitation and repression to which they are still subjected, that they sometimes respond in ways that cannot lead to constructive results. But in general he has a more favorable reading of the trend. While the Southern farm has little to offer Negro youth, many of them will seek the realization of their hopes and dreams in the urban centers of the South convinced that the rabid segregationists are a diminishing minority.

A prevalent assumption in the United States is that we have but a single minority problem—the Negro. And quantitatively, this is so. But in the Southwest, in California and Colorado, as well as in New York City, there is another significant minority, the Spanish-speaking people—the Spanish Americans, Mexican Americans, and Puerto Ricans, who, according to Professor Burma, total about 3.5 million.

Although the Spanish Americans have been in the United States for ten generations, most of the other Spanish-speaking groups have only recently immigrated and therefore face many of the problems that bedevil newcomers; since they are less well-educated and less well-trained than the native population, they find themselves at the bottom of the social-economic ladder. But, as Professor Burma says, the educational picture is constantly becoming brighter for these groups, and with better education goes better jobs and a greater opportunity for acculturation.

If one problem of American youth were to be singled out because of our overriding concern with it, it would unquestionably be juvenile delinquency. This evidence of serious social dislocation among large numbers of young people is a sharp reminder of our collective shortcomings as parents, neighbors, and citizens. Professor MacIver emphasizes that while the initial source of delinquent behavior must be sought within the family, the family in turn is much affected by the forces in its immediate environment and the larger society. Low economic status, overcrowded housing, lack of training and experience for competitive urban life, and social discrimination tend to be characteristic of high-delinquency areas. And Professor MacIver places particular stress on the vulnerability of newcomers to the city who must face the most difficult problems with the least equipment. Professor MacIver discusses the importance of preventive and rehabilitative measures aimed at eradicating as rapidly as possible the pathological conditions conducive to the growth of delinquency and at providing additional resources in the form of facilities and personnel to help reverse the antisocial behavior of young people before it becomes fixed.

This cursory review should have made at least one point clear: that there are many children and youth in the United States who continue to require special help. But large as these special groups are, they by no means include all children and youth in need of help.

INTRODUCTION

Elizabeth Wickenden in her essay on voluntary welfare services and Eveline Burns in her review of the government's role in child and family welfare assess the scope and adequacy of our social effort on behalf of children whose families are unable to provide for them.

Miss Wickenden calls attention to the strength of the American tradition of reliance on mutual aid and the important innovations which voluntary organizations have to their credit. The extent of present-day voluntary efforts is suggested by the finding that $400 million was raised by community chests during 1959 for 27,000 separate agencies in 2,000 American communities. Miss Wickenden points out that, while many families still experience economic hardship, the heart of the voluntary effort is being directed toward the prevention or alleviation of problems reflecting social disequilibrium. The more voluntary agencies contribute to the reduction of divorce, desertion, illegitimacy, delinquency, and mental illness, the greater will be their contribution to the well-being of children who are the principal victims of these social ills.

Professor Burns describes the tremendous part that government now plays in providing assistance to those in need; she then cites major shortcomings that still persist in this elaborate structure of public aid. Among the weak programs is the Aid to Dependent Children's Program which, in Professor Burns' opinion, has no clearly defined policy and which fails to provide an adequate level of support for those whom it purports to help. Professor Burns further points out that despite the acknowledged desirability of keeping children in their own homes, 70 percent of all public resources for children is still spent on foster care. More needs to be done to assist working mothers, low-income families, and children of broken homes. Professor Burns concludes her review with the hope that the American people will more adequately honor their expressed concern for the welfare of children and youth.

Dean Henry David's paper, covering the triple subject of "work, women, and children," provides a transition from the more specific problem areas and the social mechanisms available to cope with them to transformations in the larger society that affect the population as a whole. The focus of his concern is the rapid rise in the employment of women outside the home, especially married women, which has been proceeding in recent decades so rapidly that it might appropriately be called a social revolution.

Dr. David indicates that no single factor can account for this "revolution" which is connected not only with the needs of the economy but also with significant changes affecting women, including an increase in their marriage rate, a lowering of their average age of marriage, the earlier completion of their families, and an increase in their life expectancy. But it is strange that, in a child-centered culture such as ours, this revolution which impinges so directly on the child, has not been seriously studied. Dr. David concludes that such a study could not fail to provide a new range of understanding of the nation's recent social and economic history.

The remaining three essays in the volume by Nelson Foote, Eric Larrabee, and Norman Cousins are contributions of another dimension. These authors raise questions about the inner springs of American society and of the contemporary world and speculate about our present position and about what the future holds in store for us.

Dr. Foote reminds us that each generation sets its own aspirations and goals. There is no certainty of greater control over society as time proceeds; all that is certain is greater control over nature. Looking back over this century, Dr. Foote is impressed with the sharp changes in the stance of successive generations; looking ahead, he raises what he believes may become the central issue for the present generation—how to adjust to peace if the wheel of fortune makes this turn.

In a peaceful world, self-realization must be sought as much through leisure activities as through work. But Dr. Foote suggests that a Puritan culture, however much the Puritanism has been diluted, will probably encounter difficulties in learning how to live with its good fortune.

The place of childhood in American culture is the concern of Eric Larrabee. He differentiates between the need of adults to be concerned with the nurturing of their successors and the special situation which prevails in the United States where so many adult tensions and frustrations are projected onto children. Mr. Larrabee reviews the changing styles in child-rearing, which he relates to the value structure in American life during the past half-century. He argues for a basic skepticism toward prevailing doctrines of child care and for caution, so that we do not become enslaved by another tyranny of our own making. He concludes with a plea to permit the new generation to develop their own worries, believing that a little inattention will do it (and the rest of us) a world of good!

The concluding essay in the present volume, as well as in the series, is Norman Cousins' thoughtful discussion of the human commonwealth. Mr. Cousins begins by recalling some simple but often neglected facts. He argues that the rate of change in the lives of nations and peoples has greatly accelerated during the last decade, much more than most of us realize, for we all suffer from lack of perspective. He further believes that since education must always be geared to the challenge of the times, there is an urgent need to reform our educational structure if we want to control and not be engulfed by the changes that are under way.

We must begin by de-provincializing education; both East and West belong to the same human commonwealth. We must recognize the basic unity of most religions. We must discard the stereotypes that hamstring the scholar and enflame the passions of the citizen. We must recognize the human situation for what it is and help the young to understand that all men must learn to live on one planet.

Young and old, East and West, the planet itself, cannot flourish or even survive unless the lesson of "the human commonwealth" is learned—and learned quickly.

THE OLD GENERATION AND THE NEW

by NELSON N. FOOTE

THE WHITE HOUSE Conference on Children and Youth is a kind of periodic national audit of our long-term hopes for our children and their partial realization. It exceeds in perspective not only the annual reports by which we examine our progress in many other fields but also the decennial census which counts the various units of which the nation is constituted. Each decade it tries to formulate some sense of the kind of environment that would be more favorable than the current one for the kind of people that we want the rising generation to become.

To discuss the kind of environment that would favor the rising generation is to take a very special point of view. It is to generalize the roles of parent and of professional person who cares for children to the extent of considering the United States as a vast household, as if its citizens were universally interested in fostering the development of their offspring. No one who has gone through the agitation of a referendum on

Nelson N. Foote is Research Consultant, Sociology, for the General Electric Company.

a school bond issue would take that assumption for granted. Nonetheless, it is a useful standpoint from which to think about what would be possible if everyone would in fact play his role as citizen with the same seriousness as that of parent.

Aspirations and Reality

Each generation sets some bounds to what it deems possible, as well as declaring some goals. Certain bounds are fixed by nature, but others are only taken as given, and a later generation often makes up its mind to assault such limitations as unnecessary suppositions. It is often the differing assessments of what is possible and what is forbidden by circumstances beyond control by which one generation is distinguished from another. Parents may aspire to the same state of affairs as their children, but consider the risk of trying to attain it so great that they fear that their children too would only be hurt by the attempt. And sometimes they are right.

There is no certainty of progress from lesser to greater control over society as time proceeds. There is some advance in control of nature. One need not be very old to remember how uncertain life was before antibiotics, even for the young person who expects never to die. But the illusion that progress extends from the realm of technical control over natural processes to that of human relations, however stubbornly preached by self-persuaded social scientists, withers in the glare of recent history. Nuclear physics has raised the threat of total obliteration as its way of clarifying the issue. Some uncertainties of natural origin remain, like the weather, but on the whole, the kinds of restriction that arbitrarily limit how far we may develop are those we impose upon each other. And while these change from generation to generation, their obsolescence is illusory evidence on which to base a claim of progress.

Giving up the idea of progress is hard in practice even when granted intellectually, nourished as we are on the rhetoric of education and material advancement. Only last summer, for instance, I conversed in the Brussels airport with an Indian attorney from an Arabic country known for its oil riches. He told me of how justice is served in that area through the mutilation of offenders, foreigners of course exempted. I asked him what became of the victims other than those who are beheaded, and he replied that the ruler permits their hospitalization by Christian missionaries. He succeeded in briefly reviving my childhood sense that I was fortunate to enjoy citizenship in an advanced civilization. Such a sense, however, cannot survive a trip through the nearest veterans' hospital. Human beings are no less capable here than elsewhere, now than before, of treating each other horribly. I shall only mention a file I used to keep of the crimes of parents against children.

When we experience a sense of movement from worse to better in our relations with each other, it is like the movement toward the climax of a play, rather than like the steady improvements in the properties of steel over the past century. In real life, unlike the drama, each plot leads into another, but there is no necessary cumulation of happiness for the actors. The next series of events is always in jeopardy of passing from better to worse.

In facing equally this constant jeopardy of fortune, there is justice among the generations, between one generation and the next. Save in relative control of nature, which will always remain incomplete, it is as good or bad to be born one time as another. How we acquit ourselves in our own time cannot be attributed to our choice of parents, but only to how we utilize the time we have. And likewise, when we assume the role of parents, we cannot guarantee success to our children. However lavishly we set the stage for them, the stage may further but cannot control the plot or its outcome. Indeed, if we assume that our children want what we want as the outcome of their existence, and bend every resource to getting it for them, we can do them the greatest disservice, since they would not recognize the outcome as truly theirs, nor would the striving to achieve it be theirs.

What does it mean, then, to aim during the next decade toward the provision of an environment favorable to children and youth? If each lived in a world of his own making, and could work out his own fate individually, there would be no logical sense to this venture in prophecy. But for good or evil, our destinies are intertwined, across as within generations. We act in each other's plots, and while in real life there is no omniscient author as in the drama, we not only set the stage but continually cast each other in the parts we play.

Unraveling the complications of the fact that parents are particularly potent in casting their children into the roles they perform—with some assistance from professional teachers and employers—is thus no easy task. Because of the narrative concreteness of each generation's span of events, it may be helpful to look closely at recent developments before attempting further to generalize philosophically.

To this point we have argued only that each generation has its own peculiar plot to fulfill, in roles and setting which have been cast by its predecessors, but the evolution of which can neither be dictated nor guaranteed by them. There is not even a way for one generation to sacrifice itself by denying its own obligation to realize the possibilities of its own time. When this viewpoint is applied to events of the decades traversed by the White House Conference on Children and Youth, what does it portend for the next ten years?

The first of these conferences was held in 1909 at the behest of President Theodore Roosevelt. His name is reminiscent of the period during which the United States emerged from preoccupation with its own westward settlement and inferiority to Europe, and began to take pride in its own distinctive contributions to world civilization. The Great White Fleet which circled the globe and the completion of the Panama Canal climaxed this new portrayal of the country abroad. Meanwhile the several cross-currents of the election of 1912 manifested at home the desires of all segments of the population to share in the sense of having completed the building of a nation.

The next White House Conference came after victory in the war had been celebrated, the great steel strike had been lost, and the country had been increasingly transformed from being an agricultural to being an industrial nation. Except for the dethroned farmers whose wheat had been so mighty in winning the war, most people became oriented toward making money through manufacturing and commerce. With the rise of the automobile, the small town which had set the pattern for rural America was overthrown by the city. The emphasis of the forthcoming 1920s was to be on the relaxation of restriction and inhibition, on self-assertion and success.

There is no reason to expect historical events to fall neatly into decennial intervals, and they do not. On the other hand, from the viewpoint of parent and child generations, there is some grouping of events around major turning points, which sometimes occur that close together. From Armistice Day in 1918 until the beginning of the depression was not quite eleven years, and World War II began in September of 1939 with the invasion of Poland by the Nazis.

What Defines a Generation?

The traditional conception of a generation in time was thirty years, about the average period from a male's birth until the birth of his first male child. Nowadays a generation so defined is much closer to twenty years in duration, due to earlier marriage, smaller gap in age of husband and wife, and less emphasis on male children. From the beginning of this century, therefore, we may speak of either two or three generations having elapsed, speaking chronologically, with 1930 as the dividing year in the former case, 1920 and 1940 in the latter. And in either case, 1960 becomes another, if somewhat less dramatic, turning point between this generation and the next.

The turning points between generations are more sociological than chronological, despite intriguing coincidences with historical intervals. What distinguishes one generation from another is not a sequence of small gradations but rather marked qualitative divergences, occurring rather suddenly. Certain historical events usually act as watersheds, causing the thinking of those who come to adulthood before these events to flow into more or less parallel channels, whereas the orientations of those who come to adulthood afterward, while likewise conforming with their contemporaries, flow in very different directions from the thinking of their predecessors. Thus World War I, the depression and World War II have been the major turning points for American young people of this century. As of this moment, the nature of a new crisis differentiating the pre-1960 generation from the post-1960 generation is not evident, but it is imaginable. Hitherto the major turning points have regularly been provided by drastic shifts in either international relations or domestic economy or both simultaneously. Since international politics and domestic economies constitute the principal structures with which young people grow up and adults pursue their careers, it is imaginable that they will likewise be the basis for the next turning point in the formation of the new generation from the present cohorts of children and youth. Indeed, in retrospect a few years from now, we may wonder why it was not obvious to us at this moment that a great crisis in our society would be constituted by a substantial increment in confidence in the duration of peace.

If Prime Minister Khrushchev were to succeed in making the kinds of guarantees to Americans which would give them

some confidence in the peaceable intentions of Soviet
Russia, a considerable economic crisis would probably result.
Without indulging in further speculation as to the likelihood
of this being the turning point which differentiates the 1960s,
and far less stating it as a definite prediction, let us at least
recognize this possibility. It does provide an example of the
kind of turning point which would compare in universal influence with the previous turning points of this century.

The peculiar mechanism by which generations are differentiated is thus simultaneously historical and biographical. The
historical events which produce the watersheds are economic
and political shifts which affect the present and prospective
conditions of life of all persons coming to adulthood when
they occur. That is, they cause each young person's estimate
of what is possible for him to differ from the estimate made
by his parents at that same phase in their own life histories.
Biographically, membership in a distinctive generation is not
so much the result of when one is born as when he becomes
an adult, an event far less definitely placed chronologically
and one which can be quite substantially hastened or postponed by historical events. Some boys have found themselves
in combat overseas before they were out of their teens, just
as many girls are now finding themselves mothers before
twenty. On the other hand, in pursuing certain professions
requiring advanced training, the dependency of young people
on their parents is frequently prolonged through most of
their twenties. The transition from adolescence into adulthood, therefore, is to be identified realistically primarily by
the making of those major commitments which tend to

structure the remainder of one's life history—choice of vocation, choice of mate, and choice of friends and models of behavior. These major life-determining decisions tend to interlock; their intercontingency adds to their stability.

As the principal mechanism for differentiating historical generations, the biographical mechanism of making basic career choices may seem peculiar to a free society, where individuals are encouraged to make them with minimum reliance on parental recommendation. Certainly much attention is concentrated on vocational and marital selection in the United States, where it is widely believed that only voluntary commitments can be counted sound. It could be argued, however, that the same mechanism operates even in societies where parents are seemingly more authoritative in determining their children's life-plans. Most significantly, few societies remain in which the control of one generation extends to its grandchildren. And thus, even where children do not themselves openly resist parental direction, a way remains by which vast concerted changes can occur from one generation to the next.

Each generation, apart from planning its own course during adulthood, resolves to raise its children in various ways differently from the way in which it was raised by its parents. Many men and women who grew up as only children during the 1920s and '30s, for example, resolved that their children would not be only children, but would grow up with brothers and sisters. It is quite true that each generation also takes for granted that many of the ways of its parents were right, and transmits them unquestioningly and almost unwittingly to its children. Thus the scheme of generations may be said to provide naturally for both continuity and change, and it would be unrealistic to emphasize either to the exclusion of the other.

In the same manner, the coming together of a man and woman in marriage produces a domestic environment for their offspring which is likely to be different in important ways from that in which either grew up. This mixing of backgrounds through marriage increases the chance of novel outcomes, viewed from the standpoint of individual biography. From the statistical standpoint, however, it also tends toward the diffusion and assimilation of the various strains of family culture, so that cumulatively children may differ more from their predecessors than from their contemporaries.

Finally, in devoting detail to the mechanism by which intergenerational distinctions evolve, it must be noted that the various generations, as groups of actors in society, overlap in time and thus interact. It has become well recognized that the outlooks of adolescents are heavily shaped by their peers. The individual makes chums of others who are crossing the same thresholds of development, pondering the same difficult questions of belief and self-evaluation. He does not entirely think for himself, however great his insistence on independence from parental guidance, but represents the combined thinking of those members of his own generation with whom he is in intimate contact. And of course the web of such communication among age-mates is not compartmentalized within particular segments or strata of communities, but seems to spread in an unbroken web across the land, and even into other lands. Through challenge and debate, vague alterations of emphasis in values often lead not to resolution of differences and harmony, but to sharpening and polarization of views, to the crystallization of contrasts, and even to conflict between adjoining generations. One may cite as a familiar example the conscientious mutual disapproval of the ethics of financial management practiced by parents reared during the depression and children reared during the continuously upgrading prosperity since.

The New Generation

Returning then to our example of the possibility of peace as a major turning point in the planning of life-careers by the new generation, it is all too obvious that here is an assumption as unprovable as it is controversial, one that could readily polarize the population along generational lines, needlessly perhaps but effectively. It is not so long ago that it took the most brutal of facts to convince the majority of Americans that involvement in war was unavoidable. Yet a scant twenty years later, it will be equally hard for the majority to become confident that a long period of peace is possible.

Yet peace is possible, peace in the reality of a confidence sufficient to permit substantial disarmament. If peace in the world were to endure for even another twenty years, it could be argued, it would be for the first time in the history of the world that potential combatants, industriously equipping themselves to the ultimate in arms, have not used them. Yet every day we are confronted with events that are happening for the first time in the history of mankind. Many young

people are so accustomed to the surpassing of previous limitations on technological prowess that they scoff at any who
doubt the eventual success of the latest space-traveling pipe-
dream as very old-fashioned indeed.

Of course, to achieve right relations among blocks of humanity is not a similar technical problem, as we have made
plain from the outset. And just how it is to be done is
exactly the major challenge confronting the present generation, beside which the perfection of lunar rockets is a beg-
ging of the question. The kind of training for the one is
utterly different from that which has the best chance of
achieving the other, and over the appropriate training for
youth the conflict between the generations will probably
wax hotter. Indeed, on the axiom that the dominant theme
of a period always seems in retrospect as if it ought to have
been obvious to participants at the time, the plausibility of
our hypothetical suggestion that the exchange of visits between president and prime minister might prove to be the
turning point between the last and the next generation becomes uncomfortably persuasive.

For the sake of perspective, let us step back a moment to
the late 1940s, when clearly a new generation was emerging.
Following the success of the Marshall Plan in averting Communism in Europe through promoting economic recovery,
President Truman set forth his bold, new program for extending the principle to the underdeveloped nations. His
Point Four Program seemed to this writer then, and still
seems today, an ideal vehicle for mobilizing the technical
talent of the young people of this nation for accomplishing

the nontechnical objective of establishing a just world society, one that would extend the sway of our favored values without encroaching on the autonomy of other people. It might have given expression not only to the vastly more cosmopolitan public opinion that emerged from the experiences of World War II, without diminishing the emphasis on economic achievement that distinguishes us as a people. I was wrong, as was President Truman, in appraising the temper of the people. He was far more right in recognizing soon after that the majority of the citizenry of 1948 still had memories of the depression which dominated their thoughts about the future. It may be that his mistake in judgment or timing was only in not treating public opinion about international relations as consistent with opinion regarding the domestic economy. And if this were the error, it need not be repeated, at least in dealing with our more-or-less hypothetical example. In a sense, events have given to the American public a second chance to consider grand strategy with regard to domestic economy and world politics, and to members of the new generation the chance to design their lives by a different set of assumed limitations and possibilities.

The terms of the overall equation by which people calculate the outcomes to be expected from moving in various directions are different from what they were in 1948 in only a few essentials, but the balance of numbers between the old and the new generation is much changed, and the decision may well be opposite. In 1948, it may be remembered, unemployment in engineering and related professions was high, and college students were being dissuaded from entering these pursuits. Now, of course, the most common plaint is that enrollments in technical schools, already at a stupendous peak, are far below requirements, if we are to man the advanced facilities that are being constructed to match Communist or commercial competition. Secondly, instead of the economic uncertainty of that year, we have bounded briskly out of a brief recession, and foresee output climbing so vigorously that hampering effects of the steel strike are disregarded. And finally, while the aggressive competition of the Soviet Union for influence among the uncommitted nations is far more visible, the neutrals appear more ready to declare their allegiance. What we seem to have, in other words, is a clarification of a situation that may have been imminent in 1948—even with Korea included among the evidence—that what impends is not a conflict but a peaceful competition. If this interpretation is made by the younger generation of the world with which they are confronted, that the only kind of peace that is possible with the Soviet Union is an indefinite period of strenuous competition, it may seem preferable to indefinite waiting for the first missile to arrive. Certainly on the other side, Russian young people seem powerfully tempted by civilian goods and services, so tempted that they may be willing to rest their hopes for global eminence on their prowess in economic and scientific competition.

If the 1960s become a period of strenuous competition with the Soviet Union, this will be quite different from most of the 1950s, which were largely occupied with holding the Communists in check abroad while devoting resources at home primarily to upgrading the physical standard of living, to achieving affluence, as the phrase has caught it. Merely to hold back the Communists abroad and to increase the level of consumption at home are not the kind of national or societal purposes which translate readily into individual life plans, as they are almost nondirective in their implications. It is not surprising that people during this immediate period, especially those reaching adulthood, have been perturbed by the question of who they are and what they want to become —the question of identity.

In choosing as its most influential guiding document Erik Erikson's *Childhood and Society*, the White House Conference on Children and Youth in 1950 chose prophetically. Erikson's book was a penetrating formulation of the task of finding identity when restrictions on the individual's choice among alternatives are removed. Before the coming of the affluent society, it always seemed to make sense to uphold as ideal a society in which everyone could achieve the fullest expression of all his potentialities. That slogan has now become obsolete, as the surplus of possible courses of development and the absence of restrictions force one to set his own limits, choose the few paths to which he will voluntarily confine himself, if he is not to be a futile dilettante. The past ten years have taught people, especially the younger ones making their lifetime choices, to view more tolerantly those conditions of life which remain fixed, to accept as valuable the idea of permanent commitments, which can liberate more energies and personal resources than the defunct state of remaining uncommitted. The corollary of the problem posed by Erickson, that serious commitment, voluntary but nonrevocable, is a positive good, has only slowly emerged. It is in a sense the legacy of the 1950s to the '60s, which now offer the opportunity to the new generation to build upon it as a positive premise.

Self-Realization, Fun, and Morality

As we look into the '60s from this biographical premise that serious commitments are good, and from the historical premise that we can enjoy peace if we are willing to undergo strenuous competition with the Soviet Union, various further implications and corollaries of these premises can be foreseen emerging during the next decade or two. Perhaps a useful point from which to start in laying these out is to go back to another book which most aptly foretold the concern of people becoming adults during the '50s, David Riesman's *The Lonely Crowd*. Near its close, Professor Riesman suggests that, since so many people do not find self-realization in their work, the widespread growth of leisure might make it possible for them to cultivate their autonomy in play.

Even at the time of his statement of this proposition, Riesman was open to criticism for surrendering so readily the occupational realm as a sphere for autonomous self-development, for the establishment of identity. But he saw self-realization in work the privilege of only a small percentage of our population, and from the standpoint of the year in which he wrote—a year when engineers were often unemployed—he expected that percentage to dwindle. But throughout the succeeding period, the most rapid growth in the labor force has been precisely in those occupations which offer their participants a professional career. And autonomy and identity through work are close to synonymous with those kinds of occupations which can be called careers. The extent and speed of professionalization during the succeeding years has been prodigious, yet seems minor in relation to what is coming. Of this, the currently over-three-million enrollment in higher education gives only a hint. The vast rise in industrial research and development, civilian as much as military, seems likewise on the lower part of an exponential curve. And so with the rise of all kinds of professional services and institutions—medical, educational, and recreational.

In respect to leisure and recreation, David Riesman was even righter than he thought he was, because it is in the sphere of play that the new features of personal development have become most fully clarified, in the model of the advanced amateur. And it is here that the ambiguities of the relationships between work and play in personal development have become clarified, with boundless implications for society at large.

Adults play roles in society both as producers and as consumers. It is more revealing to describe their styles of life in terms of producer and consumer roles than simply of work and play, especially when work connotes only gainful employment. It is primarily in respect to play—to self-chosen interests which occupy leisure—that people's roles as consumers can and do become differentiated. To the extent that consumption refers only to necessities—food, clothing, and shelter—consumption patterns tend to be differentiated mainly with respect to quantity, and thus reflect the differing incomes associated with the various producer roles. But as the discretionary portions of incomes rise—while in the aggregate real incomes become both higher and relatively more equal—the patterns of consumer expenditures of money, time, energy, and attention can and do become more and more representative of genuine family styles of life, less and less indicative merely of the earning power of the principal breadwinner of each household. Upgrading leads to differentiation. This differentiation is most visible in connection with leisure pursuits, and more visible still as these self-chosen interests are pursued more seriously.

Where for the multitude during recent decades, work has been set off sharply from play, for the serious amateur, the competence, application and creativity of his play can be distinguished from those of the skilled professional only by his not making a living therefrom. The degree of enjoyment, the voluntary commitment of long hours to learning and practice, the multiple forms of expression of serious interest —publications, associations, advanced courses, reading, thinking, meeting, trying new techniques, which are found among serious professionals, are also common to serious amateurs.

In this paradoxical combination of seriousness with voluntary commitment to group-developed standards of performance, the growth of leisure and the growth of professionalization since the war join to shape the main outline of our coming society. The early manifestations are everywhere, in camera clubs, boating magazines, specialized shops to handle equipment, adult education courses, and inservice training seminars. What the devotees of each special interest may not have noticed is how parallel the lines of development have been among the other specialties. Also, while the movement toward serious pursuits of self-chosen interests in work and play has gone far enough for recognition as a general movement, it has not as yet embraced more than a small minority. Most of the effort to realize in full the meaning of a leisured professional society still lies ahead, although very near ahead.

Unhappily, the signs of the times are not clear enough to be immune to misapprehension. Even though, for instance, the desire of the sons of factory workers to become engineers runs far ahead of existing facilities and enrollments some vocal critics of our educational system profess that not enough high-school students are being pressed into science and mathematics. Even though Dr. Conant has pointed out the vast waste of talent in the discouragement of achievement among girls, it continues along with the waste of skilled manpower already existing among minority groups. As reported by the President's Commission on Higher Education in 1948, a high percentage of the most able high-school students still do not go to college. There is no dearth of evidence as to the abundance of aspiration to professionalization. There is, however, little recognition of and reliance on the voluntary auspices under which the younger generation wishes to conduct its affairs, its insistence, to put the matter flatly, that *work be fun*. The older generation, or at least some of its presumed spokesmen, apparently do not grant that such a demand is legitimate; they cannot grasp that it is possible for the world's work to get done, or for the world's political crises to be met, on that basis.

Yet when fun is seen neither as an escape from work nor as a preparation for work, but as a feasible means of making any worthwhile activity a path to self-realization, it is plain that fun offers as sturdy and effective a moral discipline as work. Indeed, there is no difference, because the traditional discipline of work was not really the discipline of work but of a society which imposed unpleasant toil on the majority as a condition of consumption. Work was not chosen in most cases on its own account but as a means of making a living. "Just a job" was the typical way of speaking of it, but that is not how one describes a profession. A profession offers not just a job but a career, and its morality springs from the assumption that it was entered by voluntary commitment, that one is motivated to pursue it not primarily to make a living, which is taken for granted, but to receive the respect of his colleagues and more or less directly to serve those who need what one produces.

The concept of professional ethics is familiar, but the idea that fun imposes morality on behavior, while not new, remains still a rather strange notion to many. They are familiar with the rules of games, and know that without their observance, games cannot go on. Games evince a higher degree of interest among participants in observance of rules than occurs under any form of government. The only extension of the principle involved is that the rules of the game must apply more widely as the game itself is widened to include more and more of the world's work. The serious amateur, as he becomes involved with others in his interest, plays a game with very strict rules of honor. One often sees, for example, sportsmen who are far more punctilious about the conservation of wild life and the forests and streams than are those who utilize them merely for a livelihood. The etiquette and reciprocal sensitivity among members of voluntary associations are always superior to those found where relations are compulsory. The socializing effect of games on children has long been noted by child psychologists, but only recently has it become apparent that the same principle might operate in humanizing some of the less civilized features of adult life.

In previous times, when a society became oriented toward leisure and enjoyment, it was often to the neglect of work, which was imposed on some subject group, and of decent government. Now for the first time in history it begins to appear that this outcome does not have to be feared; indeed conducted as fun, both work and government are likely to be performed with stronger conscience and higher competence than under the pressures of duty and necessity. The beauty of such a revolution is that it requires no one to arm and assault an enemy; one has only to relax and enjoy it, to relax, that is, the anxieties which inhibit serious commitment to playful purposes, and the free flow of energies which follows.

Perhaps the ability of the older generation to accept this more playful way of life is greater than the voices of alarm among them suggest. Certainly the past generation has seen family life take on a more festive aspect, along with a keener and more responsible interest in the development of children, among fathers as well as mothers. As parenthood has become more of a hobby, it has also become more of a profession. As many have said, children have become consumption items, wanted for their own sake, and not as extra hands. Not so long ago big, strong boys were the favorite choices for adoption, where now requests for baby girls are the most frequent. Professor Jessie Bernard has pointed out that nowadays the position of the child in the home has become very much like the role of the guest. Similarly with regard to occupations outside the home: when one goes to conventions of people of almost any occupation, one finds mingled the festive with the serious aspect of the professional concept.

Nowadays most people live not only long enough to see their children develop into adulthood, but also their children's children. Their span of life thus may be said to cover three generations. As parents, with their own children, they get to re-live vicariously, but by direct observation, their own experiences of growing up. But as grandparents, a higher degree of vicariousness is usually called for, if they are to enjoy the development of young people at a distance. And as grandparents, they also have to diffuse their empathic participation in the development of others over a much wider number. This necessity for taking a parental attitude toward younger generations can also be viewed as an opportunity. As stated at the beginning, the generalization by citizens of the parental attitude of concern to treating the nation as a single household is a boon to public welfare when it occurs.

The recent growth of delight in family life, while it may among parents seem to preoccupy them with private affairs, can among the grandparents who are so much increasing in numbers result in a wider and deeper concept of citizenship. The White House Conference on Children and Youth, therefore, ought to be of equal interest to all generations, not least to the oldest.

For those whose lives encompass the decades of these conferences, the succession of decades, each with its separate emphasis, thus presents a challenge to vicarious participation in the outlooks of each cohort of their successors; it also calls for an effort of philosophical integration. It has often been noted that grandparents sometimes understand their grandchildren better than they did their own children, so there is no reason to despair that the dramatic transitions from generation to generation, so important in the definition of limits and aspirations, are impossible to assimilate. Each in his own full time has a different set of generational perspectives to reconcile with those he embodied in his own young adult commitments. Thus no one is denied, each has his own responsibility to declare where the whole procession is and ought to be headed. Depression and war make us conscious that we are each dependent on all the others but they cannot take from us that we are the integrators who weave from the many strands of influence and experience the particular adult we have become. The old generation has provided the new with the materials of which it must fashion its existence; there are no other available to it. The world stage and the national are set with greater possibilities and fewer limits than any previous actors have entered upon, and thereby inevitably greater dangers. It will be a breathtaking decade in which to participate, directly and vicariously.

In 1930, when I graduated from high school, the commencement speaker chose to expound a pagan text, "When the gods rain gold, O Youth, spread wide thy mantle." His prophecy, then premature, may now be timely.

RURAL YOUTH

by JOHN H. KOLB

FAMILY and community are the nearly universal framework within which youth view themselves and look to their futures. Rural families and their farms continue to serve as seed-beds producing surplus food, fiber, and children. The North American farm family has high value ratings in the tradition of the nation. Rural communities are the exchange and experience arenas for those youth who remain in them and for those who go out to seek their fortune elsewhere.

Both rural life and agriculture now provide their own "challenge of change," contributing to and receiving from others. They never were as isolated and as static as romantic writers have described them. The "revolution," as some characterize current changes, dates to World War II when "Food Will Win the War" and "Food for Freedom" were more than slogans. They represented a social movement, an aroused determination, an impetus to set up scientific research, to apply modern technologies to farming, and to expand production plants. They were the signals for agriculture

John H. Kolb is Professor Emeritus of Rural Sociology at the University of Wisconsin.

to assume and to ask for a place of recognition and respect in the eyes of the nation and of the world. The stereotype of the farmer as the man with a hoe disappeared.

In that period two new concepts, now matured and accepted, were born: agricultural parity and social security. Farmers demanded a "fair share" of the nation's income, and during the ensuing decade the means of achieving this parity have plagued politicians, ensnared congressmen, riven farm leaders and farmer organizations into factions, and have bewildered rural youth beyond possible assessment.

Periods of rapid change in a society can be particularly perplexing to youth when they themselves are undergoing changes—changes of maturity, outlook on the world, decision-making, family relations, and community influences. Young people need time and a degree of stability around them in order to become a part of adult life and to build their own personalities. Denied these they may be thrown into uncertainties or set adrift by indecision. The swirl of changes within the family framework which now involves rural youth can be described briefly in two movements: population mobility and the change from agriculture to agribusiness.

Migration Movements

North American rural society has always been highly mobile. Before the 1930s the movements from the rural seed-beds included the vast trek of people who populated the cities. During the economic disaster of the 1930s, there was a reversal of the urbanward trend which sent many families and many young people back to the land—land that by any standard may have been marginal in production capacity. Since 1940 the movement toward urban centers has resumed but this time only toward, not into, the cities themselves. There at the urban peripheries rural migrants seeking another farm or some other occupational opportunity have been met by families moving from the city centers—a two-way movement converging to form new family patterns and new community arrangements. By 1958 government reports indicated that the rural nonfarm residents, those living in the open-country or places of less than 2,500 population but not on farms, represented one-quarter of the nation's people, while less than 12 percent lived on farms. This means that, in many areas and even in whole states, the rural nonfarm population exceeds the farm.

To complicate the problem of definition and to blur still more distinctions between rural and urban, farmers are increasingly engaged in nonfarm work. By 1957 it was reported that only 35 percent of the nation's farmers were wholly dependent upon agriculture. In that year nearly 3 million farm residents were working off their farms, mainly at nonfarm work, and slightly more than a third of them were farm women working away from their homes. Because 40 percent of the farmers account for about 90 percent of the nation's agricultural production, it follows that the majority of farmers are not confined to their farms occupationally or socially. But, they never were. In earlier years farmers worked on the roads to pay off some of their taxes, bartered in villages and towns for their supplies, and exchanged work with neighbors at planting, threshing, or barn-raising times.

For rural youth migration movements were and are severely selective processes, and this gives them their real significance. Rural to urban migration begins at about age sixteen and is largely over by age thirty. Rates vary with urban conditions and distances. Girls leave rural areas, especially farms, in disproportionally larger numbers than do boys, and at an earlier age. Boys, while less migratory than girls, travel greater distances, and the greater the distance a youth moves the more likely he is to go to some larger city. At least 50 percent of farm youth move to other occupations and to other communities. It is claimed that the expense of rearing and educating country boys and girls who live and work in cities during their productive years is an undue burden. Such claims may be more difficult to maintain in recent years with increased school aid programs, reallocation of some income and special taxes to localities, and the rising costs of farm subsidies and surplus storages.

Family-wise the selective migration takes more younger families than older ones and more of those who were operators of small rather than large farms. Tenant farm families lose more of their youth to cities than do owner families. Also, families with a number of community organization connections are less mobile than those with few such contacts. From every angle family and community are interrelated in their influences upon youth.

Qualitative aspects of these migration movements are probably even more important for society than the quantitative. In this regard there is less agreement in opinion and in research results than about the extent of the movements.

One interpretation is that the deviants leave the country for the city—the more and the less capable. Another is that farm youth are the "left-behinds," either by indecision, inertia, or low aspiration. There is evidence of relatively low levels of urban labor-market achievement by farm-reared youth, and that those rural youth who do migrate tend to have completed more years of schooling and have higher intelligence test scores than do those who remain in rural areas. These variations in estimates change with time and place, with definitions of capabilities, and with values attributed to results of various testing techniques. Some of the implications for decision-making by rural youth will be considered later.

The issue in this connection for policy-making and for continued study is how to help rural youth reorient toward the larger society of which they are to be part and parcel—not a drab, leveled-out, mass industrial society, but one of opportunities at various levels of interest, achievement, ability, and relative advantages. The traditional rubric of a rural-urban dichotomy is no longer relevant for youth either of country or of city birth. The city must have the products of the various seed-beds to supply itself with food, fiber, and workers of many kinds; and the country needs the feedback from the city of machinery, insecticides, artificial fertilizers, merchandise, and skilled workers and specialists. But to pit one segment of society against another because of differences in residence, occupation, or cultural values is inferior statesmanship. Rural youth are in need, just now, of a reinterpretation regarding the interrelationships in society. This will take a bit of doing since attitudes of opposition and contrast are deep-seated. Country parents express fears and offer resistances to having their children go away to the city for work or for school and these attitudes can often be detected in the reactions of rural youth to new situations. The old myth that the country is God-given and the city devil-derived is not easily dispelled.

Rethinking is also required at professional and theoretical levels. Newer theoretical constructs than the traditional "rural" and "urban" are needed, for neither includes all of a kind, surely not as of now, if indeed they ever did. Only when other variables are introduced can real meanings in an analysis be gained—variations in education levels, in parental experiences, in occupational opportunities, in incomes, in geographic regions, in social status. Moreover, such variables occur in complexes, combinations, syndromes. Analyses by simple dichotomies are too often misleading since there may be greater differences within each category than between them.

Agribusiness

A second movement immediately involving rural youth is from agriculture to agribusiness. In academic circles agribusiness is defined as including not only production on farms and ranches but the processing and distributing of the commodities so produced, and also the manufacturing and distributing of supplies and equipment used in the production. These services have expanded to unrealized proportions and provide occupational opportunities for millions of rural farm, non-farm, and city people.

There is a striking similarity between the up-curves of those engaged in agribusiness and the down-curves of those in agriculture in its traditional sense. Between 1929 and 1953 all workers on farms in the United States decreased by more than 3 million while workers in the marketing of farm products increased nearly 2 million. Agribusiness is reported to account for 40 percent of all consumer expenditures and to employ 37 percent of the labor force.

At the farming end of the process rapid changes have been in full swing for some time. Within commercial agriculture improved technologies and results of research have resulted in great increases in outputs per acre, per animal, per farm, and per farmer. Reports from government sources show that the physical volume of farm products in 1956 was about 50 percent above that of twenty-five years earlier. The size of farms increased 40 percent in fifteen years to 336 acres in 1954, while farm population decreased about 28 percent from 1940 to 1954. But changes occurred not only on farms but among farmers through numerous contractual arrangements. One of these features is termed "vertical integration." A farmer who operates within such an arrangement shares with one or more related businesses some of his management decisions and risks in both the producing and the marketing of his commodities.

Commercial farmers are also involved in other contractual arrangements through sales and bargaining associations, cooperative organizations for production, marketing and purchasing, through governmental inspections for sanitation and maintaining standards, and through agreements under parity provisions. Thus with the benefits of improved technologies, contract and integration plans, and with government policies for parity, present-day agriculture has piled up previously unheard of surpluses. Agriculture now finds itself operating in an economy of abundance with a theory of scarcity.

Some results of such rapid and often chaotic changes are brought into focus by a statement made by a group of younger-than-average agricultural economists.[1] They had been meeting for discussions under the auspices of the Social Science Research Council and were thus free to state the case as they regarded it professionally, not as the representatives of their respective employing institutions or agencies. They considered the period of change as critical and "the response of agriculture as confused." The statement emphasized that there is a welcoming and rapid adoption of some changes and a resistance to others that may be inevitable concomitants. A recognition that moral as well as economic values are involved in the troubled situation is very heartening.

Some consequences of the changes pointed out in the statement include: chronic distress in certain sections of agriculture in spite of public remedial measures that have grown to unmanageable size and accelerated movements of people out of agriculture; a widening of the income gap among those families who remain, between those able to adopt new

[1] George K. Brinegar, Kenneth L. Bachman, and Herman M. Southworth, "Reorientations in Research in Agricultural Economics," Report of the Subcommittee of the Social Science Research Council Committee on Agricultural Economics, *Journal of Farm Economics*, Vol. XLI, No. 3 (August 1959), pp. 600–19.

technologies and those lacking financial resources or personal capabilities; and successive areas of agriculture being increasingly controlled by outside commercial interests.

"Problem-Farming"

Chronic distress areas and those farming families which cannot close the income gap are likewise a part of the agricultural picture which rural youth must view and seek to understand when decisions are being made. These areas and families represent nearly one-half of the farm population of the nation; 48 percent was the estimate reported to Congress in 1955 by the United States Department of Agriculture. This "other half" of agriculture does not come within the compass of the rapidly changing conditions just described for commercial agriculture. Its families live in "low-income," "subsistence," or "problem-farming" areas. The various terms have similar meanings. More than four-fifths of the farms in "low-income" areas had gross sales of less than $2,500 in 1949. The concept, "low-income" farmer, is relatively new but however defined, it includes a heterogeneous group of people and represents multiple problems. The most significant fact about low-income families is that they are concentrated and they have remained remarkably stable over the years.

"Problem areas" include a majority of the rural population referred to as "minority groups": Negroes, Spanish-speaking peoples, and Indians. Many are tenants, share-croppers, and those on small farms. These are the source for regular or seasonal labor for owners and operators of larger farms.

"Problem" farm families contribute heavily to the manpower of the nation. Between 1940 and 1954 an estimated one-half of the expansion in the nonagricultural labor force was supplied by movements from the farm population and more than half of this came from low-income farming areas. The proportion of children and youth under twenty years of age is much higher in these areas, and the proportion in the productive adult ages is lower than in the rest of the farm population. Some of the families are welfare cases because of sickness, age, or broken homes.

Problems are multiple because of limited physical resources, small farming units, inadequate health protection, and children handicapped in educational opportunities. Institutional, cultural, and family patterns of attitudes and values seem to hem in these families, setting them apart. To rescue them from their own sense of low status and to improve actual opportunities for youth especially, is a major issue. Improvement programs are now under way and are meeting with success, according to government reports, but methods used for communicating with commercial farm families are not effective with the problem families. Mass media do not "reach" them. They are not members of the usual farmer organizations and their educational achievement levels limit their use of circulars and bulletins. They require more personal approaches through informal groups, including friends and neighbors.

The "boot-strap" methods, aimed at helping families to help themselves, appear to have limitations unless changes in some of the fundamental sources of the difficulties can be brought about. The question can be raised as to how long agriculture can endure half commercial, half problem.

Migrant, seasonal, transient laborer families moving in and out of the problem and other areas, serving as an accepted or considered a necessary adjunct to commercial farming in certain regions, defy description. To report that their children and youth are slow and irregular in school progress, do not participate in social activities, are not accepted by others, are often handicapped by poor health and by emotional disturbances, and that parents display seemingly little interest, is only to understate the case.

On the more hopeful and encouraging side, it can be stated that improvements are under way—more and better health clinics, medical care, camp accommodations and sanitation, provisions for food, transportation of children to specially built schools, services by churches and grants from private foundations for studies. A real promise in the situation is the surprising response on the part of children when favorable opportunities are provided. Also, by more mechanization and diversification on larger farms and ranches and within communities, the worker families are becoming somewhat less migrant. They tend to form into colonies and to settle in substandard houses on the outskirts of towns and cities. These settlements become like Toonerville, California, which gradually, over the years, evolve into a Farmersville with their own respectable schools, churches, stores, taverns, and social organizations. But there are heavy social and economic costs and sacrifices of human resources along the way. On the other hand, some of the "foreigner" laborer families of yesterday who were denied the privilege of swimming in the community pool have sons who today are wealthy farm owners and members of school and church boards. Many do not.

Career Plans

Rural youth are caught in these changing complexes of confusion and contradiction: agriculture to agribusiness, family farming to vertical integration, traditional attitudes of individualism to power politics with attempted production regulations and ridiculous surpluses, widening gaps between commercial and problem farming, and inland isolation to world military strategy. In the midst of all this and their elders' indecision, they must, sooner or later, answer the question: to farm or not to farm?

Decision-making has engaged the time, energy, and finances, not only of many rural youth, but of many researchers, especially since 1950. Before that time studies concerned with rural youth usually centered about selective migration, attitudes in regard to farming, and their apparent reactions to local problems. The more recent studies indicate that farm-reared youth who migrate to cities are relatively unsuccessful or reach only low levels of achievement in many urban occupations. This has real significance since it is estimated that about one-third of nonfarm people in the whole country were reared on farms. Low levels of aspiration in regard to occupation and education are also known to be related with low levels of achievement. Therefore, the rather widely accepted conclusion of some researchers that nonfarm youth have higher educational aspirations than do farm youth of equal intelligence has important implications.

Other studies suggest, however, that perhaps most of the difference between aspiration levels of farm and nonfarm youth can be accounted for by the low aspirations of farm boys who plan to farm. Much depends upon the meaning given to the concept "aspiration." If it means to desire something which one does not possess, then the farm boy who plans to farm is not in the race to get somewhere else. His planning to farm may have been by deliberate decision or by default of indecision. In either case the results may be tragic. If he should change his mind because of new experiences or of recognized inability to keep or to gain a foothold in farming, he is unprepared for other possible opportunities. He is likely to move into lower levels of occupation than his abilities could permit, because he lacks the necessary education and training for the higher levels. The loss is not only his, personally, but society fails to realize a potential resource.

This kind of situation is not difficult to visualize or to experience. Financial resources may not be available when $30,000 to $50,000 is needed to acquire ownership of some middle-range farms. Or some farm-reared youth may fall victim to what is termed "effective environment." They become accustomed to and oriented toward the lifeways and the social values which agriculture represents to them. Their casual contacts with other ways of life and work may even have blunted their desire to change. They are bombarded with the same kinds of movies, comics, TV programs, and other mass media but it doesn't "take." Studies indicate that many perceptions are limited within various group relations: peer groups, those of about the same age and social status; reference groups, those whose approval is sought and whose values are accepted; primary groups, those whose responses are personal, intimate, and considered important for personality development.

The planning-not-to-farm side of the story is fully as important as the planning-to-farm, especially as the trends in migration continue. This, the researchers point out, is more than a negation but must be considered as part of "an act" to enter the nonfarming world. Three factors are suggested which may result in this kind of planning: certain personality characteristics probably associated with early training, perceiving farming as unattainable for them, and being sons of parents who are more oriented to the nonfarm than to the farm world.

From every source of evidence parents and families are implicated in youth decisions: parents of those youth who plan not to farm have higher levels of education and occupation aspirations for their sons than do parents of those who plan to farm; socio-economic levels of families have an influence on children's desire for education; family background is a factor bearing on chances for academic survival; parents' participation is associated with the "drop-outs" in 4H Club youth groups; years of schooling completed by parents are associated with attitudes toward the education of their children. These and other conclusions even suggest the necessity of an early and deliberate breakup of sons' expectations that they can or should be farmers.

Many decisions may not be direct and in a straight line. Everyone familiar with rural youth recognizes that questions are often settled piece by piece, that the process may be complex and often takes a long time. Once set in train, decisions do move on but compromises and reasons are often mixed with what may appear to be fortuitous circumstances.

Open Questions

Issues involved in the context of this section of the discussion are many and complicated. Only a few will be reviewed and perhaps in too brief and idealistic phrases to suggest solutions, practical or workable. They will follow in reverse order to that of the discussion.

First, "more research is needed." This expression is found in nearly every report examined. Results reported need to be retested under different conditions and with other groups of people. Simple and direct answers to problems of decision-making are being demanded from many sources but the issue is how to be more certain of results for special application, and how to communicate those which are dependable to points of real need. Many questionnaires are being circulated among rural youth but replies of "father," "mother," "friend," "teacher," to questions regarding early influences on decisions may, upon more intensive investigation, turn out to be rationalizations, escapes from pressures to think, or be substitutes for actual unknowns.

More attention might well be turned to the area of discovery. How can rural youth be exposed through experiences to other than the farm environment? How to "stir up the gift that is within thee"? Are determinations once aroused and abilities discovered transferable to other areas of action previously considered latent, retarded, or even nonexistent? Studies are needed not only for their predictive purposes but for the more rapid improvement of facilities and personnel for counseling and for guidance at early ages.

What can be done to compensate for the low levels of education attainment on the part of farm parents? Reports indicate that nearly one-third of the nation's farmers had only an eighth-grade or less schooling. Now a high-school education is the expected level in rural society; but as was pointed out, studies show high correlation between schooling of parents and their attitudes and ambitions toward the education of their children.

Second is the issue of the fuller development of rural youth as society's great human resource. Agriculture might well give greater attention to this problem of human resources in whatever seed-beds they may have grown. A Congressional committee was told recently that the "hard core" of the farm problem is the surplus of human effort committed to farming. "Interdependence," within a national as well as an international economy, would appear to be a signpost which should be followed. How can agriculture continue trying to be separate and self-concerned, while attempting to rid itself of its own surpluses, human and material? Can such surpluses be somehow regarded as an opportunity instead of a problem? "Free-the-World-from-Hunger," is a movement proposed by the Food and Agriculture Organization of the United Nations, whose recently appointed director-general is a citizen of India, and should know whereof he speaks.

Third is the issue of how to shift some emphasis from economic production to social and personal development. There is much agreement that technologies alone will not solve all problems, but just how to shift into other channels is not at all clear or agreed upon. The truth that man cannot live by bread alone requires reemphasis with each new turn of human affairs. How can cultural values long associated with farm family living be kept unless they are given away, shared with other families—families with which farm youth will inevitably be associating—merchant families, professional families, worker families, industrial families?

Families and communities in rural society are indissoluble. Communities are families in their interdependent relationships—the framework for their youth in action. Migration movements and business farming have their counterparts in changing community relations. Two trends, among others, will be singled out for review here: the increasing interdependences of communities and the growing institutional pressures.

During the earlier periods of rural society, country neighborhoods, often relatively isolated from general society, exerted strong influences upon youth to conform to local group values and patterns of behavior. Many open-country neighborhoods have succumbed to succeeding social movements but a surprising number of the hamlet neighborhoods have survived. Some are stronger and more active than they were ten or fifteen years ago. They are more economic in their orientation than in former years and they are also more varied in the character of their influences.

For older rural youth, hamlets provide much more contact points with the outside world than earlier since not only friends but passers-by meet there. Their influences upon children must not be overlooked, especially in the so-called "problem areas" and in the small settlements on the outskirts of towns and cities. Even in the areas of commercial agriculture they serve as channels for communication and for evaluating changes. They are capable of two-way action: implementing innovations of certain kinds and protecting members from too abrupt changes when accepted modes of behavior or established beliefs seem challenged. Recent studies indicate that they have most meaning for those youth and adults who actually participate in their activities since then identification becomes action.

Village-country or town-country communities have emerged as centers of influence in rural society. However, the movement is not completed even though as population aggregates they appear to be well established. Many farmers and ranchers live in the village or town centers and some business and professional families are country residents, yet many differing interests are not fully reconciled. There are external evidences of an integrated group, but upon examination there are indications of lack of the internal requirements for community solidarity and for unified action. There are overlapping administrations and areas for elementary and secondary schools, for health and hospital services, fire and police protection, sewage disposal and water supply. In some cases, efforts for community coordination have been so strong that an ambition for self-sufficiency has developed. This tendency has made it difficult for one community to work with another for their larger mutual interests.

Of increasing importance are the nonfarm families which come to take up residence. The newcomers are less responsive than earlier residents to the personal relations with local merchants and organization officers. They go readily to other larger centers for shopping and for recreation, even religious services.

Recent population movements toward but not into cities tend to converge about centers as small as 5,000. Many smaller places, especially of less than 1,000 population, are experiencing difficulties in their social and economic adjustments to changing times.

Thus, current movements of centralization and decentralization of population, agriculture, and industry tend to meet at the crossroads of larger town-country communities and at the peripheries of cities. This defines the most important current trend in rural community relations—the increasing interdependence of communities. The desires and struggles for local community self-sufficiency and independence have been and still are very strong, especially where the processes of town and country coordination have not been fully achieved. However, many readjustments are under way among communities of varying sizes and character and these have special significance for rural youth. First of all, it is quite evident that certain social and economic services and institutions belong together within the same communities.

The trend is moving toward a clustering of certain kinds of services and a differentiating of various communities into recognized types. Plans for community development must take into account the fact that some types of communities can establish or maintain certain kinds of services and institutions, but for others they must look to other communities and assume their share of responsibility and support. Some rural communities are finding this principle of interdependence difficult to follow. As pointed out before, they seem to feel a sense of moral responsibility to provide all things for all their people, even to furnishing employment for all their maturing youth. This simply cannot be done. To attempt to supply inferior or inadequate facilities for education, recreation, religion, or other needed services in order to be "loyal to the home town" is to short-change youth.

Responses of rural youth to these changing community relations are encouraging and often refreshing. They are doing things and going places which the adults may be doing later. Those youth in smaller communities are going to larger centers for such contacts as recreation, without apologies although not always with full parental consent. Correlations were found between size of resident community and declared intention of occupational choices and with desired future residences.

Casual conversations with young people, especially of high-school ages, often bring forth complaints regarding lack of work opportunities, restricted recreational opportunities, and impatience with conservative adult attitudes. More extended discussions usually reveal recognitions of many community conditions and limitations and a real concern for the future of the communities and their own plans for further education and full employment. Checking daily schedules often showed many activities even during summer vacation periods and a multiplicity of school and church-related organization contacts during the academic year. Complaints were encountered among some families that these activities encroached upon family life. Uneven responses were found among youth to the various special interest groups and organizations represented locally. Many of the same variables were associated with the differences among adults. The mothers' reactions were often most predictive of family patterns.

A second important trend in rural community relations is the growing dominance and central orientation of formally organized groups and institutions. Since 1950 many rural organizations, both public and private, have secured the services of professional and paid personnel on a county-wide basis and with state and national affiliations. These trends often result in degrees of uniformity in organization procedures and the creation of power structures capable of controlling channels of communication and of exerting outside pressures upon the local groups concerned. Similar tendencies are even more discernible among many local community institutions such as schools, churches, businesses, and centrally organized farmer associations.

The tendency to be self-centered and self-sufficient was observed among churches during recent restudies of country neighborhoods and town-country communities. There were evidences of overlapping church areas, of church contacts criss-crossing community boundaries and of country churches operating without regard to those in nearby villages or towns. Families were traveling greater distances than in former years, seeking churches of their preference. Many differing sects were being formed, often among former, dissident members of locally established churches. These and other evidences would suggest that organized religious interests are being directed toward churches as institutions rather than toward communities as social groups. If this interpretation is warranted, many questions arise.

Some church leaders are making ardent pleas that churches must perform their community functions in order to survive. Others contend that the church should recreate the community in its own image; while others, concerned with transcendental relations, would keep aloof from the world.

A recent study showed that the "effective" churches were markedly superior to the average churches in respect to their community outlooks, that village churches rated higher in this respect than country churches, and that town churches rated higher than village churches. Among the "effective" churches the index of community relations diminished as the members of the suborganizations of the churches increased.

Tendencies similar in effect were found among some educational institutions in town-country communities. Much attention is given to policies proposed by outside central agencies. Some high schools in agribusiness communities have continued programs, both agricultural and academic, designed for past needs rather than for today's demands on rural youth. Offerings are too limited in scope and content to prepare them for expanded opportunities. In many such cases the village boy is the forgotten one since he can not usually qualify for the vocational courses because he does not have home projects available. If he does not plan to go on to college, many of the academic subjects do not appeal to him.

Branch banks and branch mercantile establishments in town-country communities have many policies and prices fixed at central headquarters. Their managers live and work in the communities but are often, not always, less identified with the local affairs than are the owner-operators of similar businesses. Industries which are much sought after by rural communities in order to provide local work opportunities usually hire employees without regard to their residences. Their managers say that they are compelled to do this because certain skills are needed and it is simpler to try to find them wherever they are than to set up local training programs. Such policies often leave only the unskilled jobs for local people. They may likewise have little regard for local customs and traditions, when, for example, they run the plant Saturdays and Sundays during the fruit and vegetable harvest.

Some of the larger and stronger farmer organizations are no longer the social, economic, or even the local marketing agencies they once were. They have become more largely pressure groups for the protection of special agricultural interests and have their paid lobbyists and their favored legislative programs at state and national levels.

If it be true that local institutions and organizations are

becoming more oriented toward themselves and their special interests, rather than to the communities of which they are a part, then it may be proposed as a basis for study that rural youth are faced with a number of alternative choices: 1) They may compartmentalize, make little or no effort at reconciliation of various teachings and value positions of the different institutions in the community. They may open and shut mental and emotional doors as they go from one to the other. 2) They may recognize and verbalize the conflicts which they experience, or the inconsistencies may lie below the surface, unrealized and unexpressed but disturbing. 3) They may invent procedures of their own and go merrily on their ways with ideas and actions which are quite deviant from those publicly accepted by adults in the community. 4) They may not be influenced or stimulated because the local institutions and organizations are silent on important community issues.

Illustrations of all these alternatives were observed during recent restudies of town-country communities. Conflicts between schools and churches were most easily recognized. In one community high-school girls were presenting petitions signed not only by parents but by church pastors, in order to be excused from certain physical education activities and regulations. In another community a small church building with a large neon-lighted cross stood across the street from the school. The principal of the school said he paid no attention to the church and that it did not influence his pupils. Conversations with the pupils put his conclusions in doubt. One community had within its area a country church whose members observed Saturday rather than Sunday as their Sabbath. Conflicts arose over when ball games and concerts should be scheduled. Another community had a large and dominant church with many organizations and activities for its young people. Non-church youth in the community complained that these interfered with and restricted school-related social programs.

The discussion in this section can be summed up by suggesting that relations of rural youth with their communities may take at least three forms: personal—the extent to which they feel accepted in the community; social—the extent to which their acceptance is converted into participation; moral—the extent to which their behavior is responsive to community norm-values.

Issues for policy-making and for further studying are also many and varied. Only two are offered here, and in brief and general terms. First, creativity in youth is the call of the day. Industry, especially, is asking for creative ability in its scientists and its engineers, and is devising batteries of tests to find it as if it were a hidden treasure needing only discovery to be exploited. How are special abilities once discovered to find expression? Youth are encouraged to be different, to assert themselves, to question education's teachings and religious beliefs. The issue presents itself as to whether schools and other established institutions can, under pressure of crowded conditions, provide opportunities and experiences which are as agreeable to the dissenter as to the conformist.

Second, and corollary to the first, youth, it is important to recall, are involuntary members of families and communities, at least in the beginning of their lives. As suggested earlier in regard to farm boys, youth do not have the freedom for choices which some research designs seem to assume. Their recognized alternatives are limited, but as they mature their desire for independence comes to the fore. There are those who believe that this independence can be best achieved within an atmosphere of confidence—confidence in the general aims and objectives of one's society. Some educators are saying that they should be more sure and articulate regarding their own aims and the roles their schools should play in contemporary communities. Without these their pupils and parents lose confidence in them.

Some political scientists are urging the need for more overall positive belief in the American system rather than for isolated refutations of the details of other ideologies. The issue, then, for rural youth in their community relations is how to secure proper balance between the need for self-confident independence and the need for social control.

NEGRO YOUTH IN THE SOUTH

by L E W I S   W .   J O N E S

CHILDREN in the South today, both white and Negro, are in circumstances such as few other generations of children have known. In some periods of change or crisis children have been cast in bewildering roles as victims of action to which they were in no way a party. Southern children today are in social situations where they must make precocious decisions about their own conduct. Influencing these decisions are interaction between children, interaction between children and adults who have different relationships to them, and an awareness of judgments being passed on them by those who observe their conduct from nearby and from afar. There is an urgency upon children of the South to choose between alternative expectations of them. The responsibility placed upon these children makes the past ten years fateful ones for the future of the South in ways that many people may not comprehend because of their intense involvement with a particular point of view or preoccupation with a selected sequence of events.

Lewis W. Jones is Director of Social Science Research, College of Arts and Sciences, Tuskegee Institute.

Children and youth have known the impact of an ideological controversy in which there have been massive efforts at persuasion to one or another point of view about the values of this society. Southern children have had to give heed to passionate indoctrination directed specifically at them. Their introduction to our social institutions, especially our political institutions, has been quite different from that given other generations of children. The general and somewhat idealized textbook descriptions may be essentially the same as before but through the mass media and from interpretations by their elders these institutions are made to appear quite different and often far from ideal. The conclusions they reach about the society and government will influence the kind of citizens they become.

Negro children all over the South are now making a fateful commitment about themselves as persons, as are all young Southerners who have had to face up to questions regarding who they are and what their futures may be. During the past decade the status of the Negro child in the South became an issue characterized by unprecedented controversy in the course of which Negro children and youth came to new conceptions of their roles in American society. Changes in the status of the Negro child are functionally related to basic culture changes in the nation and in the Southern region, including technological and economic changes, changes in social structure and organization, and changes in the value system and belief patterns. In four major areas improvement of the status of the Negro child has come to be a critical issue for the society.

1. *Manpower.* Post-war evaluations of the availability and

use of the nation's manpower resources during mobilization for World War II, both for military service and for manning the productive machinery, brought the knowledge and skills of Negroes under intense scrutiny.

2. *Citizenship.* Hardly less significant is the citizenship status of Negroes in the ideological contest between the United States and Russia for support in Asia and Africa. The United States need not disavow the disadvantages past and present generations of Negroes have known if it can demonstrate improved opportunities offered oncoming generations.

3. *Education.* Preoccupation with the quality of education given American youth inescapably emphasized the lag of the education of Negro youth behind national and regional norms.

4. *Productive Potential.* Technological and social changes in the South brought a migration of population from the region to other areas of the country where the productive inadequacies and social disabilities of migrants produced critical community problems. The experiences of migrants in their formative years in the South are held accountable for the problems they present wherever they go.

For Negro youth to share in programs to remove inequalities between the Southern region and the rest of the nation, essential conditions for Negro participation had to be established. In the process of redefinition of the status of the Negro child no component of the American institutional structure has been exempt although the courts assumed the major responsibility in prescribing a basic legal status contrary to legal precedent and entrenched custom.

An acute self-consciousness might be expected on the part

of Negro children as the range of their opportunities was extended and encouragement given them to set new aspiration levels for themselves only to encounter a determined opposition to these new prerogatives. Doubtless, the next decade will see a need to cope with personality difficulties of Negro children and related social problems as a result of their having had to deal directly with contradictory definitions of their status.

The Subcultural Matrix

The American Youth Commission studies of Negro youth in the late 1930s provide us with a baseline from which this current assessment of the status of the Negro child may be made. These descriptions of Negro youth indicate that the rural Southern subculture is the matrix from which the present Negro personality was derived. Their thesis is that Negroes' movement into the mainstream of American life can be measured in terms of the distances they have come from the place allowed them in the typical configuration of the traditionally rural Southern subculture.

Basic to this subculture was the plantation system which required that Negroes be amenable to control and lacking in effective literacy and other characteristics that could lift them out of this status. Long operation of this system, which also came to include dependent white people, ultimately brought the South to that dramatic branding as "the nation's economic problem Number One."

The social structure interlocked with this economic structure could hardly escape peculiarities. In the '30s and '40s students elaborated on what Charles H. Cooley had defined in 1912 as the "race-caste" system. Dollard, Warner and his colleagues, and finally Myrdal [1] described and documented distinctions in the rights and privileges in a society separated by a color line. Comparative opportunities of the young were found to be related to both race and class positions.

According to tradition in the South, the Negro status was supported and maintained by the structural characteristics of the society and a strongly reenforcing set of beliefs about the Negro's place in the economy. These beliefs belonged to the subculture and were shared to some degree by both Negroes and whites. For the most part a Negro's aspirations were closely geared to his opportunities. Negroes knew the rewarding economic or occupational functions available to them. Aspiration to an occupation or a status which did not fit in the opportunity pattern or have acceptance as appropriate for a Negro in the belief pattern had to be fulfilled outside of the Southern social system. Negro parents for several generations had to make the choice for their children between aspiring within the system or escaping from it.

The overwhelming majority of Negroes followed unskilled occupations, received small wages for their work, lived in the poorest of shelters, were illiterate, and had a short life ex-

[1] John Dollard, *Caste and Class in a Southern Town* (New Haven: Yale University Press, 1937); W. Lloyd Warner, Buford H. Junker, and Walter A. Adams, *Color and Human Nature* (Washington, D.C.: American Youth Commission, 1941); Allison Davis, Burleigh B. Gardner, and Mary R. Gardner, *Deep South: A Social Anthropological Study of Caste and Class* (Chicago: University of Chicago Press, 1941); Gunnar Myrdal, *An American Dilemma* (New York: Harper and Brothers, 1944).

pectancy. Their lives were lived out in a state of dependence in which major decisions as to their fortunes and those of their children were not theirs to make. If poverty and illiteracy were not effective controls, economic pressure, punitive legal action, and threat of extra-legal punishment were. There were gradations of economic positions above this lowest level that carried prestige on the Negro side of the color line. These higher status positions within the Southern social system, however, carried with them an obligation to be useful to whites, bear symbols of inferiority, and obey the etiquette prescribed for subordinate-superordinate relationships. Cowed lower-status Negroes and cynical upper-status Negroes so conducted themselves as to allow whites to enjoy an illusion of "good race relations."

As the group above the lower stratum grew in numbers Negro children were taught how to advance to these better positions. The Negro child had to acquire the social skills essential to effective functioning in this society if he expected to live in it. The upwardly aspiring Negro child had to acquire a finely balanced equilibrium, maintain security and preferential treatment from the white South, press always for a better overall Negro status, and keep the opportunities of the broad American culture in focus as aspiration targets.

This was the situation in the late '30s, when Charles S. Johnson presented his observations of youth in the South in *Growing Up in the Black Belt*. Challenges to the Southern social order were then neither boldly open nor aggressive. There was considerable social ferment within the Negro culture that was having its influence on the personality development of Negro youth. Some of his observations were:

No group in America, however, is experiencing a more rapid or profound internal change in its social composition than the Negro group. Over a comparatively brief period the cultural level of this group has been considerably advanced. Illiteracy and mortality rates have declined markedly, the standard of living has been raised to some extent, there has been a pronounced advance in the organization of family life, and there have been other equally significant changes. The external evidences of improvement have been accompanied by a less conspicuous but nevertheless intense struggle of the members of the group for position and recognition within the group. Negro youth are a part of this bitter struggle, and the period of adolescence is one in which the tensions engendered by feelings of personal inadequacy and social insecurity register their most violent shocks. . . .

The race system in the South is preserved by legal sanctions and the threat of physical violence, quite as much as by the mutual acceptance of traditional modes of behavior. Furthermore, the attitudes of the white group are constantly changing and at many points in the relationship between the two races there is a blurring of caste distinctions. In general the Negro continues to occupy a subordinate position, but the fact that he is struggling against this status rather than accepting it, and that the white group is constantly redefining its own status in relation to the Negro, indicates that in the future if one cannot safely predict progress in race relations, he can at least predict change.[2]

Change

The hopes of Negro youth today about their tomorrow are in striking contrast to the hopes their fathers held. Negroes below the age of twenty in 1960 know what immediate drastic change means. These children see respected Negro adults

[2] Charles S. Johnson, *Growing Up in the Black Belt* (Washington, D.C.: American Council on Education, American Youth Commission Studies, 1940).

and courageous Negro children in front page news, in contrast to the customary practice of ignoring Negroes except for criminal acts. The quickened concern of Southern legislatures over their education, heretofore long neglected, has projected Negro children into a sudden prominence they had never known. They realize the eyes of the world are on this drama as it unfolds with Negro children playing stellar roles for the first time in their lives, supported or opposed, as the case may be, by their white contemporaries as they make their personal decisions in a new relationship. This generation of children lives in a climate of change and they will increasingly influence its course.

The greatest change since 1940 has been the redefinition of the Negro's legal status in the South through a succession of judicial decisions that progressed from removal of specific negative legal sanctions to a positive affirmation of legal protection of common opportunity for Americans without distinction.

Changes in the status of Negroes in the South have come about as they could only come—with sweeping internal changes in the South as the economic and political positions of the South underwent change. The cultural gap between Negro Southerners and white Southerners has narrowed as has the gap between all Southerners and the rest of the nation. The New Deal, World War II, post-war economic prosperity, and the role of the United States in international affairs have all had their impact on the South in bringing greater cultural consistency in the region and that of the region in the nation. The changing citizenship status of

Negroes in the South has been influenced by their economic advances and both citizenship and economic statuses have been influenced by the Negro's changing educational status.

The economic status of Southern Negroes has greatly improved despite the fact that it has not improved as much as the economic status of whites who have favored employment opportunity. Urban Negro families earning less than $1,000 annually decreased from 90 to 40 percent from 1936 to 1949. By 1954, the median annual income of urban Negroes in the South was $2,425, which was 56 percent of the median income of urban whites. The median incomes of both rural farm whites and rural farm Negroes remained low in 1954, with the $749 median for Negroes being 49 percent of the median for whites. However, the fact that one-half the urban Negro families in the South had an income of more than $2,500 indicates a greatly improved economic status over that suffered by a predominantly rural Negro population two decades earlier. Increasing recognition of the importance of the Negro market to the economic well-being of the region causes Negroes themselves to have consciousness of the economic power it gives them.

Within the South urbanization has greatly accelerated since 1940. The increase in the urban Negro population from 1940 to 1950 (26 percent) was less than that of the white population (43 percent) since the greater movement of Negroes was to outside the region. Migration within the South showed a higher proportion of Negroes who moved into metropolitan areas going into the central cities than of whites. The rural areas and the small market towns of the

South continue to be strongholds of that Southern tradition which is least yielding to change in the Negro's status. However, population reduction in such areas is making them less important economically and politically.

The movement of the Negro population and the relative numerical importance of Negroes in different areas in the South are related directly to changes in the opportunities for employment created by changes in the economy of the South.

Students of the Southern scene have documented, statistically, the changes in the South over the past two decades. Their conclusions are in agreement with those of John M. Maclachlan and Joe S. Floyd, Jr., in their volume, *This Changing South* which describes: "strain toward consistency with national levels of economic performance" accompanied by cultural changes as aspects of the same fundamental trend.[3] Trends in the status of Negro Southerners indicate the same strain with especially aggressive action to remove invidious distinctions in their citizenship status. The result is a vitally dynamic conception of their citizenship role on the part of Negroes. Professor William G. Carleton, in the summer 1958 issue of the *Antioch Review*, expressed the view that these changes have improved the Negro status: "Groups once underprivileged and exploited are no longer underprivileged and can no longer be exploited as they were. With rising living standards and educational advantages members of once-exploited groups have come to have more

[3] John M. Maclachlan and Joe S. Floyd, Jr., *This Changing South* (Gainesville: University of Florida Press, 1956).

respect for themselves and they are demanding and getting more and more respect from others."

Circumstances of cultural change over the past quarter of a century have produced new functions, new roles, for both whites and Negroes and new relationship patterns between them are emerging. The many changes that might be described are affecting the young even more than their elders. They are learning and experiencing without the need for unlearning or forgetting. Their normal expectations in many things exceed the vague fond hopes of their parents' childhood.

Locating the Future

It has become so obvious as to be redundant to say that the future of very few Negro children is in the rural South. First of all, children are no longer a productive asset. In most types of agriculture, particularly in cotton growing, machinery has made the hand labor of children uneconomical. For many years schooling was regarded as of little importance for Negro farm children. Their futures were seen to be in the fields and the more they worked there the better they could learn what they needed to know. Farmer parents themselves needed the labor of their children to add to their poor incomes, and rationalized keeping them at work rather than in school. This has changed but there are parents who do not realize it.

The greatest demand for child workers in the South today is in vegetable and fruit production which use migratory workers for brief periods. This problem has been intensively studied during the past decade and there are agencies actively working to help children in migratory families who follow harvests from Florida to North Carolina and on out of the South to New York State. These are the most disadvantaged children in the South today. Their experiences threaten to restrict their futures to the transient life of migratory workers.

The future of Negro youth in the South, then, is in its urban areas. By 1950, 74 percent of Southern nonrural Negroes were located in 53 major cities. Maclachlan and Floyd, projecting past and present population trends, conclude that by 1970 Southern Negroes will be "predominantly urban and concentrated heavily in the region's largest metropolitan areas." Great numbers of Negro children will be urban dwellers outside of the South as a result of recent and current migration trends.

In 1940 there were 4.5 million Negroes living on farms. In 1950 this number had dropped to 3.4 million and in 1957 the estimated population was 2.8 million.

It has become increasingly difficult to enter farming since the farm business today requires a considerable sum of capital as do other business enterprises. Negro youth who aspire to farming careers will be a highly selected and doubtless a small group. Those who see their futures as farm laborers will have to possess skills very different from those their tenant fathers used. These skills will be mechanical and technical. As one farmer watching the operation of a cotton harvesting machine remarked to a visitor, "That boy's got to be smart;

he's settin' on $8,000 of my money." The future of Negro youth in agriculture appears to be in a small class of farm-owner operators and as skilled farm workers.

It has been assumed that by the end of the present decade, if the movement continues, half the total Negro population of this country will be living outside the 13 traditionally Southern states. And half of those remaining in the South will be in urban and predominantly metropolitan areas. Not only will the southern Negroes be in metropolitan areas, but they also will be inside the central cities of those areas. However, a big "if" lately has become attached to this first assumption. Tennessee discovered in the spring of 1957 that whites were moving north as fast as, and perhaps even faster than, Negroes. In March 1957, Dr. Harold A. Pedersen of the Department of Sociology and Rural Life at Mississippi State College reported that between April 1950 and July 1956 Mississippi had lost to migration 80,197 citizens, of whom 51,355 were whites and only 28,842 were Negroes. This sharply reversed a trend that most had believed as recently as 1956 was in the other direction. White urban dwellers in the South as elsewhere have flowed outward to the suburbs. The Negro movement has been to the centers of cities. The 1950 census found that while 63 percent of the white populations of southern metropolitan areas lived inside the central cities, 74 percent of the nonwhites were within the city proper. Six states had almost 80 percent or more of their metropolitan Negro populations inside the central cities rather than in the suburbs, a proportion attained only by Louisiana for the white group.[4]

Since Negro children today may confidently expect futures in urban communities, what kind of future awaits them there? The Negro migrants who have been on the move to

[4] Donald Shoemaker et al., *With All Deliberate Speed* (New York: Harper, 1957), p. 72.

urban centers increasingly since the outbreak of World War II, continue to move there. As these Negro children change residence from rural to urban areas they become beneficiaries of educational opportunities, recreational facilities, and health and welfare services superior to those available in the poorer communities from which they have migrated.

A logical conclusion to follow the prospect of urbanization is that in view of the dramatic increase in industrial plants in the South the Negro child of today may expect industrial employment. However, his opportunities for employment as an industrial worker are not too promising.

Eli Ginzberg in *The Negro Potential*[5] has described the advancement and limitations on advancement of Negroes in nonagricultural employment in the South. Between 1940 and 1950 nonagricultural employment in the South expanded by almost 60 percent for white women, almost 40 percent for white men, 30 percent for Negro men and only 7 percent for Negro women. Negroes have not been employed in the new industries locating in the South in anything like their proportion of the labor force. Ginzberg cites the Southern automobile industry as employing over 10,000 white men as operatives but fewer than 350 Negro men. However, the employment of Negroes even at occupational levels lower than those of whites in cities is a distinct advancement over their previous agricultural employment. On the basis of this employment in cities the Negro middle class has grown with

[5] Eli Ginzberg et al., *The Negro Potential* (New York: Columbia University Press, 1956).

more Negroes in professional, semiprofessional and service occupations which primarily serve the Negro population.

As the number of man-hours necessary to produce consumer goods is progressively reduced, employment in the future must be sought in types of jobs other than in manufacturing industries. Expanding opportunities are appearing in the service occupations. Opportunities in this field for Negro youth are small because traditionally there have been no apprenticeships for young Negroes in business establishments. However, the Negro market is receiving more and more consideration from business management and increasing opportunities are being provided for young Negroes to learn to manage service enterprises, especially those which serve predominantly Negro consumers.

An urban future offers expectations, responsibilities, opportunities, and a way of life that is markedly different from that of rural agricultural areas. The future of the Negro child will be one in which he will know all the benefits, critical experiences, and disabilities that belong to the process of urbanization. There will be fewer barriers to change of his status in the city because the very nature of urban life is permissive to shifts in status and roles.

The new citizenship status of Negroes in the South is related to the rearrangement of the Southern population. The relative size of the Negro population sharply declined in the decade 1940–50 and all evidence points to further decline in the period since the 1950 census was taken. Between 1940 and 1950 the Negro population in the South increased only 1.5 percent. Six Southern states—Alabama, Arkansas, Georgia, Kentucky, Mississippi, and Oklahoma—had smaller Negro populations in 1950 than in 1940.

There is evidence that increasing numbers of young Negroes are looking forward to futures in the South rather than planning to realize their hopes and dreams outside of the South. Even many young Negroes who go outside the South for their career preparation expect to follow those careers in the South. The progress of Negro communities in Durham, Atlanta, Nashville and New Orleans is evidence of this. The improvement of living conditions among all classes in these cities over the past decade bolsters the confidence that some Negroes have in the future of the South. The success of the small professional and business group of Negroes and the high standard of living they enjoy is an example before Negro children today. The gradual growth of the number of Negro voters and the attention politicians give their expressed wishes is also an encouragement. Negro children and youth see a future in the South that is emerging despite the drag of the traditional folkways, which on every hand show an ability to retard and delay, but in no place to stay, the future of an urban industrial South where all people will have fuller enjoyment of the citizenship privileges to which they are entitled.

Preparing for the Future

Transmission of the culture to the young both through formal education and informally and preparing the young for their functions and roles through various social devices are preparation for the future of the society. But education cannot prepare the young for the future when the future has not been anticipated with a reasonable degree of realism. Sometimes only a crisis will bring about the realization that the education which is being provided falls short of its intended purpose.

Few books have had such an impact on American thinking about a social issue as *The Uneducated* by Eli Ginzberg and Douglas Bray.[6] The facts presented on illiteracy in World War II were little short of astonishing. Because the mental screening by the Armed Services, as the authors say, "was mainly a measure of educational deprivation, the results of the large-scale examinations are helpful in determining the number and distribution of persons who were so educationally deprived that they were considered unsuitable for military service during the most important war in the country's history." Negroes from the Southeast and Southwest accounted for 88 percent of Negro rejections.

The Uneducated provides statistics to draw a picture in which the South may not take pride and the rest of the nation may not take comfort. Of the 716,400 men rejected for mental deficiency, 525,520 were from the South. Identified according to race, 238,260 were white and 287,260 were Negroes. Stated as rejections per 1,000 men registered, the rates were, for the country as a whole: white, 25; Negro, 152. For the states in the Southeast the rates were: white, 52; Negro, 202. The highest rejection rates for Negroes were in South Carolina

---

[6] Eli Ginzberg and Douglas Bray, *The Uneducated* (New York: Columbia University Press, 1953).

with a rate of 277 and Louisiana with a rate of 247. In addition to these rejections the Army actually inducted 384,000 illiterate men: 220,000 white and 164,000 Negro.

It is apparent that both Negroes and whites had educational disadvantages, since the white rate in the South was double that for whites in the nation as a whole, and the Negro rate in the South was one-third greater than the national rate for Negroes.

The lesson of the Selective Service reports is that a large segment of the country's youth lacked minimum literacy needed to assume responsibilities of maturity. The 1954 reports of Selective Service show that in five southern States —Alabama, Georgia, Mississippi, North Carolina, and South Carolina—more than 30 percent of the Selective Service registrants were disqualified on the mental test while none of the Southern states had fewer than 15 percent so disqualified. Outside of the South disqualifications on this test taken at random were: California 9.6, Colorado, 4.8, Pennsylvania 3.7, and Iowa 1.4.

The first real concern, nationally and regionally, about the effective literacy of Negroes came as a result of these rejection rates of Selective Service during World War II. The comparative inferiority of schools for Negroes became a consideration in the desegregation of schools as evidenced by the earnest efforts of Southern public officials to improve Negro schools even if there was no real intent to make them equal to those of whites. Since 1950 there has been accelerated investment in educational facilities for Negroes both at the elementary school and higher levels. Donald

J. Bogue in a paper in *The New South and Higher Education* concluded that "A rise in the average level of educational attainment was one of the greatest of the recent transformations in the South. The level of educational attainment climbed much faster for the South's nonwhite population than for the white. The number of nonwhite Southerners with some high school or college education increased faster than for white Southerners in all geographic divisions." [7]

In the decade 1940–1950 the gap between provision of education for Negroes and whites began to narrow. Expenditures, school plants and facilities, the length of school term, the training of teachers all showed a marked advance. Pressures brought to bear on the South brought this increase in educational provisions. "In November, 1955, *Southern School News* estimated that $2,556,500,000 had been spent or appropriated for new school construction in 16 states and the District of Columbia since 1949." [8]

In the course of ninety years those who controlled educational policy succeeded in erecting a great barrier between the Negro school and the white school in the South. Actually the segregration of schools was a mechanism for admitting some to knowledge while withholding it from others. The discerning in the South were aware of this. The president of a Negro land-grant college, discussing the institution to which he had given many years of service, summed up his

[7] Jessie P. Guzman, ed., *The New South and Higher Education* (Tuskegee Institute, Ala.: The Department of Research and Records, 1954).

[8] Shoemaker et al., *With All Deliberate Speed*, p. 93.

problems in the simple statement that: "The Negro Land-Grant college was designed and operated so as to never teach a Negro anything that would put him in competition with a white man."

Ernest W. Swanson and John A. Griffin make the point that "the out-migration of southern peoples means that the quality of public education in the South, especially that available to the Negro population, has more than academic importance for the nation as a whole and for certain selected non-southern states in particular." [9] To this it might be added that the farm-to-city shift means that the quality of southern rural education is of obvious concern to urban school systems, both South and North.

The numbers of Negro children help make it important. "There can be no doubt that the burden of educating children is much heavier in the South, particularly the rural South, than in the heavily industrialized Northeast. The differences are so great that, although the continuing urbanization of the South and migration out of the South are doubtlessly narrowing the gap, it will long remain. One of the major products of the South is babies. One of its major exports to other parts of the country is young adults." [10]

Negro children today are attending school in greater numbers, starting at earlier ages and remaining in school longer. Negro parents and Negro youth themselves are conscious of the fact they must prepare for a future that is theirs in a

[9] Ernst W. Swanson and John A. Griffin, *Public Education in the South Today and Tomorrow* (Chapel Hill, N.C.: University of North Carolina Press, 1955).

[10] Ginzberg and Bray, *The Uneducated*, pp. 188–89.

sense that other generations of Negroes have not known. This position makes them insistent that they secure the education they believe they need rather than accept an education another group may consider adequate for them.

During the past decade young Negroes have learned more about school from outside experiences than from class instruction. As an institution around which controversy has centered, the public school has come up for reassessment. Negro children now know more about the provisions and operations of public schools than most adults did ten years ago. They have to go through hostile crowds and into classrooms where they are unwelcome. No parent or friend or even advocate can do this for them. They have done it for themselves in Clinton and Little Rock and Charlotte. When Negro teen-agers made these pioneering journeys with television following their progress for other Negro children everywhere to see, the Negro child got another kind of preparation for the future. These children are aware that others may make opportunities possible for them but they alone can take advantage of an opportunity. They must be prepared for this as an unpleasant experience.

The Negro child in the South today has a better understanding of the Supreme Court, the Presidency, and the Congress than foregoing generations had. It is, moreover, an understanding that relates these institutions directly to his fortunes and welfare. Experiences of Negro youth in this decade and their discussion have provided an uncommon education in the value content of American culture, including political principles and processes of the government under which we live. Perhaps no other generation of young people has had so intensive an indoctrination in the American value system and certainly none has had the inconsistencies and contradictions so clearly presented to it. Southern children and youth have had conflicting social expectations defined for them and negations of these expectations spelled out in detail. No other generation of the young has been so confronted with the bright illusions of our political institutions or has had these illusions so ruthlessly attacked.

Final decision has not been left to legislators, public officials, or the courts. Various sorts of pressure and propaganda groups have debated the status of the Negro child now and in the future. Most adhere to nonviolent aims and methods. The championing organizations, particularly the NAACP, have been publicized, and power and influence far greater than they possess have been attributed to them. This has certainly impressed the Negro child. Negro children have learned how pressure groups are organized and the strategies and tactics they use. They are observing means that may be used to effect social and political actions as well as techniques to prevent and obstruct these by an organized minority. How they use these skills in social manipulation remains to be seen. Lessons in direct social action in subversion and in thwarting the popular will provide tools for use for ill as well as for good.

The waves of migration from the rural South to cities within and without have always brought problems. The migrants are responsible for unduly high proportions of crime, delinquency, and dependency in the cities to which they go. Despite the repetition of these circumstances over many years, no program has been developed to prepare people for migration in the places from which they go. Nor has there been a program to prepare people for adjustment in the places to which they come. This results in tremendous human waste as well as consumption of public revenue to care for those ill-adapted to urban living. Negro children have an intimate acquaintance with these social problems because many of them were not prepared for the new circumstances they face.

Negro children have learned that some action for the common welfare must be taken by the federal government and that those who argue most loudly for states rights leave undone vitally important social tasks. They know how remiss local government can be in providing for public services, for security of the person, and for enjoyment of citizenship rights. Their preparation for the future includes an expectation that the federal government can do and will do certain social tasks made essential by the magnitude of their problems.

Self-Image

The experiences of Negro children in the South during the past decade might well be expected to have affected their conceptions of themselves. Their behavior and conduct offer evidence of some attributes of their self-image. Their self-esteem ranges from pride to bumptiousness. Ideas they hold about their opportunities are expressed in striving to realize an ambition by some and demand for unearned rewards by others. Consciousness of having powerful and influential advocates of their greater opportunity is expressed in quiet confidence by some and a challenging arrogance by others. Encouragement to venture where their parents did not dare has affected the respect shown for parents and teachers who urge caution and restraint. As in all revolutionary circumstances in which a new freedom is gained there is considerable aimless, random, irresponsible behavior on the part of those who have no constructive goals. Uncertainty and a sense of inadequacy are revealed in a truculence that challenges any imposed discipline.

The one clear feature of the new self-image of Negro youth of whatever status is a sense of security expressed by assuming positive and sometimes aggressive attitudes and postures. A Southern white man who recently returned to the South after eight years in other parts of the world said that the most startling change he noticed was that "Negroes look you straight in the eye now." The newly-gained confidence that young Negroes have in themselves and their feeling of security in expressing their aspirations appear to be disturbing facts of contemporary Southern life that many Southern white people are loath to face.

The cherished illusion of Southern whites that Negroes were "satisfied" with their status and opportunities—"their place"—is being clung to despite accumulation of a mass of contrary evidence. During the decade a governor of Mississippi was positively flabbergasted when a conference of Negro educators called by him with full confidence that they would support his program for voluntary segregation refused to do so.

Charles S. Johnson wrote in 1956 what would become the valedictory to his long career of studying race relations. He said: "The present-day Southern Negro does not share the belief of the Southern white that he is inferior as a human being, even though he may earn lower wages and have fewer years of schooling. . . . What is for white Southerners most difficult to understand, in these days, is the absence of both the belief in inferiority and the simulation of this belief. The Southern Negro viewpoint is more broadly national than regional. There are very few, if any, Southern Negroes who do not want full American citizenship, even though there are undoubtedly those who, if they had it, would make no better use of it than some of their white counterparts. In philosophy the Southern Negro identification is with the nation and not with the Southern region, which is, in spirit, separatist." [11]

Negro youth strive to give the impression of not feeling inferior even if the behavior of some is clear evidence that they are over-compensating for such feeling. Unfortunately, a type of juvenile delinquency among Negro children and youth is appearing in the South. It is expressed in challenges to the traditional authority of whiteness and to that of Negro adults who occupy their positions through white authority.

Perhaps the most unfortunate aspect of the young Negro's conception of himself is that he must depend upon himself

[11] The New York *Times* Magazine, September 23, 1956.

to carry his battle with the support of few, if any, white people in his local community. Those whites who are sympathetic to his cause are silent for very good reasons of their own. Those who most loudly declare their "friendship" for him are those who do so confidently asserting they know no "good" Negro has aspirations of equality, and who denounce his heroes and threaten mayhem if he persists in pursuit of his ambitions. A state official in high office expressed this often repeated opinion: "I'm the best friend the Negro ever had but integration will come only over my dead body." If such are the Negro's white "friends," no wonder he is convinced he has none. It is certainly unfortunate when Negro youth get the idea that they must protect themselves or be prepared to do so because the duly constituted authority for preserving the security of citizens in their home communities leaves them at the mercy of enemies who would do violence to them. While their elders are cautioning them to turn the other cheek, many come to feel that their security lies in their readiness to meet violence with violence.

Another feature of the new self-image is that young Negroes are seeing themselves as leaders rather than as being in preparation for leadership. Students who suffered indignities as the first ones to enter desegregated schools, with the responsibility for persisting in their attendance despite discouraging experiences, feel this way. Students who challenged bus segregation in Tallahassee, those who staged a boycott in Orangeburg, and those who mounted a campaign to desegregate business establishments in Oklahoma have some of the feeling. The problem growing out of such a self-conception is the danger of intemperate actions that may draw reprisals.

A third feature of the new self-image is that young Negroes do not feel themselves to be a helpless minority. Instead they consider the die-hard segregationists, whatever their positions may be in the community or however important may be the political offices they hold, to be the minority. And they scoff at them as ludicrous buffoons clinging desperately to a lost cause. The young Negro in the South sees himself as belonging to the majority that includes the federal government, Negroes who have advanced outside the South, and white people of powerful influence outside the South. Problems posed by this feature of the new self-image are: 1) raising an obstruction to an early rapprochement with young Southern whites, and 2) the disenchantment possible if their allies give them too little or too tardy support.

A fourth feature of the new self-image is the belief that they hold to the great human values uncompromisingly. This is especially true in relating their struggle to the independence struggles of Asia and Africa. A problem raised by this conception is the possibility that some may join the divisive black nationalist movements in the United States, which would be a rejection of all the arduous struggle for integration and would bring further tension and conflict.

The major question the Negro youth's new self-image raises is what positive approaches can be taken in order that a constructive productive humanism can mature out of the current personality conflicts in a setting of social confusion.

SPANISH-SPEAKING CHILDREN

by JOHN H. BURMA

CHILDREN from Spanish-speaking backgrounds are very much like any other children, and, basically, their problems are the same as those of ordinary Anglo-American children, with the significant addition of acculturation, culture conflict, and assimilation. These latter may be significantly out of proportion, for they may lead to difficulties which otherwise would not have arisen or would not have been as acute.

In this discussion no inviolately rigorous use of the terms Mexican, Mexican American, or Spanish-speaking people is feasible, because of the confused use of these terms by the general public. Therefore, the noun "Mexican" will be used to mean a native of Mexico, usually an adult; the term "Mexican American" will mean a native-born citizen of Mexican ancestry, a naturalized citizen, or a child who emigrated from Mexico early in his life. "Spanish-speaking

John H. Burma is Chairman of the Department of Sociology at Grinnell College.
Considerable use is made throughout this chapter of data in John H. Burma, *Spanish-Speaking Groups in the United States* (Durham: Duke University Press, 1954), without footnoting or other special reference.

people" is used to refer inclusively to Mexicans, Mexican Americans, Puerto Ricans, and Spanish Americans. Where the group is mixed, the attempt is to designate it according to the majority of the members.

The Mexican American Child

There are in the United States today approximately 3.5 million people of Mexican origin or ancestry (the census makes no exact count), of whom possibly 1.5 million are children and youth. This large number of Mexican American youth exists because Mexicans have been likely to emigrate as families, and because of the relatively high birth rate of Mexican families. Mexican immigration was only a trickle until about 1915, but large numbers came between then and 1930. From 1930 to 1940 this flow reversed itself to emigration, but turned again after 1940 and has continued strong for twenty years. The majority of adults in this group were born in Mexico, but the majority of youth were born in the United States.

Approximately 40 percent of Mexican American youth live in Texas, another 40 percent in California, and the remainder in Colorado, Arizona, New Mexico, Illinois, Kansas, Michigan, New York—in fact, in almost every state. In numerous school districts of Texas, California, and New Mexico, Spanish-speaking children make up one-fourth or more of the total students. As a rule there exist social and residential segregation wherever there are large numbers of Mexican Americans, although where their number is small, there usually is little or no segregation. Throughout Texas,

California, and the other states with large Mexican American population, the Mexican American child suffers a special and serious handicap in becoming a successful American citizen as the result of being segregated by Anglos and of segregating himself from Anglos. It is the child growing up under these conditions with whom we are here most concerned, whether he lives in rural Texas or the slums of New York City. A relatively small proportion of Spanish-speaking children are from Puerto Rico; these will be discussed at the end of this chapter.

FAMILY AND HOME. As with all children, the family of the Mexican American child is of great importance in his development. Historically the Mexican family has been of the extended type, including grandparents, uncles and aunts, and cousins. This has the effect of giving the child a wide circle from whom he may receive emotional support, warmth of acceptance, stability, and a real feeling of belonging. These contributions are much to be desired (and have been suggested as probable factors in the lower rate of psychoses found among Mexican Americans). In this sense it is unfortunate that the extended family system runs counter to the American middle-class nuclear family pattern, hampers acculturation and assimilation, and tends to limit the individual largely to contacts with family members. These are serious handicaps for a child who is marginal (i.e., living on edges of two cultures but wholly in neither), and has contributed to the retention of the "colony" (colonia) housing pattern among Mexican Americans. The extended family and the colonia help explain why most Mexican American children have few if any Anglo friends. In the past, most recreation was found in the home and most free time was spent in the home; this is still true, but is observably decreasing. The extended family pattern is itself in a state of decline; the third generation does not want it as a day-to-day relationship, but only as a matter of frequent family get-togethers.

Other changes are occurring in behavior and attitudes toward matters relating to the family. Families plan for, and have, fewer children. The role of godparents in the life of the child is becoming negligible. There is an increasing desire by the Mexican American to function as an individual rather than as a subordinate unit in an extended family structure. This leads to "unfilial" behavior, and some consequent misunderstanding and estrangement between generations. This may become particularly acute before the marriage of the children, for under the extended family system marriage is a matter of group concern and activity; under the nucleated family system marriage is a private concern.

As acculturation increases there are changes in family roles. The father becomes less dominant, and shows more affection for the wife and children; the wife is less subordinate as the result of mutual sharing of authority and discipline; the education of the wife equals or surpasses that of the husband; the possibility of the wife working outside the home is looked upon with more favor. The gap between the freedom permitted boys and girls, although still great, is decreasing; girls are less strictly supervised, but still are more closely watched than are boys; supervision of both is least among the lower class. "Nice" girls are now permitted more dating than previously—which was almost nil—but still much less than Anglo girls. In most of these matters class differences are quite observable, with the lower and upper classes, for different reasons, most closely approaching the Anglo norm; the middle class is slowest to change, seeming to feel that their prized "family respectability" requires the perpetuation of the older attitudes and behavior patterns.

Sometimes an additional cleavage between generations results when parents who cling tenaciously to the old culture have children who seek rapid, complete assimilation. This not only causes heartache, but may leave the second generation without adequate adult models or adult guidance, and foster the formation of gangs, whose influence on the child and control of his behavior then are greater than they normally would be.

Important to any family is the home and the neighborhood in which it lives. Almost always in the Southwest, and commonly elsewhere, the Mexican immigrant lives in a segregated subcommunity. By whatever name is it known, this area is substandard and its reputation, among Anglos, is not a savory one. Nearly all these *colonias* are below the average of their parent city in such things as size and quality of housing, electricity, inside toilets, and piped hot water. The families of migratory agricultural workers have a poorer situation, for in the spring they leave their shacks for the even worse housing available to migatory laborers. Here and there public housing projects have been provided to improve this situation, but probably two-thirds to three-fourths of all Mexican American children live in substandard houses located in substandard communities. The lighter, the more well-to-do, and the more assimilated he and his parents are, the less the discrimination and the less likely he is to live in such an area.

EDUCATION. The educational opportunities and activities of any child are of great significance; this is especially true if he is the child of immigrant parents coming from a country of low average education and entering a country of high average education. Adult Mexican immigrants brought with them an average of about five years of formal education, the attitude that neither sex, particularly girls, needed a high-school education, and little belief in the general value of education for anyone except well-to-do and professional people.

Thus the chief problem relating to the education of Mexican American children before 1930 was that of getting them into school. This problem was solved with reasonable success, but there next arose the problem of segregated schools. In many areas in Texas, California, and some other parts of the Southwest, Mexican American children were required to attend segregated schools or were placed in segregated classrooms. As usual, "segregated" meant second class or worse, and from the 1930s to the middle '40s the removal of these barriers was a major concern. During the 1946–48 period, various federal courts ruled against this segregation, and in the succeeding dozen years desegregation has become almost complete. Segregation sometimes still exists through gerrymandering and the fact that schools near Mexican subcommunities are likely to be labeled "Mexican" schools and hence shunned by Anglos.

Today the chief problem is early dropout of Mexican

American students. Enrollments are good in the primary grades but then decline so that by high school they probably average no more than half the potential. Low income is a serious barrier, and since many of these parents have had little formal education they are not successful in explaining to their children why they should graduate from high school —if indeed the parents see this as desirable.

Part of the explanation for this problem also is to be found in the fact that Mexican American pupils typically are over-age for their grade placement. Either they have missed school to follow the crops, or their language handicaps have been too severe, or they started late and always have been overage. In some cases, as the child reaches adolescence the disparity between his age and that of his schoolmates is magnified for him and is a significant factor in his lack of desire to remain in school. In others, behavior which would be normal two grades ahead is viewed as alarmingly precocious by Anglo mothers who do not take into account the normal significant differences between the behavior of a twelve-year-old girl and that of a fourteen-year-old girl, even if they happen to share the same school room.

From the standpoint of the children themselves, probably their chief educational problem is their linguistic handicap. The normal educational procedure is to admit children to school at six or seven, carry on all teaching in English, and trust that they will learn the language and the content material simultaneously. This does occur under optimum conditions; i.e., when the child is bright, strongly motivated and encouraged, sympathetically taught, and wholeheartedly included by his classmates in all activities. Unfortunately such a situation is rather rare, and most commonly the child learns both language and content imperfectly. Often this language handicap, difficult at any time, becomes progressively worse until it becomes insurmountable and the child fails repeatedly and finally leaves school.

This linguistic difficulty of Mexican American pupils was used as a rationalization by those who wished educational segregation for social reasons. It was stated that segregation gave the Spanish-speaking student a "language benefit." Today professional opinion is virtually unanimous that the best way to teach English is to place the child in a class where most of the children speak English.

Another educational problem, much less dramatic than language, but equally significant, is the average Mexican American child's relatively low economic, social, and cultural level. These factors are serious handicaps for any child, and the superimposition on them of bi-lingualism, cultural conflicts, and assimilation problems often has unfortunate results. Teachers report occupational orientation and health education as problems frequently encountered. Some of the more alert school systems report considerable difficulty in presenting the Mexican cultural heritage adequately either to the majority or minority groups. Certainly an indispensable element in a complete school program for mixed schools must be the education of Anglo children to some appreciation of the Mexican culture. Most states with large numbers of Mexican American students now publish guides to aid teachers with Spanish-speaking students.

In addition to these difficulties, a significant number of Mexican American children must move about with their parents who are engaged in migratory agricultural labor. This means at best shifting schools several times, and at worst attending school only a few months of the year. Under a situation of permanent or temporary mobility the child and his parents must value education very highly to make the necessary effort and sacrifices so that the child can attend school regularly. Various educational experiments have been tried in coping with the migrant child, but none has been outstandingly successful, so the great bulk of such children attend regular community schools. Here they create problems. Sometimes they cause serious, if temporary, overcrowding. They present a difficult challenge to teachers to provide a program which has meaning and value for them, permits them to learn at their own level and pace, and which takes into account their special needs without jeopardizing the program of the permanent pupil. The best solution, a highly flexible, individualistic learning program, is good for the permanent children as well as the migrants, but unfortunately, such a program is difficult to organize and staff, and expensive to maintain.

To be successful in such a program, a school must plan an adequate method. This may be done by a "big brother" system, by a class room host and hostess, by special use of Spanish-speaking permanent students, and by practical study units on cotton, vegetables, beets, purchasing, health, family living—and Mexico. The school must have available class materials on a wide range of levels, so the migrant child may begin where he is fitted to begin and may receive individual assistance as he needs it. Account must be taken of bilingualism by emphasizing the use of oral English, yet protecting the child with a limited knowledge of the language; respect should be shown for Spanish, and at least a smattering of it should be taught to Anglo children.

In general, the educational picture for Mexican American children is a constantly brightening one. Segregation is disappearing, and schools and teachers are better equipped and more deeply motivated to handle special problems. Mexican American standards of living are improving and migratory labor is decreasing. A rapidly increasing number of pupils are children of native-born parents and bring to school a considerable knowledge of American customs and language. In short, at the chief points of tension the strain is gradually lessening, and at the same time better techniques for dealing with these problems are being developed and more widely used.

DELINQUENCY. Wherever there are sizable numbers of Mexican American youth, they have the reputation of being more delinquency-prone than Anglo youth. Although this is likely to be exaggerated, it does exist. Delinquency is related in some way to a number of factors: living in slum or substandard areas, employment of both parents away from home, educational difficulties, association with persons who break the law, low family income, poor recreation, the power of the gang, lack of occupational opportunity, lack of strict supervision, culture conflict, movement from rural to urban areas, family disorganization. All these impinge upon the average Mexican American youth more than the average Anglo youth, and hence we predict and find a higher delinquency rate among Mexican Americans. For example, most youth are rather strongly motivated to make money, to be liked, and to "be somebody." There are many avenues to achieve these goals and most of them are socially acceptable. A high proportion of the socially approved avenues are virtually closed, however, to Mexican American youth, while none of the socially disapproved avenues are closed. Thus the chances of the Mexican American youth choosing one of the disapproved methods of goal-seeking are greater than they are for the average Anglo boy—through no fault of his own but because of societal factors over which he has no control.

For all immigrants and their children, cultural differences or culture conflict are potential sources of disorganization, and this is true for Mexican Americans. For example, in Mexico it is normal for men and boys to idle on the street corner in the evening, amusing themselves and getting the day's news. In this country if boys spend much time loafing on the streets in the evenings they are likely to get into trouble with the law. Moreover, in Mexico the pattern was to release the boy from most parental controls when he was around sixteen, so that he might "become a man"; this usually meant sex, gambling, alcohol, and potentially some fighting. It was assumed that the boy would have his fling for a year or two, get it out of his system, and marry and settle down to become a respectable adult. In the United States if this kind of release occurs at the same age, the boy is only half through high school, and may be four to six years away from settling down as an adult. Here he is considered a delinquent and may be sent to a training school.

In the past fifteen years the spotlight has been on Mexican American gangs as products and producers of delinquency. From San Antonio to Los Angeles these youngsters are called *pachucos*, or simply '*chucs*, and are looked down upon by Anglos and by some Mexican Americans. Usually they are marginal persons, lost between the old Mexican world which they do not accept and the new American world which does not accept them. The core of the *pachuco* world is the neighborhood gang, not the home or school, and the members of the gang feel for it a great attachment. Their rejection of parts of the Mexican culture is closely related to the cleavage between this age group and the parent group. It is particularly unfortunate that the isolation from the parent group usually occurs before the youngsters have achieved access to Anglo society. Whenever this type of situation occurs, teen-aged gangs are strong and prevalent. Their members go out of their way to make themselves visible and to demonstrate "belonging," by ducktail and fender haircuts, special clothes, whiskers, sunglasses ("shades"), self-tattoos, and a special language, *pachucana*—part Spanish, part English, part jive, part manufactured or invented. Not all Mexican American youth who sport some of these external characteristics are actual *pachucos*; for many of them the true *pachucos* are just a reference group, one to which they feel some psychic kinship, or to which they aspire eventually, but with which they presently have no direction connection.

Group workers and probation officers say most *pachucos* are not antisocial, but are so painfully social that they are willing to make great sacrifices to achieve acceptance, status, and "belonging." The strength, uniqueness, and social cohesion of these groups undoubtedly are increased by language and cultural factors.

It must not be assumed from the foregoing paragraphs that there is a wholesale revolt among Mexican American youth against their parents. This is far from true, and the situation is a great deal more complex than such an oversimplification might indicate. Both parents and children agree on the desirability of rapid assimilation and uphold many of the attitudes and goals of Anglo culture. In such families the parents may speak only English to their children, and both may be motivated strongly toward education and upward mobility. They may seek Anglo friends, residence outside the *colonia*, and Anglo jobs. In school these children tend to achieve better than the average, to be liked by their teachers, and to find some small acceptance by the Anglo students.

The attitudes of other Mexican American youth toward this group of "squares" range from acceptance, jealousy, and grudging emulation on one extreme to almost hate on the other. Many *pachucos*, however, retain much *Mexicanissmo* and indicate great pride in their parents' cultural heritage. Anyone who turns his back on this heritage (speaking English only, for example) may be termed a *falso*, is thought to consider himself "too good for the rest of us," and may expect to be roughed up occasionally if he lives in a *pachuco* neighborhood. In actuality the great majority of Mexican American youth fall between the "squares" and the *pachucos* on the continuum. They seek assimilation, but not avidly, and retain, partly by inertia, a considerable amount of the old culture. They attend school dutifully, if without much enthusiasm, and have hopes (realistic or not) of finishing high school and getting a "good" job. Only for the "square" group is there any hope of attending college. Members of the great middle group may engage in delinquent acts, but their frequency and seriousness are likely to be considerably less than are those of the true delinquent. Obviously it is this middle group who offer the greatest hope and challenge to concerned agencies and individuals. This group has all kinds of problems, but most of them are not insurmountable in size or of such depth that they cannot be alleviated by known, normal means.

CULTURE. Of the various problems faced by Mexican American youth, none are more clearly different from those of Anglo youth than the ones related to acculturation, assimilation, culture conflict, and marginality. In the United States we tend to pay lip service to the concept of cultural pluralism—numerous separate cultures coexisting in cooperative harmony—but in actual practice most Americans tacitly expect cultural conformity and look down upon anyone whose language, color, or ways of life differ from the majority norm. This leads to pressure on any culturally different group to acculturate and to become assimilated.

Some immigrants to America fled from their homeland or in other ways forever severed their ties with the old country.

For them and their children, acquisition of the new culture was the only possibility they saw for a secure future. Such motivation has not been strong for all groups; some (Chinese, Italians, Mexicans, etc.) have contained many individuals who looked upon themselves as temporary residents and who anticipated a return to the homeland within a few years. For such persons a transfer of loyalty would be both undesirable and impractical. Elements of the new culture were accepted or rejected in terms of utility only, and any which were in serious conflict with the old culture would not be accepted; the less change and adjustment necessary, the better.

Many Mexican immigrants entered the United States with the full intention of returning to Mexico. Men brought their families with them not because they intended to "settle" but to keep the family unit intact during their sojourn. They and their children were Mexicans and intended to remain so. Under these circumstances acculturation has little utility and would have negative effects if carried too far.

Immigrants from across the seas had to accumulate a great deal of money before renewing their family and cultural ties by a visit to the "old country"; not so with the Mexican immigrant who may return to Mexico easily. Thus the accessibility of Mexico has hindered among Mexican Americans the acculturation to be found in other groups. Yet some Mexican immigrants intended from the first to become American citizens, to live here the rest of their lives, and have expected their children to do the same. These persons consciously have sought acculturation and have achieved it as rapidly as any other group. Thus second generation Mexican American children come from homes which represent both a wide range of attitudes toward acculturation and a wide range of actual acculturation. When the parents, through intent, inertia, or ignorance, cling to the old culture, and the children are sent to a public school which endeavors to inculcate in them middle-class Anglo attitudes, values, and culture patterns, misunderstanding and conflict at home and at school are almost inevitable.

It has been observed that there are three cultures with which the Mexican American child is concerned: the Anglo, the Mexican, and the Mexican-American. The Mexican-American culture often acts as a bridge for the immigrant child; he can acquire it much more easily than the Anglo culture. In general, the Mexican-American culture contains large portions of Anglo material culture and Anglo mass culture, and large portions of Mexican nonmaterial culture. The second generation boy usually has accepted much Anglo material culture, i.e., he understands and wants a bicycle, air rifle, and comic books. As a participant in our mass culture he may play Tarzan, be able to give you the batting average of Mickey Mantle, or be a rock-'n-roll addict. The material culture and mass culture are wide but shallow; the child's real problems come with the more fundamental, ethical, and value aspects of nonmaterial culture, for it is here that serious confusion or conflict occurs.

The public school, which is by far the chief acculturative agency for Mexican American children, usually teaches Anglo middle-class attitudes, values, and norms as if they were

Absolute Truth; to the extent that the school is successful, the child accepts these and either drops or refuses to adopt many of the attitudes, values, and norms presented by his family. Granted complete good will within the family, which is as unrealistic an assumption as it would be among Anglo families, conflict in these matters is inevitable. Hence the typical Mexican American youth of the second or third generation is marginal; this marginality is an anomalous condition, likely to lead to misunderstanding, frustration, and disorganization. Fortunately marginality is dynamic rather than static, and tends to reach a peak and then decline to a less disorganizing level. It is the child who is half-and-half, rather than 10 percent and 90 percent, who suffers most from marginality.

Some of the social disorganization found among marginal Mexican Americans results because such youth have freed themselves from creeds, beliefs, and other social controls which operate within the framework of the old culture, and yet have not acquired wholly the folkways, mores, and social controls of the new Anglo culture. Thus they may suffer from *anomie*, be relatively free from self-discipline or value internalization, and be more easily influenced by matters of the moment. Aimless or delinquent behavior are the frequent results, although strong, disciplined men, dreamers and reformers, as well as hoodlums, alcoholics, and criminals have come from such environments.

Marginality of children may be prolonged by parents who wish to have "the best of both cultures." At first glance this is a laudable goal; in practice it frequently works out unsatisfactorily. Basic to the failure of any such goal is the fact that cultures do not consist of many unrelated bits and pieces, but rather are a weblike, organic whole. Bits may not be abstracted from the whole with impunity, even if other bits arbitrarily are put into place. Thus it appears necessary for the Mexican American to make up his mind which culture he wishes for his own, rather than to drag on, willy-nilly, with unrelated parts of each.

A good illustration is bilingualism; for no one would argue that it is undesirable to know more than one language. Mexican American youngsters are not really taught Spanish, and commonly they read it very imperfectly, write it phonetically and incorrectly, and speak with poor grammar, construction, and vocabulary; and if they take academic Spanish in high school they meet with little more success than they do in English courses. Since such children as a rule also know English imperfectly, they have a mastery of no language. An increasing number of ambitious second generation persons who now are parents do not teach their children Spanish in the home; they fear the child will learn neither language well, and if a choice must be made, they prefer English.

Certainly conflicting values of the two or three cultures with which the Mexican American child has contact is a disorienting factor for him. Neither the Mexican nor the American culture has truly systematic values; each has some contradictory elements. Confusion of values is serious enough to warrant considerable attention by philosophers, social psychologists, educators, and psychiatrists, when only one culture is involved; how much more serious it is when the child is expected to grope toward a workable, acceptable pattern within the maze of two such cultures! That he confronts frustration, confusion, misconception, and disorganization is to be accepted as a matter of course at the same time it is greatly deplored.

The Puerto Rican Child

The second largest group of Spanish-speaking children in America today are the Puerto Ricans. Twenty years ago there were only a few scattered thousands on the mainland, and few of them were children. In 1955 there were between one-half to two-thirds of a million here (despite wild estimates of "millions"), with an estimated 80 percent of the total in New York City alone, including 40,000 to 50,000 children enrolled in the New York City schools. There, in Chicago, and in most major cities between, are found sizable numbers of Puerto Rican youth. Like other immigrant groups of the past, Puerto Ricans are poor, uneducated, lack occupational skills, have little facility with the English language, suffer disproportionately from social problems, and live in the least desirable sections of the city with their high delinquency rates, in part because of discrimination, segregation, and exploitation. Puerto Rican children and youth have serious enough problems to warrant our attention. Except that a higher proportion of Puerto Rican youth are themselves immigrants, and that they are concentrated much more heavily in large urban areas, the situations and problems of Puerto Rican and Mexican American youth are in many respects similar.

Like the Mexican family the Puerto Rican family undergoes changes with immigration. The father's authority over the wife and children declines, freedom of wife and children increases, and for the children freedom sometimes becomes license and incorrigibility. With this group, too, there is likely to be a hiatus between generations which increases misunderstanding and conflict; in part this is the result of the greater acculturation of the child and his consequent marginality, confusion, and disorientation of values and norms. As is so common and so tragic in such cases, usually parents and children each sincerely believe that they are right and the other wrong. Many Puerto Rican women work outside the home, because there is need for additional income or because there is no male breadwinner. This means children too frequently are without the mothers' care during the day, are left with neighbors or in day nurseries, or wait on the streets after school until the parent returns.

The environment of large numbers of Puerto Rican children in the New York City and Chicago school systems has caused more problems than one would expect, because of the attempt to put into practice new educational philosophies. Instead of the older rapid assimilation philosophy, the new philosophy maintains that the cultural and social contributions which Puerto Ricans and other groups can make should be utilized; that education for all children need not mean the same education for all children, but rather individualized instruction, assistance, and remedial work geared to the needs and interests of each child; and that teaching should encompass the total development of the individual for his best total adjustment. These philosophies and goals, although highly desirable, do create extra problems whenever large numbers of youngsters as different as the Puerto Rican children enter a school system. Inevitably the school to which the Puerto Rican child is assigned is much different from the one with which he or his parents were familiar in Puerto Rico, and many of the values and norms peripheral to education are different (such as participation of girls in after-school programs), so that tri-cornered misunderstandings between parent, school, and child easily arise, but are not so easily resolved.

Some of the techniques which have been evolved to meet these problems in New York City include the use of Spanish-speaking interpreters at registration time and other methods of making the parents and child feel accepted, booklets in Spanish to explain the school's aims and rules, the use of a buddy or big brother system, assignment to orientation or vestibule classes where emphasis is placed on remedial and language arts work and from which the student is moved when he is ready, a conscious attempt to involve parents as much as possible in school activities and interests, and the use of special Spanish-speaking guidance counsellors.

Unlike the Mexican Americans, Puerto Ricans never have been subjected to educational segregation, but the quality of the school systems from which the immigrant children come is such that they usually are retarded a year or more. The fact that these young people have special needs for vocational training, health, and hygiene, and community awareness makes their satisfactory education even more difficult. Almost without exception Puerto Rican students have serious linguistic handicaps, despite the fact that immigrant children have been taught some English in the Puerto Rican schools.

One of the most frustrating aspects of mainland living for many immigrant Puerto Rican children is our color bar. On the island three groups are recognized: the white, the Negro, and the *grifo*, who is mixed; there is not much discrimination against the Negro, and almost none against the *grifo* except socially; the *grifo* thinks of himself as somewhat above the Negro. When a *grifo* comes to the mainland, he finds himself not only classed as a Negro, which threatens his status, but also subjected to far more discrimination than was directed against the Negro on his home island. The results may be confusion, bitterness, frustration, aggression, or a "don't care" or "what's the use" attitude. By mainland standards from a third to a half of Puerto Ricans are colored —considerably more than by island standards. The Puerto Rican mulatto child is not only subjected to discrimination on the mainland, he faces difficulty in thinking of himself as originally Puerto Rican and Spanish, since he is looked upon by most people as a Negro. His problem of self-evaluation and self-concept may lead to psychic disturbance. Certainly this is one reason for Puerto Rican gang membership; in the gang he is accepted for what he is, stands on his own merit, and has security.

In general the problems of the Puerto Rican child are basically those which most of our immigrants have faced and overcome in the past: language handicaps, overcrowded housing in slum and delinquency areas, poverty and all its secondary aspects, discrimination and low status, educational difficulties, recreational inadequacy, and the problems of acculturation, assimilation, and culture conflict. The historic pattern on the East Coast has been for the immigrant group to settle in an ethnic slum area and there to reproduce for a generation the culture patterns of the old country. The younger people gradually move away to undifferentiated housing areas until the ethnic area, as an area, no longer exists. The "white" Puerto Ricans are following this traditional pattern, and the social world of the Negro Puerto Ricans, at first bounded by the apartment house and the street, expands more slowly. This change comes more easily for those who live outside the New York City area. The assimilation of Puerto Rican youth is hindered in New York by the absence of concrete, homogeneous norms to which to adjust. The kaleidoscope pattern of New York City produces neither a clear norm to which to conform nor the social controls conducive to conformity which may be found elsewhere. Lack of homogeneity of behavior, however, is not always a serious handicap in a heterogeneous social world.

Coming late, as they do, in our stream of immigrants, Puerto Rican children benefit from the wisdom gained by trial-and-error techniques used on other groups. Metropolitan schools and social agencies know better how to handle such problems than before. The Puerto Rican immigrant child brings with him knowledge of some elements of American mass culture acquired in Puerto Rico, and at least some knowledge of the language on which to build. He already is a citizen, and suffers little more from divided loyalty than does a transplanted Texan. For a significant number, their color will be a serious handicap from their school days forward. In short, Puerto Rican children suffer all the handicaps of any children living under comparable socio-economic conditions, plus special problems which are cultural and racial in nature; yet they have better and more sympathetic assistance in meeting all these problems than any previous group on the East Coast. There is every reason to believe that their problems will decline in the future.

The Spanish American Child

Although relatively fewer in number, the problems and prospects of Spanish American children also are of importance. There are in New Mexico several tens of thousands of Spanish American children. Although they are tenth generation native American, this group until a generation ago had clung tenaciously to its own variation of Spanish culture, and hence its children have most of the problems of Mexican American or Puerto Rican children, at least in terms of cultural differences. They suffer a mixture of ethnic and class discrimination, but not in overwhelming degree. They, too, must choose which culture to follow, and consequently are typically marginal, with all that this implies. On the other hand, many of them live in stable families in their own small agricultural communities, or in cities like Albuquerque and Santa Fe where their numbers are so great that they do not feel isolated.

Like other Spanish-speaking children their greatest handicap, other than poverty and its secondary results, is their language difficulty in school, which results in an average achievement less than that of Anglo children. Spanish Americans are a proud group, but this has not prevented many adolescent boys from needing the psychic security received from gang membership, and so-called *pachucos* are as common in cities in New Mexico as in California or Texas.

Although these children are now and for some time in the future will be handicapped by poverty, lack of economic opportunity, linguistic inadequacy, marginality, and culture conflict, their opportunities and outlook seem at least as good as those of Mexican American or Puerto Rican youth.

JUVENILE DELINQUENCY

by ROBERT M. MAC IVER

"PARENTAGE," Bernard Shaw wrote, "is a very important profession, but no test of fitness is ever imposed in the interests of the children." None the less the great majority of parents succeed, somehow or other, under all sorts of conditions and often in the face of considerable handicaps, in bringing up their children to become at least as good citizens as they are themselves. And sometimes it happens that parents of high standards have children who deviate into delinquency. There are no universals here to guide our search for cause or cure. But a growing consensus of research findings indicates that the parting of the ways, the redirection of the child toward habits of antisocial behavior, begins very frequently in the stresses and strains of parent-child relationships.

We must not, however, interpret this conclusion too narrowly. The family is not an island apart from the group and the neighborhood. Tensions aroused within it may be in-

Robert M. MacIver is Director of the Juvenile Delinquency Evaluation Project of New York City and Professor Emeritus of Sociology and Political Philosophy at Columbia University.

duced by the forces that bear on it. Parent or child or both
may be so disturbed by outside influences, by the social or
economic conditions to which they are exposed, that the
relation between the two deteriorates. To take one of many
cases, if the child is retarded educationally and has consequent troubles and frustrations in his schooling, he resorts
to truancy. The father, worried by this or by the school investigator, rough-handles him, not knowing any better, and
the process of alienation between home and school sets in.
We should not assume that the children of families in the
higher-delinquency areas are inherently more prone to misbehavior than more favored children, nor is parental failure
by any means always a sufficient explanation. The lack of
outlets for youthful energies, the cultural deprivation of the
home, the congestion of living space, the paucity of opportunities and incentives that others enjoy, and not infrequently
a sense of being discriminated against, these and other adverse influences corrode the attitudes of the young, while
the parents in turn suffer from like frustrations.

Human beings, and not least children, have a remarkable
capacity for surmounting unfavorable conditions. Even under
the conditions suggested above the large majority of children
grow up to be respectable law-abiding citizens. But with
some, either the stresses are greater or the natural disposition
is less resistant, and these, chafing at restraints and unable
to solve their problems, become disoriented in their society
and most often alienated at home, with father or mother or
both. Some of them are brought up in "broken" homes, but
more of them in emotionally "broken" homes, where often

lack of guidance, lack of reasonable discipline, or the sheer lack of understanding between the older and the younger generation confirms the process that ends in the hardened delinquent who finds his only congenial society in the company and under the code of the underworld.

If then we hold that juvenile delinquency is a problem that has its focus within the family, we do not thereby assign full responsibility for it to the family itself, and we do not imply that either therapy or prevention depends only on methods that might be brought to bear within the family circle. The emotional tone of family life is a composite of various factors. Rarely do we find a culture group so enclaved within its own traditions that family standards are sheltered from such impacts. This is the case, for example, with the Chinese colony in lower Manhattan, where, incidentally, we find a complete absence of the juvenile delinquency characteristic of congested city areas. In like manner certain religious groups anchored in a highly distinctive orthodoxy are in degree immunized from social influences and trends.

Socio-Economic Factors

The importance of the socio-economic factors, as they react on family life, must be grasped if we are to interpret the incidence of delinquency or are concerned with remedial policies. Under socio-economic factors we include particularly the complex consisting of low economic level, deteriorated and overcrowded housing, lack of training or experience for the competitive urban life, and subjection to some degree of economic and social discrimination. This is precisely the complex that characterizes our high-delinquency areas. Such areas the incoming groups inhabit, groups generally of different ethnic or racial origin from that of the surrounding population, and the combination of resourcelessness and residential restrictions has resulted in increasingly congested and deteriorating housing, with multiple families occupying the space where a single family dwelt before.

It is the children of groups so situated that swell the delinquency statistics. For example, in New York City, in the first five months of 1959, 39 percent of the delinquency petitions before the Children's Court concerned Negro children, many of them from recently migrant Southern Negro families, and 22 percent concerned Puerto Rican children. The elementary and junior high-school enrollment in New York City public schools was given (October 31, 1958) as Negroes 21.3, and Puerto Ricans 16.3 percent. Various other evidences suggest that for the children of these two groups educational retardation is an important factor in the causation of delinquency.

The simple distinctions of delinquency incidence already drawn, which could be much more fully developed by a breakdown of delinquency statistics across the country, may be sufficient to refute some current misconceptions about the nature of the problem. In the first place, delinquency is not to be understood, as is sometimes done, as being essentially a "lower-class" phenomenon or as a product of "lower-class morality." Delinquency occurs among the youth of all classes, though in the more prosperous classes it may be less visible or less exposed and there is less among them of the petty filching that tempts the poor. Where delinquency is most prevalent, it is where particular evocative conditions exist, and these are to be found, not among the poor as a whole but especially among newly urbanized groups, ill-adjusted to city life and too frequently suffering the effects of social and economic prejudice and discrimination. We have therefore no ground to assume that the higher delinquency rates of these groups are attributable to inherent inferiority or native viciousness.

These considerations strengthen the prospect that the volume of juvenile delinquency can be definitely reduced by well-directed measures, based on an understanding of the conditions that foster it. If the higher rates are socially conditioned they should be amenable to constructive change in the conditions, including the timely provision of outlets, opportunities, and requisite training for the children who are beginning to seek illegitimate substitutes for them. But this is a topic to be developed later.

What the Statistics Really Mean

On the face of it, the growing delinquency statistics look quite alarming. In the decade 1948–1957 the number of juvenile delinquency court cases doubled for the country as a whole. The percent increase has been greatest in the last few years. If we project the 1957 rate it means that some 12 percent of all children between the ages of ten and seventeen will during their adolescence be involved in at least one court appearance on a delinquency charge. The number of youngsters who come to the attention of the police, without court appearance, is probably around three times as large. And when we note that boys are involved about five times as often as girls and also that considerably more urban boys are apprehended than rural boys, we reach the conclusion that any boy brought up in certain urban areas is almost as likely as not to run some time into some trouble with the law.

The delinquency problem is certainly a quite serious one, and clearly our attempts to deal with it have had little success. But again we shall misconceive both its dimensions and the nature of its demands on us unless we interpret aright these mounting figures.

Let us observe, to begin with, that the coverage of juvenile delinquency laws has become very wide, including a whole range of offenses from relatively trivial misbehavior to felonies. According to a somewhat old Children's Bureau report (1945)—more recent country-wide figures are not available—one-third of all charges, excluding traffic charges, before juvenile courts were on the ground of truancy or running away—forms of escapism that may not imply any evil intent. The proportion of very serious crimes, such as robbery or aggravated assault, was around only 2 percent. Moreover, the number of arrests depends somewhat on the activity of the police, and when the public is aroused by some flagrant juvenile crime the police are likely to apprehend a larger number than previously, which they can easily do because of the wide range of offenses that come within the scope of the delinquency laws. Potential arrests within the law are always greater than actual arrests, for adults and juveniles alike, and the disparity is lessened when there is public outcry. The other side of the picture is suggested in the fact that around half the cases brought before the courts are dismissed or discharged.

It may also be, as is frequently asserted, that greater public concern has been aroused in the needs and problems of our youth, and that in consequence more activity is displayed in reporting, recording, and handling cases of youthful misconduct. Youth welfare organizations, family organizations, clinics and institutions for delinquents have certainly increased, and a rather considerable proportion of the cases that come before our courts are referred by schools, psychiatric clinics, welfare organizations, and parents themselves. Another factor is a change that has come over the fights between youthful gangs. Scraps between teams or gangs of boys are probably as old as history, but in an age inured to violence the modern urban gang has taken to new and more deadly weapons. Instead of using fists and sticks and brickbats the embattled gang resorts to zip-guns and switch-blades and sawed-off shot guns, resulting in more serious and sometimes fatal casualties. When this happens, there is a public outcry for stronger measures of control, the police are alerted, and one way or another more youthful offenders come into evidence.

While, then, the vast increase in the reported rates of juvenile delinquency may not signify a *corresponding* increase in youthful misbehavior, it still reveals the gravity of the problem. Whatever affects youth affects the citizenship of tomorrow. The train of evils that follow from the disaffection, alienation, and lawlessness of youth is incalculably great—the squandering of energies, the degradation of families, the injury done to neighborhood and community, the mortgage on the society of the future, as well as the vast cost to the nation of crime itself. In some of our great cities the percentage of arrests for serious crimes has risen well over the earlier national average cited above.

What makes the problem more formidable is that in spite of the much-expanded agency activities directed to the control of delinquency the number of cases calling for such activities continues to increase. Is it then that these activities have little success, or should we assume that, had it not been for them, the increase would have been considerably greater? We might note in this connection that in 1956 and 1957 the number of juvenile court cases throughout the country rose more rapidly than in any preceding year.

Combating Delinquency

More light is needed on this whole subject. While some good studies have been made of certain institutions for delinquents and some exploration has been made of the efficacy of particular modes of treatment, the problem as a whole needs much fuller investigation. The public, while much concerned, is beset by a futile controversy between the advocates of strict disciplinary measures and the advocates of a social-service approach. Discipline is a necessary element of all upbringing, but mere discipline without effective appeal to mind and heart, so that it becomes one with self-discipline, is barren and causes revulsion. Discipline enforced by punishment alone neither improves the offender nor makes him less ready to offend again—but rather has a contrary effect. Those who believe sheer enforcement will stop delinquency—obviously it does not *reform* the delinquent—should learn something that criminology emphatically confirms, viz., that punishment, or more severe punishment, has never proved an effective deterrent of crime. Or they might consider, for example, the study of 500 delinquents made by the Gluecks, which found that 70 percent of the fathers were too strict or too erratic in the exercise of discipline, while 25 percent were lax or indifferent. It is time, then, we got beyond this unworthy controversy and faced the genuine issues.

In doing so, we should first distinguish between the two objectives of an overall program for the control of delinquency—prevention and rehabilitation. Much the major portion of the energy and expense devoted to the problem is concerned with rehabilitation. Too seldom do we find any well-thought-out project directed specifically to prevention. Yet practically all our authorities in this field agree that a preventive program—one planned to reach and re-orient young people at an earlier stage, when symptoms of incipient delinquency appear—has much the greater promise.

REHABILITATION. Let us look first at the rehabilitation problem. Here the agencies primarily involved are the police and the courts, though in a broader way we may regard the great majority of welfare agencies, both public and private, as having a significant part in it. The police on the one hand bring the large majority of cases before the courts, and on the other—since three-fourths of all youth dealt with by the police are not brought before the courts but simply ad-

monished, warned, sent back to their families, or referred
to some agency—have often the first opportunity to bring
influence to bear on erring youngsters. The degree to which
the police utilize this opportunity is very variant, depending on
the "philosophy" of the police department and the extent
to which they have a properly trained juvenile bureau or
division. It is wholly up to the courts to determine the degree
and kind of rehabilitative treatment for more serious cases.

Aside from such admonition and guidance as the particular
judge may offer in the brief process of the hearing and adjudication, the court has mainly the alternatives of probation
or institutionalization for cases that are not discharged or
dismissed. Around three times as many cases are put on
probation as are committed to institutions. Probation is certainly the more desirable alternative wherever there is no
clear necessity for institutional commitment, wherever, that
is, the youth can remain in his home environment without
serious peril to himself or to society.

While in principle the commitment of a juvenile to a cus-
todial institution, whether it be designated "training school,"
"residential treatment center," "youth camp," or otherwise,
is not punishment but a remedial or rehabilitative measure,
it none the less deprives him of liberty and relegates him for
a period ranging generally from around eight months up to
two or more years to a restrictive unnatural environment. He
is cut off from home and associates and neighborhood. His
effective society consists of a group of similarly resentful delinquent youth, under the control of a body of officials and
professional workers. No matter how devoted and how skilled

this latter body may be, they are often unable to make headway against the "underworld" spirit that develops in the rebellious youth. The relatively innocent ones among them may learn more evil ways from the tougher ones, and the latter are likely to bully the former and subject them to indignities and even to the pent-up sexual desires that are roused under such conditions. The recidivism rate is generally quite high.

These are adequate grounds for preferring the alternative of probation wherever it is admissible. Since, however, some cases do call for institutional custody and care, every precaution should be taken to limit the risks of this process. Experience shows that small-scale institutions are preferable to large-scale ones. Small-scale institutions admit of more specialization, closer personal relations, and more experimentation. The broad term "delinquency" covers many different kinds of behavior trouble, requiring differential treatment. And when delinquent tendencies are associated with particular physical or mental ailments, specialized institutions to deal with different types of problem are clearly indicated. Wherever feasible, small urban residential shelters and group foster homes should be developed, and most of all for such delinquent boys or girls as may be institutionalized because their proper homes are deemed unfit for them to live in.

Whatever may be achieved in the above-mentioned respects, the alternative of probation offers the greater promise, for all except the very serious or difficult cases. But it has to be effective probation. Too often probation is a wholly perfunctory service. Too often it is understood to mean merely a routine check every few months to find whether the youngster has been in trouble again. Caseloads are often far too heavy, and even where reasonable qualifications are set up for probation officers the screening is too often ineffective and the salaries are too low to attract an adequately equipped staff. There are some outstanding exceptions, where the nature and the requirements of a probation system for juvenile offenders are properly realized. But the country as a whole is very far from having attained this level.

Since probation is the primary service provided under the courts for the rehabilitation of erring youngsters, it must be developed to serve as far as possible this objective. The probation officer should have the qualification, the time, and the opportunity to offer help, protection, and guidance. He should have the ability to recognize the different types of trouble that affect young delinquents and to enlist the appropriate services of voluntary agencies and official ones alike. He should familiarize himself with the family background and the youth's case history. He should either be in frequent contact himself with the youth or else find some "big brother," settlement worker, or good neighbor who will do so. The requisite service places a high responsibility on the probation officer and involves the additional cost of a considerably larger probation staff than is usual. But the extra cost per youth is quite small compared with the cost of institutionalization and weighs a trifle in the balance against the benefit of rehabilitation.

PREVENTION. From rehabilitative measures we turn to preventive ones. As already pointed out, the potentialities of well-thought-out preventive services still lie largely in the future, though in recent years some definite advances have been made. We have more knowledge of the conditions under which delinquency develops, of the early indications of delinquent tendencies, and of the different types of behavior disorder that we lump together under the term "delinquency." This growing knowledge is beginning—though only beginning—to result in more promising action-programs. We are beginning to realize the high importance of early screening so as to discover the tensions and problems of children, as a pre-condition of providing guidance and needed care. Here is a function the schools are peculiarly well situated to fulfill, and in various school areas throughout the country programs are being inaugurated or developed for this purpose. We are learning that the mere provision of more playgrounds and better recreational facilities and occasional summer camps, valuable as these are in themselves, does not reach the heart of the deeper-seated conflicts and troubles that beset the disoriented children of our congested slums and semi-ghettos. And maybe we are also beginning to perceive that the social work approach, however valuable for the rescue and redirection of juveniles who are getting into trouble, does not suffice to change the environmental conditions and the socio-economic factors that breed the habits of delinquency.

The prevention of delinquency may be thought of in two ways. In the broader sense, whatever can be achieved in the upbringing and education of children, whatever influences can be brought to bear to arouse constructive interests in them, whatever parents first, then school and church and associations, can do to understand the problems and the needs of youth, to evoke their capacities and to sustain their morale —all such up-building influences are preventives of serious delinquency. But these generalities have no bite. Possibly, if we take them from the reverse side they may have more practical relevance. Thus, delinquency is prevented by whatever can be done to guide parents to avoid either laxness or too rigid discipline with their children, by whatever can be done to enable young persons to find their own interests and discover their capacities, by whatever the school system can do to insure more stimulating and personalized teaching, particularly for pupils who are irked by schooling or who are slow to learn.

In a more specific sense the prevention of delinquency may be regarded as the rescue of those young persons who are showing symptoms of delinquent tendencies or forming habits or making associations that may well lead to a delinquent career. It is necessary, however, to distinguish between mere prankishness, mischief-making, and boyish aggressiveness on the one hand and the more ominous indications of disaffection, alienation, and antisocial attitudes on the other. We proceed to cite three types of specific preventive programs classified according to the breadth of their operation.

1. The first type centers directly on the affected young people, on the individual boys and girls who exhibit the earlier signs of behavior trouble which, unless arrested, may develop into confirmed habits of delinquency. Such "predelinquents" may be reached through school contacts, agency referrals, or neighborhood investigation. It is a first-aid service,

endeavoring initially to enlist their interest, cooperation, and friendship, offering them help in their troubles and problems, seeking to redirect their attitudes, endeavoring in the process to understand their situation, to deal with such sources of conflict as may lie in their family relationships, school relationships, or peer-age associations, and seeking to provide for them outlets and opportunities they lack. It is a task that requires much patience and skill. For some cases special professional service, medical, psychiatric, or other, may need to be called in.

While such programs can and do render quite valuable service—and the earlier they get to the disturbed child, the more successful they are likely to be—there remains always the serious danger that the continued impact of an unfavorable environment may undo this temporary effect.

2. The second type of program seeks to minimize this danger. It concentrates on the neighborhood itself and endeavors to provide for young people within it some of the sustainment that otherwise is lacking. Under this type we include, for example, the Chicago Area Project, which is distinctive in that its primary concern is to set up areal organizations composed of residents of high-delinquency areas, so as to enlist them in active concern for the welfare of neighborhood youth. Such organizations are not likely to arise spontaneously in these areas, and in any case they need outside resources. The Project, while scrupulous to leave decisions in the hands of the residents themselves, has been successful in mobilizing such organizations and in aiding them to carry out a variety of programs for youth recreation and for

the training of delinquent juveniles, as well as campaigns for measures of community improvement. The Area Project recognizes that neighborhood organizations of this kind offer by no means the whole answer to the delinquency problem, but regards the alerted participation of neighborhood residents as an essential aspect of it.

Another kind of neighborhood planning, which in the first instance is not specifically directed to the delinquency situation but has important implications for it, is that of the All-Day Neighborhood Schools of New York City. There are now nine of these schools situated in the neediest and most run-down areas of the city. While regular elementary schools under the Board of Education, they utilize special services extending beyond school hours and are occupied with community activities in the evening. The core of the operation is a team of six "group teachers," with an administrator. These teachers work from 11 to 5, carrying on flexible educational programs through the school hours and from 3 to 5 conducting various recreational programs through "clubs," one for each grade. The "clubs" are composed of children whose parents work late and others who may particularly need this opportunity. During the recreation period the psychiatric social worker unobtrusively observes and gives aid to children in need of special attention. Other services are provided through volunteers, and the school receives additional equipment and resources through the local branch of the Citizens for the All-Day Neighborhood Schools, an organization that has done much to support the system. (Special programs are also carried on during the summer.) Every effort is being made during school hours and beyond them to provide some cultural enrichment for these deprived children.

The schools are open evenings for meetings and discussions of neighborhood issues. The ADNS plan seeks to enlist the interest of the adults both in the work of the schools and in the civic and social needs of the neighborhood. It is hard sledding under the circumstances, but some progress is achieved. In addition to the group teacher staff each school has an ADNS administrator; three have also a special "community coordinator," and the whole system is in charge of a devoted director who has under the Board of Education been the principal founder and formulator of the ADNS plan.

Even a casual visitor to an ADNS school can hardly fail to be impressed by the spirit animating it, by the happy responsiveness of pupils, and the friendly relations between teacher and taught. They are not all equally successful in these respects—it takes some time for the plan to catch hold in new schools—but the prevailing attitude contradicts the old conception of the balky child, "creeping like a snail unwillingly to school." Truancy is conspicuously less frequent than is characteristic of schools situated in slum-like areas, and since chronic truancy goes hand in hand with delinquency we can reasonably infer that the ADNS schools have preventive efficacy. A study is now being planned to test this inference.

As a third example of a neighborhood-oriented program it may be in order to mention one recently inaugurated in New York City under the sponsorship of the President of the New York City Council and of the Juvenile Delinquency Evaluation Project. The Project in question, set up by the mayor in 1956, is the first investigation so far undertaken of the whole operation of a great city in the field of juvenile delinquency. It studies and reports on the functions, the problems, the needs, and the interrelations of all the official agencies involved, and also considers the role played by a considerable variety of voluntary agencies. In addition the Project has now undertaken, with the support of the city's Youth Board, to organize an experimental program for the prevention of delinquency in one high-delinquency neighborhood in the Bronx.

In briefest outline the program is directed to reach the near-delinquents or pre-delinquents, establishing a system of continuous contacts with the people and the agencies of the neighborhood, to bring them "first aid" through the ministrations of its own staff, to guide them to needed agency services, to inquire into their family relations, school relations, and other possible sources of trouble, to provide recreational and other outlets and assist them in matters of training and potential employment, and to keep a thorough record of case histories, of services rendered, and of services called for but not adequately available. At the same time the program is promoting a neighborhood council for the well-being of neighborhood children and a body of local volunteers to assist the professional staff in the discovery of neighborhood needs.

3. Finally, we turn to the third and most far-reaching type of preventive program. Our second type went beyond the first

by envisaging the neighborhood as a whole—endeavoring to mobilize it for the service of its youth in trouble. Our third type, taken in its totality, is perhaps nowhere fully realized, though some approaches to it exist, and others are now being planned. It would thoroughly renovate the physical neighborhood itself, removing the conditions that stimulate and confirm habits, attitudes, ways of living that in themselves are prejudicial to decent citizenship—the congestion, the litter, the promiscuity, the decaying multi-partitioned housing, the cramped ugly yards, the whole physical impoverishment that in certain city areas is the accompaniment and the accomplice of economic and social impoverishment.

We have here in view not the sporadic delinquency that occurs in every area, among every class of the population, but the more concentrated and formidable volume of delinquency that characterizes the deteriorated areas of our great cities. These high-delinquency areas are typically areas to which incoming groups, usually of a different ethnic or racial stock from the surrounding population, entering the great city from an agricultural background and at the lowest economical level, have accommodated themselves. A whole complex of conditions work against their proper integration into the fabric of American society and turn the areas they inhabit into festering slums that have a deleterious effect on the welfare of the city as a whole. Every adverse factor helps to perpetuate every other—the physical setting, the impoverishment in a land of plenty, the abrupt change from old ways of living, the cultural denudation as the traditional culture loses hold on the young and the new one is slow to be acquired, the lack of training and of adequate opportunities and outlets for youthful energies, and the social and economic discrimination that so frequently is aroused by the rest of the complex. Perhaps one should rather be surprised that so large a proportion of those subjected to these conditions are able to surmount them than that a sizable minority of the young go seriously astray.

While some steps are being taken to improve certain of these conditions, no more than very partial success can be looked for so long as the delinquency-breeding physical slum continues to exist as the habitation of these new urban groups. Great housing schemes under public auspices are certainly of high merit, especially if those who go to live within them are given accessory social services. But they merely bound the areas of deterioration and are in danger of being infected by them. A thorough program of renovation, reconstruction, maintenance, inspection, limitation of subdividing, and overall control is a major need, with adequate provision for recreation, youth clubs, and other neighborhood amenities. With this physical basis other programs for neighborhood upbuilding, such as those already described, would have much better prospects. As for the cost of these measures, it would be repaid abundantly in the ultimate economic saving, and many times over in the social and moral gain to the city as a whole, and most of all to its troubled youth.

To organize all-out neighborhood programs for the areas of in-migration it would be advantageous for such large cities as are involved to set up special commissions, one for each incoming group. Such a commission would investigate the needs and problems of the group and the conditions of any neighborhood in which it settles. It would include housing experts, educators, and representatives of relevant city agencies and of welfare organizations. An all-out enterprise of this sort would, for the first time in our history, assure that these incoming groups would start afresh, protected against the demoralizing conditions to which in the past they have so often been subjected, and thus enabled to develop their proper contribution to our multi-group society.

We observe in conclusion that programs for the prevention of juvenile delinquency have the great advantage over programs of rehabilitation in that they benefit whole groups, while reaching to those who are in special danger. And the more thorough the program of prevention the more far-spreading is the service it renders. A full-scale neighborhood program is of benefit to the whole community. While it saves some from becoming delinquents it contributes no less to the well-being of the many who are resistant to that danger, and to their elders as well. Wherever we find a high rate of delinquency we can be sure that the root trouble lies not in the youth themselves, but in the social and environmental conditions to which they and their families have been exposed.

FRONTIERS IN VOLUNTARY WELFARE SERVICES

by ELIZABETH WICKENDEN

ALMOST all Americans know something about voluntary social welfare services for children and young people. The annual Community Chest campaign with its familiar red feather symbol; the Boy Scouts, Girl Scouts, and Camp Fire Girls; the American Red Cross; the YM and YWCA; the youth-serving and children's programs of their own religious denominations; the Salvation Army; the family service, child welfare, and settlement house agencies in their own communities; the Travelers Aid beacon when they travel: these and many others are familiar aspects of the American social environment. But not everyone, even when actively involved in these programs, has paused to consider just how any particular method of making provision for the needs of children and young people differs from the many other organizational devices used to meet similar needs and how it is related to the evolution of the social structure as a whole. A broad appraisal of the way in which American social insti-

Elizabeth Wickenden is Consultant on Public Social Policy to the National Social Welfare Assembly.

tutions are serving or failing our younger generation in this pivotal year of 1960 must necessarily take into account the evolving pattern of social welfare services under voluntary auspices.

There are three aspects of this question. First, we are here concerned with a specific *function*, known as "social welfare," with characteristics that distinguish it from other youth-serving functions such as education, health, and recreation. Second, we are discussing these services under *auspices* described as "voluntary" to distinguish them from those provided by governmental bodies under the compulsion of law. What relationships and distinctions exist between these two auspices and how have they developed? Third, our appraisal focuses upon welfare services in a particular *setting*—the United States at this period in its history. No function is more directly the product and the instrument of the society it serves and hence more dependent upon the immediate setting within which it operates. But understanding this present, with its implications for the future, requires in turn historical perspective.

The Functional Evolution

Two functions are basic to any society: protection of children through their dependency period and their induction into the culture of the society in which they live. In all human societies these functions are shared with the individual mother by a widening circle of other individuals cooperating for these purposes under a variety of institutional patterns. First to join the mother in this responsibility is the father, and their continued association in the task of child nurture creates the fundamental social institution, the family. Around the nuclear family there develop broadening circles of responsibility, initially bound by ties of consanguinity and marriage, and subsequently by propinquity, a common base of economic operation, and a shared culture.

In a society which is relatively localized, stable, and simple in its functioning, the family, village, or tribal pattern of relationship adequately meets the socially recognized needs of children in virtually all circumstances. More organized social measures for this specific purpose are not only not available but, under prevailing social standards, they are neither needed nor missed. In such a society the larger family circle simply closes around and absorbs the child who suffers any failure in parental care. Similarly in this kind of social setting cultural assimilation of the up-coming generation proceeds along traditionally prescribed lines until outside influence or basic changes of social organization disturb the pattern.

BEGINNINGS OF SOCIAL WELFARE. Organized welfare services appear on the social scene when something happens to upset the elementary equilibrium between individual, family, and society. This most commonly results from basic changes in the methods and organization of economic production affecting in turn all other social relationships. Or, it might result from large-scale migration disrupting the family and cultural pattern, or from war or conquest. Outside influence might be brought to bear through trading or colonization or evangelization—or, in our more popular modern terms, technical assistance and the communication of ideas. Any such disturbance of the status quo can set off a chain reaction of social readjustment wherein the former pattern no longer meets the needs of children.

At the same time any change in social organization and social aspiration inevitably affects the objectives and methods of child-rearing. This is clear in our own era with its steadily increasing complexity of social organization. The task of rearing children to independent adult functioning takes longer, involves the application of more specialized knowledge, and becomes constantly more costly and progressively more complex. Individual parents are less able to fulfill their obligation to or their aspirations for their children without the aid of organized social support. The almost universal development of schools to share the parental task of cultural preparation is a clear example of this. Social welfare services are likewise a way to supplement and support the family in assuring to children the help they need in growing up into a complex, hazardous, and challenging social environment.

Social welfare is simply the organized measures through which society provides assurance that the recognized social needs of individuals will be met and that those social relationships and adjustments considered necessary to its own functioning will be facilitated. Social welfare services for children are, therefore, correspondingly those which supplement, support, or, when necessary, substitute for the family in providing the standard of protective care and nurture a particular social group deems necessary for its dependent members; and those considered necessary to facilitate the social assimilation of young people as functioning members of that particular society or social group. The term "social standard" describes this interaction of social entitlement and social obligation underlying the welfare function.

No definition comfortably fits the facts of social welfare experience unless it recognizes the variability of this standard in different settings, stages of historical evolution, and among individual groups in a pluralistic society. These variations in social standard provide the central dynamic in the evolution of the social welfare function.

EARLY INSTITUTIONS. Organized child welfare service seems typically to begin as congregate care in institutions. Misleadingly called "orphanages," these institutions have generally made provision not for children who had lost their parents but for children who would benefit by being segregated from the prevailing low level of care available in their homes. Beginning in the Middle Ages children's institutions, usually under religious sponsorship, not only provided care for the orphans created by the wars, pestilence, and social change of the period, but also pioneered in the new educational and health services demanded by a changing social order. The Elizabethan Poor Laws also made institutional provision for children under governmental auspices through the almshouse. Both types were brought to this country by its settlers to serve as forerunners of present voluntary and public child welfare programs. The general-purpose children's institution seen today in less-developed countries outlived its historical purpose in our own country when changing social standards demanded more specialized services and decried the isolation of children from the mainstream of family and community life.

DEVELOPMENT OF DIFFERENTIATED CHILD WELFARE SERVICES. Toward the end of the nineteenth century social services for children began to develop rapidly in terms of scope and differentiation, and thus required more complex organization and specialized staffing. Out of these and related needs the structure of modern social welfare and the profession of social work were born. The change in children's services can be attributed to three factors: changes of attitude regarding children's developmental needs, changes in social needs and organization resulting from industrialization, and—for the United States—the peculiar task of assimilating millions of newcomers into our social structure. Each of these factors helped to shape American social services in this generative period.

Social and psychological sciences emphasized the essential role of individual family nurture in child development, especially in the early years. Consequently a variety of services directed toward assuring an adequately functioning family base for every child gradually displaced the earlier reliance on institutional care. Special children's agencies were organized to bring together parentless children and childless couples through adoption and to find temporary foster family care for those requiring it. By the same logic every effort was made to hold together families threatened by psychological tensions or economic deprivation. Charitable organizations (predecessors of today's family service agencies) provided counseling services, economic aid, and other services to such families.

Other services developed that were directed toward supplementing family care in order to meet special needs requiring the more specialized services opened up by advancing science. Social welfare often plays a pioneering role in this respect by initiating services which later become programs with a broader base of social responsibility. Many specialized educational, health, recreation, and related programs began in this way as charitable undertakings of particular religious or other voluntary groups. This aspect of the welfare function derives from the fact that particular groups are committed to a standard of social obligation toward children not yet accepted by the whole society. Through voluntary association they pioneer in new areas which in turn raise the sights and ultimately the standards of others.

A third type of welfare service is related to the problem of acculturation and particularly to the processes by which young people are prepared for the social responsibilities of adult life. This became a major task when millions of immigrants were coming to this country, and early American social work took much of its own coloration from historical circumstance. Child-rearing became an especially complex task when children were growing up in a culture new to their parents. Such parents found it difficult to assist their children and parent-child conflicts were aggravated by these differences. Socially organized measures were, therefore, increasingly necessary and rapidly expanded under the auspices of religious bodies, settlement houses, and other voluntary organizations. At the same time the shift from a frontier-type agricultural economy to one characterized by large-scale industrial production and urban living created tensions and problems of adjustment for young people that still persist.

Social welfare also sought to help children in a fourth and broadly pervasive way: by striving for an adjustment of prevailing social values and existing social institutions in order better to meet their needs. This crusading aspect of the welfare function played a major role in its formative years. Efforts to achieve protective legislation, limitations on child labor, better public welfare programs, improved juvenile courts, changing attitudes and opportunities for the children of minority groups, and the successive White House Conferences on the needs of children launched in 1909 are all examples of this area of welfare activity.

Voluntary and Government Auspices

Social welfare services perform the same social functions under either voluntary or governmental auspices. No absolute distinctions can be made, especially in our social system that encourages pluralistic approaches to the same problem. Whether the adoption of a particular child is arranged by the welfare agency of his parents' faith, by a nonsectarian voluntary agency, or by the local public welfare department, its social purpose is the same: to provide him with a home. There are, however, certain attributes in each which tend toward a differentiation in functional emphasis.

In general voluntary services reflect the active concern of particular groups within a society, while those under government auspices are largely directed toward needs so widespread or so compelling that the authority of law and the taxing power are brought to bear on meeting them. Thus voluntary services tend toward variability and those under government toward universality. But services which are initially varied may move toward universality as the need or desire for them becomes more widely recognized. Historically this has produced a steady movement from voluntary toward governmental sponsorship for widely accepted welfare services, a movement fostered by the voluntary agencies themselves as the scope of particular needs became apparent in their own selective undertakings.

Voluntary welfare has, however, continued to carry forward its own adaptive function by pioneering in the development of new services, continuing as pacemaker in some fields entered by government, and focusing on functions for which they feel a special competence or responsibility. Religious agencies, especially those of minority faiths, feel a compelling obligation to provide services for the children and young people of their own group in order to protect their religious and cultural heritage. The American tradition of reliance on mutual aid has also helped to sustain the vitality of voluntary welfare and leads to continuous invention, of which recent examples might be seen in such peripheral developments as the union health and welfare fund, Alcoholics Anonymous, and the cooperative nursery school.

There are also countervailing factors tending to becloud these characteristic distinctions. As public welfare has become universally established and widely accepted, it has developed a wide variety of new services which not only parallel those of voluntary agencies but may, in particular communities, outstrip them. At the same time private agencies have been increasingly financed by tax money in the performance of functions the government considers essential. This confusion in traditional social role has not yet been assimilated in social welfare theory, much of which derives from the time when voluntary agency pioneering was creating a new social function and a new profession.

INFLUENCES ON VOLUNTARY WELFARE. Modern social welfare services were largely initiated under voluntary auspices. Though minimal governmental protection against dependency had existed since Poor Law days, the scientific and professionally oriented approach of the new agencies was more a protest against this undifferentiated and humiliating public program than its progeny. The impulse and drive for the new services came from many sources. Religious conviction then and now played an important role and religious bodies lent their institutional support, both as sponsors of services for their own members and backers of community effort. The volunteer, contributing his effort as well as his money, is intrinsic to any successful voluntary welfare undertaking. The established agency of today was once created from nothing by dedicated people whose breadth of vision was their only professional qualification for the new field of social welfare. The philanthropic impulse which led successful community leaders to discharge their sense of social responsibility toward newcomers and other disadvantaged neighbors in financial support for these new agencies was indispensable to their growth. In time this burgeoning social welfare field also developed a source of strength and support in the profession of social work, itself largely fostered by the early voluntary agencies.

THE INFLUENCE OF PUBLIC WELFARE DEVELOPMENT. Voluntary social welfare led the way, but, under the pressures of economic and social change, governmental welfare development was not far behind. From the turn of the century governmental programs expanded rapidly, and they were vastly accelerated by the depression. This growth, encouraged by voluntary agencies that saw clearly the need for broader-based measures than they could provide, has inevitably had a profound impact in turn on the functioning of the voluntary agencies, an impact that can be considered in three ways.

In the first place large-scale public programs, especially those that prevent or relieve economic need, have greatly modified the character of voluntary programs. The various Social Security measures, launched in 1935 following earlier emergency relief provisions, have virtually eliminated the need for voluntary agencies to give economic aid to the needy except in unusual circumstances. By providing for needy children and the survivors of insured workers, these programs have also virtually eliminated dependency as a cause of child placement. Governmental programs in the fields of health, education, housing, vocational placement, race relations, and many others have likewise affected the character of voluntary welfare activity for children and their parents.

Governmental financing of voluntary agencies to perform welfare services in its behalf is a second important influence. This may take several forms. Most common is the purchase of a specified service from a voluntary agency by the public welfare agency or children's court in behalf of a particular child or family for which it has assumed responsibility. Less widespread is the outright governmental subsidy paid to a voluntary agency to underwrite its performance of a needed welfare function, for example, day care for the children of working mothers, or services directed toward potential delinquents. Another device, more widely used in the health field, involves grants to voluntary agencies for research and demonstration projects in a particular problem field. And finally the federal government gives substantial financial aid to nonprofit agencies by authorizing the deduction from taxable income of individual, corporate, or foundation contributions to organizations engaged in recognized charitable, educational, and related activity. Similar concessions are made by state and local governments in exemptions from property, excise, sales and other taxes.

Governmental influence is also applied directly through regulation and the power to enforce suspension of activity. This usually takes the form of licensing, which requires that individuals or agencies performing certain services meet specified minimum standards. Child-caring agencies are commonly licensed and generally welcome this limited public regulation in order to protect the standards of child welfare practice from unscrupulous or poorly qualified individuals and organizations. The solicitation of funds for charitable purposes is also subject to regulation in many states in order to prevent fraud.

THE INFLUENCE OF FEDERATION. Another major influence on voluntary welfare development has been the rapid growth in the last forty years of federated fund-raising at the community level as a means of channeling philanthropic giving through one annual campaign and one allocating mechanism. At present 2,027 American communities with approximately 115 million residents are served by community chests, united funds, and similar organizations. Approximately $400,000,000 was raised during 1959 to provide funds for 27,000 separate voluntary agencies.

Federation plays such a dominant role in shaping the prevailing voluntary welfare philosophy that its impact is difficult to appraise. On the one hand it has served to reduce public irritation arising from a multiplicity of fund appeals, has encouraged efficient use of community and professional energies in a single concentrated campaign, and has subjected the operation of all participating agencies to periodic review by an objective citizen group—thus protecting the public and encouraging the agencies to adapt to changing needs and concepts. A logical corollary has been the development of community welfare councils, now functioning in 438 communities, to plan and coordinate welfare and related community services. On the negative side there has recently developed some revolt against federated fund-raising on the ground that it dilutes the principal asset of voluntarism, its capacity for giving practical expression to the aspirations, particular interests, and special needs of different groups in the population.

THE INFLUENCE OF CORPORATE GIVING AND THE LABOR MOVEMENT. Two other influences of growing importance in voluntary welfare are those of the corporate giver, as represented by industry and foundations, and the labor movement. Forty percent of the money raised by community funds comes from business and 40 percent from workers, the latter actively encouraged by their unions. The former represents an important source of contribution which, because it is passed on to the consumer and tax-payer, seems relatively painless. Again, however, it tends toward dilution of one of the traditional values of voluntarism: the close rapport between giver, service, and beneficiary. This is offset to some extent by the growing labor representation in voluntary welfare management and financing, since the unions tend to think of themselves as representing both the giver and the beneficiary. In both cases, however, an additional organizational structure is added to the voluntary equation.

The Current Social Setting

In our time, as in all others, the particular characteristics of social welfare services for children and youth depend upon: 1) the special problems of adaptation confronting our society; 2) the social standard it applies to the rights, obligation, and role of its children and their families; 3) its economic capacity to provide the benefits and services required by the first two; and 4) the extent to which children's needs are met by nonwelfare measures. The interaction of these factors is sharply revealed when efforts are made to export the standards and supporting institutions of one society to another with differing adaptive problems. For example, the social standard represented by child labor laws is quite impractical in a country where the very survival of children depends on their productivity and where there is no educational system to occupy the years thus added to their developmental period.

In our own setting the startling growth of productive capacity (now approaching a money value of $500 billion a year) has made possible a national income which not only does not depend upon the employment of children but provides a substantial surplus which can be applied to their extended rearing. Thus a primary characteristic of our society is the prolongation of the period of youthful dependency and the greatly increased social investment, both through family expenditure and socially provided services, in the upcoming generation. The growing proportion of this investment financed by government in the form of public schools, public health, public recreation, public welfare, and other public services has affected both family budgeting and voluntary services.

THE PRESENT CHALLENGE. At the same time the rapid change in institutional structure, population distribution, social attitudes and values that has been necessary to produce this rising standard have, in their turn, produced new problems of social adaptation, especially for the young. These tensions and maladjustments today constitute the principal challenge to voluntary social welfare. The time when poverty and economic insecurity spawned the major social problems is gradually giving way to one characterized chiefly by changes in social relationships and values. While pockets of economic injustice remain, the disequilibrium between individuals and their social environment that more particularly characterizes our time is revealed in such widespread symptomatic social problems as divorce, family desertion, illegitimacy, juvenile delinquency, alcoholism, drug addiction, mental illness or personality disturbance, and the phenomenon called by social scientists *anomie* or alienation between individuals and the society in which they live.

These problems offer a particular challenge to voluntary agencies. This is true whether they are regarded as transitional problems arising from the struggle of contemporary man to move to a higher level of social functioning or, as some maintain, to a decline in basic morality and standards of social responsibility. In either case—and they are not mutually exclusive—the adaptive capacity of our pluralistic democratic system is directly challenged. It is twice challenged, since it is also being subjected to critical testing by the growth abroad of a competing system characterized by unitary authority rooted in a concept of predetermined historic dynamic. The conflict between democracy and Communism is more likely to be resolved by the relative effectiveness of the two systems in resolving these social problems of our day than by a clash of arms that would destroy both.

Children are the inevitable victims of social disequilibrium, for their emotional and social development depends upon the emotional and social health of the individuals and institutions surrounding them. Emotionally disturbed or immature parents leave the emotional needs of children unsatisfied. Broken families deprive them of the social matrix on which their best development depends. Prolonged economic dependency of young people intensifies normal tensions between generations and extends the gap between biological maturity and the time when marriage is economically feasible. Rapidly shifting social patterns and values complicate the already difficult transition from childhood to adulthood represented by adolescence. Tensions created by past wars, the cold war, and the threat of future war—including the interruption of normal living caused by compulsory military service—encourage withdrawal from social responsibility on the part of some young people whether in the guise of indifferent conformity to the status quo, the active rebellion of juvenile delinquency, or the passive anarchy of so-called "beat generation" disaffiliation. Growing up in our time presents all of these hazards for young people. Even though many find within themselves and their immediate social environment the sources of their own growth—as previous generations have done before them—voluntary welfare agencies find the emphasis of their traditional adaptive role shifting to these developmental problems and pressures, seeking to ease their impact on individuals and advance compensatory institutional change.

The central role of the family in child nurture remains undiminished by the changes in its composition and functioning that have accompanied changes in the total institutional pattern. In fact, the strength and stability represented for the child by his own family becomes proportionately more crucial as the larger society imposes the heavier demands implicit in rapid change and increasing complexity. At the same time the family is subjected by these same factors to pressures that constitute a direct challenge to social welfare. The shrinkage in family size and its isolation from binding identity with a larger social group have placed an unprecedented burden on the nuclear family and especially on the parent-child relationship. Frequent movement from one locality to another tends to intensify this isolation. Early marriage, seemingly a product of youthful insecurity, the widespread employment of mothers outside the home, the changing social pattern in masculine-feminine roles, and the uncertain application of psychological theory to family relationships have all contributed to the current insecurities in family life. To the extent that these insecurities derive from social causes, the remedy likewise must be found in social measures.

Voluntary welfare agencies seek to strengthen the family, both in its normal functioning and in times of crisis, by three types of help. Family agencies help relieve internal tensions by bringing objective counsel to bear on emotional and other family problems and by helping secure more specialized assistance, such as psychiatric or other forms of therapeutic service, when needed. Welfare agencies of many types also help relieve the family by providing supplementary services for its children. Visiting housekeeper service that helps keep families together when the mother is ill or absent from the home clearly demonstrates the institutionalization of a service formerly assured by the larger family or neighborhood. With almost one-third of the mothers of children under eighteen working, day care centers meet a pressing realistic need and, many social workers believe, contribute to family stability by easing social and emotional pressures that many mothers cannot otherwise withstand. Recreational and other group activity for young people outside the home, including summer camping, are also characteristic ways to strengthen the family by supplementing its benefits and relieving its internal pressures. Parent education and discussion groups offer the traditional reassurance of shared experience, reinforced by objective counsel. Controversies surrounding the institutionalization of many social functions formerly centered in the home seem to miss the reciprocal value of this trend in freeing the basic emotional vitality of the family relationship.

Welfare agencies also continue to find, when and if family care fails, substitutes in the form of adoptive or foster home placement. Increasingly, however, these children are the victims of social maladjustment rather than economic conditions or death in the family. Illegitimacy, family breakdown, or emotional difficulties account for an increasing proportion of these children. The close relationship between child placement and family service is thus emphasized and many combined agencies have resulted. Religious agencies are especially, though not exclusively, concerned with the provision of these substitutes for family care, partly because of charitable tradition and partly because of the principle, incorporated in many state laws, that children should be assured religious rearing in their own faith. Couples seeking children for adoption continue to outnumber the available supply except where children of certain minority groups and those with special handicaps are involved. This fact—together with upheavals abroad and widespread travel by Americans in military or foreign service—has resulted in the increasing adoption of foreign children with concomitant legal and social problems for welfare agencies to resolve.

In providing services for children with special needs, the welfare function changes conspicuously as new needs develop and as well-established services are taken over by others. Thus services for blind and deaf children—to cite one example—initiated under welfare auspices are increasingly incorporated into the educational system. At the same time welfare agencies carry forward their traditional pioneering function by spurring the development of experimental or intensive service in such fields as the treatment of children with severe emotional disturbance, the mentally retarded, and rehabilitation of the physically handicapped. As the need for general-purpose orphanages has diminished, institutional care for children has centered on those requiring highly specialized treatment and those whose own developmental needs are better served by group living arrangements.

Voluntary welfare agencies are also concerned with children whose special needs derive from minority or newcomer status as with the Negroes and Puerto Ricans in many cities, from the migratory nature of the family occupation, from the military service of the father, or from the fact that they are away from home or traveling. Another important area of voluntary welfare service involves aid to needy children overseas. This includes both direct aid in the form of food, clothing, and medical supplies, and technical assistance to help countries develop their own child welfare programs. Many have also sponsored international student exchange, work-camp, and study-tour programs for young people as their contribution to helping prepare for life in a shrinking world.

The transition from childhood dependency to adult self-reliance and social responsibility is not easy in any age or culture. In our own time it seems especially difficult for many young people for such reasons as changing social values, increasing organizational complexity, world tension, excessive pressure on the family, prolonged dependency, and heavy social demands in such forms as military service, technical knowledge, widening scope of social identification, and unceasing adaptability.

Voluntary agencies help bridge the gap by sponsoring programs that combine group association on a peer basis with mature leadership. These programs are often under religious sponsorship—such as the YM and YWCA, the YM and YWHA, Catholic Youth Organization and Jewish Center programs—both as a means of preserving cultural and religious traditions and as a logical link between home and the larger society. The neighborhood is also a natural center and many housing projects make provisions to house a voluntary welfare agency for this purpose. This is a peculiarly institutional function, since the family cannot effectively wean its adolescents itself and self-organization by adolescents may isolate them from the very society they are seeking to join.

Juvenile delinquency represents one measure of the failure

of this process and today constitutes a major, and in some cities critical, challenge to the welfare function. Voluntary welfare services are directed both to the prevention of overt antisocial activity by rebellious young people and to the salvaging of those already involved, including those coming before the juvenile courts. An interesting example of preventive work involves the assignment of social workers by neighborhood houses and other agencies to work with youthful street gangs in an effort to channel their mutual loyalty and cohesiveness into constructive outlets. Agencies have also assigned caseworkers to seek out on a so-called "aggressive" basis the families of potential delinquents in an effort to strengthen the family base and hence the child's development. Many voluntary agencies also operate institutional and other programs for delinquent children who are either committed to them by the courts or sent by their parents or guardians on a voluntary basis. Here again religious motivation often plays an important role, but programs under both denominational and secular auspices have increasingly added psychiatric concepts of treatment to the traditional vocational training of such schools. Post-institutional aid and supervision is also provided by many voluntary agencies.

The social problems of children today can never be solved through the provision of more and better welfare services. In fact one of the frequent criticisms directed at social welfare is that it attempts to bale out the ocean of social maladjustment with the teacup of individual services. This criticism is justifiable only to the extent that welfare agencies, especially the voluntary agencies with their greater freedom in this respect, fail to use their knowledge of individual problems to remedy the social conditions that cause them or to improve the social institutions that might prevent them. There are three ways voluntary agencies can do this. Through research, both especially organized projects and analysis of their regular programs, they can establish the facts regarding children's present problems and the efficacy of existing measures. Through planning devices—community welfare councils, conferences, and the many committees that characterize social welfare organization—they can pool their knowledge, bring out differences of viewpoint, and devise new or modified programs and proposals. Through social action programs they can put their facts and their proposals before those who make social policy, whether in the arena of government, the economy, or organized voluntary association. All of these methods are being increasingly used by welfare agencies at this time in a reviving recognition that their responsibility is not only to individuals but to society itself.

The Challenge Ahead

The future of America's children will be determined by institutional adaptations that go far beyond the scope of social welfare. Will a rule of law replace armed might as the instrument of international relations or will we choose to revert to the caveman's level of social organization? Will equilibrium between the world's population and its productive capacity be reached at a level of well-being for all or in a holocaust of struggle for the resources of survival? Social welfare can anticipate no role in the latter alternatives for its values are tied to a complex level of social organization and a productive capacity well above survival limits. Its own contribution to a secure future lies rather in the third area of contemporary challenge: the values represented in the social relationships among people and between individuals and their social institutions. If in the name of economic efficiency our society should sacrifice its capacity to produce responsible individuals who so shape and order their own institutions as to meet the full needs—social and spiritual, as well as economic—of all its people, including its children, then it will destroy itself from within as other civilizations have done before it. If, on the other hand, the symptoms of social maladjustment that today confront us are transitional, pointing the way to a higher plan of adaptation, social welfare must play a more creative and spirited role in moving our society toward this goal.

THE GOVERNMENT'S ROLE IN CHILD AND FAMILY WELFARE

by EVELINE M. BURNS

ALTHOUGH it is generally accepted that the family is our basic social institution and that it has primary responsibility for the well-being of its members, and in particular for the well-being of children, all modern countries have found it necessary to support the efforts of the family by action on the part of government.

This development has taken place for several reasons. First, the economic ability of the family to provide for the basic physical needs of children is conditional upon the ability of the family head to earn, without interruption, an adequate income. In our present-day economy this is not always possible. Governments have responded in various ways. Social security systems, usually consisting of some combination of social insurance and public assistance programs, are by now universal in all highly developed societies. Other efforts include minimum wage laws, vocational rehabilitation, training, assistance to families to move from depressed

Eveline M. Burns is Professor of Social Work at the New York School of Social Work, Columbia University.

areas, and broader measures to raise the levels of employment and productivity in distressed areas themselves.

A second set of considerations leading to government action in the interests of children and families has been the inability of some families to meet the basic emotional needs of children. When this happens governments step in in the interest of the child and may remove him from his own home and provide other care for him. At one time this alternative care took the form of placement in an institution, more recently, of placement in foster homes. There is, too, a new emphasis on early permanent planning for children which has led, among other things, to an increased stress on adoption. Other efforts include the provision of homemaker services, or casework and counseling with the child and his parents, or day care centers and similar facilities.

A third stimulus to governmental action stems from the fact that some actions of individuals and families may not always be in the best interests of society as a whole. For example, if the decision is left to their parents, some children, for economic or other family reasons, may not receive an education of the level that is necessary if they are to function as responsible and effective producers and as voting citizens in a democratic society. Therefore, compulsory education up to certain ages has been instituted and, to overcome the financial obstacles, this level of education has normally been provided at public expense. Or, economic pressures may lead some families to require that children work and contribute to family income. Hence we find child labor laws. Or, the way in which individuals spend their incomes when left to their own devices may not always be in the best interests of society as a whole, and laws prohibiting the sale of narcotics to all and intoxicating liquor to minors are necessary.

Finally, government, acting as the implementing agent of a democratic society, has undertaken certain functions bearing directly on the welfare of the family. National defense, a police and court system, environmental health are some of these functions. Moreover, in addition to education, which has already been mentioned, governments make available in varying degrees such commodities or services as low-income housing, medical care and rehabilitation, school lunches, free holiday transport for mothers and children, and the like. And recently it has been seen that many recreation needs, whose satisfaction involves the provision of parks, playgrounds, and large unspoiled natural areas, can be satisfied only if government takes a major responsibility for their provision.

Government's Role, 1950–1960

INCOME SECURITY. By the time of the 1950 White House Conference state and city governments were playing an important role in child and family welfare. In this chapter we shall concentrate primarily, although not exclusively, on the social security and the welfare programs as generally understood.

By 1950 the Old Age and Survivors Insurance program covered some 35 million persons by a system which, in return for the payment of social security taxes by employers and their workers throughout their working life, made available monthly payments of a predetermined amount (varying with the recipient's previous earnings) to retired workers aged sixty-five and over and to the survivors of covered workers. But the payments were low (the average monthly benefit for a single worker in 1949 was only $26.50, for a worker and aged wife $41.40 and for a widow with three children only $54.00) and many millions of families lacked any such protection because the breadwinner was employed in "uncovered employment."

In the intervening ten years the contribution of the program to family well-being has been vastly increased as a result of a series of amendments. First, coverage has been extended (notably by the amendments of 1950 and 1954) so that today 9 out of 10 jobs are covered. Second, benefits have been increased, not only for future beneficiaries but also for those on the rolls at the time the changes were made. In addition, it has been made possible to exclude 5 years of low earnings when calculating the benefit amount and to disregard all years of no earnings due to disability. These changes have led to a sizable increase in average benefits. By January, 1959, the average monthly benefit awarded to single aged workers had increased to $67.50, that for a man and eligible wife to $119.40, and that for a widow with three children to $171.70.

Third, a new risk area has been provided for. Since 1956 totally and permanently disabled workers, fifty years of age or over, have been entitled to social insurance benefits, and since 1958 their dependents have also been able to claim benefits. Of special interest to children was the 1956 amendment which provided that if a child of a deceased worker was totally physically or mentally disabled prior to reaching the age of eighteen, he could continue to receive his orphan's benefit until death, instead of losing it at age eighteen.

In contrast to the amendments of the OASDI program, which have so greatly enhanced economic security of families and children, changes in other social insurance programs during the 1950–60 decade have been either insignificant or have failed to adjust the programs to changing economic conditions. For the individuals affected by unemployment (who have averaged between 1.9 and 3.4 millions annually during this period and reached 5.4 million at the peak) unemployment insurance is a major potential resource. Coverage of this program was extended to include firms employing four workers or more by an amendment to federal law in 1954 but the states covering all employees increased only from sixteen to eighteen during this decade. Benefit amounts have been raised in most of the states but in general have failed to keep pace with rising wages: as a result the ratio which they bear to a worker's previous wages has fallen far below the 50 percent which was the objective when the system was inaugurated, in all except six states, averaging for the nation as a whole only a little more than a third of weekly wages. Of more serious concern to families is the absence of legislation providing benefits for dependents; the states with such provisions increased only to eleven at the end of 1958 as against five in 1949.

Duration of benefit has been increased in most states during this period; yet in 1958 the number of workers exhausting such benefits as their state laws entitled them to became so large that the federal government enacted a Temporary Unemployment Compensation Act to assist the states in paying benefits beyond the normal duration. Not all states took advantage of this legislation, which in any case expired in mid-1959.

In the last ten years no state has followed the example of the four which by 1950 had enacted temporary disability laws: the existing laws have however been frequently amended and are somewhat more liberal than they were.

Special categories of families such as veterans and railroad employees benefit from special income security programs. Both of these have been significantly liberalized in the last decade.

Despite the remarkable expansion of social insurance protection of families against various risks to continuity of income, the incomplete coverage of some programs and the gaps in risk coverage of the system as a whole mean that many millions of families whose sources of income have temporarily or permanently dried up must still be supported by public assistance. During 1950 there were more than 8 million persons drawing social insurance and related benefits of one kind or another. By March, 1959, the corresponding number had grown to over 20 million. Yet in the same period the number of persons receiving public assistance had increased from 5.5 million to over 6.5 million. Of these public assistance cases in 1959, 2.9 million were receiving Aid to Dependent Children payments, while about half of the 480,000 persons receiving general relief had children (averaging 2.9 per case with children).

During the ten years that have elapsed since the last
White House Conference significant improvements have
taken place in public assistance. Of direct concern to children was the broadening of federal aid in the Aid to Dependent Children program in 1950.

In this ten-year period amendments to the Social Security
Act have considerably liberalized the federal grants to the
categorical public assistance program, so that the federal
share in the cost of all types of assistance has risen from
45.1 percent in 1950 to 50.4 percent in 1958. Particularly
noteworthy were the changes enacted in 1958 whereby the
states were given more flexibility in adjusting the size of
grants in individual cases without prejudicing the extent of
federal reimbursement and whereby a beginning was made,
through the variable grant principle, in providing relatively
more federal aid to the poorer states. Since 1956, too, the
more liberal grant-in-aid arrangements have fostered the provision of more adequate medical care for public assistance
recipients. But while average monthly assistance payments
have increased much of this has been offset by rising prices.

Yet a third major step forward in public assistance must
be noted. The amendments of 1956 radically revised the
concept of the purpose of public assistance by extending government's responsibility for assurance to eligible needy persons of cash payments, needed medical care, and various
services. These services are to help aged recipients attain
self-care, to help the blind and the disabled to attain self-
support or self-care, and in the case of recipients of Aid to
Dependent Children, to help maintain and strengthen fam-

ily life and help parents or relatives "to attain the maximum self-support and personal independence consistent with the maintenance of continuing parental care and protection." Although it is too soon to assess the full impact of this broadening of the objectives of public assistance, the first reports of the states to the Social Security Administration of the services they are rendering and of steps they are taking to utilize to the maximum other community agencies providing similar services suggest that the amendment has already had a stimulating effect.

But a major stumbling block has not been removed. The 1956 amendments, which so greatly broadened the responsibilities of public welfare, quite logically included authorization for additional federal money to train more personnel and to undertake needed research, but to date Congress has not voted the authorized appropriations.

In contrast to the developments that have taken place in the categorical assistance programs, little has happened in general assistance (or relief). No federal aid is available for this program and in many areas of the country it is nonexistent or highly restrictive.

SPECIAL SERVICES FOR CHILDREN. During the last decade, social services developed specifically for children have in general failed to keep pace with the growth in both the child population and the increasing wealth of the country. The stimulus to the development of child welfare programs through federal grants provided under Title V of the Social Security Act has been intensified by increases in authorizations and appropriations. Yet, although the former have risen from $3.5 million in 1949–50 to $17 million in 1959–60 and the latter from $3.5 million to $13 million, it is note-worthy that after 1949–50 smaller sums have been appro-priated than were authorized, and in most years the states utilized less than the sums appropriated by Congress. More-over, the number of children served by public child welfare programs has not kept pace with the increase in the child population, falling from 55 to 51 per 10,000 children be-tween 1946 and 1957. The decline has been particularly noteworthy in urban states where the proportion served fell from 62 to 49 per 10,000 children during this period. Only in the rural states has the percentage served increased (from 40 to 63 per 10,000 children), a situation which reflects the preference given to rural areas in the distribution of federal funds. Recognition was given to the needs of urban areas, both metropolitan and suburban, by an amendment in 1958 which eliminated the references in the allocation formula to predominantly rural areas and areas of special need.

Furthermore, only limited progress was made during the last decade in improving the caliber of staff in the public child welfare programs. Although between 1950 and 1955 the number of child welfare workers with professional de-grees rose from 19 to 28 percent of the total, there remained 33 percent who had had only some graduate study and 39 percent who had none at all in an accredited school of social work.

OTHER SOCIAL WELFARE PROGRAMS. In the public programs, other than those concerned with income maintenance, less progress can be reported for the decade 1950–60. (Because programs dealing with health fall within the scope of another chapter in these volumes, no mention is here made of the notable developments of public and publicly subsidized programs in the field of health.) Although the Housing Act of 1949 offered the promise of a revised and much enlarged low-rent program by authorizing federal loans and contributions for not over 810,000 additional dwelling units over a six-year period, subsequent legislation severely cut the number of dwellings to be initiated each year. From 1950 to 1957 inclusive, only 238,000 low rent public housing units were started. In 1956 less than 5,000 units were started.

Among the more narrowly protective services, too, there was only limited progress. The minimum wage rate under the Fair Labor Standards Act was increased from 75 cents to $1.00 an hour in 1955. But efforts to raise the minimum to a level more in keeping with current price levels have been unsuccessful and the gap in federal legislation has not been filled by action on the part of the states.

Since 1950 there have been no legislative changes in the child-labor provisions of the Fair Labor Standards Act. Amendments that became effective in 1950, notably modifying the agricultural exemption, have resulted in getting more children off farms and into school. Between 1951 and 1958 school enrollment of rural youth, ten to fifteen years of age, rose from 86 to 94 percent while the urban rate remained stable at about 98 percent.

The Future Role of Government

That government, in the interest of the community as a whole, should take action on behalf of children is clearly no longer questioned. The realistic issues today concern rather the scope of that action, the specific policies to be applied, and the effectiveness of the measures adopted.

To a significant degree the role of government with regard to children has shifted from the narrower "police" function of protecting the community from the delinquent child and of protecting the helpless and neglected child from those (parents, employers, or institutions) who would take advantage of him, to a wider concept. The modern view of the use of government increasingly emphasizes developmental and positive (as opposed to narrowly protective) action and focuses more upon the child as a member of a family group than as an isolated individual. This approach broadens the potential role of government: public policy in the interest of children no longer is restricted to "child welfare services" as such but embraces all governmental measures affecting the well-being of all American families.

The precise role of government during the coming decades will depend primarily on three major considerations: first, the extent to which social, economic, and demographic developments create problems for the family which the family alone and unaided cannot resolve to the satisfaction of the community; second, the extent to which nongovernmental supra-family organizations or associations can deal effectively with the situation independently of government help, and, finally, the extent to which the nation as a whole evidences both a concern about the existence of such problems and a willingness to pay the price in terms of the money, time, and effort needed to develop suitable solutions.

The social stresses facing the family in the years immediately ahead fall into two groups: those which arise out of developments in the past for which social provision, although well under way, is not yet complete, and those which can be expected to arise as a result of more recent social, economic, and demographic changes, some of whose effects can already be predicted.

In the first group it is evident that the need for income security has not yet been fully met. The widely expressed preference for social insurance as the technique for assuring family and individual economic security has not yet been fully implemented. Coverage for unemployment insurance is far from complete. Workmen's compensation laws, also limited in coverage, have lagged far behind the newer social insurance programs. Benefits of all social insurance programs (and notably of unemployment insurance) have not kept up with rising wages and prices and call for constant scrutiny and revision. For the millions dependent for their incomes on public assistance, the situation is even more unsatisfactory. Most disturbing of all, in view of the nation's expressed concern for the welfare of its children, is the disadvantageous position of the 2.25 million children who are supported by the Aid to Dependent Children program. Because federal aid for this program has from the beginning been much less liberal than for the other categories (matching only up to $30 per child as against $65 per person in the other programs), the monthly payments per child ($28.68 in March, 1959) fall far below even the modest payment to the aged ($64.34), the disabled ($63.66), and the blind ($68.86). Furthermore, the limitation of the payment to children in families where the father is dead, absent from the home, or disabled, means that many needy children are denied public aid, especially in those states that deny public assistance to employable persons and in those where general assistance is grossly inadequate. In some cases the program operates to perpetuate or even encourage family break-up as the only way to secure public aid.

Nor does the ADC program embody any consistent social policy. Supposedly developed in order that the mother would not have to seek employment and thus would be able to remain at home to provide care for her children, the payments are almost nowhere adequate enough to remove all inducement to the mother (and sometimes the children) to seek paid employment. Indeed, in some communities pressure is put on the mother to do precisely this. And if it be the case that children need a sense of stability then the ADC program must again be held lacking: not only may payments be reduced from time to time on account of inadequate appropriations but eligibility for them may be endangered by action by the mother which runs counter to certain requirements, or the amount may be reduced by the extent of earnings so that no incentive to independence remains.

Public policy has indeed recognized the special need for services to children. But despite the stimulus given by federal grants since 1935 to the development of child welfare services, by 1959 almost half of the counties in the nation, accounting for a quarter of all children, had no fulltime public child welfare workers.

Furthermore, despite the growing emphasis on the importance of preventing family breakdown and enabling the child to remain in his own home, over 70 percent of the resources devoted to child welfare services are still spent on foster care. In December, 1957, only 38 percent of the children receiving casework services from state and local public welfare agencies were in their own homes as against 62 percent who were in foster homes, institutions, or elsewhere, and the figures for voluntary welfare agencies were much the same. Even more disconcerting is the fact that between 1946 and 1957 the number of children receiving service (unrelated to financial assistance) in their own homes increased by only 22 percent whereas those in foster homes increased by 37 percent.

Inadequate as the provision for constructive and rehabilitative services to children is as such, the status of corresponding provision for adults and families is even more unsatisfactory. We have no measure of the extent of this type of service rendered to the 5 to 6 million recipients of public assistance but all the evidence points to the fact that it is small. In some communities, public assistance recipients do not even receive the minimum physical care and medical attention to render them self-supporting. The major public rehabilitation program, Vocational Rehabilitation, as late as 1958, rehabilitated only 74,317 people annually plus another 18,584 persons who had been prepared for employment but had not found jobs. The insignificance of these figures is revealed when it is pointed out that there are estimated to be some 2 million handicapped persons who could be rehabilitated and that every year a quarter of a million persons become in need of vocational rehabilitation services.

Vocational counseling services for young people in schools and public employment agencies are still very inadequate and will become more so during the coming decade when the population expansion of the postwar years begins to affect the labor market, unless vigorous steps to expand these facilities are taken.

The gaps and inadequacies so far discussed are "unfinished business." They indicate the extent to which the nation, by 1960, had succeeded in grappling with the threats to family and child welfare due to social and economic developments of the past. But as we look ahead, it is clear that the impact on some or all families of problems created by recent developments, of trends even now evident, will call for further social provision.

One significant social change is the increasing tendency of mothers to work. In the ten years, 1948–58, the number of mothers in the labor force increased by 80 percent and the proportion of all mothers who work, by almost 50 percent. Many of these are mothers of preschool children. While fewer of these mothers work full-time (16 percent of those with preschool children as against one-third of those with older children), this still means that a problem of assuring adequate care during the mother's absence exists for a large proportion of the 3.6 million preschool children whose mothers were in the labor force in 1957.

Group day-care centers present themselves as one type of facility which might be developed to meet this need. A nationwide study conducted in May, 1958, showed that nearly 400,000 children under age twelve had to care for themselves while the mother worked and 138,000 of these children were less than ten years old. Among children under twelve with working mothers, 1 child in 13 had to look after himself for varying periods, and in the age group ten to eleven, 1 child in 5 was without any care while the mother was at work. Over a million children were looked after by nonrelatives.[1]

The inadequacy of the facilities for day-time care of children of working mothers serves only to throw into relief the larger problem of society's failure, as yet, to provide appropriate arrangements for the care of children when parents are unable to carry out their normal functions for whatever reason. While some of these arrangements may be institutional in character (day-care centers, nursery schools, school lunch programs, etc.), others involve the rendering of services in the home. In the last decade increasing attention has been devoted to homemaker services. Yet despite the great potentialities of this form of family aid, in the spring of 1958 there were only 143 agencies (serving 2,188 families) providing homemaker services, all but 33 being private agencies.

Arrangements for substitute care of children in groups or in the home may be provided on a commercial basis or by public or private welfare agencies either free or on a fee basis. Experience has shown the necessity for licensing and supervision of commercially operated services. Private agency-

[1] See the forthcoming study by the Children's Bureau, *Child Care Arrangements of Full-time Working Mothers.*

operated services are growing, but slowly, and serve primarily low-income groups. If the need is to be adequately met an expansion of public activity seems inevitable.

Another development which bears upon the role of government is the upward trend of family breakdown in the nation as a whole. On the one hand more babies are being born out of wedlock; on the other hand, there appears to be an increase in the break-up of marriages and more divorces involve children. In 1956, the illegitimacy rate of unmarried women aged fifteen to forty-four (20.2 per 1,000) was almost three times as high as in 1940 and such births constituted 4.65 percent of total live births as against 3.79 in 1940. And although the proportion of illegitimate births accounted for by teen-agers has declined (40 percent in 1956 as against almost 50 percent in 1940), and despite the trend to earlier marriage, 1 in 7 of all girls fifteen to nineteen years of age who bore a child was not married.

The divorce rate per 1,000 married women, although far less than its postwar peak of 17.8, is still above that of 1940 (9.2 in 1957 as against 8.8 in 1940) and in 1958 the number of married women who reported themselves as separated from their husbands was nearly as great as the number reporting themselves divorced. And with the trend to earlier marriages and earlier child bearing, more of the divorces involve children. About half of the divorces granted in 1956 were to couples with at least one child under eighteen and 1 in 9 divorcing couples had as many as three children.[2]

[2] The data in these paragraphs are derived from "Facts about Families," *Social Security Bulletin* (May, 1959), pp. 9–14.

As against these developments, only one cheerful fact can be noted: full orphanhood is on the way out. As a result of improvements in medical science and social protective measures, fewer women die in childbirth and fewer workers die because of industrial accidents or occupational diseases. By 1957 the number of orphans with both parents dead was estimated to be only 55,000, while there were 1,890,000 with the father dead and 800,000 with the mother dead.

Public recognition of the fact that the social problems of dependent children are primarily problems of broken homes rather than orphanhood has come slowly. Great progress has been made in devising social measures to protect the economic welfare of the orphan, primarily as a result of the OASDI program. But against this effective provision for the economic needs of the orphan, social provision for the equally large number of children affected by broken homes has lagged. In 1956 it was estimated that some 2.5 million children lived with the mother in a broken home and some 200,000 children lived with their father only. Hitherto public provision for the economic needs of such children has taken the form of Aid to Dependent Children, which has increasingly become a "broken families" program as OASDI has shouldered more and more of the responsibility for the orphaned child. At the end of 1958, 59.8 percent of the fathers in ADC families were divorced or separated or had deserted the family or were not married to the mother. This preponderance of broken families, together with the sharp upward trend of ADC recipients (from 599,000 families and 1.52 million children in 1949 to 775,600 families and 2.24

million children in March, 1959), has exposed the program to much adverse criticism.

Some of this criticism is uninformed, and fails to take account of the facts cited above relative to the trends of divorce, separation, and illegitimacy in the nation as a whole and of the increased child population. Furthermore, it seems probable that part of the remarkable increase in broken families in receipt of ADC reflects the fact that when government accepts financial responsibility for the support of certain precisely defined categories of persons their true number becomes known for the first time (just as the number of disabled children under eighteen qualifying for OASDI benefits exceeded the estimates made before benefits became available to them in 1956). It is highly probable that before the days of ADC there were large numbers of broken families living below public assistance levels, but no statistical count was made of them. Unfortunately, too, public attention focuses on the inadequate parents and not on the hundreds of thousands of ADC mothers who make a decent home for their children despite shockingly inadequate monthly payments. Yet even when allowance is made for these facts, it remains true that family breakdown has now to be recognized as a major cause of income insecurity among children.

Popular resentment of the large numbers and steady growth of the broken home ADC recipients has led to actions which gravely jeopardize the welfare of children. Sometimes efforts are made to refuse payments after a second or third illegitimate child is born, or to force the mother to seek paid work, or to remove the child from the family. Elsewhere, the low level of ADC monthly payments per recipient probably reflects the general disparagement of this category. The effect upon these children, who will be the citizens of tomorrow, of meager and uncertain living standards, and of social disapproval, denied as they are in any case the benefit of normal two-parent home environment, seems often to be forgotten in the concern of communities to keep down illegitimacy and dependency rates.

All this is not to deny that the broken home has become a major social problem calling for more knowledge of its causes and more constructive and imaginative programs for its prevention and control. Hitherto society has attempted to discharge its responsibilities through a single program, ADC, providing a meager income and limited casework service, supplemented by a very inadequate system of specialized public and private child welfare services. No greater challenge faces a nation professedly concerned with the well-being of children than a reassessment of social policy in relation to the broken home. Such a reassessment would have to place much greater stress on prevention. It would explore more imaginatively the contribution that could be made by organizations and institutions additional to courts, correctional agencies, and those now thought of as "welfare agencies," such as the schools, the churches, trade unions, and the like. Above all, it would be postulated upon the assumptions that the major concern is to strengthen the family and the major test of achievement is the welfare of the child.

A third development pointing to a larger role for government is the fact that during the last ten years the average American family has become steadily better off. The median money income for all families from all sources rose from $2,530 in 1944 to $4,970 in 1957. Even after allowing for price increases and the higher tax rates of recent years, this is a sizable improvement. As the general level of economic well-being rises, it throws into relief the position of groups who have not shared in the general prosperity. The number of families of whom this is true is disturbingly large.[3]

The disparity in average per capita income between the richest and the poorest states is still great, ranging as it does from $968 in Mississippi and $1,122 in Arkansas to $2,744 in Delaware and $2,678 in Connecticut in 1955–57. In the poorer states not only are average family incomes much lower, but the ability of the community at large to support needed public or private welfare services is restricted. Families who derive their living from agriculture have also failed to keep pace with the general prosperity.[4] The median money income for rural farm families in 1954 was only $1,973. Furthermore, agricultural workers are currently excluded from most governmental protective legislation, such

[3] For the facts about low-income families, see U.S. Congress, Joint Committee on the Economic Report, *Characteristics of the Low-Income Population and Related Federal Programs*, 1955; and *Low-Income Families*, Hearings before the Sub-Committee on Low-Income Families, 84th Cong., 2nd Sess. (Washington: G.P.O., 1955); and the series of reports issued by the New York State Interdepartmental Committee on Low Incomes.

[4] For a vivid account of the living and working conditions of agricultural wage-earning families, see *Report on Farm Labor* (New York: National Advisory Committee on Farm Labor, 1959).

as the Fair Labor Standards Act, Unemployment Insurance, Workmen's Compensation, the Taft-Hartley Act, and Child Labor Laws. Most disadvantaged of all are the 380,000 American migrant workers and their families, while the approximately 500,000 foreign migrant workers in agriculture, although in most cases given more protection through agreements with their national governments, are almost as badly off. The migrant family has low and uncertain income, unsatisfactory housing, inadequate health facilities, and, in some communities, limited access to social services because of its "nonresident" status. The child in the migrant family frequently works in the fields with his parents, he suffers from inadequate and interrupted schooling, and he and his family lack the sense of stability and security that comes from a feeling of "belonging" to any community.

The average level of incomes of minority groups, notably Negroes, Puerto Ricans, and Mexicans, also falls below the general average: their housing conditions are less favorable, their educational levels are lower, and their health records are poorer than those of the general population.

In general children who are members of large families have also failed to share in the general prosperity. Income increases as the size of the family increases only up to the point where there are two children in the family. Thereafter, income actually decreases quite rapidly as the family size grows. In 1954 the median income of the two-child family was $4,506 while that of the five-child family was only $3,155, with three extra people to support. It has been estimated that whereas only 14.8 percent of all families with two children in 1954 had annual money incomes equal to less than half the city worker's family budget, 19.4 percent of three-children families, 31.7 percent of four-children families, 47.8 percent of five-children families, and over 51.8 percent of families with six or more children were in this situation. (The city worker's family budget is a measure of the dollar cost of maintaining a family of a specified size at a level of living which meets prevailing standards of health, efficiency, nurture of children, and participation in community activities. It describes a "modest but adequate," rather than a "luxury" or "subsistence" standard.) When it is recalled that 54 percent of the nation's children are in families with three or more children, these facts give rise to serious concern.

Finally, all those families or individuals dependent on socially provided income, whether social insurance or public assistance, constitute another large segment of the population who have failed to keep pace with the general rise in living standards.

Many of the measures needed to ensure all American families a level of living in keeping with current standards of adequacy and consistent with our steadily increasing national product necessitate action by both government and the individual citizen, such as measures to eliminate discrimination. Others are of a kind that only governments can take. They include extension of minimum wage laws and laws governing the employment of children to cover all employments and all children. They call for federal aid to the poorer states greater in proportion to that given to the richer in order that families dwelling therein may not be denied access to the commonly accepted level and range of social services.

They suggest both assistance to families to move away from depressed areas to others of greater opportunity and also aid to revitalize certain depressed areas. They call for the extension of educational opportunity and training and vocational guidance facilities for all children, for all studies demonstrate that as a group the low-income families are characterized by poor education and lack of skills, and their position will become even more disadvantaged as automation and advanced technology create greater demands for well-educated and skilled workers. They include revision of our social security programs to ensure that benefits keep pace not only with prices but also with the rise in average standards of living. They may even involve the adoption of some system of children's allowances or other special aids to members of large families to offset the disadvantages suffered by children therein, for the only current public policy in the interests of large families, income tax exemptions for children, helps only those families who would normally pay sizable taxes and in any case does not put any additional money into the homes with the lowest incomes.[5]

All signs point to a continuance of the high mobility of the American population and even to some increase of the

---

[5] It has been estimated that the percentages of families with incomes of less than the tax exemptions to which they were entitled in 1954 were: families with one child, 14.6 percent; two children, 16.6 percent; three children, 25.5 percent; four children, 44.5 percent; five children, 66.6 percent; six or more children, over 76.9 percent. James C. Vadakin, *Family Allowances* (Miami: University of Miami Press, 1958), p. 163.

rate as the shift of families from the cities to the suburban areas gathers momentum. The need for adequate community facilities in both the city and its suburbs is thereby intensified. In the newer communities, facilities have to be brought into existence. The older cities face even more serious problems due to the draining away both of the better-off families who seek the living amenities of the suburbs and of business enterprises seeking lower costs of operation outside the highly taxed or high-rent cities. Thus they are being left with a population that in general is poorer and more likely to be in need of social services including, notably, subsidized housing and community facilities, while at the same time their tax base has shrunk. Unless the cities and the families remaining within them are to suffer progressive deterioration and "urban blight," there will have to be more extensive and vigorous public action in the form of urban renewal, public housing, development of recreational facilities, and the like.

The broadening of objectives in housing policy to include urban renewal has created new and challenging problems such as the relocation of tenants from the condemned areas, and the provision of adequate and well-coordinated community facilities and services in the redeveloped areas. In addition, it is increasingly realized that the provision of satisfactory housing for the nation's families is not assured merely by making available "decent, safe, and sanitary dwellings." Underprivileged families from the slums need help in raising their standards and adjusting to new conditions. And the problem is complicated by the fact that existing income limits as a condition of eligibility tend to make the housing project a concentration of low income groups, among whom public assistance recipients (and notably ADC mothers) and minority groups form, inevitably, a large proportion.

The Contribution of Non-Governmental Institutions

Whether or not these developments, which affect the well-being of some or all children in varying degrees, will, in fact, lead to an expanded role for government will depend in part on the extent to which other social institutions are interested in, or are able to take, action which is beyond the power of the individual family. For our society is characterized by the existence of a large number of voluntary associations formed by individuals or families to deal with certain problems that no one family or individual could deal with alone and unaided. Workers have formed trade unions, which have fought not merely for higher wages but in recent years also for various guarantees of income after earning ceases or for group provision of services needed by all families even when earning power is not interrupted. Many millions of families and their children benefit today from such privately negotiated benefits as retirement pensions, supplementary unemployment compensation, health insurance, and the like. But spectacular as has been the growth of these arrangements in recent years, they cannot substitute for governmental programs. First, not all families have breadwinners who are employed in highly organized industries, and these include many of the families most in need of help or protection.

Such additional benefits, over and above decent wages, are typically not found in agriculture, or in small firms, or in struggling industries. Second, even where such programs exist they do not do the whole job: they are additional to the basic provision by government. It is significant both that their great growth has followed the assumption by government of responsibility for assuring basic minimum security, and that they are known as "fringe" benefits.

Families also combine with others to deal with common problems in other areas. Since World War II, there has been a remarkable growth of associations initiated by parents of children with specific physical or mental disabilities. But while some of these organizations have succeeded in raising sizable sums of money to finance research and other programs of their own, it is significant that a considerable fraction of their energies is directed to exerting pressure on governments to make special provision in school systems, health services, and the like for the children whose interests they represent.

Private philanthropy is another institution which supplements the ability of families to deal with social and economic problems and which at one time was in a very real sense an alternative to government action. But some of the problems today are of such magnitude and involve the raising of such large sums of money as to be beyond the capacity of even the most generously supported private welfare organizations. The function of assuring basic economic security is now generally agreed to be one that government, rather than private philanthropy should assume for this very reason. Indeed, leading private welfare agencies now vigorously support more adequate governmental income security programs on the ground that unless government accepts this responsibility the private agencies cannot carry out their own responsibilities. But in other areas, too, private welfare is no longer seen as an alternative to government but rather as carrying out certain functions which, for religious, cultural, or other reasons are believed to be more appropriately performed by nongovernmental bodies.

One area in which private welfare has played a very important role is the provision of casework services to children. Yet even here, in June, 1957, in the country as a whole, of about 404,000 children receiving casework services, public agencies were giving primary service to about 281,000 children and secondary services to another 50,000 served primarily by private agencies, while the latter were giving primary service to about 123,000 and secondary services to another 2,000. Thus public agencies were serving 43 children per 10,000 child population while the private agencies were serving 19. These figures exclude most of the children in families receiving public assistance some of whom undoubtedly receive governmental services, and also those receiving services directly from juvenile courts and probation departments. Inclusion of such children would still further increase the preponderance of the public sector. Furthermore, in some cases, although the private agencies were rendering services, their cost was met wholly or in some degree by government.[6] To the extent this occurs, sponsorship ceases to be purely "private" as opposed to "public," for decisions as to the extent of subsidization and the desirability of providing services indirectly through private agencies rather than directly by government move into the realm of public policy.

The role of voluntary welfare is dealt with more extensively in another chapter in this volume. Here we are concerned only with the extent to which private philanthropy can realistically be regarded as an alternative to government in grappling with the major social problems facing families in the coming decades. All the evidence suggests that its role can only be that of an important supplement although it will inevitably be greater in some functional areas than others. In 1955, for example, private agency expenditures for family and other child welfare services were a little more than 3 times as large as the corresponding public expenditures (excluding services rendered under the public assistance programs). But the inadequate and underdeveloped state of these services throughout most of the country and the many unmet needs for additional services caution against any inference that the vastly greater sums needed to equip the country with an acceptable volume and level of service could be secured from private philanthropy. Between 1945

[6] Slightly over 43 percent of all payments for foster care by state and local public welfare agencies were payments for children in homes or institutions supervised or administered by voluntary agencies. *Child Welfare Statistics, 1957*, Children's Bureau Statistical Series 51, Social Security Administration, U. S. Dept. of Health, Education, and Welfare, 1959, p. 26. In 1952 the United Community Funds and Councils reported that 12.5 percent of the total income of voluntary services providing specialized services for children came from public funds.

and 1955 expenditures from philanthropic contributions for health and welfare purposes (excluding education and religious purposes) are estimated to have increased from $1.2 billion to $1.9 billion. During the same period the corresponding public expenditures rose from $8.1 billion to $22.2 billion.[7]

The Degree of Citizen Concern

The extent to which the people of the United States will be willing to make use of the instrument of government to implement the pledges made to their children at the 1950 White House Conference will depend upon their willingness to pay the necessary price in money, time, and effort. It must be recognized at once that the money price, in terms of the additional tax monies needed, will be stiff. It will be necessary to devote a larger proportion of national income to these social programs if existing deficiencies are to be made good and if even a modest effort is to be made to grapple with the newer problems created by current economic, social, and demographic developments. Moreover this social provision will have to be made for a rapidly growing number of children. Between 1950 and 1958 the number of children under eighteen increased from 47.0 million to 61.3 million, and it is expected to increase to 79.0 million in 1970.

But increased tax revenues do not necessarily mean proportionately increased tax rates. How much incomes avail-

[7] For data on public social welfare expenditures, see Ida Merriam "Social Welfare in the United States, 1934–54," *Social Security Bulletin* (October, 1955), pp. 2ff., and "Social Welfare Expenditures in the United States, 1956–57," *ibid.* (October, 1958), pp. 22ff.

able for private spending would be reduced by additional expenditures on governmental programs in the interests of children and families will depend upon the rate of growth of national productivity. In the recent past, national product has been increasing at the rate of 3 to 3.5 percent a year. It is this increase which accounts for the fact that although public social welfare expenditures for all purposes (including education) have risen from $7.8 billion in 1936–37, to $16.5 billion in 1946–47 and to 37.9 billion in 1956–57, we are still devoting a smaller percentage of our total economic output to such ends (8.8 percent in 1956–57 as against 8.9 percent twenty years earlier). It is this rise of productivity, too, which has enabled the average income receiver to dispose, as he wishes, of a steadily rising income even after payment of all taxes for social welfare, defense, and other purposes. Current estimates suggest that in the years immediately ahead at least this rate of economic progress can be anticipated and some authorities put it even higher. (The National Planning Association uses an average of 4.2 percent as the most probable figure.) To the extent that these forecasts are borne out, the burden of financing more adequate public social welfare services (in the widest sense) will be lightened. Nor must it be forgotten that many types of social welfare expenditure result in additions to the nation's productive potential or save other costs. The disabled worker who is rehabilitated, the child who secures a better education, the family which is helped to attain self-support, yield economic returns for the public investment in them. And the families which are prevented from breaking up, or the child who is saved from delinquency represent a saving in social costs in future years.

Even so, it would be unrealistic not to expect that effective development of publicly provided goods and services will require the devotion of a larger proportion of national income to these programs. Whether or not this will happen will depend upon prevailing values, on how much people care about the well-being of children and families, and how much they know about the nature of the problems and the effectiveness of the measures for dealing with them. That people are willing to spend more of their income on publicly provided goods and services when they are convinced of the worthiness of the objective and the effectiveness of the program is shown by the growth of expenditures on social insurance (from \$3.86 per capita in 1936–37 to \$73.37 in 1956–57). If there is an equal concern about the broken family or unsatisfactory housing, they will be willing to spend on the relevant programs more than the \$4.44 and \$.70 per head which they spent in 1956–57.

WORK, WOMEN, AND CHILDREN

by HENRY DAVID

THERE IS an obvious measure of truth in the frequently heard assertion that the society of the United States is strongly child-centered. No other major society in the world, for example, provides as many or as varied educational opportunities for its young. Probably no other society is as responsive to the consumption desires of its young—or to adult beliefs about what the young want and need in their pursuit of happiness. No other society allocates as large a volume of goods and services to the satisfaction of these consumption desires. Probably no other society has fashioned as elaborate and extensive a system—and this implies no judgment on its adequacy—of public and private agencies and services for dealing with the problems and needs of its children and youth.

More subtle qualitative evidences may also be invoked in support of the characterization of Americans as a child-centered people. Thus, in contrast to the peoples of other

Henry David is Executive Director of the National Manpower Council and Dean of the Graduate Faculty of Political and Social Science at the New School for Social Research.

Western societies, Americans seem to be more self-conscious in their search for and adoption of what is alleged to be the newest and, of course, the best mode of child-rearing. The market for books and periodical and newspaper articles which offer "scientific" advice on the care, rearing, and development of children at all ages is enormous. However uncertain they may be about the psychological significance of the concept, Americans seem to share a universal concern with giving their offspring a sense of "security." Currently, they seem to be dedicated to the proposition that the young should not be "frustrated" in their growing-up experiences and in their relationships with one another or with adults.

To some foreign observers these signs of a child-centered society testify to an excessive, perhaps even a neurotic, preoccupation with the young at the expense of adults. This kind of critical observation about the posture of Americans toward their children is, of course, traditional. In part, it grows out of the fact that Americans have long seemed far less disposed than other Western people to define a "place" for their children, or to act on the belief that children should have a place and be kept in it whatever "it" might be. In the nineteenth century, Anthony Trollope found it unfortunate that American children were "never banished, snubbed, and kept in the background," as children were in England. More recent European visitors have been struck by the extent to which American children participate as equals in many aspects of adult life from which the young in other societies are normally excluded. Europeans also frequently find it odd that American adults encourage their young to voice opinions on the most complex and difficult social, economic, and political issues and that they manifest respectful attention to the views that children express on these issues. One English visitor is reported to have remarked that the schools of the United States and American middle-class family life seem to be conducted according to the principle: "The child knows best."

On the surface it appears true that the world of the adult and the world of the young are less sharply differentiated in the United States than in other Western societies. It may even be argued that, since early in the nineteenth century, considerations of equality and freedom and the value placed upon early self-dependence have conspired, in combination with other influences, to blur the lines between these two worlds. The fact that years alone do not seem to establish a claim for superior status and deference, as they do in many societies, and that rigid distinctions are not maintained between the young and adults with respect to dress, patterns of social behavior, recreational activities, freedom of personal conduct, and the like, may be taken as additional marks of a child-centered society.

In spite of a preoccupation with the young, however, it also remains true that most Americans appear to have been singularly indifferent to the import that one of the major social transformations which the United States has experienced during the present century may have for the rearing and development of their children and youth. That transformation is the one which has taken place in the employment of women—more particularly in the employment of wives and mothers—outside the home. At first glance, one might expect that changes of almost revolutionary proportions in the normal pattern of women's lives and in the functions of married women would be seized upon as having far-reaching consequences for the form and substance of family life and for the care and rearing of the young. One might further expect that, in a society which values its young so highly and which is presumably so concerned with their healthy development, changes of this character would immediately stimulate serious reflection and inquiry. Neither of these expectations, however, has in fact been realized.

The scale of the change which has taken place since the close of the nineteenth century in women's employment outside the home is suggested by the following comparisons: In 1890, the Census Bureau counted about 4 million gainfully employed women who represented one-sixth of the nation's working population and the same proportion of the women in the United States aged ten and over. In the last several years, however, between 21.5 and 23 million women have been in the labor force in the course of any one month. In the course of any year, about 28 million women have been employed outside the home. In recent years, moreover, women have accounted for about 30 percent of the nation's total labor force, and about one-third of all women fourteen years and older have been employed outside the home.

The most recent United States Department of Labor data on employment show that out of a total civilian labor force of just over 70 million in October, 1959, 23.5 million—or one third—were women. In that month, better than a third of all women aged fourteen and over were employed outside the home. About 33.9 million of the 63.5 million fourteen and older—or about 54 percent—who were not in the labor force were engaged in keeping house, while another 4.7 million were attending school.

Explanations of why women have come to play so important a role in the nation's labor force require no detailed treatment here. It is sufficient to note, as the National Manpower Council remarked, that: "To make clear the variety and the complexity of the factors which have affected the demand for and the supply of women workers during the present century would require retelling the history of the United States. Growth and change in the economy, advances in science and technology, an expanding urban population, developments in education, the role of government as an employer, the crisis situations of war and depression, social values and attitudes, patterns of marriage, childbearing, and life expectancy—all have contributed significantly to the revolution in women's employment." [1]

More significant than the increases in the numbers of women employed either full time or part time outside the home, and more significant than the steep rise in the proportion of the working population accounted for by women are the changes which have taken place since the close of the nineteenth century in the age and marital characteristics of women workers. More than half of the women workers in 1890 were under twenty-five years old, and only 15 percent

[1] National Manpower Council, *Womanpower* (New York: Columbia University Press, 1957), p. 9.

of the employed women were over forty-five. In recent years
however, less than one-fifth of all women workers have been
under twenty-five, at least half have been more than forty
years old, and almost two-fifths have been over forty-five. As
late as 1940, women above forty-five accounted for only a
little more than one-fifth of all women in the labor force,
while those under twenty-five still constituted one third. At
the turn of the century, peak participation in the labor force
occurred among the twenty-year-old women, and in 1940
among women eighteen and nineteen years old. During the
last several years, however, women around fifty are as likely
to be in the labor force as those of any other age. Currently,
about the same proportion—that is, almost half—of all the
fifty-year-old women in the nation, as of all the twenty-year-
old women, are engaged in work outside the home.

In October, 1959, a larger percentage (49.7) of all forty-
five to fifty-four-year-old women were employed than of
those in the eighteen to twenty-four year age group (47.5
percent). Moreover, labor force participation rates for
women between forty-five and forty-nine ran higher than
for those eighteen and nineteen years old. In that month,
the actual number of women between forty-five and fifty-
four who were counted as employed exceeded by almost
300,000 the number reported not in the labor force who were
engaged in keeping house.

Implicit in the changes which have taken place in their
age characteristics are the equally radical alterations which
have occurred in the marital status of working women. Early
in the century, the typical working woman was not only

relatively young, but she was also single. Today, she is married. Over the last several years, the married women have accounted for 6 out of every 10 women in the labor force. At the end of the nineteenth century, while employment outside the home was common among married Negro women, it was relatively exceptional among married white women. Even though gainful employment was more common among immigrant women than among the native born whites, only 2.5 percent of the white married women in the United States in 1890 were reported by the Census as gainfully employed. Now, employment outside the home among married women is nearly as characteristic for whites as for Negroes, and is found among all socio-economic groups.

The full significance of the replacement of the single woman by the married woman in the labor force appears in the fact that for several years now better than 30 percent of all the married women in the country have been employed outside the home. Even more important from the viewpoint of the rearing and development of the young, is the fact that an even larger proportion of all the mothers of school-age children in the nation—at least 4 out of every 10— are currently found in the labor force.

Most of the striking growth in the employment of wives and mothers has come about during the last two decades. In commenting upon the participation of married women in the labor force, Simeon Strunsky, writing at the close of the 1930s, could still point out that what deserved recognition was the vastly greater number not engaged in work outside the home. Observing that some "three million married women were in gainful employment outside the home in 1930," he went on to remark: "In absolute numbers and the peculiarly intricate nature of their problem, the married women workers are obviously a major social factor of our day. Yet the married women workers are little more than ten percent of all the married women in the nation. Eight out of every nine married women still have the home as their sole economic interest. The married woman worker is a problem to herself and society, but she is not the typical married woman of the times." [2]

Now, almost one-third of all the married women living with their husbands are employed outside the home. On the other hand, less than 4 out of every 10 widowed or divorced women, as well as of the married women not living with their husbands, and less than 5 out of 10 single women are working.

Since the eve of World War II, the rise in the employment of married women has been spectacular. Thus, between 1940 and 1955, among thirty-five- to forty-four-year-old married women living with their husbands, the proportion in the labor force more than doubled. During the same period, there was almost a tripling in the proportion of married women aged forty-five to sixty-four who were employed outside the home. From 1947 to 1957 alone, participation in the labor force among married women increased by half.

A Census Bureau report noted that in March, 1957, "The number of married women in the labor force—either em-

[2] Simeon Strunsky, *The Living Tradition. Change and America* (New York: Doubleday, Doran, 1939), pp. 55–56.

ployed or seeking jobs—was at a record spring level of 12.7 million. . . . During the period since World War II, there has been an average yearly increase of about one-half million in the number of working wives." It should be noted that only 1.2 million of the 12.7 million wives then employed outside the home were not living with their husbands. In March, 1957, almost one-third of the more than 50 million women in the United States with children under eighteen were in the labor force. Among the more than 11 million mothers with children of school age, two-fifths were working. At that time moreover, there were more than 2.5 million mothers in the labor force whose children were of pre-school age. These working wives represented 17 percent of all mothers with pre-school children, and almost all of them were living with their husbands.

The recession of 1957–58 did not discourage participation in the labor force among married women. In 1958, reported the Census Bureau, "a little over half of the women in the labor force" were "working wives living with their husbands," and only one-fourth of the working women were single. In March, 1958, the number of wives in the labor force had reached a new high of 13 million, and all but 1.2 million of them were living with their husbands. It may be noted that a tiny minority of these working wives, somewhere between 1 and 2 percent, were holding more than one job. In March, 1958, more than 4.6 million mothers with children between the ages of six and seventeen—or over two-fifths of all such mothers in the nation—were employed outside the home. Moreover, one-fifth of all the mothers with children under six were at that time counted in the labor force, and of these 2.8 million working mothers with children of pre-school age, less than half a million were living apart from their husbands, or were widowed or divorced.

In recent years, only about one-third of all the women in the labor force have been full-time workers. The other two-thirds have been either part-time or part-year employees. It is significant, therefore, that a special survey conducted in 1958 for the Children's Bureau by the Census Bureau provided fresh information on the extent of full-time employment among working mothers. The data showed that in May of that year, the mothers of some 2 million children under six years of age were full-time workers. In addition, there were about 3 million children between the ages of six and twelve whose mothers were working full time.

The rapid increase in the employment of wives and mothers outside the home in recent years may be viewed as the product of an expanding economy and of growing and changing labor force requirements, which exerted a steady high demand for women workers at a time when the supply of men workers was inadequate because of the low birth rates two decades earlier. But this is only a partial view of a development which represents a new pattern of life for women. Work outside the home normally occurred in the past during the earlier years of a woman's life. It is less than thirty years since marriage meant the withdrawal from gainful employment for most women who had worked when they were single. Generally speaking, early in the twentieth century only those who were compelled to work by economic necessity or who were motivated by strong career drives continued to remain employed after they married. Now, as has been seen, employment outside the home is a characteristic experience at two distinct stages of a woman's life— during her younger years and after marriage when her last child has reached school age.

A substantial minority of girls enter the labor force while they are still in high school, and it is customary for young women to work before they marry and even after. Rather than marriage itself, it is the first pregnancy which is likely to result in the young wife's departure from the labor force. While many mothers of very young children, as has been seen, continue to be employed outside the home, largely for compelling economic reasons, the labor force participation rates among mothers with preschool-age children are relatively low. Once their children reach school age, mothers display a strong tendency to return to the labor force or to enter it for the first time.

This tendency is shown by the rise in labor force participation for women after they reach thirty and by the fact that the proportion employed outside the home is at least twice as great among mothers with school-age children as among those with children under six. Employment increases steadily with advancing years until about age fifty, so much so that there is ground for speaking of a large-scale "return to work" movement among women in their thirties, forties, and fifties—that is, among mothers who are uncertainly described as "mature" or "older." The decline in employment outside the home begins after fifty, but it is not until after the sixtieth year that a significant drop in the labor force participation rates occurs. Thus, in October, 1959, the percentage of women in the fifty-five to sixty-four-year age group who were in the labor force was slightly larger than that among the twenty-five to thirty-four years olds.

Of the variety of developments which have led to the present patterning of work in the lives of women, four merit special attention. One is the increase in the marriage rates. According to population experts, under present conditions less than 7 percent of American women never marry. The extent to which Americans reject the unmarried state is revealed by the fact that the number of married couples in the United States increased by 5.5 million during the decade beginning in 1947. Not only does a larger proportion of American women marry than in the past, but they marry at an earlier age. Currently, half of the women in the United States marry before they are twenty-one, and, with the exception of the small number who remain single, almost all women marry before they reach their thirtieth birthday.

Related to early marriage is the third development connected with the tendency for married women in their thirties to enter or reenter the labor force. That is the reduction in the period of time within which the family is completed, even though there has also been a marked increase, since the depressed 1930s, in the number of children per family. Seventy years ago, when twenty-three was the median age of marriage, half of the women had their last child when they were thirty-two. Consequently, half of the women were only a year or two away from forty when the youngest child entered school. Now, however, the median age of women when they bear the last child is only twenty-six, which means that their median age is thirty-two when the youngest child enters school. The earlier age of marriage, moreover, means that most women will not have reached fifty when the youngest child marries.

The fourth development, the rise in average life expectancy, has also contributed to the tendency of women in their thirties, forties, and fifties to work outside the home. Under present conditions, 3 out of every 4 women can expect to live to sixty-five, and 1 out of 4 to age eighty-five. There is now a long period of years during which mothers are relieved in greater or lesser degree from the more onerous and more time- and energy-consuming responsibilities of child care and homemaking. Average life expectancy for a woman of forty today is about seventy-six, but at the opening of the century it was only sixty-nine. A woman can now expect to live about thirteen years longer after her youngest child reaches school age than she could sixty years ago. Then she could look forward to only thirty years of life on the average after her last child entered school.

Existing patterns of work outside the home are not likely, under any series of reasonable assumptions, to alter drastically in the near future. Careful projections indicate that adult women—most of whom will be wives and mothers— will play a critical role in the anticipated expansion of the working population. Thus, U. S. Department of Labor studies estimate that "women 35 years and over will contribute over 4 million of the total labor force growth of 10½ million between 1955 and 1965. The number of women 25–34 in the labor force will probably show no change . . . ; women 20–24 will increase by about a half million because of sharply rising numbers in the population." [3] To the 13 million increase projected for the 1965–1975 decade, it is expected that adult women will also contribute significantly.

It was observed earlier that the growing employment of wives and mothers did not prompt intensive inquiries into its implications for the rearing and development of the young or for other aspects of family life. Generalizations about the feelings and behavior of Americans as a whole—or of any other people, for that matter—should always be regarded with suspicion. Nevertheless, there is ground for contending that Americans adapted to and accepted, in spite of traditional attitudes toward the "proper" functions of women, the new place which work outside the home came to occupy in the lives of married women and the new significance of wives and mothers in the labor force.

Furthermore, it is possible to argue that while some Americans may have felt that having more and more married women employed outside the home produced some socially undesirable results, or threatened men's job opportunities, most of them seemed to act as if that development was, on balance, to be welcomed. Finally, it may be stated with greater assurance that there was no great sense of urgency to discover precisely how the children and youth of the nation were being affected by the virtual revolution which had occurred in women's employment outside the home.

[3] Sophia Cooper, "Labor Force Projections to 1975," *Monthly Labor Review* (December, 1957), p. 1445.

This last observation is strongly supported by the comment made as late as 1957 by Mrs. Katherine Brownell Oettinger, Chief of the Children's Bureau, that "we do not yet have dependable research evidence, one way or the other," on "the effects of maternal employment per se" upon children.[4] A recent review of the research on children during the decade 1949–1958, reported to the Children's Bureau Clearinghouse for Research in Child Life, suggests that relatively few thoroughgoing investigations had been made into the consequences of maternal employment upon child development or upon the needs for and availability of child care and other welfare services, in the light of recent levels of participation in the labor force among younger mothers. While many Americans believe that there is a positive relationship between maternal employment and delinquency, and that the children of working mothers are badly neglected, this review of a decade's research on children underlines the paucity of reliable data on these popular generalizations. The plea for "more solid information than we now have about . . . maternal employment" as a possible cause of delinquency is frequently heard.[5] Two recent thoughtful papers [6] which deal with the relationship between the employment of mothers and child development make

[4] National Manpower Council, Work in the Lives of Married Women (New York: Columbia University Press, 1958), p. 141.

[5] See, for example, Catherine E. Harris, "A Decade of Research Concerning Children," Children (July–August, 1959), p. 148.

[6] Eleanor Maccoby, "Effects Upon Children of their Mothers' Outside Employment" in Work in the Lives of Married Women, pp. 150–72; John Rose, M.D., "Child Development and the Part-Time Mother," Children (November–December, 1959), pp. 213–18.

it clear that current knowledge in this area is not only limited but also speculative in character.

Only recently have national data become available on the means relied upon to provide care for the children of mothers employed outside the home, but not, it should be noted, on the quality of the care these children actually receive. The special Census Bureau survey mentioned earlier indicated that in May, 1958, about two-fifths of the 2 million children of pre-school age whose mothers were in the labor force "were taken care of by relatives other than their parents, including older children in some cases. Another fifth or so were looked after by their own fathers or mothers who either worked different shifts or whose working conditions were such as to permit the children to stay with them. In some cases, the mother worked at home, in family business or farms, in schools, or in other places where it was possible to keep her children with her during working hours. Roughly one-fourth of the children were cared for by neighbors or other nonrelatives while their mothers were working, but only 5 percent were placed in 'group care centers,' such as day nurseries, nursery schools, settlement houses, etc." [7]

Some 24,000 children under three and 67,000 between six and twelve, whose mothers were employed, were looked after in one fashion or another by older children in the family or by adults, but a substantial number of them were expected to care for themselves while their mothers were working. Apparently, among the ten- and eleven-year-old chil-

[7] U. S. Department of Commerce, Bureau of the Census, Current Population Reports, Series P-50 (January, 1959), p. 6.

dren, 1 out of 5 was expected to care for himself while the mother was at work.

The absence of the mother from the home is a point of major concern in many of the comments made about the effects of maternal employment upon children. And this is understandable. Not only is care of the child taken to be the primary responsibility of the mother, but it is also widely assumed that the mother's physical proximity to the child, and, therefore, her constant availability to respond to his needs, is an essential pre-condition for adequate care. Perhaps the more distinguishing features of a child-centered society are the beliefs that the healthy development of the child depends almost exclusively upon the central mother-child relationship, and that parents are ideal companions for their children. "It is a peculiarity of parents, especially of mothers," remarked Katherine Anthony many years ago, "that they never entertain a modest doubt as to whether they might be the best of all possible company for their children." [8]

It is, of course, almost self-evident that it is not so much the physical proximity of the mother to the child, or the constancy of the attention she provides that matters profoundly, but the quality of the care that the child receives from the mother, or from both parents, or from a substitute parent. In the more recent considerations of the bearing of maternal employment upon child development, this point is repeatedly stressed and supported by clinical and other evidence.

[8] Harold E. Stearns, ed., *Civilization in the United States* (New York: Harcourt Brace, 1922), p. 336.

All this invites speculation about the character of child-mother relationships in the past when fewer mothers worked outside the home, but when industrial homework was far more common than it is now, when part-time work by women was probably far less common that at present, when housework was physically more exacting and time-consuming, and when wives produced within the home many of the goods and services they purchase today. Thus, from one point of view, what may be of special significance in the change in women's work is its shift from within to outside the home, and, the resulting longer periods of continuous *separation* between the mother and child, rather than any major reduction in the *total amount of time* which the mother devotes to child care. It is, of course, easy to forget that what constitutes a full-time job in number of hours worked today would have been regarded as a half-time job in many occupations and industries sixty and seventy years ago.

In any case, if the changes in women's work during the present century constitute a major social transformation—as it seems evident they do—their significance for the children and youth of the nation will not be illuminated solely by more intensive and extensive studies of altered patterns and practices of child care, however important they are. What is required is a series of inquiries into the full range of consequences which presumably flow from having so large a proportion of wives and mothers engaged in employment outside the home. If it be objected that this is merely an invitation to reexamine many facets of American life which are already being actively studied from other vantage points, the simplest and briefest reply is, "Why not?" Each new vantage point skillfully utilized for research purposes provides fresh insights and information, and there is every reason to expect that this one would do no less.

At present, all too little of a reliable nature is known about the implications which the new patterns of women's employment have for the meaning of work in the society, for the educational opportunities and experiences of the young, for the duration of marriage and the incidence of divorce, for the interpersonal relationships of husbands and wives both within and outside the family unit, for the parental role and functions of fathers, for family income and spending, for the availability of free time and the nature of leisure, for the character and adequacy of welfare policies and services involving children, and for a host of other subjects.

It was pointed out earlier that an explanation of how the twentieth-century revolution in women's employment came about "would require retelling the history of the United States." It is no less true that an examination of the society's contemporary life from the viewpoint of employment outside the home by wives and mothers would provide a new range of understandings of the nation's recent social and economic history.

CHILDHOOD IN TWENTIETH-CENTURY AMERICA

by ERIC LARRABEE

CHILDHOOD in America is not only admired; it is looked upon as a national asset, somewhat on a par with the Declaration of Independence or the Mississippi River. We like to think of it as a good in itself, and to lament its passing. We hang onto the images of youth that are thought to be traditional—the barefoot boy, the old swimming hole, the sandlot games—though in fact few of us may ever have known them in life. *Tom Sawyer* is a dominant picture of boyhood, just as *Huckleberry Finn* is almost a national epic; and the loss of innocence is a persistent theme in our literature.

So it is for other nations too, and I mention these qualities to describe us rather than set us apart as unique. Yet one can imagine attitudes toward childhood different from ours. Children can be thought of as vessels to be filled, animals to be restrained, plants to be encouraged, or simply as adults in the process of becoming. And though surely children are

Eric Larrabee is Executive Editor of *American Heritage*.

universally loved, the state of being a child is not universally
esteemed. In some societies it may be no more than an interval spent in training for maturity, to be got through as rapidly as possible. The comparison has of course been made—
so often as to be commonplace—between American children
and their European peers, who have been taught to act like
little grown-ups, and are startlingly "well behaved" by contrast.

Childhood in America is also something that adults experience vicariously. It plays a large part in the national diet
of stories and symbols. Children are continuously observed
and recorded in the act of being themselves, and their documented behavior is everywhere available, from the consoling
normalities of Spock and Gesell to the revolutionary defi-
ance of Dennis the Menace. Short stories about children, as
many magazine editors have commented, make up a discon-
certingly large proportion of the manuscripts sent in by fic-
tion writers, since those attracted to emotional nuance so
often find their favorite subjects in the very young or very
old, who are supposed to escape the uninteresting routines
of getting and spending, and live mainly in their senses. But
the place where children are most prominent of all is in
advertising. There they frequently play the role of the ultimate audience, whose approval of a product is spontaneous
and unpurchasable, and therefore greatly to be respected.

They are looked upon as important, however, largely in
adult terms. Though children are increasingly entitled to be
labeled as a "market" in their own right, they do most of
their consuming through adult proxies. Toys are less often

designed to please children than to please adults' ideas of what children should like, and the father who forces on the family the electric train he really wants for himself is a familiar figure in our folklore. "For the children's sake" is one of the most unanswerable arguments in the conventional repertoire of American conversation; it removes virtually all questions from the realm of debate, particularly those that involve one's neighborhood or style of life and are likely to be subject to the worst anxieties. The mass migration to the suburbs of the postwar parental generations has drawn heavily on this argument, even where it was obvious that "for the children's sake" actually meant: "In order not to have to be bothered by the children."

Some of the disillusionment with suburban utopias may come from the discovery, made by those who fled there in such high hopes, that suburban children can no longer be brushed out into the backyard and ignored until mealtime. The city dilemmas follow close behind and, as each new community becomes in its turn overcrowded and overequipped, the skillful managing of schedules and facilities is ever more exigently required of the parents. That they are little more than chauffeurs for their sons and daughters is another of the current clichés, but it has its somber side: the half-humorous dismay over problems of family organization may tend to replace the accepted parental image of a loving authority—as, to a degree, it already has been replaced—by that of a manipulative expediter. *Life* magazine has run several features which encourage this tendency, showing mothers on the one hand who are overpowered and exhausted by their offspring, and children's parties on the other hand which have been suavely arranged for a minimum of adult wear-and-tear. The assumption, in each case, is that children are a "problem" to their parents.

What seems to be happening here is an invasion of childhood's world by a set of adult demands. First of all we demand to have children—a demand so great as to overturn the predictions of demographers and outrun the resources of adoption agencies—as if they were the natural prerogative, if nothing else, of a prosperous normality. That an adult feels entitled to children, or guilty at not having them, is bound to be a burden on the children themselves, whether they are natural or adopted; and at worst it invites the parents of low humane capacity to treat their charges like part of the expected middle-class furniture, and harass them for being insufficiently decorative and creditable. Among the varieties of modern parent that, as a nonparent, I find least easy to admire are the ones who present their children as adjuncts of their own personalities, and treat some trivial misbehavior as though it were a defect in themselves, thus prolonging and exacerbating a painful and unnecessary embarrassment.

Society uses childhood to initiate its apprentice members, and we need not be surprised that its methods are sometimes harsh. They have to be. But there is a difference—or there ought to be—between the understandable concern of adults over their successors, and the use of children as an outlet for adult tensions and frustrations. Under a system of arbitrary parental administration, in the small-town world where they could roam at will, children were often able to construct a semi-independent enclave insulated from adult distractions. But with the decline of unquestioned adult authority, and the drawing in of family life to limited quarters, there has come to be a premium on cooperativeness and "understanding," and with it a weakening of childhood's traditional defenses against its eternal enemy.

Child-training is an expression of culture, just as much as sonnets or postage stamps, and behavioral scientists of every stripe have found it a happy hunting ground for evidences of social change, psychological theory, or national character. One would expect that a newborn baby, within reasonable limits, would always be pretty much the same kind of animal; but of course different societies in different ages have persisted in picturing it quite differently—pictures that are, in fact, society's changing picture of itself. Nor have we escaped from this in our time. What may seem to be a statement of desirable practice with infants can still turn out, on examination, to be a statement of adult attitudes toward other adults.

One of the most striking expositions of this idea was made by Martha Wolfenstein in an article for the *Journal of Social Issues* in 1951, called "The Emergence of Fun Morality." In it Miss Wolfenstein compared the various editions—over the years since 1914, when it was first issued—of the *Infant Care* booklet published by the Children's Bureau of the United States Department of Labor. This is a presumptively neutral and authoritative document—representing, as Miss Wolfenstein writes, "at any given time a major body of specialized opinion in the field"—and it has been widely used (by 1952 over 28,000,000 copies had been distributed). But the most remarkable thing about it is the manner in which it changed between 1914 and 1945.

In the 1914 edition the infant is represented as a creature of strong and dangerous impulses. "The child is described as 'rebelling fiercely' if these impulses are interfered with," Miss Wolfenstein writes. "The impulses 'easily grow beyond control' and are harmful in the extreme: 'children are sometimes wrecked for life'. . . . The mother must be ceaselessly vigilant; she must wage a relentless battle against the child's sinful nature." Quite clearly the writers of this early edition thought they were stating nothing but the self-evident facts of infant nature, yet in retrospect it is obvious they were doing nothing of the kind; they could far better be described as reflecting the strong, continuing tradition of American puritanism, which still could view the emerging emotions as demons to be feared and tamed.

Time was bound to catch up even with the authors of a government pamphlet, and by twenty years later there had been drastic revisions in the text. "We find in 1942–45," Miss Wolfenstein goes on, "that the baby has been transformed into almost complete harmlessness. The intense and concentrated impulses of the past have disappeared. Drives toward erotic pleasure (and also towards domination, which was stressed in 1929–38) have become weak and incidental. Instead we find impulses of a much more diffuse and moderate character. The baby is interested in exploring his world . . . Everything amuses him, nothing is excessively exciting."

In this contrast we can see a change taking place, not in the nature of babies, but in the climate of opinion about the nature of impulses. Is it good to do what one likes? asks Miss Wolfenstein. "The opposition between the pleasant and the good is deeply grounded in older American morals (as in many other ascetic moral codes). There are strong doubts as to whether what is enjoyable is not wicked or deleterious. In recent years, however, there has been a marked effort to overcome this dichotomy, to say that what is pleasant is also good for you. The writers on child training reflect the changing ideas on this issue.

"In the early period there is a clear-cut distinction between what the baby 'needs,' his legitimate requirements, whatever is essential to his health and well-being, on the one hand, and what the baby 'wants,' his illegitimate pleasure-strivings, on the other. This is illustrated, for instance, in the question of whether to pick up the baby when he cries. In 1914, it was essential to determine whether he really needs something or whether he only wants something. Crying is listed as a bad habit. . . . In 1942–45, wants and needs are explicitly equated. 'A baby sometimes cries because he wants a little more attention. He probably needs a little extra attention under some circumstances just as he sometimes needs a little extra food and water. Babies want attention; they probably need plenty of it.' What the baby wants for pleasure has thus become as legitimate a demand as what he needs for his physical well-being and is to be treated in the same way." Thus was "permissiveness" endorsed, these many years ago, by the Department of Labor.

The change that chiefly interested Miss Wolfenstein was a related one in the attitudes toward play. "Where impulses are dangerous and the good and pleasant are opposed, play is suspect. Thus in 1914, playing with the baby was regarded as dangerous; it produced unwholesome pleasure and ruined the baby's nerves. . . . The mother of 1914 was told: 'The rule that parents should not play with the baby may seem hard, but it is without doubt a safe one. A young delicate and nervous baby needs rest and quiet, and however robust the child much of the play that is indulged in is more or less harmful. It is a great pleasure to hear the baby laugh and crow in apparent delight, but often the means used to produce the laughter, such as tickling, punching, or tossing, makes him irritable and restless'. . . . The dangerousness of play is related to that of the ever-present sensual impulses which must be constantly guarded against."

To this the later editions oppose a completely contrary view. Play is now connected with the healthy, exploratory activities of the infant human organism: "A baby needs to be able to move all parts of his body. He needs to exercise." Furthermore, this impulse and all like it are now diffused, and involve both mother and child. The pleasant and the good are not only identical; they are fused together in a new combination called "fun," which is obligatory for everyone. "Mothers are told that 'a mother usually enjoys entering into her baby's play. Both of them enjoy the little games that mothers and babies have always played from time immemorial.' [This harking back to time immemorial is a way of skipping over the more recent past.] 'Daily tasks can be done with a little play and singing thrown in.' Thus it is now not adequate for the mother to perform efficiently the routines for her baby; she must also see that these are fun for both of them. It seems difficult here for anything to become permissible without becoming compulsory. Play, having ceased to be wicked, having become harmless and good, now becomes a new duty."

Previously, in the picture Miss Wolfenstein derives from these pamphlets, parenthood itself had been a test of moral strength; there were frequent allusions to the mother's "self-control" and "unlimited patience." But in the recent period parenthood is defined as a source of mutual enjoyment to all concerned, including the father, who had hitherto been little mentioned. There is a new imperative: "You ought to enjoy your child"—and there is no place in the new universe for the parent or child who cannot "enjoy" those tasks which formerly had been defined as merely necessary. "Fun has become not only permissible but required."

The moral of Miss Wolfenstein's story is a double one; not only should we be wary of the new tyrannies which masquerade under the banner of release from the old, but we should also cultivate a saving skepticism about the going theories of child care. They are of their time, no more, no less, and there may be much in them even now of fashion and the misconceptions made palatable only through general acceptance. Indeed, the pendulum swings today so rapidly that we may react against a given school of thought almost before it has a chance to add its characteristic fragment of truth to the communal store. There is already under way an attack on "progressive" education—and the demand for a return to the supposed "standards" of the old-fashioned school—while it is still a question whether we have yet learned to be anywhere near "free" enough. Compared to the old, the modern tyrannies have the advantage of being almost invisible; but they bear down with no less weight on the emerging unorganized personality.

To take another example from the literature of social science, there is a vividly illuminating article called "The Middle-Class Male Child and Neurosis," by Arnold W. Green, which appeared in the *American Sociological Review* in February 1946. Green takes the position that two of the frequently accepted "explanations" of mental ill health— that it originates during childhood in thwarted love, or because of the arbitrary exercise of authority, as in the old-fashioned home—do not in fact explain one of the common neuroses of American males. Instead, under the modern mantle of demonstrative affection and mild rule, Green finds even greater danger of a child's inner integrity being weakened or violated.

Green begins by describing, as a basis of comparison, the life of lower-class Polish families in the Massachusetts industrial village in which he himself grew up. Their homes appear to be brutal and devoid of warmth; the sound of blows and voices raised in anger issue from them so continuously as to warrant little or no attention. Yet the children do not become neurotic. However harsh the parental authority, it remains—so Green writes—"in a sense, casual and external," the parents having neither the means nor the opportunity to invade the essential core of the child's self. There are likely to be many children, offering many models of possible behavior and yet presenting a united front in rebellion against the older generation's poor English, attachment to the "old country," or lack of sophistication about American ways. The houses are neither clean nor filled with objects of value, so that the child "is spared the endless admonitions which bedevil the middle-class child not to touch this or that."

Under such circumstances, child-training is haphazard and easygoing, "very similar to the training received in many primitive tribes," and it makes a sharp contrast to that of the typical native-white, Protestant, urban, college-educated, middle class. Here the heart of the parental attitude toward children is ambiguous. The father finds that his duties and obligations are increasing, while his rights steadily diminish. The mother, interrupted in a career half-seriously begun, has been thrown into household tasks—even with a plenitude of gadgets—which her training defines as drudgery and encourages her actively to dislike. No matter how deeply loved and desired, children in such families cannot help but seem a psychological and financial drain, a continuously limiting factor on career and social life.

Here the mother, as Green writes, "is her single child's sole companion. Modern 'scientific child care' enforces a constant supervision and diffused worrying over the child's health, eating spinach, and ego-development; this is complicated by the fact that much energy is spent forcing early walking, toilet-training, talking, because in an intensely competitive milieu middle-class parents from the day of birth on are constantly comparing their own child's development with that of the neighbor's children. The child must also be constantly guarded from the danger of contacting various electrical gadgets and from kicking valuable furniture. The middle-class child's discovery that the living-room furniture is more important to his mother than his impulse to crawl over it unquestionably finds a place in the background of the etiology of a certain type of neurosis, however absurd it may appear."

Without companions, tied down to a restricted area, the child's animal expansiveness and boredom inevitably involve him in what his culture defines as "trouble": "screaming, running around the apartment, upsetting daddy's shaving mug, rending teddy-bear in two, emptying his milk on the rug to observe what pattern will be formed. This 'trouble' is all a matter of definition. Similar behavior, in modified form, would not be interpreted in primitive society as 'trouble,' and neither would it be by Polish parents in the community described above."

With the emphasis that the modern period puts on love, especially within the middle classes, the most effective response to "trouble" on the parents' part is to threaten to withdraw their love. "The more ambivalent the parents are toward the child, the more seriously is the 'trouble' he causes them interpreted. He should not act in such a way because of the sacrifices they have made on his behalf, and the least he can do is show his gratitude by 'loving' them in turn, i.e., keeping out of 'trouble'. . . . Mamma won't like you if you don't eat your spinach, or stop dribbling your milk, or get down from that davenport. To the extent that the child's personality has been absorbed, he will be thrown into a panic by this sort of treatment, and develop guilt-feelings to help prevent himself from getting into further trouble. In such a child a disapproving glance may produce more terror than a twenty-minute lashing in little Stanislaus Wojcik."

Later, when the middle-class child begins to emerge into middle-class society, he discovers that his attempts to escape from guilt within the family involve him only in guilt outside it. He is now expected to be purposeful, independent, and competitive. "He is expected to 'do things,' to accomplish, perhaps to lead in some endeavor, like other children. . . . At first he felt guilty only if he failed to love and obey, and his guilt could be assuaged by the propitiation of submission; now, however, the god-monsters will be appeased only by a combination of submission in his role of child-in-family, and assertiveness in his play-group, school-pupil, and other roles enacted outside of home. An integration of these conflicting roles is impossible. . . . He is damned if he does and damned if he doesn't. He is embraced by a psychological Iron Maiden; any lunge forward or backward only impales him more securely on the spikes."

He has been victimized by adults.

Admittedly, these inroads into the child society are made without great calculation or intent. It is rare enough for adults to remember that they once were children, let alone to reconstruct imaginatively their own childlike incomprehension of the adult world. The two universes are opposed,

yet that of the child is continually eroded by the leakage of
its members into maturity, and the veil of forgetfulness that
falls between them and their past. One may view this partial
amnesia as fortunate or unfortunate—certainly it is the latter for novelists, whose childhood is their prime source of
fresh and glistening sense impressions—but in either event,
it is a permanent obstacle to adult interpretation of childhood's major experiences.

To the child, the most evident and annoying fact about
grown-ups is that they do not understand—they do not take
in an event directly, in the fullness of its happening, with
all of its qualities intact. To the child, so much is occurring
for the first time that events come through to the mind
complete, carrying their full load of atmosphere and conno-
tation. He lives immersed in the state of nature which adults
can attain only by a supreme effort, in which no fact is
without value and the mind can consciously apprehend more
dominions and powers than it can find words to describe.
The human brain is a matchless device for screening and
filtering out the messages sent to it by the senses, and converting them into "intelligible"—that is, previously recognized and labeled—patterns. But the penalty of perfecting
it is a narrowing wave-length, like a loud speaker that will
convey only a sodden, restricted band of the total spectrum
of sound.

Just as a dog can hear a whistle pitched above the human
limit of audibility, so a child may "hear" a range of phenomena denied to adults. Having just emerged from the
preverbal culture of infancy, he still retains some of its

capacity for nonverbal intelligence, while for adults what cannot be put in words might just as well not exist. If a house is filled with hate, a child will often know it long before he has learned to explain, even to himself, what his sensations are telling him. And it is this evident disparity between the world as he knows it and the world as officially described that often gives him his extraordinary sense of rightness, of being in tune with the cosmos, regardless of what "they" say. In favorable circumstances, he may even share this conviction with other children.

Shared conviction is a prerequisite of "play," in so far as play is considered as the self-contained ritual by which children exclude other realities than their own. "May I play with Johnny?" Play has a definite starting point and stopping point, a moment when its own terms take hold and a moment when their spell is broken. The material of the drama ("what shall we play?") is unimportant; what matters is the assertion of a superior reality, of being drenched in organized meaning and cleansed—as the adult imagination can be cleansed by art—of the psychic dust and dirt accumulated in the daily round. The fact that play is patronized by adults is high on the child's agenda of dissatisfaction with them; he resents both their intrusion on its sacred precincts and their apparent ignorance of its beguiling and ennobling potentiality.

The idea has by now been thoroughly popularized that primary emotional patterns are set in childhood, yet this period is still only partially credited with its considerable contributions to the world of work and worry. Look, for example, at that most "American" of methods for the accomplishment of tasks: the combat team. What is it but the "gang" of American childhood, recapitulated in adult terms? Characteristically, we break down any organizational situation, no matter how large, to the half-dozen or so of our immediate, face-to-fact colleagues, the manageable unit that temperamentally accords with our earliest memory of a "group." There is always the leader, though he or she may not be the senior, nor assured of tenure; just as there are always the stalwarts, the goof-offs, and the one or two siblings dragged along for the ride. Childhood created it, childhood trains us in it long before we see the inside of a schoolroom, or discover the voluminous duties that organized adulthood is prepared to impose.

The "iron maiden" that Arnold Green describes is in itself not a bad introduction to what Erik H. Erikson has called (in *Childhood and Society*) the "dynamic polarities" of American life: between migratory and sedentary, competitive and cooperative, individualist and conformist, radical and conservative, responsible and cynical, and so on. It must help us to have handled when we were young at least one set of irreconcilable alternatives. As Erikson puts it, "the American, on the whole, lives with two sets of 'truths' . . . [he] must be able to convince himself that the next step is up to him and that no matter where he is staying or going he always has the choice of leaving or turning in the opposite direction if he chooses to do so . . . for the life style (and the family history) of each contains the opposite element as a potential alternative which he wishes to consider his most private and individual decision."

In this the novelists do us a disservice when they persist in treating childhood as the lost abode of a fugitive and an irretrievable innocence. The child, in their hands, has become a kind of twentieth-century equivalent of the eighteenth-century Noble Savage, a repository of our fears and fantasies. The result is a mounting concentration of adult attention—too much attention, and for the wrong reasons—on a time of life that is difficult enough without it. Already adolescence, as a period of fruitful immaturity, is showing signs of disintegration under the massed assault of its anxious elders. Their compulsive concern over such irrelevancies as teen-age delinquency, rock-'n-roll, or steady-dating (so Edgar Z. Friedenberg maintains, in *The Vanishing Adolescent*) has made it increasingly difficult to *be* an adolescent—and, therefore, to grow up. Perhaps, Friedenberg suggests, age is overly interested in youth to the extent that age finds itself uninteresting.

There have been some admirable efforts to visualize and describe the self-contained society of the child, among recent ones the comic strip *Peanuts* or Robert Paul Smith's best seller, "*Where Did You Go?*" "*Out.*" "*What Did You Do?*" "*Nothing.*" Smith is especially successful in describing the small-town childhood of an earlier generation, with its strong streak of self-reliance and disdain for all other values than its own. Who now knows how to play mumbly-peg, Smith asks? What has become of all the arcane lore that children faithfully passed on to younger children? Why do they now have an overabundance of toys and yet are always asking for "something to do?" Why, indeed? The same question could be asked of their elders. For even this intelligent evocation of a vanishing way of life bears the mark of our other motives, our worries about an America that is in so many senses too prosperous—in short, about ourselves. The members of a new generation deserve at least the chance to develop their own worries. A little inattention might do them a world of good.

THE HUMAN COMMONWEALTH

by NORMAN COUSINS

EDUCATION for membership in the human community of the twentieth century is not a matter of an expanded syllabus. It goes beyond subject matter into attitudes, into values. It involves a sense of adventure in seeking new truths about man. It has to do with a respect for the inevitability of change and the need for change.

Education does not exist apart from history. It is at its best when it serves history most, when it deals with the needs and changes produced by human experience. In this sense, education today is far more difficult than it has ever been.

History stopped crawling about eighty years ago and began to catapult. The danger so well described by Whitehead—the danger that events might outrun man and leave him a panting and helpless anachronism—is by now much more than a figure of speech. We have leaped centuries ahead in inventing a new world to live in, but as yet we have an inadequate conception of our own part in that world. We have surrounded and confounded ourselves with gaps—gaps

Norman Cousins is Editor of *Saturday Review*.

between revolutionary science and evolutionary thought, between cosmic gadgets and human wisdom, between intellect and conscience. The clash between knowledge and ethics that Henry Thomas Buckle foresaw a century ago is now more than a mere skirmish.

Confronted with this sudden and severe "upset in the metabolism of history," as Professor Donald H. Andrews of Johns Hopkins calls it, what is it we expect education to do? No single answer can possibly have enough elasticity to be all-inclusive. We expect it to narrow the gap between the individual and society. We expect it to shorten the distance between individual capacity and collective needs. We expect it to produce the rounded man. We expect it to enlarge the ability to think and the capacity for thought. We expect it to be helpful in creating constructive attitudes—both on an individual and a group basis. We expect it to impart basic and essential general knowledge for rounded living, and basic and essential specialized knowledge for specific careers. We expect it to develop ethical values. In short, we expect education to furnish the individual with the necessary intellectual, social, moral, and technical clothing for a presentable appearance in the world community.

But yesterday's clothing no longer fits. Is there sufficient education for vital participation in the world community? Is there sufficient emphasis on the most important science of all—the science of interrelationships of knowledge—that critical area beyond compartmentalization, where knowledge must be integrated in order to have proper meaning? Is there sufficient awareness in the individual that this time is unlike any other time in history, that the human race has exhausted its margin for error? Is there enough of a sense of individual responsibility for group decision? Is the individual equipped to appraise the news and to see beyond the news, to see events against a broad historical flow?

These questions are not academic. They are as real as a long walk in the hot sun, as real as a lost pay envelope, as real as any immediate problem that directly affects the welfare of the individual. For we live at a time when the problems of human destiny are no longer philosophical abstractions reserved for posterity but our own special and immediate concern. Ultimate questions have become present imperatives.

These are vaulting responsibilities; the apparatus of education cannot be expected to assume the entire burden. But at least those responsibilities offer something of a yardstick by which education can measure its own part and place in the total picture.

The problem may be complicated and confounded by many insufficiencies, but at least one of them is not an insufficiency of new knowledge. In fact, new knowledge is being generated so rapidly that it can hardly be classified, much less be absorbed. We know virtually everything except what to do with what we know. We are being hurt or threatened not by what we don't know but by what we do know that we can't put to good use. Our facts are even more out of hand than our machines.

How can education make new knowledge obedient to human purposes? Another way of asking this perhaps is: how do we educate for change?

The main business of a rational society is the business of living with change, comprehending it, and, if possible, making it subordinate to the human situation. In a more limited sense, whether the idea of America survives in this world may depend less upon the amount of destructive force we can develop or use than upon our ability to deal with the problem of change in our time.

There is not a single critical situation in the world today that does not involve the challenge of change. It makes little difference whether we are talking about our relations with the rest of the world or our economy or even our hopes. There is a fast-moving current of change that ties all our problems together. They are tied together in the sense that all of them make insistent demands on us: Either we understand the vital problem of change involved in each case or we are left on an historical siding.

To return to our opening theme: There was a time in the life of nations and civilizations when the pace of change was glacial. The problems of the period of the Enlightenment, for example, were at least two hundred years in the making. The effects were spread out over another century or more. The lifeblood of Greece may have run out in large measure during the Peloponnesian Wars, but the causes fed slowly into that conflict and the consequences distributed their hurt over long years. In fact, ours is the first generation in history that has had to absorb the kind of changes that heretofore took thousands of years to produce.

From 1945 to 1960 we have seen change overtake a large part of the body of systematic knowledge. The one event represented by the liberation of atomic energy may have greater significance than any previous utilization of the scientific intelligence of man. The conquest of earth gravity, as represented by the man-made space ship, may have an even more profound effect on philosophy than upon physics. A sudden new perspective bursts upon the mind. The human brain now begins to perceive, however dimly, the meaning of a universe in which the earth and, indeed, the solar system may occupy a position in relationship to the whole no larger than the atom itself is to this planet.

Nothing has been more difficult in the evolution of thought than for man to depart from his view of himself as central in the universe. But now we have to begin to live with the idea that life, life with intelligence, may exist on millions or billions of planets and may even, in many cases, be far superior to our own.

Meanwhile, even as we prepare to take off for other worlds we seem to be doing our level best to get rid of this one. The means now exist and stand primed for instant use—means that can expunge in a few seconds the work and culture of man that required thousands of years to put together piece by piece. No one knows whether it took man a quarter of a million years to evolve into his present being, or a half million years, or two million years. What we do know is that he has now employed his evolved intelligence in the creation of explosives that would put an end to his place on this earth at least.

Whether the explosives go off or whether this planet becomes a safe place for human life depends not on magical solutions but on the ability of man to understand the challenge of change.

If the use of nuclear military force no longer can achieve victory but threatens universal extinction, then it becomes important to understand this change and attempt to devise means that can be effective in enabling us to preserve our freedoms and values and also serve the cause of humankind in general.

If our security today no longer depends on the pursuit of force but on the control of force, then it becomes necessary for this change to be known and acted upon. Tied to this is the need to educate in connections. That is, to educate in our relationships with the rest of the world.

If we are challenged by a powerful ideology, we can recognize that the only time we need fear an ideology is if we lack a great idea of our own—an idea great enough to encompass change, great enough to unify man and set him free, give him reasonable peace, and make the world safe for his diversity.

Education, which is essentially a process of conversion, can deal with the new conversion skills that are now needed to master change. Humans convert beautifully in the fields of science and technology. They can convert the face of nature into a countenance congenial to human life. They can convert sand, stone, and water into gleaming and wondrous towers. They can convert fluids into fabrics. They can convert the invisible atom into an infinity of power. They can convert the rush of water into the whirling fantasy of the dynamo and thence into the magic impulses that banish darkness or turn wheels or carry images and voices over empty space. They can convert air, agitated by the spin of a blade or the thrust of a jet, into the lifting power that enables them to rise from the earth and fly over the mountains and the seas.

But these are not the conversion skills that are now most needed. What is most needed now by man is to apply his conversion skills to those things that are essential for his survival. Of these, the most urgent and overriding need is to convert facts into logic, free will into purpose, conscience into decision. He has to convert historical experience into a design for a sane world. He has to convert the vast processes of education into those ideas that can make this globe safe for the human diversity. And he will have to learn more than he knows now about converting the individual morality into a group ethic.

Our failure to develop these conversion skills has converted us into paupers. The plenty produced by our scientific and physical skills has not relieved the poverty of our purposes. The only thing greater than our power is our insecurity. All our resources and all our wealth are not enough to protect us against the effects of irrational ideas and acts on the world stage. It makes little difference how magnificent are our new buildings or how impressive are our private kingdoms. If no answer is found to war, all men will die poor.

The universe of knowledge, systematic and unsystematic both, is the key to the new conversion process. It can furnish the basic materials that must go into the making of the new purposes and designs. And, quite possibly, it may furnish some of the motive power for the decision behind the effort itself.

Now some people may take the fatalistic view and say it is too late. They may say that man cannot possibly develop the comprehension necessary to deal with change in the modern world, that he will require many centuries before his conversion skills can be developed as they now need to be developed in the cause of human survival.

But there is a larger view of man—one that history is prepared to endorse. This view holds that the great responses already exist inside man and that they need only to be invoked to become manifest. For man is infinitely malleable, infinitely perfectable, infinitely capacious. It is the privilege of all those concerned with education to appeal to these towering possibilities.

By education I am not thinking of schools alone. I am thinking of all those who work on the frontier of ideas. Education begins with ideas. And ideas, if they are big enough, can unfreeze man and make him effective in turning back the largest threat he has ever known.

So far we have been considering the historical mandate in education. We have been considering the fact of change and the challenge of change. We have been considering the general approaches, the attitudes, the values. All these come before syllabus. But syllabus is the point of prime contact with reality in education. In addition to creating an atmosphere in which new approaches become clear, we must define the courses of study, select the textbooks, and draw up a time-table for getting from here to there.

How, then, do we go about educating the individual for membership in the human community of the twentieth century? We do this first of all, I believe, by de-provincializing education. We can rescue education from the notion of a compartmentalized world, a world in which peoples and civilizations have been assigned to two big bundles neatly marked "East" and "West." We can maintain an essential and proper respect for the legacy of Western civilization, but we can also recognize that it no longer serves a useful purpose to talk about the "destiny of Western man" or the "uniqueness of Western man" or the "prospects of human civilization."

The central meaning of living history is that human civilization has at last emerged on a single stage. The problem is to develop a consciousness of this reality and an education and a philosophy equal to it. Whatever an individual's pride in belonging to the West or to the East, it now becomes necessary to develop complementary allegiances, affiliations, and sense of connection. A world geographic unit, to repeat, has created a single arena for the human community. If that community has no sense of itself, if it is lost in its own anchronisms, then it will never meet its needs.

What is it that justifies the term, "uniqueness of Western man?" Is it philosophy or literature or political science or a common yardstick of values? Is it Christianity that defines the oneness of the West? Is there a magical biological fluid that circulates through his body, creating a natural kinship between Europeans and North Americans and South Americans?

First, let us consider the origin and distribution of the species. A not uncommon error is to confuse anthropology with philosophy. "Western" man is Greek and Roman, but he is also German and Scandinavian and English and Portuguese and Spanish and Polish and Russian and much more. If you go back far enough, there is a common stock, of course, but by going back just a little farther you can also include the people of Asia and Africa. Does living in Europe endow a person with a special chemical attraction for anyone who lives in the Americas? And what part of the Americas are you talking about? Canada? Puerto Rico? The United States? Argentina?

Is there a biological oneness felt between Germans and French so that neither party can possibly feel for, say, the Egyptians? And how would you classify a substantial part of the Mexican population, with Spanish and Negro and Indian blood flowing together? Are North American Indians to be considered East or West? They are authentic Americans; in fact, they once owned the place, but the anthropologists relate them to Eastern races. When we talk about the destiny of Western man, then, do we include the Indians of North and South America?

Or perhaps we are thinking of our political heritage. Classical Greece, in particular. True, Greece was the vital ground in which the political roots of democratic government were planted. It was here that the operation of society became a political science. The concept of constitutional government, separation of powers, limitation of tenure, direct responsibility of officeholders to the people, rights and duties of citizens—in all these respects Greece made a towering contribution to history. When we add to this the Roman science of laws, we have a legacy that is deeply felt, deeply valued, deeply expressed—and rightly so.

Yet even this is not enough to tie the West together and enable us to talk of Western man as a recognizable and complete democratic entity. The history of the West shows far longer periods of monarchy, autocracy, oligarchy, and totalitarianism than it does periods of democratic government. It may be argued that the true lessons of Greece did not begin to be learned for two thousand years; yet even if we confine our scope to recent history we can see that the principal threats to democratic institutions have come from within the West itself. Nazism and Communism, with their nihilism and authoritarianism, are prime disorders within the body of the West. When we think of the citizen as a mighty source of freedom, are we thinking of the individual German under Hitler or the Argentinian under Perón? The fact is that there is neither a political compact in the West nor even a general grouping around commonly accepted values.

If the case for the uniqueness of Western man moves from the political to the intellectual, here again we can pay our debt to the Greek teachers, philosophers, historians, and theoreticians. And we can pay an even greater debt to their disciplined rational intelligence than we do to the actual results of their intellectual labors. If more attention had been paid to Aristotle as an example of the creative thinker rather than as the sovereign monarch of all knowledge, perhaps there would have been less intellectual stagnation after the fall of Rome. As for Plato, it should also be recorded that many of his ideas on the perfection of man were to become distorted by numberless self-appointed Platonists, and that some of these ideas were to be used against man himself. The fact that versions of neo-Platonism played into the hands of advocates of a master race and brutalitarians is not to be held against Plato, of course, but it at least indicates that there is no firm agreement in the West about what he tried to say or about the practical application of his thought.

Long before Plato ideas on the need for perfection in man and his institutions were being voiced and heard in Asia— especially in China, India, and Persia. The moral code of Zoroaster, aiming at the triumph of virtue not only over the material world but over the spiritual world as well, actually helped to fertilize Greek thought. Confucianism is almost synonymous with individual virtue and applied ethics, and has influenced far more people in the East than have been influenced by affirmative Platonism in the West. Similarly, it is doubtful whether the logic of Aristotle has made a more profound impact on any nation than it has upon Persia, possibly not excluding Greece itself.

The only generalization worth making about East and West is that there is far more cross-fertilization of ideas than has been generally acknowledged. A few Western scholars, such as Gilbert Chinnard, H. G. Creel, John Dewey, Lewis

Mumford, George Sarton, Gilbert Murray, Horace Kallen, Jacques Barzun, Arnold Rowbotham, Bertrand Russell, Ralph Turner, and F. S. C. Northrop, have been concerned with the cross-currents and cross-penetration of ideas that have been associated with geographic East and West. But too little of this has percolated through to the general body of our knowledge of scholarship.

More ought to be said about the mission of the Jesuits to China in the sixteenth and seventeenth centuries, and the impact upon them of Confucianism. They were accused in Europe of having been converted themselves. The favorable accounts of Confucianism they sent back made an important contribution to the development of the French ideas of equality. The Jesuit Le Compte was especially impressed by the absence among the Chinese of hereditary nobility and the absence of caste or other distinctions. The Physiocrat School, so important in the making of the French Revolution, formally acknowledged its great debt to Confucianism, as interpreted by the Jesuits. In turn, Benjamin Franklin and Jefferson acknowledged their debt to the Physiocrats.

It is unimportant whether such influences were primary or secondary. What is important is that neither East nor West held any monopoly, as Jefferson himself pointed out, on the concept of equality. It is interesting, too, to observe the basic similarity in the thinking of Jefferson and Confucius, especially in their concern for the farmer, their cordial disdain for mysticism, their belief in the natural rights of man, their strictures against authoritarianism, their emphasis upon education as a proper function of government, their belief in the full development of the individual's potential, and their unending search for public and private virtue.

Those who are accustomed to making pronouncements about the "mission of Western man" or the "destiny of Western man" will claim that we have so far slighted one fact of mountainous importance: Christianity. Isn't Christian civilization, they will ask, synonymous with Western man? Isn't this what gives Western man the right to think of himself as different and special?

The main trouble with this line of reasoning, of course, is that it assumes that Christianity itself is an entity. Is there general agreement about the meaning of Christ and the teachings of Christ in the West? Is there common acceptance of the same articles of faith? Indeed, are not Christians divided by their beliefs into numberless and occasionally opposing denominations? In a certain sense this is inevitable. So long as they have the capacity for creative interpretation, so long as they can exercise the right of free choice, they will be unable to devise and stay within any single institution or credo. This is natural and right. There is strength in such diversity. But this strength is misapplied if it tries to segregate or compartmentalize humanity into Christians and non-Christians, Eastern and Western man, or make something unique of one man as against another. The province of Christianity is not the ennoblement of Western civilization but the ennoblement of man.

The greatest paradox of all, however, is that the truest expression of Christianity today is to be found, not in the

West, but in the East. In India countless millions of people are living out the ideals of Christ, though they do not call themselves Christians and are unfamiliar with Christian theology. They are the poor and the meek and the merciful and the pure in heart. They regard life as sacred and will not harm it in any of its forms. They practice renunciation. They believe in nonviolence and they worship the memory of a human being who perhaps has come closer to embodying Christianity than anyone in modern history. Interestingly enough, Gandhi's struggle was directed against a Western Christian nation.

Are we to overlook the basic unity of most religions? The code of Hammurabi, the Koran, the Talmud, the Analects, and the Bhagavad-Gita have many of the same fundamental tenets defined in the Sermon on the Mount. What we call the Golden Rule has its parallel expression in almost all other religions. The Islamic faith is as closely related to the Jewish and the Christian faith as the latter two are to each other. It is astonishing to find how little is known about the Islamic religion in otherwise well-educated circles in Europe and the Americas. The extent to which the Mohammedan belief incorporates many of the fundamentals of Judaism and Christianity is overlooked in the frequent references by many Western thinkers to "Judeo-Christian" traditions or civilization. This is properly regarded by the peoples of the Near East as another example of our philosophical and theological provincialism.

"When will the West understand, or try to understand, the East?" asked the Japanese philosopher, Okakura-Kakuze,

more than fifty years ago. "We Asiatics are often appalled by
the curious web of facts and fancies which has been woven
concerning us. We are pictured as living on the perfume
of the lotus, if not on mice and cockroaches. It is either im-
potent fanaticism or else abject voluptuousness. Indian spirit-
uality has been derided as ignorance, Chinese sobriety as
stupidity, Japanese patriotism as the result of fatalism. It has
been said that we are less sensible to pain and wounds on
account of the callousness of our nervous organization!"

The East, of course, is no more a political or cultural or
anthropological entity than is the West, although those who
talk with such careless ease about Western man generally
juxtapose him against Eastern man. What common center
fuses an Afghanistan Moslem with a Filipino Catholic? Or
a Ceylonese Buddist with a Chinese Taoist? The religious
Hindu is as appalled by the paganism of some of his Chinese
neighbors as are the Episcopalians by Jehovah's Witnesses.
Conversely, some Chinese are as baffled by Indian mysticism
and theosophy as many of us are, though it must be recorded that theosophy is a product of the West. And the big-
gest ideological threat in Asia today, Communisn, is not an
Eastern idea but a Western one. What all this adds up to is
not an Eastern entity but a vast complex inside a complex,
with no single unifying thread.

The Asians—1.5 billion of them—happen to share a continent which is a formal geographic unit only by human
designation and not by divine insistence. To make grooved
and rutted generalizations about these people is to commit
a sin against good scholarship and the human community

at a time when a vast expansion is needed in man's awareness and comprehension of man.

It is astonishing to see how often university conferences in Europe and the Americas on the problems of philosophy or politics in the modern world will allow stock references to Asian peoples and cultures to go unchallenged. One hears about the "disdain for action" or about "lack of systematic thought" or about the "Oriental love of vagueness" or about the "Eastern mentality" or about "typical Eastern mysticism" or about the "propensity for negation."

What is most unfortunate about these remarks is not the polite arrogance which assumes that failure of communication is necessarily the fault of the next fellow, but the unscholarly technique of placing "Eastern" philosophers inside a single academic enclosure. Anyone who has attended a philosophical meeting, whether in Japan or China or Indo-China or India or Pakistan or Turkey, is able to bear witness to the same spread of ideas and approaches, the same display of argumentation over ends and means, the same contrasts of lofty thoughts and plodding trivia that enliven similar meetings in Paris, London, or New York. Imagine, then, a meeting of Filipinos, Japanese, Chinese, Indians, and Pakistani being characterized as though the ideas of only a single philosopher were being examined.

It must also be said that the East has its own provincial philosophers and scholars who lack an adequate background for an understanding of Europe and the Americas and who make the error of dealing in stereotypes and nonexistent entities in writing about the "iniquitous and materialistic

West." Even when they are friendly, they excuse our "rashness" and "impulsiveness" because of our youth. We are "precocious," "mechanistic," "frivolous," "irresponsible," "ambitious," lacking in "perspective," "wisdom," "insight." As yet, however, Asian scholars have not proclaimed any missions for Eastern man, nor have they endowed him with a special claim on human destiny.

What an Eastern philosophical conference has most in common with a Western philosophical meeting, perhaps, is an apparent disposition to invest geographical entities with fixed cultural, ideological, or philosophical components. Thus it is not unusual to hear Western philosophy criticized as lacking in sufficient appreciation of the "vital intangibles" or "elusive but central values." Along with this is the criticism of "Western thought" as being overly concerned with systems and techniques and not enough with the domain beyond man's limited intelligence. This criticism, of course, is merely the Asian manifestation of a philosophical provincialism which is not centered in or confined to any single area.

So far as the overriding needs and purposes of man today are concerned, it is irrelevant to attempt to determine which set of stereotypes came first or which is more unscholarly or unfair—that of the West or that of the East. What is important is that a major effort be made by all concerned to get away from the entity complex. It would be well, perhaps, if the world of scholarship would enter into a sort of compact on specificity. It should be made clear whether when we use the term "East" we are thinking of everything from the Bosporus Straits to the Bering Sea, or whether we have a specific area or culture in mind. Proper distinctions should be made between Japan and China and India and Pakistan and Indonesia and Siberia and Iran and Syria and Israel. Similarly, when Asian scholars comment on Europe and the Americas it would be helpful to know whether they are thinking primarily of the Balkans or Scandinavia or South America or France or Canada or whatever.

In addition we can liberate ourselves from some of the harmful misconceptions that are so much excess baggage. Consider, for example, the frequent remark mentioned above that the East has a "disdain for action." It is said that it is virtually impossible for Asians to get beyond opinions and into operations. Thus we have heard about Chinese lethargy, Indian passivity, Balinese serenity, and so forth. In the light of recent and current history, that picture can stand some revision. The Civil War in China, stretching over fifteen years, was conspicuous for its lack of lethargy on all sides. Indeed, the missing ingredient appears to have been, not action, but thought. Japanese aggression in concert with the Axis only a few years ago was sharply in contrast to the prevailing conception of an Oriental nation as lacking in drive or dynamics. It is worth noting, incidentally, that industrialization, militarization, mobilization, aggression, and colonization—all of which dominated Japanese life for perhaps a quarter of a century—had previously reached advanced development in the West. So far as India is concerned, the widespread outside impression of an almost universal passivity or impassiveness must be modified in the light of observable facts of life in India for at least fifty years. Passive resistance and noncooperation were the most vital parts of a real *action* program. After independence, intense political activity on the extremes of both left and right—activity from which Indian men of learning and letters sought no immunity or exemption—made India one of the least passive places on the face of the globe. Bali, too, more closely resembles a hot-bed of Balkan intrigue than it does the glamorous, languorous land of Covarrubias sketches.

As for the complaint of "Oriental vagueness," I have searched my memory but I can recall nothing more tangible or more vividly conveyed than the needs and hopes of Asian peoples I was able to meet. Most memorable of all was the emphatic detail with which they documented their desire to maintain their freedom and self-respect, and their deep resentment at being regarded as inferior beings fit only to be servants or subjects. Exclusion acts and humiliation by legislation leave them with no vague reaction. If anything, the response is severely normal—almost to the point of being terrifying. True, some Asian writers and philosophers may have cultivated vagueness for vagueness' sake, but it ought not to be difficult to draw up a list of Western writers and philosophers who have some fairly well-developed abilities in that direction themselves.

Then, of course, there is the matter of the "mystical, mysterious, spiritualistic, and occult East." This is becoming more and more of a travel-poster slogan for tourists and less and less a description with any substance behind it. The most populous nation in Asia has had more disdain for the popular conception of mysticism and the occult than perhaps any country in the world. The intensely practical and down-to-earth philosophy-religion of Confucius and Lao-tzu has little scope for higher metaphysics.

Is there nothing, then, that distinguishes the peoples of Asian countries from the peoples of Europe and America? Such differences as exist cannot be separated into two large spatial bundles conveniently tagged "East" and "West." Many of the distinctions are national rather than continental, and even here it is important to take into account whatever pluralism may exist inside the nations themselves. In addition to the pluralisms are the paradoxes. Indeed, not until the paradoxes are located and defined does the essential nature of a culture begin to reveal itself. The finest observers, historians, and anthropologists have all been paradox hunters. Hunting and comprehending paradoxes is infinitely more challenging and rewarding than the pursuit of incredible entities.

We may live in the two worlds of "East" and "West," but we have only one planet to do it on. As L. L. Whyte has written in *The Next Development in Man*, the separation of East and West is over, and a new history opens rich in quality and majestic in scale.

Our courses of study, therefore, should be directed to the entire human arena in today's world, and, more particularly, to the human situation. They may not be able to embrace the whole of comparative cultures, but they can at least develop the grand approaches and an acquaintance with the essentials. They can also deal with the nature of the contact points among contemporary cultures. They can help prepare the individual for direct experience in those cultures. They can attempt to deal with the problem of working relationships. They can educate in common problems.

Language studies represent a wide field for expansion—both in terms of early availability and teaching techniques. Advanced school systems are now considering the feasibility of foreign languages in the lowest grades of elementary schools. We can go beyond that. We can utilize the nursery school and thus take advantage of the most responsive period for natural education in languages that an individual can experience. We can use the earliest building blocks of the education process. Tomorrow's well-educated American will be not merely bi-lingual but tri-lingual. In addition to English and French or Russian or German or Italian or Spanish, he will have proficiency in Hindi or Urdu or Chinese or Japanese or several others. He will see no weakening of his loyalty to his own country in the development of a loyalty to the human commonwealth. His awareness of his place in the human family will not run counter to his pride in the history and achievements of his nation. The widening of allegiances, in fact, is a mark of human evolution.

Most of all, of course, the well-educated man in the human community will be able to see a direct connection, not solely between himself and his society at its largest, but between his awareness of the needs of that society and his effective reach in helping to meet them.

SUGGESTED READING

THE OLD GENERATION AND THE NEW by NELSON N. FOOTE

Carr, Edward Hallett. *The New Society*. London, Macmillan, 1951.

Erikson, Eric H. *Childhood and Society*. New York, Norton, 1950.

Galbraith, John Kenneth. *The Affluent Society*. New York, Houghton, 1958.

Mannheim, Karl. "The Problem of Generations," in *Essays on the Sociology of Knowledge*. Oxford, Oxford University Press, 1952.

Riesman, David, Nathan Glazer, and Reuel Denney. *The Lonely Crowd*. New Haven, Yale University Press, 1950.

Stevenson, Robert Louis. *Virginibus Puerisque*. 1881.

RURAL YOUTH by JOHN H. KOLB

Biddle, William W. *The Cultivation of Community Leaders*. New York, Harper, 1953.

Hollingshead, August. *Elmtown's Youth*. New York, Wiley, 1949.

Loomis, C. P. and J. A. Beegle. *Rural Social Systems and Adult Education*. New York, Prentice-Hall, 1954.

Sanders, Irwin T. *The Community: An Introduction to a Social System*. New York, Ronald Press, 1958.

————. *Making Good Communities Better*. Revised ed. Lexington, Ky., University of Kentucky Press, 1952.

NEGRO YOUTH IN THE SOUTH by LEWIS W. JONES

Davis, Allison and John Dollard. *Children of Bondage: The Personality and Development of Negro Youth in the Urban South.* Washington, D.C., American Council on Education, American Youth Commission Studies, 1940.

Davis, Allison, Burleigh B. Gardner, and Mary R. Gardner. *Deep South: A Social Anthropological Study of Caste and Class.* Chicago, Chicago University Press, 1941.

Dollard, John. *Caste and Class in a Southern Town.* New Haven, Yale University Press, 1937.

Frazier, E. Franklin. *Negro Youth at the Crossways: Their Personality Development in the Middle States.* Washington, D.C., American Council on Education, American Youth Commission Studies, 1940.

Myrdal, Gunnar. *An American Dilemma.* New York, Harper, 1944.

Warner, W. Lloyd, Buford H. Junker, and Walter A. Adams. *Color and Human Nature: Negro Personality Development in a Northern City.* Washington, D.C., American Council on Education, American Youth Commission Studies, 1940.

SPANISH-SPEAKING CHILDREN by JOHN H. BURMA

Burma, John H. *Spanish-Speaking Groups in the United States.* Durham, Duke University Press, 1954.

Griffith, Beatrice. *American Me.* Boston, Houghton-Mifflin, 1948.

McWilliams, Carey. *North from Mexico.* New York, Lippincott, 1949.

Mills, C. W., C. Senior, and R. K. Goldsen. *The Puerto Rican Journey.* New York, Harper, 1950.

Padilla, Elena. *Up From Puerto Rico.* New York, Columbia University Press, 1958.

Tuck, Ruth. *Not with the Fish.* New York, Harcourt Brace, 1946.

Welfare Council of Metropolitan Chicago. *Institute on Cultural Patterns of Newcomers.* Chicago, 1957.

JUVENILE DELINQUENCY by ROBERT M. MAC IVER

Aichorn, August. *Wayward Youth*. New York, Meridian Books, 1955.

Bloch, Herbert A. and Frank T. Flynn. *Delinquency: The Juvenile Offender in America Today*. New York, Random House, 1950.

Cohen, Albert K. *The Culture of the Gang*. Glencoe, Ill., Free Press, 1955.

Healy, William and Augusta Bronner. *New Light on Delinquency and Its Treatment*. New Haven, Yale University Press, 1936, 1950.

Robison, Sophia M. *Juvenile Delinquency: Its Nature and Control*. New York, Holt, 1960.

FRONTIERS IN VOLUNTARY WELFARE SERVICES by ELIZABETH WICKENDEN

Boy Scouts of America. *Study of Adolescent Boys*. New Brunswick, N.J., 1956.

Child Welfare League of America. A *Statement of Principles and Policies on Administration of Voluntary and Public Child Welfare Agencies*. New York, 1958.

Coyle, Grace L. *Group Work and American Youth*. New York, Harper, 1948.

Fredericksen, Hazel. *The Child and His Welfare*. San Francisco, Freeman, 1957.

Girl Scouts of America. *Study of the Adolescent Girl*. Part I. New York, 1958.

Gordon, Henrietta L. *Casework Services for Children: Principles and Practices*. Boston, Houghton-Mifflin, 1956.

National Association of Social Work. *Social Work Year Book*. New York.

THE GOVERNMENT'S ROLE IN CHILD AND FAMILY WELFARE by EVELINE M. BURNS

Blackwell, Gordon W. and Raymond F. Gould. *Future Citizens*

All. Chicago, American Public Welfare Association, 1952.

Hill, Esther P. "Is Foster Care the Answer?" in *Public Welfare* (April, 1957).

Housing and Home Finance Agency. *Children and Youth in an Urban Environment.* Washington, D.C., 1959.

United Nations. *Economic Measures in Favor of the Family.* New York, Columbia University Press, 1952.

WORK, WOMEN, AND CHILDREN by HENRY DAVID

Gross, Irma H., ed. *Potentialities of Women in the Middle Years.* East Lansing, Michigan State University Press, 1956.

Myrdal, Alva and Viola Klein. *Women's Two Roles: Home and Work.* London, Routledge and Keegan Paul, 1956.

National Manpower Council. *Womanpower.* New York, Columbia University Press, 1957.

————. *Work in the Lives of Married Women.* New York, Columbia University Press, 1958.

Women's Bureau. *1958 Handbook on Women Workers,* Bulletin 266. Washington, D.C., Government Printing Office, 1958.

CHILDHOOD IN TWENTIETH-CENTURY AMERICA by ERIC LARRABEE

Erikson, Erik H. *Childhood and Society.* New York, Norton, 1950.

Friedenberg, Edgar Z. *The Vanishing Adolescent.* New York, Beacon Press, 1959.

Liberman, Sally. *A Child's Guide to a Parent's Mind.* New York, Schuman, 1951.

Riesman, David, Nathan Glazer, and Reuel Denney. *The Lonely Crowd.* New Haven, Yale University Press, 1950.

Smith, Robert Paul. *"Where Did You Go?" "Out." "What Did You Do?" "Nothing."* New York, Norton, 1957.